cool creatures, hot planet

exploring the seven continents

Marty Essen

ENCANTE
PRESS

Published by:

Encante Press, LLC
P.O. Box 850
Corvallis MT 59828
www.EncantePress.com
SAN: 850-4326

Printed in Canada

Cover photograph of Marty Essen by Deb Essen
Cover and interior layout by 1106 Design

Publisher's Cataloging-in-Publication
(Provided by Quality Books, Inc.)

     Essen, Marty.
        Cool creatures, hot planet : exploring the seven continents / by Marty Essen.
        p. cm.
        Includes bibliographical references.
        LCCN 2006904124
        ISBN-13: 978-0-9778599-7-9
        ISBN-10: 0-9778599-7-5

        1. Essen, Marty–Travel. 2. Essen, Deb–Travel.
     3. Voyages and travels. 4. Animals. I. Title.
     II. Title: Exploring the seven continents

     G465.E86 2006   910.4
                         QBI06-600195

10 9 8 7 6 5 4 3 2 1

To Stephanie Manley:
With thanks,

Contents

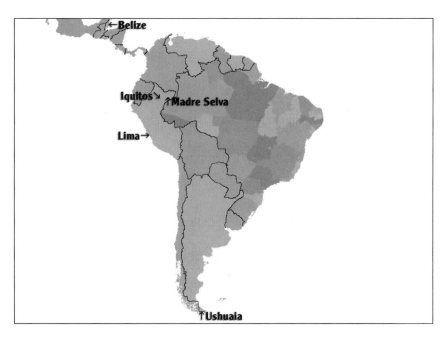

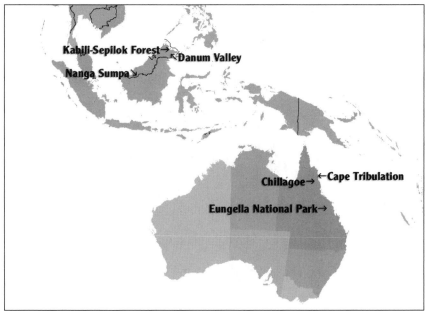

All maps © 2004 Cartografx Corporation

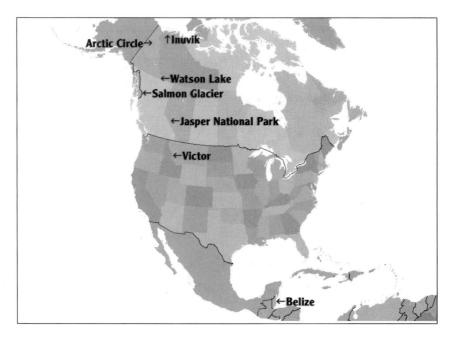

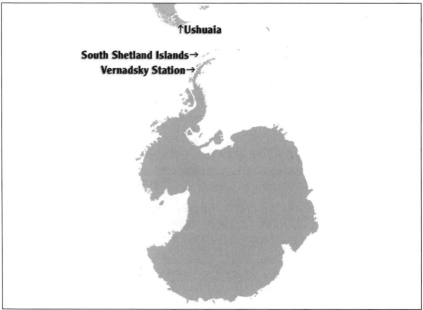

Introduction

Travel is fatal to prejudice, bigotry, and narrow-mindedness,
and many of our people need it sorely on these accounts.

—MARK TWAIN, *THE INNOCENTS ABROAD*

I solved my midlife crisis. My brain consulted with my fingers, toes, and knees, and we collectively refused to be conformists participating in the aging process. My birth certificate claimed I was thirty-nine years old, but we weren't about to believe a piece of paper with an illegible signature from the year the Rolling Stones became a band. My brain and the rest of my twenty-seven-year-old body were going traveling.

When my wife, Deb, and I embarked on our first international trip together, I had no thoughts of turning our adventures into a book. I just wanted to go on vacation. I started work early in life, and by the time I confronted my midlife crisis, I had built from scratch both a successful talent management agency and a telephone company—and become a workaholic in the process. Between the ages of nineteen and thirty-nine, I had indulged in only five week-long vacations and never missed a day of work because of illness.

While I'm pleased with the direction my life has taken, I sometimes wish I had pursued my childhood dream of becoming a herpetologist. Observing and interacting with wildlife gives me pleasure no business transaction can match. If given the choice between finding a rare snake and landing a lucrative business deal, I'd choose the snake every time.

On the other hand, if I had become a herpetologist, I wouldn't have met Deb. I was working as a talent manager, in 1984, when the stunning blond-haired-woman-with-a-brain walked into my life. Seven months later we were married. I changed careers to telecommunications while Deb and I were living in Minneapolis, Minnesota. Then, in 1996, our thirst for nature lured us west to the Rocky Mountains near Victor, Montana.

Moving to an area with abundant wildlife had a positive impact on my psyche. Now each time I stepped out the front door of our home I'd have a good chance of seeing a deer, moose, bear, or turkey. As for the impact on my telephone company, the competitive advantage of doing business in a rural state was outweighed, at least initially, by a small prospective employee pool. I ended up working harder than ever.

Deb and I discussed taking time off for travel, but events in my office kept pushing our plans further into the future. As my fortieth birthday stared me in the face, I realized my business would continue running our lives as long as I let it. Finally I declared, "No more delays! We need to get out and have some fun."

Cool Creatures, Hot Planet: Exploring the Seven Continents grew from a much shorter version of the Amazon chapter I had written for two Montana newspapers. The Australia chapter also ran in abbreviated form as a newspaper article, but by then the industrious side of my brain had kicked in to say, "Hey, this can be *more* than just fun. Wildlife encounters on all seven continents would be a great subject for a book." Once a workaholic, always a workaholic.

Deb and I were international-travel neophytes when this project began. I had visited Canada once, and she had been out of the country a few times, but neither of us had ever attempted anything close to the kind of travel we did for this book. Specifically, we avoided popular tourist destinations and sought out remote areas where we could observe wildlife in undisturbed habitat.

In addition to the hundreds of animal species we encountered, Deb and I met people from more than twenty-five different nations. Consequently, I got a good feel for how citizens of other countries viewed the United States and was amazed by their detailed knowledge of our political system and its leaders. I often found myself wishing average Americans shared the same awareness of their own country.

In recent years, the United States government has pursued self-serving policies that ignore the needs and interests of other nations. Our travels confirmed the irresponsibility of such policies. We live on a small planet, and what we do in America affects the rest of the world.

Deb and I commenced our first adventure on George W. Bush's Inauguration Day and completed all eight trips for this book during the initial three and a half years of his presidency. Although Bush had little effect on our early adventures, once he started selling the invasion of Iraq, his actions became an inseparable part of our travels.

While political issues weave through the chapters, the focus of *Cool Creatures, Hot Planet* is on animals. Throughout the course of our travels, Deb and I had many unforgettable wildlife experiences. Often we just happened to be in the right place at the right time—or in some instances, the wrong place at the wrong time. As I wrote about our encounters, I occasionally wondered if anyone would believe me. Trust me: every story is true.

I learned so much while writing and researching this book that I felt as if I were working on doctorates in both herpetology and zoology. Thankfully, I was able to skip the animal dissection courses. Books, direct field observation, and knowledge passed on by local guides all contributed to my education. Sharing with you the best of what I've learned gives me great pleasure.

Four technical notes:

- I have changed the names and physical descriptions of some of the people mentioned in this book to protect their privacy.

- I took liberties when determining the gender of some animals. If I knew their correct sex, I used it. If not, I took my best guess based on size, coloring, and behavior. Referring to animals I shared moments with as either "him" or "her" seemed more appropriate than using a generic "it."

- While conducting background research, I found the size and weight specifications of animals varied by reference source. Therefore, I either averaged the specifications or selected the measurements most closely matching my personal observations.

- I use *rainforest* and *jungle* interchangeably in this book. Although technically a jungle is the dense tangle of vegetation often associated with the regrowth of a logged or otherwise disturbed rainforest, in common use the difference between the words is insignificant.

Completing *Cool Creatures, Hot Planet* would have been impossible without Deb. Not only did she accompany me on every trip, but she was also my primary sounding board during the writing process. Sometimes I'd spend hours wrestling with a single sentence or paragraph. Just when I'd reach the pinnacle of frustration, she'd suggest a solution to the problem from her unique perspective. Though her ideas were often too far out of character for me to use, she always helped me past the ruts.

Whenever I give presentations about our adventures, someone invariably asks me, "And your wife went with you *willingly?*" Frankly, I couldn't have left Deb at home if I wanted to. She's tougher than any man I know, my best friend, and a damned good travel companion.

I dedicate this book to Deb.

1
Belize May I Take a Vacation?

I was psyched! Deb and I were finally going on a trip. We hadn't taken a vacation in six years, and now we were packing for Belize.

I first became interested in Belize when a neighbor in Minnesota showed me photos from trips he'd taken there. As time passed I almost forgot about the country. Then, after Deb and I moved to Montana, a friend asked me to critique the Belize episodes of his syndicated fly-fishing show. Though I'm not a fisherman, watching the stunning tropical scenery behind the action rekindled my interest in the country and inspired me to suggest it to Deb as the destination for our much-needed break. She immediately concurred.

Belize sits on the Caribbean Sea with Mexico to the north and Guatemala to the south and west. Its population is 266,440. For comparison, the state of New Hampshire is about the same size but with a million more people. Once known as British Honduras, Belize became an independent nation in 1981 and still maintains ties to the United Kingdom as a member of the Commonwealth of Nations (an association of fifty-four sovereign states, most of which were once linked to the British Empire).

We scheduled our trip for the week of January 20–27, 2001. Though I once spent a day in Thunder Bay, Ontario (180 miles north of where I grew up in Duluth, Minnesota), this would be my first extended international visit. In anticipation of the event, I educated myself about Belize by reading guidebooks and surfing the Internet. Deb helped with the research, and together we came up with numerous possibilities for things to do during our stay.

Deb and I have a lot in common. Physically we stay in shape through evening walks and weekend outdoor activities, and mentally we have similar values and a relationship that lets us talk for hours. Where we differ is on how we like to play. My love is wildlife photography and hers is scuba diving.

Belize, with its reputation for amazing wildlife and spectacular diving, would be an ideal location for us. Rather than debating about how much time we'd allocate to diving versus looking for wildlife, we each planned half our vacation. I booked the first half at Black Rock Lodge near the Guatemalan border, and she booked the second half at Blackbird Caye Resort on the Turneffe Islands.

When Deb and I travel by air, our trips begin and end at the Missoula International Airport. Airports often display items to entertain waiting passengers, but here, in perhaps the tackiest airport in America, passengers encounter taxidermic animal displays at every turn. All that's missing is a sign proclaiming, "Welcome to Missoula, where dead things are considered art."

Flying from Missoula to anywhere can be a time-consuming process. Our flight to Belize stretched over two days, with an overnight layover in Minneapolis and a three-hour layover in Houston.

While we walked between gates at Houston's George Bush Intercontinental Airport, I noticed a crowd gathered around one of the televisions. George W. Bush would soon be sworn in as president of the United States.

I tried not to be too pessimistic about what the coming years would bring, but in a catty sort of way, I felt we'd picked a particularly appropriate moment to travel to a foreign land. I boarded the airplane, hopeful of reaching international airspace before the change of leadership became official.

As a first-time traveler to an undeveloped country, I naturally had some feelings of anxiety. Midway over the Gulf of Mexico, my mind wandered to a newspaper exposé I had read about corrupt customs agents in Central America. Though I couldn't remember which country had been mentioned, by the time we landed I was prepared for heat-lamp interrogations and body-cavity searches—I have a very vivid imagination.

In contrast to my fears, clearing customs was both painless and noninvasive. Uniformed men looked us over but didn't stop us from proceeding into Belize's only major airport. The facility was small, well kept, and quiet—kind of like the Missoula airport, minus the dead things.

We stepped outside to the curb and inhaled the hot humid air. The change from the snowy weather at home felt delightful. As we absorbed our new surroundings, a short wiry man in his late sixties approached us.

"Mr. and Mrs. Essen?"

"Yes."

"My name is Alejandro. I drive you to Black Rock Lodge."

I was surprised the man found us so quickly, until I realized Deb and I were the only light-skinned people in sight.

Alejandro's heavily accented speech was somewhat difficult to understand. English is the official, though not necessarily the preferred, language in Belize. I suspected he was most comfortable conversing in Spanish, the language I heard most often in the airport.

Alejandro loaded our bags into his compact van. Then, as soon as I settled in the front seat and Deb climbed into the back, he launched us onto the streets of Belize City. We brushed past a cluster of bicyclists, zipped by a row of tiny stores with painted stucco walls, and whizzed along a road bordered by dilapidated wooden houses.

Approximately one-third of Belize's population resides in or around Belize City, making it the country's only true urban area. A city tour would have been interesting, but we headed straight out of town.

To reach Black Rock Lodge, we would travel from the Caribbean coast to the far western side of the country. The Western Highway would take us most of the way. Because the narrow two-lane highway passed through several villages, the seventy-mile-long drive was supposed to take two hours. Alejandro, however, seemed determined to cut the time in half.

Sharp corners, steep hills, and railroad tracks meant nothing to him. If a vehicle ahead threatened to slow our progress, he'd gun the engine and recklessly swerve into the opposite lane—oncoming traffic be damned! We rocketed across the country with pistons pinging like popcorn in a cheap tin pan. I braced my hands against the dashboard and meditated on a calmer place: "Ahhhh, rush-hour traffic in Minneapolis."

Just past the town of San Ignacio, Alejandro slowed the van and veered onto a gravel road. We skirted farmland for a few miles before turning into the jungle. (Belize doesn't have a true rainforest, as its rainfall is neither consistent enough nor high enough in volume to meet the requirements. Locals called the moist tropical forest "jungle," and I will do the same.)

Trees towered around us as we crept along, avoiding numerous ruts and washouts. When the road dropped abruptly into a shallow stream,

Alejandro remarked, "During rainy season we ride horses from here. River now low enough, we drive directly to Black Rock."

We reached the lodge after another mile or so. As we stepped out of the van, I noticed a handful of *cabañas* (in Belize the Spanish word *cabaña* is preferred over the English word *cabin*) surrounding a larger building. The entire complex paralleled the Macal River. Although the darkening sky limited my view, I was pleased to see that all the structures had natural wood exteriors and were obviously built to blend in with the jungle.

"Wait here," said Alejandro. He disappeared into the central building and returned accompanied by a gray-haired man with a ponytail. "This is John, the manager. He'll show you to your cabaña. I'll be back on Wednesday to take you to Belize City."

We waved good-bye to our driver and shook hands with our host, an American who looked like he was stuck in the 1960s. "Stuck in Belize" would be a more accurate description, however.

"I didn't expect to find an American in charge," I said. "What brought you to Belize?"

"I came here on vacation many years ago," he replied. "I just never got around to returning home."

"I can't blame you. From what little I've seen of the country, it's beautiful," I said.

John escorted us down a path. "How was your trip?" he asked over his shoulder.

"The plane flight was long and boring—" Deb began.

"—but once we landed, the trip got exciting," I finished. "Alejandro seemed reserved until he got behind the wheel. I've never been on a more hair-raising ride in my life."

John chuckled. "You need to understand, automobiles only recently became popular in Belize. Many of the locals are still learning to drive, and Alejandro is no exception."

The lilt in John's voice made me suspect he wasn't being totally serious. Nevertheless, I turned to my wife and smiled. "Honey, would you like the front seat for the return trip?"

We soon reached our cabaña. It was the last building on the path, and the one with the best view of the river.

"Have either of you stayed in an eco-lodge before?" John asked as he opened the door to let Deb and me inside.

"This is a first," I answered.

"Your accommodations have electric lights, a hot-water shower, and a flush toilet. Everything is powered by batteries, which are charged by solar panels. Please be sure to turn off the lights when you're not using them."

"Of course," I said. "One of the reasons we selected Black Rock is because it's solar powered. I read in one of my guidebooks that most of the other lodges along the river use diesel generators."

John nodded as he set our bags at the foot of the bed. "Yes, and the noise carries a long way. You'll hear them if you canoe downriver. Solar power is definitely the way to go."

I looked around. We didn't plan to spend much time inside our sparsely furnished cabaña, but since the windows had storm shutters instead of glass, all the outdoor sounds flowed inside. We were fortunate to be far away from growling generators.

John excused himself, and shortly thereafter I had my first Belizean wildlife encounter. When I flicked on the bathroom light, a huntsman spider, with a body bigger than a quarter, glared down at me from the wall above the sink. I swatted at him with a newspaper, but after he deftly avoided several strikes, I came to admire his fortitude. The cabaña was big enough for the three of us to share.

"Deb, come here. We have a new pet."

As my wife joined me in the bathroom, I pointed at the arachnid. "Wow, is he big!" she said.

"What should we call him?"

"How 'bout Spike?"

"Perfect!"

To make amends for my assassination attempt, I brought Spike a nice juicy fly for dinner and decided to continue feeding him throughout our stay. If he was going to be the resident bathroom attendant, adding a little weight might make the next guests think twice before trying to kill him.

Once Spike was too full to wander about the cabaña—or so we hoped—Deb and I crawled into bed. Our long day of travel was finally over.

Each day of our trip began the same way. I would get up before dawn and Deb would sleep until breakfast. As any morning person can attest, the thirty minutes before and after sunrise comprise the best hour of the day. Nothing beats the feel of cool morning air while watching the first light appear on the horizon.

I awoke on Sunday, eager to become acquainted with Belize. The path we had taken the night before didn't end at our cabaña. Instead, it angled a short distance down to the river and then paralleled the riverbank. I sauntered along it, looking for wildlife and photographing exotic tropical plants.

Of all the hikes I would go on during our travels, this one had the fewest events to write about. For me, however, it was fascinating. Since it was my first walk in a tropical forest, everything was new. I felt as if I were in a giant greenhouse, without the pots. All the vines, trees, and ferns were vivid green. Every leaf glistened with dew, and a sweet fragrance hung in the still air.

Other than wild pineapple and a type of *Heliconia* called lobster claw, I didn't recognize specific species of flora. For a moment, I wished for a better knowledge of botany, but rather than fret over identification, I enjoyed the vegetation for its lushness and beauty.

I walked for more than an hour but didn't travel far because each step presented another interesting distraction.

When I returned to the cabaña, Deb was dressed and ready for breakfast. We strolled up the path to the main building. The open-air structure had a thatched, dome-shaped roof, which sheltered the dining room and bar, and next to it was a large sundeck overlooking the Macal River.

John and the kitchen staff served all guests family style at a long table. Joining us for a breakfast of fruit and cereal were three couples from the United States and two men from Germany. The Germans didn't speak English, but we introduced ourselves to everyone.

While John poured a round of coffee, I asked him, "Does Black Rock have a set schedule of activities, or do we make our own arrangements for the day?"

"This is your vacation," he said. "The other guests are traveling by four-wheel drive to some Mayan ruins. You two can go with them or plan your own itinerary."

"The Mayan ruins sound interesting," I said, glancing at my wife, "but I'd rather explore the jungle."

"I agree," said Deb. "How 'bout doing our exploration on horseback? Are there trails we can follow?"

"Sure, there's a great trail that goes up to Flour Camp Cave," said John.

"We have horseback riding experience," I said. "Do we ride on our own, or do we go with a guide?"

"Tamo will accompany you. Just give me an hour to find him and get the horses ready."

Deb and I went back to our cabaña to grab flashlights for exploring the cave and then walked along the river for a while. When we returned, Tamo was waiting at the bar.

Our guide was a handsome young man with straight black hair wrapped in a bandana and a shy smile on his face. Even though English was his second language, he had a deliberate manner of speaking that was easy to understand.

Judging from the giggles of the teenage girls working at the lodge, Tamo was the local heartthrob. As we followed him through the kitchen, one of the girls playfully punched him in the shoulder. He ignored the blow, but the gleam in his eyes gave him away—he was enjoying the attention and knew how to look just disinterested enough to keep the girls in pursuit. Some things are the same, no matter where you go.

We mounted our horses and clip-clopped down the gravel road we had taken with Alejandro the day before. Every so often Tamo halted his horse and shared with us his vast knowledge of local history, plants, and wildlife. The fuzzy red fruit of a lipstick tree, for instance, could be used for making dyes, and the cottony fiber inside the fruit pods of kapok trees could be used for stuffing pillows and life jackets.

Eventually we angled off the road and cut across a plantain farm. "Plantains are a type of banana," he explained. "Very popular in Belize. Not sweet, like regular banana. We cook and eat them like a potato."

A narrow trail led from the farm back into the jungle. The three of us rode quietly in single file, listening to birds calling from the palms and other broadleaf trees. An hour or so later, the vegetation opened to reveal a small, grassy hill. The terrain didn't look unusual, so when we dismounted on the hilltop, I assumed we were stopping to rest our horses.

"Unexcavated Mayan site," said Tamo. He guided us around to the far side of the hill and pointed at a hole near our feet. "There."

I looked down and saw an exposed four-foot-high section of stone blocks. Obviously much more of the structure remained hidden beneath the soil. I smiled, thrilled by the unexpected treat of seeing a nearly undisturbed ruin.

At one time Belize was at the center of the Mayan Empire. From AD 300 until their decline six hundred years later, the Mayans had one of the most advanced civilizations in the world. The reason for their society's deterioration remains a mystery. Was it disease, natural disasters, crop failures, or war? Perhaps one day someone will find the definitive answer among the pyramids and structures the Mayans left behind. Archaeologists have excavated major sites, such as Caracol and

Xunantunich, but an estimated thousand lesser sites remain either undeveloped or undiscovered.

As our horseback ride continued, I scanned the jungle, hoping to spot a snake, toucan, monkey—or any other animal for that matter. At home I enjoy watching nature television shows, but here I had to remind myself that each program condenses days, perhaps weeks, of work into a single episode. Shows such as *The Jeff Corwin Experience* and Steve Irwin's *The Crocodile Hunter* wouldn't be interesting if their hosts spent entire episodes searching for animals and only found a few frogs or skinks.

Admittedly, I secretly fantasized I could be like Steve Irwin: I'd sneak through the jungle, stop, put a finger to my lips, dive under a thicket, and emerge with a ten-foot-long boa constrictor!

Contributing to the apparent lack of wildlife was that Deb's and my jungle observation skills were in their infancy. Although our skills would improve on future trips, in Belize we could have passed within ten feet of a troop of monkeys without noticing them.

We followed the trail for another hour before reaching Flour Camp Cave in the mountains above the lodge. With flashlights in hand, we dismounted and ducked through an opening near the base of a towering limestone wall. The cave branched into multiple chambers, each adorned with stalactites and stalagmites and other calcium carbonate formations. Some of the formations were smooth and wet, and others were rough and dull. The most beautiful resembled waves of blown glass.

"Vampire bats," said Tamo.

"Really? Where?" I asked.

Tamo aimed his flashlight above us to reveal dozens of brown bats, clinging to the ceiling, twenty feet overhead. I had noticed an odor when we entered the cave, and now I knew what it was—bat guano. As far as animal excrement goes, bat guano doesn't stink too badly. It smells kind of like a locker room in a dusty old high-school gymnasium, only more concentrated.

"I'd love to find some bats we could get closer to, so I can take some pictures," I said.

"Follow me," said Tamo.

Our guide led the way through a slender opening in the wall, and we climbed to a smaller chamber. Numerous bats flew out as we entered, but a handful remained. I had to hunch over to avoid hitting them with my head. The tiny vampires were roughly the size of a house mouse. Deb shined her flashlight on one while I focused my camera within inches of his face. I was surprised how brave the little guy was. Had I been equally brave, I could have easily reached up and touched him. Getting rabies shots on vacation, however, wasn't my idea of a good time.

As Tamo watched, he commented, "You're not city people, are you?"

"No, we're not," said Deb. "Why do you say that?"

"A lot of the visitors don't like it here so much. The bats scare them."

Vampire bats are often exterminated when humans move into their territory. The bats are holding their own, for now, but they're a good example of what can be lost if humans indiscriminately kill off "undesirable" species. Once a plant or animal is eradicated, so are all the potential medical benefits it could have provided. People surviving heart attacks or strokes after being given the blood-thinning drug Draculin owe their lives to bats. Draculin is derived from the anticoagulant found in vampire bat saliva—the most effective anticoagulant known to man.

After I photographed the bats, Tamo led us into a small room where pottery shards littered the floor. "Missionaries came to Belize many years ago and tried to force people into Christianity," he explained. "This was once a hiding place for those who wanted to practice traditional beliefs."

"Why do so many people feel it's perfectly okay to impose their brand of religion on others?" I muttered.

Tamo shrugged.

Deb bent down to examine the shards. "Were the pots used for cooking?"

"Some were, but breaking pottery was also part of traditional religious ceremonies," said Tamo.

"Did the missionaries ever find the people hiding in the cave?" I asked.

"I'm not sure," he said, "but nobody stayed in one spot for too long."

Our tour continued through several more chambers before we popped out into the bright sunlight. Thankful that hiding out in a cave was something we'd probably never have to do, we mounted our horses and headed back to the lodge.

Upon our arrival, Deb and I handed the reins from our horses to Tamo and thanked him for the enjoyable ride. As our guide walked away, Deb looked at me and wiped her brow. "I'm parched," she said.

"Me too. After a hard day of letting the horses do the work for us, a beer would be most appropriate."

The two of us walked—slightly bowlegged—into the main building and sat at the bar. John, doubling as bartender, handed us each a Belikin beer. Though other beers could be found in Belize, Belikin was essentially the national beer. In fact, no one gave us an option of buying any other brand during our trip. Luckily, it was a tasty brew.

"Tamo must have liked you two," said John, grinning. "Your ride was scheduled for four hours, and you were gone for six. If he doesn't like the people he's with, he usually brings them back early."

"I'm glad he liked us," said Deb. "We had a great time."

I wanted to ask John a question but was afraid he'd think I was insane. I started a second Belikin before blurting out, "Are there any fer-de-lances around here? I'd really like to find one."

John tilted his head and looked at me out of the corner of his eye. "Why the *hell* would you wanna do that?"

"Snakes have fascinated me since I was eight years old—the bigger or more dangerous the better. In the Western Hemisphere, no snake is deadlier than the fer-de-lance."

Fer-de-lance is the common name for *Bothrops asper* and other related pit vipers. My reason for calling it the deadliest snake in the Western Hemisphere wasn't because of venom toxicity—a few species produce venom that is more potent. I was referring to the total number of snakebite-related fatalities, a statistic led by the fer-de-lance because of its quick strike and tendency to live in areas frequented by humans.

"We don't normally look for fer-de-lances, but we do occasionally see them," he said.

"Recently?" I asked.

John glared at me as if I were inquiring about a taboo subject. "Fer-de-lances aren't something to mess around with. I know of two recent bites. A friend of mine was bit last year. Lucky for him, the bite turned out to be dry [no venom injected]. Then, just a few weeks ago, a fer-de-lance bit one of the horses in the field below your cabaña."

"Did the horse live?"

"The fer-de-lance dropped it dead in its tracks."

"Are you *sure* it was a fer-de-lance? Did you see it?"

"The bite happened during the night. When I examined the horse in the morning, I noticed two fang marks on its leg. I didn't see the snake, but only a fer-de-lance could have killed a healthy horse like that. Based on the size of the marks, the snake had to be big—at least seven feet long."

"I want to find *that* snake."

John looked at me and shook his head as if saying, "This crazy American is going to get himself killed."

"Don't worry. I won't take unnecessary chances or do anything stupid. All I wanna do is photograph it."

Though in John's mind the mere act of looking for a fer-de-lance was "doing something stupid," the determination in my eyes convinced him to help me out. With a deep breath he stepped out from behind the bar, led me onto the sundeck, and pointed to an area midway between our cabaña and the river. "That's where the horse died. Look there first."

"Thanks, John!"

Deb and I finished our beers before walking to our cabaña. While she retired to the porch with a book, I loaded my camera with film and hurried into the field. Even though I had drunk two beers at the bar, I wasn't HWI—*Herping While Intoxicated.* (*Herpetofauna* is an all-inclusive word for reptiles and amphibians. Herpetofauna enthusiasts are called *herpers,* and searching for herpetofauna is called *herping.*) My head was clear, and I intended to be careful. If I spotted the fer-de-lance, I planned to maneuver just close enough for a good photo. The greatest danger would be not seeing the snake until it was too late.

A fer-de-lance fortunate enough to reach seven feet in length wouldn't linger in the open field where horses could trample it. Instead, it would probably be in the tall grass along the perimeter or at the base of one of the scrubby trees between the field and the Macal River.

I cautiously combed through the grass and scrub, checking every possible hiding spot. My heart pounded as I inched into vegetation blocking the view of my bare calves. I thought about the rattlesnakes I had photographed in Montana. Searching for them was restful in comparison, as I knew they'd likely raise a racket if I got too close. A fer-de-lance couldn't give me such a distinctive warning—I'd be lucky to hear a rustle or a hiss.

I grew bolder as my search continued, but I didn't see or hear any sign of the horse-killing snake. Eventually darkness forced me to give up. I trudged back to the cabaña, disappointed but confident my herping luck would improve in the coming days.

For Monday's adventure, Deb and I decided on an eleven-mile canoe float down the Macal River. After breakfast, John showed us a map of the route, warned us about some rapids, and handed us our lunches.

"Hmmm," I thought as we set off downstream, "I hope we don't miss the spot where we're supposed to meet our ride at the end of the float."

The size of the Macal River corresponds with the time of year. Since this was the dry season, it meandered along at an average width of fifty feet. Had we visited during the rainy season, the Macal would have been an awesome spectacle. I could see evidence of previous high-water levels displayed in the trees along the banks. Hefty stumps and clumps of vegetation were wedged between branches ten feet above us. That the river could rise so high was hard to imagine.

We let the gentle current carry us as we scanned the riverbanks for wildlife. This was a bird-watcher's paradise. Scores of birds sang in the trees, swam in the river, and soared above us. Deb and I were surprised to spot species that were common in the United States, such as belted kingfishers and rufous hummingbirds. Then we reminded ourselves: birds have to go *somewhere* when they fly south for the winter.

Birds, however, weren't foremost on our minds at that moment. We wanted to see iguanas. Tamo had told us they were common in trees along the river, but when we first looked, we didn't see any.

The lizards were there. We just had to train our eyes to recognize that what initially appeared to be long bulges on the topside of branches were actually the reptiles we were searching for. Green iguanas between two and three feet long were the most common, but we also spotted several gorgeous, orange, six-foot-long males. We usually found both varieties sunning themselves in the trees overhanging the river—the orange ones frequently lounging a little higher than the green ones.

We were enjoying a glorious sunny day. The temperature was a perfect eighty degrees, and we had the river to ourselves. Sometimes we'd stop paddling and just listen to the gentle gurgle of water under our canoe and the melodic songs of nearby birds.

Raaaaaaawwrrrrrrrr!

"What was that!" we exclaimed in unison.

I looked for the source of the roar but saw only jungle. "Could it be a jaguar?"

"I have no idea," said Deb.

Khwa-alk. Khwa-alk. Loud snorts emanated from the direction of the roar. We paddled toward the sound.

Weeeeeeee! Weeeeeeee! Weeeeeeee! When the snorts gave way to squeals, I determined that the source of the commotion was less than thirty feet from the water's edge. We pulled alongside the bank, searching for a place where I could get out of the canoe without capsizing it. The water beneath us was deep, and a thick wall of foliage jutted over the river. Climbing onto land would be tricky.

*Raaaaaaawwrrrrrrr!—*on the other hand, I wouldn't want to interfere with the course of nature.

Another round of squeals and snorts followed the roar. When the sequence was completed, I knew with reasonable certainty what was making the noise. "They're peccaries," I said. "Two, possibly three, are having a dispute."

"I think you're right," said Deb.

Peccaries are close relatives of pigs, known for their pungent odor and aggressive temperament. While I couldn't smell them, their piglike squeals were unmistakable.

Deb and I hung near the riverbank for a few minutes listening to the confrontation. After two more roars and three more squeals, all we heard were occasional snorts. Apparently, the peccaries had settled their differences.

As we drifted away, I had second thoughts about my decision to stay in the canoe and said, "What if I was wrong about the roars and we were eavesdropping on a jaguar attacking a peccary? I may have missed out on the photo opportunity of a lifetime!" I paused while Deb stared at me. "Then again, I might have also missed out on becoming a jaguar chew toy."

I glanced at my watch. We were supposed to conclude our float by four o'clock, but as near as I could tell, we were a half hour behind schedule. We abandoned the pleasure portion of our journey and paddled hard for the last several miles.

We neared the takeout shortly after our appointed time. Any fears I had of floating past our ride vanished when we spotted Alejandro waving to us from the riverbank. We pulled ashore and within minutes were bumping along the rutty dirt road toward Black Rock Lodge.

After Alejandro dropped us off, Deb and I retired to the bar to discuss the day's events. John served us white chocolate martinis.

"*Oooh,* this is good!" I said.

"I'm glad you like it," replied John. "I use a special kind of vanilla you can't buy in the United States."

Deb took a sip. "Oh, this *is* good—a perfect complement to an excellent day!"

"So you must have had a good time on the river," said John.

"We had great time," I said. "The rapids weren't a problem, and we saw tons of birds and iguanas."

"And the scenery was just stunning," added Deb.

"I think we heard some peccaries fighting," I said.

"And the float was so peaceful," added Deb.

"I still haven't found a fer-de-lance though," I said.

"And *believe* me, he's tried," added Deb.

John shot me a sideways, "haven't you given up on that yet?" look.

I took a long sip of my martini to draw out the silence. Then I said, "Tomorrow is our last day here, and I want to make the most of it. I think I'd have better luck finding a fer-de-lance if I got into undisturbed forest, but your activity list doesn't include off-trail hiking."

"We don't have much call for that. Most people prefer to float the river, ride the horses, or explore the Mayan ruins."

"Do you ever arrange activities that aren't on your list?"

"Sure, occasionally." He paused for a moment. "I have just the thing for you. Black Rock sits on 250 acres of privately owned jungle. Once a year the owners want us to inspect the perimeter. I was going to have Arturio walk it next week, but I can have him do it tomorrow, and you can go with him. The jungle is thick in spots—Arturio will have to cut the way with a machete—but it'll be your best chance to find a fer-de-lance."

"That sounds great. Thanks!"

John just shook his head.

After dinner, and a few more white chocolate martinis, Deb and I retired to our cabaña for the evening. Although I had put on a confident face, I was apprehensive about the coming day. We would be slashing our way through the jungle, and visibility underfoot would be limited. I tossed and turned in bed, envisioning hidden creatures taking bites out of my exposed calves. I fell into a fitful sleep.

By morning my apprehension had changed to excitement. I was ready to go. Deb and I strolled into the bar, where John and Arturio were waiting for us. Arturio was short and muscular and had a machete half his size strapped to his side. Since he didn't speak English, John gave him instructions in Spanish. I couldn't understand their conversation, but when John mimed a chopping motion with his arm, I became concerned. He had told me several fer-de-lance stories over the past two days, and most of them ended with the snake losing its head. I'd feel terrible if my hunt produced the same result.

Had John instructed Arturio *not* to kill the fer-de-lance, or had he directed him to kill it *after* I finished photographing it? To make sure we had the same goal in mind, I looked him directly in the eyes and said, "Please tell Arturio that he's *not* to kill any snakes we find."

John nodded and relayed my instructions.

Our trek commenced with Arturio leading us away from the river and into the Maya Mountains. Since Deb and I were in good shape from hiking in the Rocky Mountains at home, I didn't expect much of a physical challenge other than dealing with the heat and humidity. After all, the mountains here were mere hills by Montana standards—or so I thought.

Soon after we started, I realized the thick jungle cloaking the terrain had caused me to underestimate our task. The first part of our hike was so steep that at times we had to scramble on all fours.

Surprisingly, the difficulty of the climb had no effect on Arturio or his effortless machete work. Following him was like following a machine. By the time we reached a plateau, Deb and I were breathing heavily and sweating profusely. Arturio, on the other hand, looked as if he were starring in a TV commercial for a new Belizean antiperspirant.

One thing I learned as a kid was that snake hunts often lead to finding something good, even if it isn't a snake. In this case, we observed leafcutter ants in action for the first time. The aptly named ants were diligently cutting off pieces of leaves and carrying them in well-organized lines to their massive nest. Leafcutter ants don't eat the leaves they harvest. They use them as a substrate for growing a special fungus, which is their sole source of food. Watching the half-inch-long ants carrying leaf pieces, several times their size, made my back ache in sympathy. If I had proportionate strength, the horse I rode two days earlier could have ridden me instead.

Another interesting find was a cowfoot tree. The large, funnel-shaped, needle-sharp growths covering its trunk made it the nastiest looking tree I'd ever seen. At first, I was relieved to have spotted it before bumping into it. Then I flashed on a mental picture of Madonna in concert wearing a bustier. The likeness was uncanny. I quickly tried to erase the image from my mind, but it was too late. I was stuck on her song "Like a Virgin" for the rest of the day.

Upon reaching the highest point on Black Rock's property, we shrugged off our daypacks and reveled in the breathtaking view of the Macal River valley. When I had pictured Belize before the trip, I never envisioned being on a mountaintop and in the jungle at the same time. Yet here we stood, bounded on three sides by towering trees, while the fourth side dropped precipitously to the valley floor, where the river cut through a solid blanket of tropical forest.

Our hike continued with a climb down the opposite side of the mountain. Descending was easier, as the terrain wasn't as steep. Even with stops to check out likely snake hiding spots, we reached the lodge earlier than expected. Though I was disappointed about not finding a fer-de-lance, enough daylight remained to squeeze in another adventure.

One of Black Rock's standard activity options was floating the river on inner tubes and riding over the five-foot-high waterfall in front of the lodge. The prospect of shooting the falls had come up in our conversations with other guests, but so far no one had had the nerve to try it. Now that Deb and I were hot and grimy from our jungle trek, the falls looked irresistible.

We followed John to the storage hut, where he pulled out inner tubes and paddles for us to use. Although I looked forward to cooling off in the river, I was apprehensive about the possibility of having to swim. My wife and I are opposites when we're in the water. She's graceful and confident, and I'm clumsy and insecure. With my limitations in mind, I asked John for advice on the best way to go over the falls.

"No matter what you do," he said, "don't let go of your inner tube handle."

Deb and I lugged our gear a mile upstream before wading into the river. Getting used to the cool water took only a moment. Soon we were leisurely floating downstream, comfortably reclined in our inflatable donuts.

We soaked up the sun, watched herons feeding along the banks, and kept an eye out for boulders lurking below the surface. The river varied in depth from three to six feet, and the water was so clear we could see fish swimming beneath us. Despite the water's clarity, every so often one of us would overlook a boulder and receive a firm "kick" in the rear end.

As the roar of the waterfall grew louder, we agreed that going over one at a time would be the safer approach.

"Since you're the better swimmer, do you wanna go first?" I asked.

"Sure," said Deb.

Moments later I could see the falls. Or to be more accurate, I could see where the river dropped from sight.

As my adrenaline began to flow, my male ego took over. That I swam like a drunken house cat no longer mattered. With a few quick paddle strokes, I pulled even with my wife. "Do you mind if I go first?" I asked while passing her by.

She just smiled.

From the top of the falls, the drop looked twice as far as it looked from land.

"Holy shiiiiiiiiiiiiiiiiiiiiiiiiiiiiiit!!!" I yelled, drawing out the word as I plunged over the liquid precipice.

From Deb's vantage point, I looked like Wile E. Coyote going over a cliff in a *Road Runner* cartoon: straight out, straight down, and out of sight!

I smacked the churning water at the base of the falls. My goal was to stay upright and blissfully float to the riverbank. Everything went as planned, for a split second. Then I flipped backward into the waterfall.

The rushing water thrust me under! The weight of the falls plunged me deeper! As my toes strained to touch the river bottom, I looked up. My arms were stretched above my head, and my hands were still clutching the inner tube handle and paddle. I noticed a shaft of light penetrating the turbulence and futilely gasped for air. I tried not to panic, but as I choked, all I could think was, "So this is how it ends."

I never learned how deep the water was, because the buoyancy of the inner tube reversed my descent before I touched bottom. I popped to the surface—coughing and wheezing—hooked an arm over the inner tube, and kicked my way to the riverbank. I'd made it!

I stood on the rocks and looked for Deb. She was backpaddling above the falls, waiting for my signal. When I waved, she let the current carry her forward as she screamed, "Aaaaaaaaaaaahhhhhhhhh!"

Her ride went pretty much like mine—minus the inhaled gallon of water. When the falls spit her out, she was beaming like a child after a roller coaster ride. "That was *great!*" she yelled.

Soon Deb joined me on the riverbank, where the two of us compared adventures. Although I could now laugh about what happened, I was eager to dry off and unwind with a drink. We climbed the steep path from the river and headed directly to the bar.

We had been so involved in our float that we hadn't noticed the other guests watching us from the sundeck. When they waved us over, we joined them for an impromptu cocktail party. Our ride over the falls had been a big hit, but despite our encouragement, no one was willing to duplicate our feat.

When the party broke up, Deb and I wandered to our cabaña to sit on the porch and watch the river go by. I enjoyed just relaxing for a bit, listening to the babbling water and singing birds.

As the sun dipped below the horizon, the annoying buzz of a small but fierce contingent of mosquitoes replaced the pleasant sounds of the day. Soon the little bloodsuckers were dive-bombing us from all directions. I caught a few of the juicy pests for a bedtime snack and hurried inside.

When I presented the freshly killed mosquitoes to Spike, he seemed most appreciative of my efforts and devoured the last meal I would give him before our departure. My portion of the trip was over. We had to return to Belize City the next day to catch a boat for the Turneffe Islands.

Alejandro picked us up on Wednesday morning for another white-knuckle ride down the Western Highway. Our schedule allowed us time for a side trip to the Tropical Wings Nature Center—a native-butterfly research facility near San Ignacio.

Tino, the curator, met us at the entrance to the center and led us to his outdoor workstation. "Normally I'd take you right in to see the butterflies," he said, "but they're just beginning to warm up in the morning sun. If we wait a few minutes, they'll open their wings and be easier to photograph."

Tino's workstation was primarily a collection of jars containing caterpillars and chrysalises. I noticed two colorful chrysalises on the corner of his table and asked, "What species of butterfly will come out of these?"

"I don't know," he said. "I found them in the jungle. I'll be as surprised as anyone when they emerge."

Tino removed the lid from a jar containing a caterpillar and handed it to me. "Sniff."

I put my nose to the rim and inhaled. A harsh almond smell jolted the back of my nostrils.

"Cyanide," he said.

"Butterflies are poisonous?" I asked.

"Yes, many of our butterflies are poisonous. But they're most toxic during the caterpillar stage, when they're feeding on leaves."

A caterpillar's poison is a defense mechanism, which protects it from being eaten. Poisonous caterpillars aren't exclusive to Belize, but this was my first time witnessing the phenomenon.

The caterpillars represented only part of the cycle of chemical warfare going on around us. The cycle begins with plants producing cyanide as a defense against caterpillars that eat them; then certain caterpillar species develop immunity to the defense, and the cyanide buildup in their bodies makes them poisonous as well. Since any bird eating a toxic caterpillar would have an unpleasant and possibly fatal experience, the caterpillars appear to be the victors of the war. The caterpillars better not gloat, however, because someday birds may also develop an immunity to cyanide, become poisonous, and rule the jungle.

After Tino finished showing us his workstation, he led us into the butterfly house. More than two hundred butterflies lived within the confines of the plant-filled, sixty-foot-long, two-story-tall, screened enclosure. While some fluttered about, others clung motionless to the vegetation.

As the facility's sole visitors, Deb and I leisurely moved among the butterflies without anyone getting in our way. Of the fifteen or so species we observed, our favorites were the appropriately named clearwing butterflies, the brilliantly colored blue morpho butterflies, and the hand-sized owl butterflies (named for the large spot on each wing that resembles an owl's eye).

I could have spent the entire morning photographing butterflies without a hint of boredom, but we had to stay on schedule if we were going to reach the harbor on the far side of Belize City in time to catch the semiweekly boat to Blackbird Caye Resort. Missing the boat would have been disastrous, but with Alejandro at the wheel, only a head-on collision could make us tardy. He whisked us across the country and dropped us at the port with time to spare.

From Belize City we raced east across the Caribbean Sea on a thirty-two-mile-long speedboat ride to the Turneffe Islands atoll (a collection of coral islands surrounding a lagoon). The voyage was similar to Alejandro's driving—speed, not comfort, was the goal. Our single-cabin boat skipped from wave to wave, giving us spankings along the way. By the time we reached our destination, my entire body was vibrating.

Blackbird Caye Resort is situated on a four-thousand-acre, jungle-covered island, which it shares with the Blackbird Oceanic Society Field Station. At the time of our visit, the resort's layout included a main building, twelve beachfront cabañas, a triple-sized cabaña, and staff quarters.

Aside from the tropical decor, the resort felt more American than Belizean. All of the current guests were from the United States, as were the majority of the frontline staff. We would even pay our bar tab with U.S. dollars. I had mixed feelings about this. Even though spending a familiar currency and communicating with people who spoke like me would be convenient, the Americanisms diluted much of the cultural flavor from the experience.

With three-, four-, and seven-day reservations available, groups arrive at Blackbird Caye Resort at different times and have overlapping stays. Since the holdovers have already established relationships with other guests and staff, the staggered scheduling can make new guests feel like outsiders.

On this day, two couples arrived with us on the speedboat: Mark and Carolyn from New Jersey, and Greg and Andrea from Pennsylvania. Mark was a musician, Carolyn was a graphic arts recruiter, and Greg and Andrea were chiropractors. Everyone in our group was between thirty and forty-five years of age.

The six of us walked into the main building for an orientation on scuba diving and other activities. The large, single-room, high-ceilinged, tropical-themed structure had a reading area near the entrance, a bar on the left, and tables arranged in a semicircle around the center post and breakfast counter. Eighteen people from a Minnesota-based scuba club occupied the tables on the right side of the room. They were in the midst of a boisterous, alcohol-splashed, post-dive party.

As the sober new arrivals, we felt like high school freshmen entering a cafeteria full of rowdy upperclassmen and chose the table farthest to the left. Although the six of us had exchanged only a few words on the boat, we instantly became friends and would share several meals and activities during our stay.

After orientation, Deb and I unpacked and went for a stroll along the wide, sandy beach. As we walked hand in hand, numerous thoughts wandered through my mind: "Something about this place seems familiar. The palm trees, the thatched-roof cabañas . . . I know. This is as close to *Gilligan's Island* as you can get in real life. What were the castaways thinking! Who would want to escape from this?"

When we reached a sandbar at the end of a point, we stopped to let the gently rolling waves wash over our bare feet. Both of us were eager to see more of Blackbird Caye, but since the sky was growing dark, we sauntered back and settled into our cabaña for the night. I took the upper hammock, and Deb took the lower one.

Okay, we didn't really sleep in hammocks. Once inside our cabaña, the primitiveness of *Gilligan's Island* was replaced by modern conveniences including air-conditioning, a hot-water shower, and yes—a comfortable bed.

I awoke before sunrise. While Deb slept, I eased out of bed and threw on a T-shirt and shorts. Our cabaña sat on the southeastern side of the island, and a path led north from our porch into the jungle. With my flashlight and camera in hand, I hiked down the path until it petered out. From there, I picked my own route through the trees. As I walked slowly among the first shadows of dawn, a glint of something shiny froze me in midstep.

"Whoa! What is that?" I shouted.

Floating on a huge web, millimeters from my nose, was the fiercest looking spider I'd ever seen. It had a long body—the size of a tube of lipstick—oversized fangs, and legs that stretched out as far as my fingertips. Since I hadn't seen anything like it before, I presumed I had discovered a rare new species of spider and promptly dubbed it a *Belizean fangs-o-death*.

I shivered thinking about what might have happened had I taken another step. I envisioned the spider grasping my face, injecting deadly venom between my eyes, and sucking out my brains. Soon my imagination had the spider rivaling the creature from the movie *Alien*.

I took a deep breath and returned to reality.

Once I realized the Belizean fangs-o-death wouldn't leap from her web to attack me, I began to appreciate what a beautiful creature she was. Her shiny golden-brown body was covered with speckles of red, yellow, and white—she would have made a great Christmas tree ornament.

I engrossed myself in photographing the spider until I noticed the sun was about to rise over the horizon. I couldn't pass up the opportunity for an ocean sunrise shot and turned to dash for the b—

"Whoa!" Once again, I froze in midstep.

The sky was now bright enough that I could see more easily where I was going. Somehow, in the twilight, I'd walked the perfect route into a massive cluster of webs. Left, right, everywhere I looked was another spider. I was surrounded by fangs-o-death!

So much for it being a *rare* spider.

I ducked under a web, zigzagged around another, and squeezed between two more. Spotting an opening, I raced toward the ocean, reaching the beach just in time to capture a sequence of stunning sunrise images.

The human guests on the island were still asleep, but I wasn't alone. Sharing my sunrise—and obviously enjoying it in their own way—were several billion sand fleas. The nearly invisible insects took advantage of my distracted state and indulged in a hearty breakfast of Marty legs. While I'm all for supporting the resident wildlife, the fleas took my generosity too far. My legs would itch for the rest of the trip and then some.

Although the sunrise was dramatic, something more spectacular caught my attention—further down the beach several brown pelicans were fishing. I've watched birds fish before, but nothing compares to the technique used by brown pelicans. From high above the water they'd suddenly drop headfirst into the ocean. The human reaction to seeing them hit the water for the first time can be summed up in one word: Ouch!

An interesting fact about brown pelicans is that they're the only pelican species that dives from the air to catch their food. Other pelicans swim, often using cooperative herding methods, to capture their prey.

Having survived the Belizean fangs-o-death, admired the sunrise, and cringed at the pelican splats, I headed back to the resort.

(I learned later that the Belizean fangs-o-death was actually a mildly venomous golden orb weaver subspecies. How boring is that? You gotta admit: my spider name is better.)

I reached our cabaña just as the other guests were stirring to prepare for a day of scuba diving. Of the resort's twenty-four guests, I was one of three who hadn't come to dive. I love most outdoor activities, but all my life I've struggled to overcome both my fear of heights and my fear of water. Once, despite my aversion for heights, I managed to parachute out of a perfectly good airplane, but thanks to a cruel, head-dunking, cigar-smoking swimming teacher I had as a child, even the thought of going underwater with scuba gear makes me hyperventilate.

Deb, on the other hand, was eager to go underwater and explore the pristine reef surrounding the islands. In many popular diving locations, the reefs are in poor shape due to carelessly dropped boat anchors and divers who insist on touching everything they see. Here, the boats weren't allowed to anchor on the reef (the captain follows the divers' rising air bubbles), and proper diving protocols were enforced.

Deb went on three dives during our stay—two on the first day and one on the second. When she returned after her first outings, she wasn't as enthusiastic as I expected her to be.

"I enjoyed the dives," she said. "The reef was in great shape, and the variety of sponges, corals, and fish was amazing. There was even a barrel sponge so big I swear I could've fit inside it. The one negative was that most of the group just wanted to cruise over the reef. I would've much rather gone slower and explored a smaller area."

"Speak up next time," I said. "You're paying for your dives just like everyone else."

"I know, but I was outnumbered and didn't feel right telling the others what to do."

"Keep in mind, the dive club has been here all week, and tomorrow is your last chance."

"Let me see how things go. Perhaps I will say something."

When Deb was diving, I was exploring Blackbird Caye. A sandy beach ringed the southern end of the island, and thick mangroves fringed the northern end. After walking the entire beach, I found the mangroves impenetrable and turned my attention to the heart of the island. Much of the interior was swampy and thick with coconut palms, ferns, and broadleaf plants. Snakes? While the habitat looked ideal for them, it was possible that none lived on the island. Rather than engage in a futile search, I wandered back to the resort to get some advice.

I found David, the manager, in the main building. He had a serious demeanor that didn't match his dark tan, windblown blond hair, or tropical-print shirt. I'm not sure how long he had worked at the resort, but based on the surprised look he shot me, I was obviously the first person to inquire about the island's legless inhabitants.

"Snakes, huh?" he said. "Interesting you should ask. Just the other day I saw a boa constrictor under your cabaña. Boas are common around here, but they're not something we normally advertise to our guests."

"Excellent!" I said. "I had two boa constrictors when I was a kid. Finding one in the wild would make my trip."

Boa constrictors are heavy-bodied nonvenomous snakes, which grow up to fourteen feet in length. That Blackbird Caye would have a sufficient food supply for such a large snake was unlikely. Instead, it would probably support one of the many dwarf island subspecies, which reach five feet in length or less. For me, size didn't matter. Finding a slender three-footer would give me as much pleasure as a fourteen-foot-long behemoth.

I was confident of success. After all, how hard could it be to find a common snake on a small island?

After a break for lunch, I began my boa constrictor search. First, I looked beneath every cabaña. Then I meandered through the jungle scanning tree branches and checking under anything that could hide a snake. My hunt didn't produce the result I wanted, but I did find dozens of green iguanas and small lizards. Unlike the iguanas on the mainland, which were usually high in the trees, most of the ones I found here were on or near the ground. In fact, on several occasions I was able to sneak up and give them a pat before they scurried away.

While I found exploring the island's interior to be a fascinating experience, it was an uncommon activity. Most guests stay at Blackbird Caye Resort solely to enjoy the Caribbean Sea. If not scuba diving, they were usually tanning on the beach, snorkeling over the reef, or kayaking in the lagoon.

The resort's staff was probably relieved their guests didn't do much on-land exploration. Although I was pleased to find sections of the island untouched by human activities, I was sickened to discover that an area behind the resort was being used as a garbage dump. How could anyone justify using the island as a trash receptacle? To learn the answer, I marched back into the main building to find David.

"I was out looking for snakes and was shocked to come across your garbage dump. Why would you pollute such a beautiful island?"

David shook his head in agreement. "I know the trash isn't pretty, but it has to go somewhere. Where do you suggest we put it?"

Before I could answer, a staff member shouted from the door that the dive boat had returned. David had to excuse himself to help unload equipment.

I considered approaching him later to press the issue, but I had already made my point. He knew I was upset. If enough people spoke up, the resort would have to do something about the problem.

(Once back in the United States, I made multiple inquiries about the dump. In August 2005, I received an e-mail from the owner assuring me that a barge now comes out to the island every month to haul garbage away.)

Following our first full day on the island, Deb and I joined Carolyn, Mark, Andrea, and Greg for dinner. The resort served excellent food, and we always had our choice of a surf, turf, or vegetarian entrée. Halfway through our meal, one of the dive crew rushed in from the dock to announce that a crocodile had come for a visit.

A wave of excitement flowed over me. If I couldn't find a boa constrictor, a croc would make an excellent consolation prize. I dashed into the darkness with the others close behind. When we reached the dock, a lamp provided just enough light for us to make out the eight-foot-long American crocodile smiling from the shallow water. He was truly a beautiful reptile—shiny and brown, without a single visible scar.

According to the International Union for Conservation of Nature and Natural Resources (IUCN), American crocodiles are a "vulnerable species." (Every IUCN status cited in this book comes from the *2004 IUCN Red List of Threatened Species.*) Despite their diminishing numbers, they maintain a stronghold within the Turneffe Islands. Consequently, one of the warnings given to us at orientation was to resist the urge to go skinny-dipping at night.

I was surprised how unafraid the crocodile acted, until I learned he was a regular visitor who showed up around dinnertime for scraps of chicken. Humans should never feed wild animals, but that complaint could wait for another day. Since the croc looked like he'd stick around for a while, I ran to my cabaña and grabbed a flashlight and both of my cameras.

When I returned, I handed the flashlight to Deb so she could aim it at the crocodile while I focused my cameras. Unsure of what would work in the challenging lighting conditions, I used different film and settings for each camera and snapped multiple shots.

The crocodile provided the perfect opportunity for my travel gods to make their first international appearance. Based on business trips and the few domestic vacations I had taken with Deb, I knew travel gods accompanied me whenever I was away from home. I'm not sure how many of these fun-loving, occasionally sadistic deities exist, but I'm pretty sure of three: one who likes me, one who despises me, and one who thinks he's a comedian. The practical joker is definitely the ring-leader. When I go on business trips, he always hides my belt.

The travel gods delight in making me do stupid things—far be it for me to take credit for the acts. In this instance, they decided I wasn't close enough for a good photo and convinced me to lie on the dock and lower a camera inches from the water, well within the crocodile's strike range. Since I couldn't look through the viewfinder, I had to guess at my aim and lens settings. Luckily, I ended up with some great croc shots from a unique perspective—and as an added bonus, I got to keep my fingers!

Friday, our last full day in Belize, had arrived, and I was determined not to waste a moment of it. I set off into the jungle before sunrise to continue my boa constrictor search.

I was bolder searching through the vegetation here than I would have been on the mainland. Because I was on an island, the sur-rounding water would keep me from getting hopelessly lost, and there probably weren't any dangerous creatures to worry about—unless I disturbed a crocodile. The only time I felt uneasy was in swampy areas, where deep mud threatened to suck me down and deposit me at the Earth's core.

After several hours of scouring the jungle without luck, I trudged back to the resort to meet Deb for lunch. While I had been snake hunting, she had been on the morning dive boat.

"I can tell by your smile you had a good dive."

"Yes—it was *soooo* much better than yesterday."

"You must have talked to the dive master, then."

"I did, but it really wasn't necessary. Most of the people from the dive club had decided to sleep in, and everyone else was into doing a macrodive." (A macrodive is a slow-moving dive for exploring the nooks and crannies of the reef.)

"That's great! Tell me about it."

"Well, I spent an hour in crystal clear water at a depth of twenty-five feet. I found a huge moray eel under a coral shelf, and cleaner wrasses were servicing him by picking parasites from his teeth and gills. Then a sea turtle, the size of a dinner plate, swam up from behind some coral and floated in front of my face to pose for pictures. I also found a lob-ster colony crammed into a crevice and an *incredible* variety of fish, including French angelfish, parrot fish, puffer fish, and others I didn't recognize."

"Cool! I'm glad you finally got the dive you wanted."

"It was wonderful! So—how was *your* morning?"

"Pretty good. No snakes, but lots of lizards. . . ."

When we finished eating, Deb and I met up with Mark and Carolyn for a sea-kayak outing in the lagoon on the western side of the island. The four of us enjoyed the warm, sunny afternoon, paddling about in the clear water and keeping an eye out for crocodiles.

Upon our return, Deb persuaded me to go snorkeling with her. The last time I tried snorkeling I almost drowned. As strange as it may sound, snorkeling combines my fear of water with my fear of heights.

My near-drowning experience occurred fifteen years earlier on the island of Maui, Hawaii. I hadn't snorkeled before but agreed to try it so I could get a taste of what Deb experienced when she scuba dived. On that day, both my lack of buoyancy and the worst head cold of my life combined to work against me. Not only did I have trouble floating on top of the water, but I also had difficulty breathing through my snorkel.

I practiced near shore, snorkeling for a minute or two each time before having to stand and catch my breath. My snippets of underwater observation helped me appreciate Deb's fascination with scuba diving. The fish were so intensely colored they appeared to radiate from an internal light source.

As I continued practicing, my technique improved. Eventually my confidence grew to where I felt comfortable following Deb away from shore to a section of reef in eight feet of water. Although I could no longer touch bottom, I blissfully cruised along without incident.

When I reached the far side of the reef, the ocean floor unexpectedly dropped off, and I found myself looking down through forty feet of clear water. A new sensation overcame me—I felt as if I were teetering on the edge of a cliff.

Logically, I knew that snorkeling in forty feet of water wasn't any more difficult than snorkeling in eight feet of water. I also knew I wasn't going to fall from the surface of the water and break my neck on the ocean floor. As I struggled to think rationally, a microscopic Cro-Magnon man emerged from the recesses of my brain and shouted, "Panic! Get out of the water now! Breathe as fast as you can or you'll drown! Thrash your arms and legs—it's the *only* way to keep from falling to the bottom! The shore is too far away! You'll never make it! Paniiiiiiiiiiiiiiiiic!"

Unable to ignore the commotion in my brain, I flailed toward shore, frequently trying to touch bottom, each time misjudging the depth and pistoning under the water in midbreath. Soon I was exhausted and hyperventilating. I didn't have much left, but I forced myself to swim until my toes connected with solid ground.

Bloated from trying to drink the ocean dry, I labored out of the water and rolled onto the beach. I looked for Deb and spotted her floating over the reef, unaware of what had happened.

Now, as I stood on the beach at Blackbird Caye, I tried to purge my memory of the Maui ordeal. I wasn't thrilled about snorkeling again but knew giving it another shot would make my wife happy—I'm such a good husband.

This time I wouldn't be able to practice near shore, as the reef was in fifteen feet of water, three hundred feet straight out from our cabaña. Deb and I paddled our sea kayak to the edge of the reef, slipped on our masks and fins, wrapped our lips around our snorkel mouthpieces, and eased into the cool water.

I kicked my feet and floated for one or two heavenly seconds—then the ghost of my childhood swimming teacher swooped down and shoved me underwater!

I struggled to the surface and launched myself into the kayak.

"This isn't gonna be easy!" I said, spitting the harsh, salty taste out of my mouth.

"Just relax," said Deb. "You'll be okay."

"Oh, so *that's* the problem. I just need to relax while inhaling the ocean."

I tried again, this time floating for nearly a minute before my lungs seized. I rolled back into the kayak, angry with myself for not doing better.

"This is pathetic!" I said, knowing Deb was underwater and couldn't hear me. "Everyone at the resort, even the housekeeping staff, has a reef exploration story to tell—except me."

As I draped my legs over the side of the kayak, psyching myself up for another try, the ghost of my childhood swimming teacher coughed. I glanced up and he smiled a sinister smile—his lips eaten away from puffing thousands of cigars. I was no longer an easily intimidated eight-year-old boy. This time he wasn't going to defeat me. I slid back into the water.

Still holding the kayak, I stretched out and willed myself to float. I let go and drifted over the coral. Soon Deb glided alongside me, pointing out highlights of the reef. We snorkeled side by side for a bit, then separated while I followed a school of tiny blue fish.

I was heading to my left when Deb grabbed my wrist and pulled me to the right. The excitement in her eyes pierced the window of her dive mask. I immediately thought, "Shark! Crocodile!"

She pointed down with an exaggerated gesture, but when I looked, all I saw was coral. She pointed up and we popped our heads above the water.

"There's a *huge* moray eel below us! He swam out of the coral to look at me before retreating into a hole. He probably won't come out again, but keep an eye out for him."

Moray eel attacks on humans are rare, but any animal that grows to ten feet in length and has razor-sharp teeth deserves an extra measure of caution. Giving the eel plenty of space wouldn't be a problem for me. I wasn't a good enough swimmer to be diving underwater and sticking my nose where it didn't belong anyway. I circled above the coral, hoping for the thrill of seeing a moray, but he never showed himself again.

The one advantage I had over Deb was that my struggles to stay afloat kept me warm. After an hour, she was chilled and ready to go ashore.

Although the fish on this minor section of reef weren't as large or as brightly colored as the ones I had seen in Maui, just being able to observe the underwater life without hyperventilating was a victory for me. I can't say I mastered snorkeling, but at least I had a reef story of my own to tell at dinner that night.

The smell of shish kebabs sizzling on the grill drifted into our cabaña as we changed into dry clothes. Deb and I, along with most of the guests, would be leaving for the mainland on the morning boat. To say goodbye, the resort staff was hosting a barbecue and beach party.

As we joined the festivities, the bartender handed us each a glass of rum punch and proclaimed, "Drinks are on the house!"

The evening was perfect: the temperature was ideal, and a gentle breeze wafted in from the ocean. We sat on the beach chatting with Greg, Andrea, Mark, and Carolyn. I can't remember what we talked about, but I can still feel the warm sand flowing between my toes and the contentment of being with people I liked.

When the sun went down, a wave of sand fleas rose up and forced us inside. As on the day we arrived, the dive club from Minnesota preceded us to the bar. This time, however, the freshman class feeling was gone. Together we finished off the rum punch and laughed into the night.

Morning came far too quickly. Deb and I rushed to pack our bags and down our breakfast before meeting everyone on the dock. Leaving such a paradisiacal island was difficult, and the bumpy speedboat ride punished everyone who had drunk too much the night before.

Physically I felt okay, but mentally I was just beginning to sort out my thoughts. The disadvantage of goal-oriented travel is that failure is always a possibility. My unsuccessful boa constrictor and fer-de-lance searches had left me feeling simultaneously frustrated and invigorated. Even though the snakes had eluded me, the time I spent combing through the jungle was far more enjoyable than any vacation I could have had lying around on a beach all day.

As we sped toward Belize City, I realized I was hooked. I hadn't even finished this trip, and I was already contemplating where to go next to look for wildlife. Costa Rica came to mind first, but then I thought about the Amazon rainforest—I'd always wanted to go there. "Yes, that's where I'll go," I thought. "But will Deb go with me?" I decided to wait until we got home before springing the idea on her.

The boat dropped us at the port with a half day to burn before our flight departed for the United States. Every local guidebook I had read proclaimed that visiting the Belize Zoo was a must. Though I'm not a fan of zoos, the Belize Zoo was unique, and a visit would make good use of our time. All we had to do was figure out how to get thirty-one miles west of the city without a car.

Our problem was instantly solved when a taxi driver met us at the end of the dock and offered to take us to both the zoo and the airport for a flat fee. His price was so reasonable that haggling was unnecessary. We just hopped into his car and headed west.

The one thing we had missed at the beginning of our trip was a Belize City tour. Now, traveling at a relaxed speed, I could look out the windows without worrying about oncoming traffic. What immediately stood out was the lack of a visible middle class. I saw several palatial mansions, which our driver said political leaders and corporate figures owned, and hundreds of rundown shacks, which the general population occupied.

"Are there any midsized houses?" I asked.

"No," he said. "Belize has a few rich people and everyone else is poor."

Statistics backed up his statement. The annual per capita income in Belize was only $3,260 (U.S.), a figure that didn't leave much room for a middle class.

Upon reaching the zoo, our driver pulled into the parking lot and said, "I'll wait for you here. You have at least two hours before we have to leave for the airport, so take your time."

The Belize Zoo was worthy of the hype. Unlike traditional zoos, which are virtual jails, here the majority of the animals lived in large open-air enclosures resembling their natural habitat. The zoo was started in 1983, as a project to save native animals that had been used in the filming of a documentary, and it had grown to 125 animals by the time of our visit. All the inhabitants were native to Belize and were either born at the zoo, rescued, rehabilitated, or received as gifts. Over the years, the zoo has made a significant impact locally by teaching the importance of protecting Belizean wildlife, and earned a worldwide reputation for its conservation efforts.

I especially enjoyed my visit because I could observe all the animals I might have seen in the jungle had I been lucky. Since the zoo seldom used traditional cages, photographing the animals without bars getting in the way was easy. Even the jaguars, which by necessity had to be caged, looked at home in their large tree-filled living quarters.

Once we returned home, I'd be tempted to show off my zoo photographs accompanied by grand stories such as: "I snuck up on this jaguar and snapped these ten close-up photos. Then I noticed the jaguar was stalking a spider monkey, so I took a few photos of it as well. And here's where things really get interesting. The spider monkey was watching a coatimundi, who was following this jabiru stork, who was trying to avoid this fer-de-lance. . . ."

Content that we had now seen most of the major animal species in Belize, Deb and I rendezvoused with our taxi driver and proceeded to the airport.

While I waited to board the airplane, I flashed back to my high school American history class and a lecture my teacher had given on why all other countries were inferior to the United States. With just one visit to a foreign country, I learned that *different* was a more appropriate word than *inferior.* I liked different. Belize had whetted my appetite for world travel and was the perfect first step in a journey that would lead me to discover what different meant all over the world.

2
Amazon Encounters
of the Venomous Kind

After we arrived home from Belize, I was still feeling discouraged about my failure to find a snake. I felt as if I were a modern day Saint Patrick who had rid the entire country of snakes. Wait a minute . . . that was it. I was Saint Martin of Belize! Soon statues of me would be going up all over the country, parades would be held in my honor, a day would be named after me, Belikin would brew a special beer. . . .

I reveled in my new sainthood for a while before realizing that being a living saint would be a lot of work. First my followers would want me to bless everything; then they'd want more miracles. Who wants to live under that sort of pressure? I'd rather find a boa constrictor or fer-de-lance anyway. And you know, as soon as I went somewhere and found a snake, I'd be promptly "decanonized."

Of all the places in the world to look for snakes, I couldn't think of anywhere I'd have a better chance for success than the Amazon River and rainforest region of Peru. I just needed to convince my wife to go with me.

Deb and I had been married for seventeen years, yet as international travel partners we were newlyweds. Even though I knew her outgoing personality well, I wouldn't fully appreciate her bravery until further into our travels. Therefore, I approached her tentatively about the Amazon, half expecting her to declare such a trip would give her the creeps. To my surprise she replied, "I'll go with you to Peru, if you promise to go with me to Australia after that."

I asked for one trip and received two instead. Did I marry a great woman, or what? Perhaps she was the saint, not me. We were headed for Peru, a country with far too many snakes for either of us to rid in a single visit.

While the decision to travel to the Amazon happened quickly, it was actually the culmination of a dream hatched back in grade school when I wanted to become a herpetologist. In my mind, such a journey was like a religious pilgrimage to a holy site—a virtual requirement for anyone who loves herpetofauna. Although my career plans changed when I grew older, my Amazon dream would now become a reality.

From sixteenth-century Spanish explorer Francisco de Orellana's claims of a female warrior race to tales of poisonous snakes, man-eating piranhas, huge spiders, tropical diseases, and headhunters, no place on Earth surpasses the Amazon for mystery and perceived danger. When I informed family and friends of our travel plans, most thought we were insane. My mother burst into tears, and my attorney insisted we immediately draw up our wills. While the adult in me was touched by their concern, my evil inner child couldn't help blurting out, "And my goal is to photograph a fer-de-lance, up close!"

As with other trips in this book, we had options for accommodations that cater to people who like visiting exotic places without giving up the conveniences of home. This was especially true along the main body of the Amazon River, near the city of Iquitos, where one lodge even advertised a chlorinated pool and waterslide. Deb and I had no interest in such luxuries, however. We wanted to experience the rainforest, not just a resort located in the rainforest.

After we eliminated everything near Iquitos, an Internet search led us to select an eco-tour expedition service called Margarita Tours. Accompanied by American guides, Dr. Ben Schmitt and Dr. Devon Graham, we would travel from Iquitos by boat eighty-four miles down the Amazon River and thirty-two miles up the Rio Orosa (a south-bank tributary). We would sleep three nights on the boat and three nights at a biological research station.

Traveling from the Missoula International Airport to Iquitos, Peru, was a frustrating chore. Before we even departed, the airline changed our flight schedule five times and added an extra day to our trip. Our final schedule had us leaving Missoula on Thursday, July 5, 2001, with overnight layovers in Minneapolis and Lima before arriving in Iquitos on Saturday. Even that almost didn't work out when the airline misplaced the records of our e-tickets to Lima and nearly stranded us in Houston during an aircraft change.

When we touched down in Lima, a crowd of several hundred shouting Peruvians met us at the airport exit. Naturally I assumed they were proclaiming the arrival of Saint Martin of Belize, but as we walked the gauntlet, only a few people showed interest in us—and they just wanted to carry our bags or give us rides. Deb and I spotted our shuttle driver on the far side of the crowd, holding a sign with our names on it. He knew only a few words of English, but that was all he needed to direct us to his van and whisk us to our hotel.

Lima is a huge city that covers 390 square miles and has a population of 7.5 million people. My exposure to Peru's capital during our ten-minute ride was enough to make me glad we hadn't reached our final destination. Judging by my view from the van, it was a dirty, overcrowded, and hectic metropolis.

We spent the night in an old hotel, not far from a busy street. Our room wasn't much larger than our bed, but that was fine. The problem was that the walls were so thin we could hear commotion from the street all night. What little sleep I got came in fits and starts.

At breakfast, we met Dr. Ben Schmitt and our fellow expedition participants (Dr. Devon Graham would join us later). Two Californians, two Texans, and a Spaniard made up the small group. Ben, the trip leader, was one of the Californians. He was a tall man in his fifties with a crew cut and closely trimmed beard. The other Californian was Megan, an athletic woman in her mid-thirties. She was a receptionist at a veterinary clinic and had been on a previous Amazon trip. As for the Texans, Jack and Mary were a down-to-earth couple in their mid-fifties. They owned a successful business and were obviously looking forward to escaping phones and fax machines for a while. Rounding out the group was Terese, a graphic artist from northern Spain. She was in her late forties and had long graying hair and a warm personality that could instantly light up a room.

The seven of us crammed into a shuttle van and weaved through traffic to the airport. The only reason we had flown to Lima was because we couldn't fly directly to Iquitos. Having overshot our destination, we now had to fly six hundred miles to the northeast.

The Lima airport was small in proportion to the population it served. Passengers waiting to get on the morning flights occupied every chair, and the overflow of people sat wherever they could find a smidgen of floor space.

The din of hundreds of voices made deciphering the flight announcements, which were given only in Spanish, nearly impossible. When everyone in the gate area rose and started squeezing through the doors, Deb and I followed. We walked onto the tarmac and stared at four identical 727-sized airplanes—all with their steps pulled down. I looked back for the rest our group, but they were out of sight.

"Which plane is ours?" I asked.

"Hell if I know," said Deb.

Since people were boarding more than one aircraft, we couldn't be sheep. When I spotted a woman dressed in an airline uniform, I asked, "Which plane do we get on for Iquitos?"

She tilted her head, as if she didn't understand, then pointed vaguely toward the four airplanes and shouted, "Iquitos!"

Being six feet tall has its advantages. I glanced over the shoulder of the man in front of me and saw he had a ticket for Iquitos. He was moving with purpose, so we followed him up the steps of one of the airplanes. Once inside, a multilingual flight attendant greeted us and confirmed our seats. Relieved to be in the right place, we settled in for takeoff.

Our flight path led us over the Andes Mountains. Since the sky was mostly clear, the view out my window was spectacular. The Andes are the second-highest mountain system in the world. Some of the peaks below us towered twenty thousand feet above sea level. I noticed occasional tiny villages, surrounded by massive peaks, far from other visible signs of life. That anyone could live in such a harsh environment amazed me.

When a sheet of clouds blocked the view, my mind wandered to *Alive*, the movie about the 1972 Andes plane crash that forced the Uruguayan rugby team into cannibalism. I pondered what might happen if we ended up in a similar situation. Luckily, I was in good shape. I'd be tough and chewy and could avoid being on the menu for a while. The plump woman in front of me would definitely go first.

The plane shuddered! Moments later the PA crackled on and the first officer announced something in Spanish.

We listed sharply to the left, as if one of the engines had died, then plunged toward Earth!

"This is it!" I thought. "We're going to be in the Andes plane crash sequel!"

Click, click, click, passengers hurriedly fastened their seat belts.

"Umm, umm," the first officer cleared his throat before beginning a second announcement—this time in English. "We'll be landing in Iquitos momentarily. Please bring your seat back to an upright position and fasten your seat belt. You!—the blond-haired American clutching his armrests. Cease your paranoid fantasy about cannibalism. It's disgusting and it's *not* going to happen!"

Iquitos sits alongside the Amazon River and has a population of 370,000. Rainforest surrounds the city, and the only way in or out is by boat or airplane. Rumors of a road project linking Iquitos to the outside world have persisted for years, but at the time of our visit, the farthest anyone could drive was fifty-five miles to the isolated community of Nauta—and even that road was impassible during periods of heavy rain.

A shuttle van transported us directly from the airport to our boat. Our schedule would return us to Iquitos for an overnight visit at the end of the expedition, but for now our curiosity about this unique city would have to wait.

As we stepped from the van, several teenage boys converged on us, hoping to sell us trinkets. They were polite yet persistent.

"We can't buy anything now because we're going on the river for a week," I said.

"But we will buy something when we get back," added Deb.

"My name is Michael. Buy one necklace from me now."

"I will when I get back," said Deb. "I promise."

"I'm Alfredo. My brother painted these postcards."

"They're very well-done," I said, "but if I take them on the boat they might get wet. I'll buy some when I return. I promise."

The boys reluctantly waved good-bye as our group walked onto the dock and boarded the *M/N Tucunare*. We had reached the Amazon River!

The captain eased the boat away from shore and steered downriver. While others unpacked gear, cracked open beers, and immersed themselves in small talk, I stood alone near the tip of the bow. I wasn't being unsociable. I had waited more than thirty years to make my pilgrimage to the greatest river on Earth and wanted a few moments to soak in the grandeur of it all. The Amazon was a mile wide (the river's widest point varies between seven and twenty-five miles across, depending on the season) with a wall of rainforest on each side. I felt as if I were floating down the center of a giant cathedral.

Geographers have traditionally considered the Amazon to be the second-longest river in the world behind the Nile. Recent findings, however, suggest that the more than four-thousand-mile-long Amazon may actually be the longer of the two rivers. While the debate will continue for years, one statistic not in dispute is overall volume. The Amazon is the world's largest river, carrying one-fifth of all the freshwater that drains into the oceans.

I popped open a beer and explored the *M/N Tucunare*. The boxy, seventy-two-foot-long, green and white riverboat was made out of native hardwood and powered by a 136-horsepower diesel engine. The vessel's main features included an upper deck, which contained the pilothouse and a partially canopied open area for lounging, and a lower deck, which contained six double sleeping berths, a kitchen, a dining room, and two compact bathrooms with showers.

Waste from both toilets flushed directly into the Amazon, joining the raw sewage from other boats and the city of Iquitos. Conversely, the water for our showers was pumped directly from the river. Although this wouldn't be a trip for the germ obsessed, the water wasn't as repugnant as you might expect. The river didn't stink, and I didn't see any floating trash. I did, however, make a mental note to keep my mouth shut when showering.

Dr. Ben Schmitt was the expedition's official leader, but since he was along primarily as an advisor, the title of "host" might have been more accurate. Margarita Tours has a staff of experts who take turns leading expeditions. Though Ben's doctorate was in chemistry, and seemingly unrelated to his duties here, he was a highly qualified Amazon authority and an accomplished wildlife photographer.

Tropical ecologist Dr. Devon Graham had been waiting for us on the *M/N Tucunare* when we arrived. The forty-year-old Floridian ran the Amazon operations for Margarita Tours and was the person actually in charge of the expedition. He had a lean build, short brown hair, and—as I would learn later—a razor-sharp wit.

In addition to the American staff, we also had five Peruvians assisting with the expedition: boat captain, Fernando Rios; chef, Danilo Amasifuen; steward, Emerson Torres; and naturalist guides, Cesar Peña and Segundo Rios. While we would have limited interactions with the first three men, Cesar and Segundo (both in their mid-twenties) would accompany us whenever we explored the rainforest. In all, staff members outnumbered paying participants seven to six.

Our journey to Madre Selva Biological Station would take a total of nine hours, but since we'd make some stops along the way, we wouldn't reach our destination until the following day. My first Amazon adventure occurred a mere four hours into the expedition. At Ben's request, Captain Rios pulled to the riverbank, two hundred feet beyond where a stream emptied into the Amazon. The doctor wanted to do some netting to find out what species of fish inhabited the confluence.

Devon announced our stop would be brief. We could either remain on the boat or follow him and Ben to the stream. After a moment of indecision, we all elected to check out the fish and hurried to our sleeping berths to grab our knee-high rubber boots (the recommended footwear for the expedition).

Devon and Ben were well on their way by the time Deb, I, and the others descended the ramp to the wide flat riverbank. Our Amazon visit was taking place during the dry season, and the river was dropping rapidly with the diminishing rains. Although it didn't occur to me at the time, the riverbank had likely been underwater within the past week.

As would become apparent all too soon, part of the mystery of the Amazon is that things aren't always as they appear. The riverbank *looked* solid, but beneath a thin crust of sun-dried mud was a mixture of sediment and water not quite ambitious enough to be quicksand. Without thinking to follow in the doctors' footsteps, I blissfully took the most direct route to the stream.

Fifty feet from the boat, I broke through the crust and sank to my shins in sludge. I tried to step out, but the crust crumbled around me, widening the hole. The more I struggled to escape, the deeper I sank. Warm mud flowed into my boots.

Deb circled me from ten feet away and giggled. "I can walk on the bank just fine. It's good to be the girl!"

"Ha-ha," I said as I struggled some more. "See if you can find me a stick."

As Deb scanned the edge of the rainforest, others in our group, who had been watching from a distance, joined the search.

"I found one!" said Terese. "Here." She tossed the seven-foot-long stick to Deb, who in turn tossed it to me.

Now, hip deep in sludge, I thrust the stick into the bank and watched its entire length disappear beneath the crust. When I looked up with a blank stare, everyone laughed.

I knew what I had to do. I just didn't want to do it. First, I leaned backward until my torso was flush with the riverbank—Amazon ooze seeped through my clothing. Next, I concentrated on pulling my right knee toward my nose. *Shloooop!*—the wallow released my foot with a loud sucking sound. Finally, I concentrated on my left knee. *Shloooop!*—I was free! I rolled onto my stomach, crawled to firm ground, and stood, covered with mud from head to toe—the *Author from the Black Lagoon.*

By the time I escaped, Devon and Ben were already returning from the stream. I had missed out on the fish but was duly initiated. I trudged back to the *M/N Tucunare* for my first cold Amazon shower.

We proceeded downriver until sunset, then tied ashore for the night. Shortly after the captain cut the engine, eight people from the Yagua tribe emerged from the rainforest to check us out. One was in her teens and the rest were younger. They stood on the riverbank—totally silent—staring through our cabin windows and observing our every move. The novelty of our presence made us the evening's entertainment.

At the time, strangers watching me as if I were an animal in a zoo felt unnerving. In retrospect, I should have interacted with the Yaguas. When I retired to my sleeping berth and pulled the curtain for privacy, I failed to recognize that the novelty went both ways and passed up a unique learning opportunity—literally staring me in the face.

I awoke at first light. The crew was already hard at work preparing the boat for departure. As often happened during our expedition, a rainstorm had moved in overnight, which would dissipate by breakfast. When I peeked outside to check on the weather, the Yaguas were still there. Had they watched us all night? I wish I could tell you.

We said good-bye to the Amazon River and headed south on the Rio Orosa. The Amazon tributary was roughly seventy feet wide and fifteen feet deep. Like the main river, its dimensions were subject to change. According to Devon, during some dry seasons it shrinks to an unnavigable stream.

Other than Yaguas paddling in their dugouts (a skinny canoe carved from a log), we had the Rio Orosa to ourselves. When we passed the occasional tribal village, children would eagerly paddle toward our boat and gleefully ride the waves of our wake. Though most of the children looked younger than ten years old, they had complete mastery over their dugouts. Sometimes, being swamped by the waves was just more fun than riding over them.

Now that we were on a narrower river, I could feel the snakes. I knew one had to be within my field of vision. But where? Was it high in the trees, in the aquatic plants near the riverbank, in the leaf litter on the forest floor? My shoulders tensed in anticipation. The snakes might have shut me out in Belize, but this was the Amazon rainforest. Surely, at any moment my eyes would lock onto my goal.

Then I saw him in the water, moving up and down ever so slightly. "Anaconda!" I shouted as I pointed. "Right there!"

"That's a stick," said Devon.

"We've passed him, now. But if you look where I'm pointing, you can still see his head jutting out of the water."

"You mean the stick."

"He's gone now, but it was definitely an anaconda."

"Or a stick."

I turned away from Devon, fuming that he had the nerve to call my anaconda a stick. I grabbed a beer and moved to the far side of the deck to sulk. Devon was right, of course—but I wouldn't be ready to admit my mistake to anyone, including myself, for a long time.

We reached Madre Selva Biological Station on Sunday afternoon. The station was located on the east bank of the Rio Orosa, thirteen river miles from the Amazon River. It was a simple facility with a few rustic thatched-roof buildings, a trading post, and a medical supply center. Madre Selva was one of three stations (the others were Paucarillo and Saballillo) run by Project Amazonas, Inc., a nonprofit conservation, education, and humanitarian organization founded by Margarita Tours and various Amazon enthusiasts as a way to give something back to the local environment and its people.

The crew moored the *M/N Tucunare* to the wooden dock in front of the station. Though we would now spend the majority of our time on land, we would still return to the boat for meals and socializing.

Danilo would labor in the tiny kitchen tucked away behind the engine room and consistently come up with tasty creations—works of art, really. A typical meal would include a fish (catfish or piranha) or chicken dish, a fancy salad, rice, boiled eggs, and fresh fruit.

While meals were usually something to savor, on this day lunchtime coincided with our arrival at Madre Selva. I wolfed down my food and impatiently waited for everyone else to finish. Yes, every glass of juice had to be emptied, and each morsel of food—to the last crumb—had to be leisurely consumed. Then, and only then, would we be ready to head out on our first jungle hike. Never had fifteen minutes taken so long.

Because of my stuck-in-the-mud experience on the previous day, I decided to try different footwear. Instead of rubber boots, I put on leather hiking boots. Not only would they be easier to walk in, but they'd also give my feet more protection if I found a fer-de-lance. As for the rest of my clothing, I wore a T-shirt, photo vest, shorts, and baseball cap.

Deb and I—along with the four other expedition participants, plus Devon, Ben, Cesar, and Segundo—stepped off the dock and into the rainforest. I was immediately glad I had left my rubber boots on the boat. The trail was firm, with just a few scattered puddles—ideal for hiking boots.

"Before we start," said Devon, "I need to warn you about a few dangers. Don't stick your hands or feet into any holes you can't see inside of—venomous snakes could be hiding there. Watch out for wasp nests—they're often hanging on the underside of leaves. You may also see some scorpions and spiders. Whatever you do, don't touch them."

We all laughed in agreement.

"Plants can also be dangerous. Some palm trees have long, sharp spines. If you run into a spine, you'll be very sorry. Other plants can give you a nasty sting. Even if the plants themselves don't hurt you, the ants climbing along them can give you a wallop. The bottom line is to avoid touching anything unless you're sure of what it is."

Devon scanned the forest before pointing to a mud nest at the base of a tree. "See the large black ants crawling out of there? Those are bullet ants. You *definitely* want to avoid them. Last year a bullet ant stung a man here at the station and he passed out from the pain."

We all put our arms to our sides and nodded.

Although we had plenty of things to stay away from, no one seemed frightened. The world is full of naïve tourists, but few people travel to the Amazon region without some expectation of dangerous flora and fauna.

In my case, bullet ants were the only surprise. I expected various types of biting and stinging ants but had no idea anything as extreme as a bullet ant existed. Even from a distance, they looked menacing. They had oversized mandibles and were roughly an inch long from head to stinger—these were definitely the bad boys of the jungle.

Some entomologists consider bullet ants to be the world's most venomous insects. The ants earned their name because their sting is supposed to feel like a hit from a bullet. I could only assume that in the interest of accuracy someone actually compared the two sensations: "Okay, Joe, shoot me in the left leg. *Yooooooow!* Good. Now put that big ol' ant on my right leg. *Yooooooow!* Yep, feels the same."

Devon and Ben led our group along a trail through the rainforest. Deb and I, engrossed in exotic new sights, lagged behind the others. For safety, one of the Peruvian guides always brought up the rear when we went hiking. In this instance, Segundo lingered back with us.

I looked around with wonderment. The rainforest of the Amazon differed significantly from the moist tropical forest of Belize. By definition, a rainforest has a closed canopy (where touching treetops shade the forest floor) and year-round rain. Our dry season trips to both a moist tropical forest and a rainforest exemplified the primary difference between the ecosystems: in Belize we didn't see a drop of rain, and here a shower would pass through almost every day.

I snapped photos of the rainforest flora: strangler figs, bizarre fungi, fiddlehead ferns, heliconias, and philodendrons, to name a few. Deb stepped between the huge buttress roots of a kapok tree and spread her arms. My five-foot-four-inch wife looked like a small child next to the tree. The roots began their run to the ground from five feet above her head and spread out for ten or more feet past her fingertips before disappearing underground. We saw big trees in Belize, but nothing close to the size of some of the giants we saw here.

"Snake! It's a fer-de-lance!" yelled Megan.

"Marty, come here! Hurry!" shouted Ben.

I bolted up the trail. From conversations on the boat, everyone knew how badly I wanted to see a fer-de-lance. I could hear their excited chatter as I skidded to a halt by the doctor's side. "Where is it?"

"On the leaves next to the path," he said.

A moment passed before my eyes made out the well-camouflaged snake. It was coiled less than six feet from where I was standing. "There she is!"

The three-foot-long snake was looking directly at me. I squatted, focused my camera, squeezed off two shots, moved closer, and refocused. A sharp pain shot up my leg!

"Aaahhhhhhhhhhhhhhhhhh!" I screamed.

I twisted to look behind me. My eyes widened—a bullet ant had its stinger and jaws firmly planted in my calf!

"Shiiiiiiiiiiiiiiiiiiiiiiiiiiiit!"

I ripped the ant from my calf and flung it aside. I wanted to jump up and down from the pain but knew not to do so with the fer-de-lance so close to my feet.

I took a deep breath and returned my concentration to the snake. This moment had been too long in coming for just one sting to stop me. I aimed my camera—another bullet ant scurried up my leg! I was dedicated to the cause but wasn't about to take another sting. I brushed the ant away and jerked sideways when yet another ant marched toward me! This time I spooked the snake.

The fer-de-lance opened her mouth, as if ready to strike, then turned and glided out of sight. I had successfully avoided a second sting but lost the snake.

Since no one's ever shot me, I can't compare the pain of a gunshot wound to a bullet ant sting. My guess is that the initial jolt from both is equally unpleasant. The lingering effect of the venom made the sting particularly nasty. I felt as if my calf muscle would burst through my skin at any moment. I walked with a limp but finished the hike under my own power.

Once back on the *M/N Tucunare,* I popped open a beer and joined the rest of the group on the upper deck. Because of all the crawly things on the rainforest floor, I hadn't had the opportunity to examine my wound. I sat in a chair and rotated my leg to the proper angle. Two large red welts—one from the bite and one from the sting—covered my calf. The ant had definitely given it to me with "both barrels."

My leg would feel better within twenty-four hours. Worse than the pain was the debate over what kind of snake we had actually seen. The rainforest is full of harmless creatures that mimic dangerous creatures. Had we seen the genuine fer-de-lance or the mimic? With the excitement of the find and the bullet ant attack happening in rapid-fire succession, no one could be sure of what he or she saw. Devon conjectured that the snake was the mimic; Ben surmised it was the real thing; and the Peruvian guides didn't have a clear enough view to even make a guess. While the definitive answer would have to wait until my photos were developed, I knew in my heart we had seen a false fer-de-lance. The snake's head wasn't as triangular as it should have been, and when it opened its mouth I didn't see fangs—fer-de-lances have exceptionally long fangs.

Bullet ants, incidentally, are so fierce they have their own mimic: a cerambycid beetle. Where was *that* mimic when I was photographing the snake?

We ventured back into the rainforest after sunset. This time I wore rubber boots to protect my calves. Wildlife spotting was supposed to improve at night, and we had brought flashlights from home specifically for that reason. Still, wandering around in the dark seemed like a counterproductive activity. How could we find any animals using only the narrow beams of our flashlights?

Deb, I, and the others followed in single file behind Devon and Ben. Since a heavy rainstorm had recently passed through, the heat and humidity were stifling. If sweating didn't get us wet first, the plants would finish the job. Every leaf supported a tiny pool of rainwater waiting to dribble on us at the slightest touch.

Walking through pitch-black jungle for the first time sharpened my senses. I wasn't nervous, but I was concerned about stepping on the wrong thing. I continually listened for the sound of movement in the leaf litter.

My concern dissipated as we started spotting new and interesting creatures. The goal of an Amazon night walk isn't to find big animals, such as jaguars or monkeys. It's to find little animals, such as insects, frogs, and snakes.

As I soon learned, the advantage of searching for creatures in the dark was that a good pass with a flashlight would reflect off multiple sets of little eyes. An investigation into the eyeshine could produce anything from tiny lizards to giant spiders. Because of the difficulty of taking pictures at night, we captured and bagged many of the creatures to photograph and release the following day.

On this night, I came to appreciate the value of having Cesar and Segundo on our expedition. The two Peruvians, with their exceptionally keen eyesight, found more animals than the rest of us combined. A leaf-mimic frog pointed out by Cesar provided a good example of their spotting prowess. When I tried to photograph the frog, it blended in so perfectly with the leaf it was on that I had trouble locating it in my camera's viewfinder.

By the time we completed our night walk, we had collectively counted forty-five species of animals. My contributions included a teapot-sized marine toad (the world's largest toad species) and a ground bird called a tinamou. Other finds included geckos, walkingsticks, poison dart frogs, rain frogs, conehead katydids, wax-tailed plant-hoppers, leaf-mimic lizards, pink-toed tarantulas, banana spiders, wandering spiders, web-throwing spiders, praying mantises, armored millipedes, tailless whip-scorpions, and pigmy toads.

One of the night's many pleasant surprises was that the mosquitoes (which technically raised our species count to forty-six) had been only a mild annoyance. When I first scheduled the trip, I had visions of fighting off perpetual clouds of biting insects. Now I looked forward to seldom needing to apply bug repellent.

Deb and I retired to our tent after an exhausting yet fascinating day in the jungle. Everyone had the option of either sleeping on the boat or sleeping in tents. We all chose the latter. Unlike the sleeping berths on the *M/N Tucunare*, which were hot and stuffy, the tents sat on a wooden platform, which allowed for air circulation. The three-foot-high platform stood 250 feet from the Rio Orosa in a grassy area surrounded by rainforest.

The tents, however, were not for sound-sensitive sleepers. The rainforest came alive at night with a countless variety of bird, frog, and insect calls. A tape recorder would have been great to have along. I tried to commit the sounds to memory but soon fell asleep.

Raaaaaaawwrrrrrrrr!

A loud roar awakened me. Ben Schmitt—infamous for his snoring—was two tents over, but even he couldn't snore that loud.

Raaaaaaawwrrrrrrrr!

I touched my wife's shoulder and whispered, "Deb. Wake up. I think I heard a jaguar. It's very close."

I sat up so I could hear better.

Raaaaaaawwrrrrrrrr!

The roar originated from high in the trees, not at ground level as I had originally thought. I touched my wife's shoulder again and whispered, "Deb. Wake up. I think I heard howler monkeys. They're very close."

"Wha . . . umm . . . what is it?" said Deb in a groggy stupor.

"Howler monkeys, in the trees."

Raaaaaaawwrrrrrrrr!

"Are you sure?"

"It's either monkeys or Ben is having a *really* bad night."

The roaring soon stopped, and Deb immediately fell back asleep. I tried, without success to do the same thing, but nature was still calling. I flicked on my flashlight, crawled out of the tent, and checked my boots for scorpions before putting them on—so far so good. I descended the steps. The outhouse was only fifteen or so paces from the platform, but in the jungle any number of dangerous creatures could be lurking at foot level, and whatever had been roaring could be lurking, well . . . anywhere.

I swept the ground with my flashlight before proceeding. A few tiny eyes reflected back, but they were probably just insects. I hurried across the grass to the outhouse, opened the door, and—

"Holy shit!" The outhouse spider had struck again!

Madre Selva had two side-by-side outhouses. Earlier in the day, I had discovered a spider web stretched across one of the toilet seat holes. A swipe with a stick had removed the web, but now, less than eight hours later, a densely woven web was covering the hole once more. The spider would scurry under the throne whenever anyone opened the door, making identification difficult without a heroic effort. Whether it was big or small, deadly or harmless, I had to admire any creature that would work so hard just to catch a piece of ass.

I returned to the tent and fell asleep.

At first light, I went looking for Devon and found him on the dock, cleaning mud off his boots.

"What was roaring so loud last night?" I asked.

"You mean Ben snoring?"

"No. It was even louder than that—some animal."

"You heard greater anis. They're quite common around here."

I shook my head in disappointment. A jaguar or a howler monkey would have been exciting. A greater ani, on the other hand, was a bird. Not that birds can't be exciting, but I had awakened my wife over a call made by a type of cuckoo!

Greater anis are large birds, measuring eighteen inches from the tip of their beak to the tip of their tail, and they have shiny black plumage. After Devon pointed one out to me, I started noticing them in the trees along the river. Other than their roarlike call, what makes them unusual is that the females of the flock lay their eggs in a large communal nest and cooperatively share egg-incubation and chick-feeding chores.

Dolphins were among the animals I most looked forward to seeing on the expedition. My pretrip research led me to believe that sightings of either of the two species of river dolphin would be uncommon. Therefore, I was delighted when they appeared almost daily. Gray dolphins, called *delfines* in Peru, reach six feet in length and are one of the world's smallest dolphins. Pink river dolphins, called *bufeos* in Peru, are pink and gray in color and reach eight feet in length.

Deb and I had just finished breakfast on the *M/N Tucunare* and climbed to the upper deck when one of each dolphin species surfaced near the boat. Though they were far enough apart that their mutual appearance probably had more to do with food availability than interspecies socialization, this was the first time I had seen delfines and bufeos together.

I tried to capture them on film, but their surfacing was unpredictable, and their blowholes often barely cleared the water before they submerged again. The bufeo was particularly difficult to photograph. Inevitably, the few times he rose high enough to expose his body, my camera was either by my side or aimed elsewhere. I felt as if he knew my intentions and was teasing me. Then again, he was an Amazon deity with a reputation for cunningness.

Some native people believe dolphins—especially bufeos—have a variety of supernatural powers, including the ability to take on human form to seduce the beautiful young village women. With that in mind, I glanced at my wife as she sipped her coffee and watched the dolphins. I was standing a safe distance from her, as she's not a morning person. On this morning, however, she wore a smile of contentment and looked unusually radiant. Maybe it wasn't greater anis I heard roaring last night. Maybe . . . no.

While some people smirk at beliefs that don't fit the mainstream and call them myths or superstitions, I could think of worse things to believe in than *Encantados* (enchanted shape-shifting beings, such as dolphins and snakes) that live under the water in *Encante* (a heavenly city of riches that can instantly move from one place to another). Like mainstream religions, these Amazonian beliefs provide plausible explanations for the unknown. Shape-shifting bufeos, for example, could explain unexpected pregnancies (a dolphin entranced her) and birth defects (a baby's deformed hand might look like a flipper). Also, the drowning or sudden disappearance of a loved one is less painful if viewed as an abduction to Encante.

From my point of view, the best part of believing in Encantados is that it protects dolphins and snakes from being overhunted. Who would dare kill a deity? Unfortunately, as missionaries and other outside influences erode the old beliefs, the animals are paying the price.

Dolphins are smart. They usually wait until nighttime before taking on human form. During the heat of the day, the cool river is the best place to be. As a human, incapable of shape shifting, I dealt with the extreme heat and humidity by perspiring so hard and fast that my pores literally ached from exhaustion. While my body would eventually adapt to the climate, I made the current situation worse by insisting on wearing my photo vest.

Part of being new to tropical travel is learning things the hard way. Photo vests, which have numerous large pockets, are a nice concept—if you don't mind the geeky look. Extra film, lenses, filters, and other vital items are always within easy reach. The problem with my particular vest was that it was as warm as a heavy wool shirt. On future trips, I'd ditch the vest in favor of a daypack.

Splasssssshhhhhh!

"The water feels great!" shouted Devon, looking up at Deb and me from the river. "You two should try it."

Of course, cooling off in the river was possible without shape shifting into a dolphin—as long as we didn't mind swimming with piranhas and electric eels. At that moment, an old man was sitting nearby on the riverbank catching piranhas, and earlier someone had seen an electric eel under the dock.

Frankly, the aquatic animals were the least of my worries. As you know from the previous chapter, I don't get along well with water. To me, jumping off the *M/N Tucunare* into a deep, moderately fast river just seemed like a great way for an unplanned visit to Encante.

"I'm gonna take a dip," said Deb. "Marty, are you joining me?"

I hesitated a moment to allow my male ego to kick in, then answered, "Of course, dear."

Deb hurried down to the sleeping berth to change into her swimsuit. I decided the shorts I was wearing would work just fine. A few minutes later, we met up at the edge of the upper deck.

"Getting out of the water is a bit tricky," said Devon, who was now drying himself off. "Pull yourself up at the far side of the dock, but be careful. It's slippery."

"Here I go!" yelled Deb. She pinched her nose between her thumb and forefinger and launched herself into the air.

Splassssshhhhhh!

She surfaced, flicked the hair out of her eyes, and looked up at me with a smile. "The water feels wonderful!"

"Good thing you plugged your nose, or there wouldn't be any water left for the fish."

"Ha-ha! Are you gonna jump or just stand there and make nose jokes?"

"I'm coming."

The drop from the deck was about twelve feet. I hit the water with perfect form.

Splassssshhhhhh!

All right, *perfect* is an overstatement. But I was straight enough to plummet deeper than anticipated, and that I didn't touch bottom was a surprise. In all, my jump was anticlimactic. The eel didn't shock me, the piranhas didn't skeletonize me, and the current didn't carry me to Encante—I didn't even swallow my usual gallon of water.

I practiced some swim strokes and enjoyed the cool river. When I looked up, Deb was back on the upper deck.

"Watch out below. I'm jumping again—and this time I'm not plugging my nose!"

"*Noooooooooooo!*" I yelled. "Don't do it, Deb! You'll kill the piranhas!"

"And the boat!" screamed Devon. "It'll smash to smithereens on the river bottom!"

"Aaaaaahhhhh!" shrieked the old man as he grabbed his fishing pole and sprinted from the riverbank.

Splassssshhhhhh!

Okay, Deb says I have to tell you I made up the part about her second jump. But just as I exaggerated the dimensions of my wife's beautiful, perfectly formed schnoz, most reports of man-eating piranhas are also blown out of proportion. *Webster's Third New International Dictionary, Unabridged* provides a good case in point, calling piranhas "remarkable for their voracity, in spite of their small size often attacking and inflicting dangerous wounds upon men and large animals."

We had been swimming with red piranhas, the most notorious piranha species. Had they lived up to Webster's definition of *often*, you might have just finished reading a very gory section describing Devon's leap into the river.

Piranhas, in fact, rarely attack anything bigger than themselves. Some species subsist mostly on fruit, and red piranhas prefer to eat the fins of other fish. Yes, on rare occasions piranhas have attacked people, but such attacks are usually limited to times of stress, when water level and food supplies are low. A little common sense can go a long way toward avoiding an attack. Again, I'll use my wife to illustrate. In the morning, she's like a piranha in low water—probably safe to approach, but why push your luck? Just wait an hour or so and be virtually guaranteed of encountering a pleasant person. The same concept applies to piranhas. Rather than pushing your luck, just wait until their habitat returns to normal and be virtually guaranteed of encountering pleasant fish.

(Legal disclaimer: Wild animals are unpredictable. Readers who swim with piranhas do so at their own risk, and the author and publisher assume no liability for any injuries that may occur. For the safest experience, always have Devon swim first.)

While we're discussing aquatic life, no Amazon story would be complete without mentioning the dreaded candiru. The skinny one-inch-long catfish is without a doubt the most feared creature in the river—at least among nature writers. If you urinate underwater, a candiru can supposedly follow your urine stream, swim up your urethra, and lodge itself there by spreading its hooked gill spines. The only way to remove the fish is through surgery.

Whether candirus actually swim up human urethras is debatable. Reputable wildlife books, such as *Smithsonian Institution Animal,* report the dastardly act as if it were fact, while John Kricher in *A Neotropical Companion* reports that he was unable to find a single documented instance of a candiru-plugged urethra. My response to the conflicting reports—why push your luck?

On Monday afternoon, we all did our own thing. Jack tended to Mary, who had come down with a flulike illness, Megan played on her laptop computer, and Terese taught Deb the finer points of siesta—relaxing with a cool drink on the upper deck while watching a band of squirrel monkeys move through the treetops.

As for me, I spent the afternoon with Ben taking pictures of the many insects, arachnids, lizards, and frogs we had caught the night before. Even though photography had been a longtime hobby of mine, working with the doctor was a valuable learning experience. Without him, I would have photographed all the animals in the field as we found them. Now, I could take advantage of the natural light in our makeshift studio on the tent platform.

We worked side by side, using tripods and macro lenses. We'd pull a creature from one of the bags, set it on an appropriate leaf or stick, and take turns capturing the image. Upon completion of each session, we'd release the subject back into the rainforest.

We had quite a collection of animals and weren't always sure what they were. Some of our invertebrates looked as if they could have been from another time or planet. My favorites included a two-inch-long red-and-yellow beetle that I could have sworn was hand painted, a spider that mimicked a white orchid flower, and a giant ceiba borer beetle that appeared to be made out of yellow, green, and maroon aluminum foil.

Of all the creatures we had, katydids (a relative of the grasshopper) came in the widest variety of shapes and sizes. After a while, I began to think that whenever Ben didn't recognize an insect, he automatically called it a katydid.

"What kind of insect is this?"

"That's a wasp-mimic katydid."

"What kind of insect is this?"

"That's a moss-mimic katydid."

"What kind of insect is this?"

"That's a leaf-mimic katydid."

"What kind of insect is this?"

"That's a dead-leaf-mimic katydid."

As you've probably deduced from the descriptive names, katydids are masters of camouflage. The wings of the dead-leaf-mimic katydid, for example, were not only the color of a dead leaf, but they were also ragged, as if in the midst of decomposition.

Ben and I moved on to the reptiles and amphibians. The herpeto-fauna didn't let the katydids have all the camouflage fun. Many of our lizards and frogs had skin patterns that allowed them to blend in with their surroundings. One of the lizards virtually disappeared when I placed it onto the spine of an appropriate leaf. Other lizards disappeared in a more traditional manner—zipping into the rainforest seconds after being placed in front of my camera lens.

Of all the herps in our possession, my favorites were the poison dart frogs. Although they looked huge through my macro lens, most were small enough to comfortably sit on my thumbnail. Poison dart frogs belong to the Dendrobatidae family, and their common name refers to the toxic skin secretions they produce, which some tribes apply to darts or arrows. Of the 120 or so species within the family, only about thirty-five are significantly toxic, with three being potent enough for use on weapons. Ben and I didn't have weapons-grade frogs, but after handling them, we did have to avoid rubbing our eyes.

Some varieties of the poison dart frog live exclusively within a small home range. Consequently, as scientists probe deeper into the rainforest, the identification of new species is inevitable.

In theory, spotting the frogs should be easy. Unlike the camouflage masters, poison dart frogs are among the most brightly colored creatures on Earth. Instead of whispering, "You can't see me," they yell, "Watch out! I'm dangerous!" For example, of the frogs we admired on this day, one had a black body with bright orange and yellow stripes, and another had a two-tone green body with bright yellow stripes.

After our successful photo shoot, Ben and I released the last of our subjects and returned to the *M/N Tucunare*. Soon everyone, except Jack and Mary, would head out for another after dark adventure. Mary's condition hadn't improved, and though we all felt sorry for her, we couldn't do anything other than secretly hope we didn't catch whatever she had. Our plan for the night was to take the skiff (a small flat-bottomed boat) several miles up the Rio Orosa and then forge up a shallow blackwater tributary.

The Rio Orosa and the Amazon are whitewater rivers—the color of coffee mixed with milk. Many of their tributaries are blackwater rivers—the color of weak tea. The type of water in a river depends on the soil it drains through. Whitewater rivers are laden with sediment, and underwater visibility is limited to a few inches. Blackwater rivers, though tinted from tannins and other organic substances, allow several feet of visibility.

Segundo started the outboard motor, and we sped off in search of wildlife. The skiff's flat bottom would allow us to navigate in shallow water—a feature we needed as we veered off the Rio Orosa and puttered up the blackwater tributary. A blanket of water hyacinth and other aquatic plants covered much of the river. Before long, the engine stalled from the vegetation snarled around its propeller. Rather than constantly working to free the propeller, Segundo switched to a dugout paddle, and the rest of us assisted him by grabbing handfuls of vegetation to pull ourselves along.

The going was slow, but that was the idea anyway. We'd ooze ahead a short distance, use our flashlights to scan the river and trees for animals, creep forward some more, and so on. Along the way, we collected frogs and watched schools of tiny fish in the gaps between floating plants.

The muddy-bottomed river was roughly fifteen feet wide and eighteen inches deep. A half mile in from the Rio Orosa, the aquatic plants became almost impenetrably thick. We considered turning around but decided to push on.

Shortly thereafter, the vegetation broke up, the river widened by more than a hundred feet, and the depth increased as well. Our persistence had paid off. We were now in more of a swamp than a river.

"There's a snake," said Cesar.

"Where!" I asked.

He aimed his flashlight at a small tree overhanging the water. "There."

"It's an Amazon tree boa," said Devon.

"Can we catch it?" I asked.

"We can try," said Devon.

After Segundo maneuvered the skiff beneath the tree, Devon stood on the bow seat and stretched for the snake. The six-foot-two tropical ecologist was about four feet too short. He attempted to bring the snake to him by pulling on the lower branches of the tree. When that didn't work, he gave the tree a sharp shake.

"Here, use my snake stick," said Megan.

Devon took the stick—which resembled a golf club with a hook instead of a head—and reached again. This time he got a hold on the boa, but it promptly slipped the hook and climbed out of range. "Sorry, Marty. I lost her."

"Damn! That would have been so great."

I was sitting in the stern, one seat in front of Segundo. Though he didn't speak English, when I aimed my flashlight toward the rear, he nodded to me in sympathy.

We backed the boat away from the tree and continued through the swamp. The water was clear enough to use the outboard motor for a while, but when floating plant life seized the propeller again, we resumed paddling and grabbing whatever we could to pull ourselves along.

Because of the darkness, I had difficulty keeping myself oriented. All I knew for sure was that we had entered what was perhaps the eeriest place on Earth. Giant trees stood in the water on tall spidery roots, treetops blocked out the stars like thunderheads, and vines dangled down from the darkness like tentacles of a jellyfish. If headhunters still roamed the jungle, this is where they'd be.

Compared to the previous night, the rainforest was quiet. The only sounds were the occasional *bruuuurp, bruuuurp* of the frogs and the *shhhhhhhhh, shhhhhhhhh, shhhhhhhhh* of water hyacinth scraping the bottom of the skiff.

"There's a caiman," said Cesar softly.

"Where!" I whispered. (Unlike snakes, which have a limited ability to hear airborne sounds, caimans have good hearing.)

Cesar pointed with his flashlight, and a pair of shiny red eyes flashed near shore. "There."

"Oh—it's a *black* caiman," whispered Devon. "They're rare around here. We need to catch this one."

He leaned over the gunwale as Segundo stealthily maneuvered the skiff alongside the caiman. Devon lunged! "Got him!"

After a brief struggle, he hauled the three-foot-long caiman into the skiff and held him up for us to see. The reptile was an extraordinary find. Classified as "conservation dependent" by the IUCN, black caimans closely resemble American alligators and are capable of reaching twenty feet in length. Once everyone had a proper look, the doctor carefully slid his catch under the skiff's false-bottom grate for safekeeping. We'd have to wait until the light of day for closer examination and photography.

As we worked our way back to open water, we painted the swamp with our flashlights, searching for more creatures of the night. When I aimed my light into the water, I glimpsed something resembling a wide olive-green belt. "Wow, what is that!"

When everyone turned their lights to where I was looking, I could clearly see the six-foot-long creature, swimming parallel to the skiff.

"That's an electric eel," said Devon.

"Aren't you gonna catch it?" I asked.

"No, Marty. This one's all yours!"

Electric eels aren't true eels—they're a type of knifefish. The electric part of their name, however, isn't a misnomer. An adult, like the one next to our skiff, could deliver a jolt of 550 volts.

Before departing the swamp, we returned to where we had seen the Amazon tree boa. All of us swept our flashlight beams across the trees but saw only a wall of foliage. We were about to move on when the glint of snake eyes caught my attention.

"There she is!" I shouted.

"Where?" asked Devon.

"Six or so feet above where she was before," I said.

"Well, we tried, Marty," said Devon. "But there's no chance of catching the snake way up there."

Segundo stood and said something in Spanish.

Devon provided the translation: "Segundo says he feels like going for a climb."

I exchanged smiles with the sturdy Peruvian as he squeezed past me on his way to the bow. The Amazon tree boa was in a skinny, smooth-barked cecropia tree that looked barely strong enough to support a grown man.

Climbing would have been difficult in the daytime, and now Segundo had only the shadowed beams of our flashlights to illuminate his way. I watched in disbelief as he scaled the tree like a lineman climbing an electrical pole.

Once he captured the snake, his job grew more difficult. Now he had to return to the skiff with one hand clutching the snake and the other grasping the tree. Somehow, he made it all look easy.

"*Muchas gracias*—thank you!" I said.

Segundo smiled and held out the four-foot-long Amazon tree boa for me to admire. Like the caiman, we'd take the snake with us—this time using a cloth bag for storage.

Contented with our successful evening, we proceeded to Madre Selva. Upon our arrival, everyone headed directly to the tents. I contemplated staying up and taking the boa out for a closer look, then reconsidered when I thought about how badly I'd feel if she escaped into the darkness. Sunrise couldn't come soon enough.

Tuesday morning, immediately after breakfast, I picked up the snake bag and climbed the stairs to the upper deck. Deb and Megan looked on as I untied the knot at the top of the bag.

"Amazon tree boas are all teeth," Megan said sternly. "They never calm down. If you don't grab its head, it'll bite you!"

"No, she *won't* bite me. All I have to do is be gentle. Once the snake understands I won't harm her, she'll be fine."

"You don't know what you're talking about!"

I reached into the bag and pulled out the snake. When she cocked her neck and stared at me, I thought I was going to eat my words. But instead of striking, she coiled into a tight ball around my hand.

Amazon tree boas are unusual because they come in a wide variety of colors and markings. Some have gorgeous orange or yellow skin with little or no pattern, and others have drably colored skin with distinct markings. My boa was off-white with two-tone-brown saddle markings.

Like all boas, Amazon tree boas are nonvenomous snakes that kill their prey by constriction—a process of suffocating, not crushing. Unlike their heavy-bodied cousins the boa constrictor and anaconda, Amazon tree boas are slim. My boa was a little thicker than a broom handle.

Just because she was slim didn't mean she wasn't strong. As I walked around the deck, wearing the boa like a mitten, my fingers slowly turned purple. I tried to unwrap the snake with my free hand, but her grasp was so tight that peeling her off by myself could have injured her. When Deb noticed my predicament, she offered to help. Together we applied the proper combination of support and strength to accomplish the task.

I carried the boa from the boat, placed her on an isolated tree near the tent platform, and snapped a picture. Okay, I confess—I actually shot about sixty photos. A bit compulsive, I admit, but life would be boring if you couldn't indulge in a good obsession now and then. Once I finished, I released the snake at the edge of the forest, snapping one final photo—okay, three—as she slithered to freedom.

One the most enjoyable aspects of this expedition was its lack of structure. People were always free to relax on the boat while others pursued activities that were more strenuous. On this morning, the majority of us went on a jungle hike. While I continued searching for snakes, Ben looked for slime worms (terrestrial flatworms).

Slime worms? Okay, even I had trouble relating to worms as a goal. Still, I must admit, the ones he found were quite stunning. Each was about three inches long, with shiny black and white stripes running lengthwise.

Any day spent walking in the rainforest is a great day, but when we returned from our hike having seen only a few animals, I felt a twinge of disappointment. What I didn't know was that our animal-viewing backup system was about to kick in.

On the day we arrived at Madre Selva, Devon passed word to the Yaguas what our various animal interests were. Since that time, tribal members had been busy "rainforest shopping" for us.

The concept of native people bringing us animals felt unsettling at first. Black market trading of wildlife is a worldwide problem, and here we were giving the Yaguas trade items in exchange for their finds. The difference with this situation was that our actions were beneficial. By trading with the Yaguas, we were giving them an opportunity to earn items they wanted and at the same time teaching them that wildlife was more valuable alive than dead. As for the captured animals, their inconvenience was temporary. After a brief photo and "ooh and aah" session, we'd promptly release them back into the rainforest.

From the pre-expedition checklist, I knew we'd have opportunities to trade with the Yaguas and that batteries and T-shirts were their preferred items. Several years earlier, I had acted on one of my more harebrained ideas and opened a side business selling "No Newt is Good Newt" T-shirts. When Newt Gingrich abruptly resigned from Congress—obviously due to all the people wearing my T-shirts—I became stuck with several boxes of excess inventory.

Now my T-shirts would have a second life. Even though the Yaguas didn't know who Newt Gingrich was, they were happy to trade for the shirts. I chuckled at the possibility of an influential American politician visiting the region and stumbling across tribal members proudly displaying the No Newt logo and caricature on their chests.

The Yaguas' initial finds included two monkey lizards, a spectacled caiman, and a dwarf caiman. While I'd enjoy observing all the animals, the best find arrived when I was off doing photography with Ben.

When I returned to the boat, Devon handed me a cloth bag. "One of the boys brought you something very special."

"What is it?"

"A rainbow boa."

"Oh, that's great! Let's have a look."

As I undid the knot, Megan, who had been standing nearby, interjected with the same stern warning she had given me for the Amazon tree boa. "Rainbow boas are all teeth. They never calm down. If you don't grab its head, it'll bite you!"

"No, it *won't* bite me. All I have to do is be gentle—"

"You think I don't know anything about snakes but I do! Just because you're gentle with a snake doesn't mean it won't bite you!"

I reached into the bag and pulled out the boa. The six-foot-long snake looked at me, as if trying to decide which part of my body would produce the best steak, then curled into a tight ball. Soon I was holding him cupped in my hands like a jeweled orb. Once I was sure he wasn't going to bite me, I glanced at Megan and smiled. She clenched her fists and stormed off the boat.

The rainbow boa was full-grown and in good shape except for a missing eye that had healed over. His skin was deep rusty-red with black circular markings filled with a hint of burnished gold. True to his name, he glistened in the sun with the colors of the rainbow.

I carried the boa around for a while before placing him back into the bag. At Jack's request, a return to the wild would have to wait. Mary was still trying to sleep off her illness and would want to see the snake when she awoke.

Later that afternoon, most of our group relaxed on the upper deck admiring the monkey lizards the Yaguas had brought to us. The lizards were a rare find because they lived high in trees and were likely captured only after someone did some serious climbing. The larger of the two lizards had a six-inch-long body with a twelve-inch-long tail, and the smaller one was half that size. Both were bright green with bands of yellow.

Aside from being colorful and uncommon reptiles, what made them special was how docile they were. Megan sat in a chair with the small lizard and I did the same with the large one. As tree dwellers, the lizards' primary desire was to move to the highest point. When we released them on our laps, they didn't try to run away. Instead, they slowly climbed our bodies and perched atop our heads. Everyone laughed as Megan and I tried to hold a serious conversation while wearing our lizard "hats."

Before releasing our two entertaining reptile friends, Ben and I carried them to a tree near the tent platform for some natural habitat photos. I shot first, capturing images of the monkey lizards from several angles. When Ben took his turn, he decided the larger one wasn't positioned properly and attempted to pull her off her branch.

The lizard was happy where she was and grasped the branch with all her might. If the doctor absolutely had to move her, he could have gently pried her fingers loose. Instead, he just yanked harder.

"Stop it, Ben!" I screamed. "You're going to hurt her!"

"The lizard will be fine."

"She's not gonna let go. You'll break her fingers!"

"I'm the human here! The lizard will do what I want it to do!"

I've never hit anyone in my life, but at that moment, I almost decked Ben. We were visitors to the rainforest, and the animals we had come to enjoy deserved our respect. When Ben pulled on the lizard again, I gritted my teeth and turned away, too furious to watch. As far as I know, he successfully got his shot.

My anger toward the doctor continued when we took the black caiman and the rainbow boa to an open area near a stream to photograph. The shots of the caiman went exactly as planned—Miss July couldn't have posed better. Then Ben removed the rainbow boa from the bag and positioned him in a coil. When the boa spotted a nearby tree and attempted to crawl to safety, Ben grabbed him and returned him to the pose he wanted. The boa refused to stay still, however, and in the ensuing battle of wills, the doctor grew rougher.

I seethed as I watched him repeatedly reposition the snake. Finally, I couldn't take it any longer. "Ben! Stop it!"

Whap! The snake tagged him on the hand—vigilante justice, boa style.

As blood oozed from the doctor's wound, I couldn't resist smiling. Megan was right—rainbow boas were all teeth.

The snake had one more job to do. I carried him back to the *M/N Tucunare* and found Jack sitting on the upper deck.

"How's Mary feeling?" I asked.

"I checked in with her a few minutes ago. She's woozy but better."

"I'm glad to hear she's improving. Let me know when she's up to seeing the rainbow boa. I'd like to release him as soon as possible."

"I'll go ask her now." He disappeared down the stairs and returned moments later. "Come on down."

I followed Jack into the bowels of the boat. When Mary saw us coming, she propped herself up to a sitting position. She looked pale and miserable.

"Hi, Mary, I brought you a present."

"Oh, isn't he beautiful. Does he bite?"

"Only people he doesn't like. You'll be fine." I maintained a light grip on the boa's neck, just in case.

Mary reached out, gave the snake a few gentle strokes, and smiled. "He feels nice—so smooth and cool."

The three of us continued with a few moments of small talk before I wished Mary well and excused myself so she could go back to sleep.

The rainbow boa had earned his freedom. I carried him to a secluded spot near the river, shot the obligatory series of good-bye photos, and watched him slither out of sight.

Now that the snake was gone, my thoughts returned to Ben. I was still fuming about what had happened and needed to talk to my wife. I hadn't seen her for several hours and had to search before finding her organizing gear in our tent.

"You won't believe what Ben did today." I said, launching into a recap of events.

Deb listened until I finished, then said, "Well, you can stew on it and let it ruin the rest of your trip, or you can forget about it and enjoy yourself."

Though a logical reply wasn't what I wanted to hear, she was right. This trip was the realization of a lifelong dream, and I couldn't let one person ruin it for me. Besides, as much as I disapproved of Ben's actions, he was still an asset to the trip. I was definitely benefiting from his vast wildlife knowledge, and some of the photographic techniques he taught me were helpful as well. If he got rough again, I'd stop him. In the meantime, I just had to accept that his view of animals was cold and scientific compared to mine.

We boarded the *M/N Tucunare* for a two-hour southbound excursion to the Paucarillo Forest Preserve. The preserve was the last permanent structure on the Rio Orosa, and beyond it were miles of virgin rainforest. We would spend Tuesday night at the preserve and return to Madre Selva in the morning.

Paucarillo was smaller than Madre Selva—just a shower, an outhouse, and a simple platform sheltered by a thatched roof. For convenience, we'd sleep on the boat.

Shortly after our arrival, we followed Devon to the platform, where he became involved in a conversation with the Yagua caretaker. Since I couldn't understand the Spanish the men were speaking, I wandered away to check out a cluster of butterflies near the riverbank.

Terese, on the other hand, had no problem understanding the conversation and soon hurried after me. "Marty," she said with a broad smile, "you're going to be very excited when you see what the caretaker has for you."

"What does he have?"

"Well . . . it's a surprise. I better let Devon tell you."

I waited until Devon finished his conversation before I approached him. "Terese said the caretaker has something for me."

"I don't know what he could possibly have. She must have misunderstood."

Ever since I mistook a stick for an anaconda, Devon had been capitalizing on my enthusiasm to give me a hard time. I could relate to the humor but after a while grew tired of trying to guess whether he was kidding or serious. Although this time I suspected something was up, I shrugged and walked away.

Deb joined me moments later. "I think they have a fer-de-lance for you."

"*Noooo* . . . really?"

"Go see Devon."

As I neared the doctor-turned-practical-joker, he held up a large ziplock bag and grinned ear to ear. "The caretaker caught a small fer-de-lance for you."

My first thought was that since the snake was in a plastic bag it must be dead. I cautiously peered inside—it was very much alive. While I was delighted with the surprise, I immediately became concerned about the fer-de-lance's health. "We need to open the bag so she doesn't suffocate."

"Snakes don't need much air," said Ben, who was standing nearby. "If you want to photograph it, we have to keep it in the bag until we return to Madre Selva. It will be too hard to control here."

I knew reptiles didn't breathe at the rate of mammals, but I was skeptical about leaving the snake in the bag all night. "Can we at least open the seal a few times to give her some fresh air?"

Ben hesitated before answering, "Yes, we can do that."

I looked in at the fer-de-lance again. She was just a *baaaby* pit viper—perhaps a foot long. Sure, she could inject a deadly dose of venom—just like an adult—but that didn't make her any less cute.

Though I would have rather found the snake myself, or at least been part of the search, this was an occasion to celebrate. The only other time I had seen a live fer-de-lance was at the Belize Zoo. Now, I could look forward to observing and photographing the deadliest snake in the Western Hemisphere without a pane of glass between us.

Before going on, I'd like to address my readers who are herp aficionados: Yes, I know that in some circles the common name "fer-de-lance" applies only to the *Bothrops caribbaeus* and *Bothrops lanceolatus* species of the West Indies, and that those same people call the *Bothrops atrox* the caretaker found a "common lancehead." However, by a consensus of nature writers, nature show hosts, local opinion, and even dictionaries, the name fer-de-lance also applies to the *Bothrops asper* of Central America and *Bothrops atrox* of South America.

Besides, I love making up songs for important events in my travels, and I'm not nearly a good enough songwriter to come up with lyrics that rhyme with "common lancehead." Instead, I came up with a catchy little ditty that I'd be stuck on for the remainder of the expedition. You too can be stuck on the song, if you join me now in singing it. To the tune of "The Duke of Earl," here we go. One, two, three—

> *Lance, lance, lance*
> *Fer-de-lance, lance, lance*
> *Fer-de-lance, lance, lance*
> *Fer-de-lance, lance, lance*

(Sing repeatedly until strangled by companions.)

Other than the fer-de-lance, lance, lance, Paucarillo wasn't as productive as Madre Selva for wildlife finds. We partook in both day and night hikes and encountered mostly insects and arachnids. The most bizarre finds were a large spider that looked as if it were made entirely out of white pipe cleaners and a caterpillar that mimicked a mound of gray belly button lint.

Where Paucarillo excelled was in its flora. Everywhere I looked were enormous ferns and giant trees draped with vines. Devon provided names for some of the flora, which included ant plants, balsa trees, cacao trees (used for making chocolate), cannonball trees (named for their large, hard fruits), cat's-claw (used for making an herbal remedy), fig trees, kapok trees, and paddle trees (used for making dugout paddles). One plant that had us all laughing was a three-foot-tall shrub called a "hot lips" or "lady's lips" plant. As the names suggest, its bright red flowers resembled a woman's lips puckered up for a kiss.

Before our morning departure, Cesar and Segundo went out on their own and brought back two snakes: a *Xenopholis scalaris* and an unidentified mystery species.

Many of the animals we found on the expedition weren't well-known enough to have common names. If we were lucky, Devon or Ben would produce a scientific name, but sometimes even that wasn't possible.

The *Xenopholis scalaris* was an eighteen-inch-long nonvenomous snake that mimicked the deadly coral snake. It was so docile it posed exactly how Ben wanted it to pose. The mystery snake was equally docile and *presumed* nonvenomous. It was two and a half feet long and had an elegant two-tone-gray skin pattern with a red spot on each cheek.

One of the most exciting aspects of exploring a remote rainforest region is that you never know when you'll discover a new species. The mystery snake had such potential.

The procedure to confirm, describe, and publish first-time finds can take several years and often starts by sending photos to experts for examination. Devon told me that sometimes only one person in the world has the appropriate knowledge to make a confirmation—particularly in the case of insects. In this instance, Ben sent photos of the mystery snake to a respected herpetologist. While the snake initially appeared to be an unrecorded species, it was ultimately identified as a *Liophis typhlus*. Though it wasn't a new discovery, it was still a special find. The reason for the delay in identification was because Cesar and Segundo's *Liophis typhlus* was significantly larger than other specimens recorded in the region.

We boarded the *M/N Tucunare* and headed north. Instead of going directly to Madre Selva, we pulled ashore at the Yagua village of Santa Ursula. We had stopped at the village the day before to schedule a trading session, so the residents were anticipating our arrival.

For trading I brought along several harmonicas to supplement my supply of No Newt is Good Newt T-shirts. Even though I used to be a talent manager in the music industry, I personally have no musical ability whatsoever. I can't sing (count your blessings you didn't have to hear me sing the fer-de-lance song) and I can't play any instruments. The harmonicas were remnants of my last attempt to be musical. The only reason I had several of them was because I kept hoping that upgrading to better models would improve my playing.

Deb and I each had a trading goal in mind. She wanted a weaving, and I wanted a dugout paddle. Much of the village (except for the men) had brought their wares to a central area, sheltered by a thatched canopy. The trading started like a typical junior high school dance, with the twenty or so Yaguas standing on one side and us on the other. Since trading stops at Santa Ursula were uncommon, I'm sure our appearance intimidated them.

As for the Yaguas' appearance, their dress was surprisingly modern. A few of the women wore skirts with a tank top or blouse, and everyone else wore cotton shorts and T-shirts (items most likely acquired from occasional trips to the town of Yanashi or trades with previous visitors). I was struck by what a good-looking race of people they were. The children were adorable—especially when they smiled—and many of the women, with their high cheekbones, dark eyes, and smooth skin, were classically beautiful.

I approached a pretty, young woman who was holding a woven handbag and a dugout paddle—one-stop shopping, Amazon style. Using hand gestures, we quickly negotiated a deal: her items in exchange for a T-shirt and a harmonica. While the woman smiled sweetly and seemed happy with our trade, I immediately felt guilty. From my point of view, I had come out much better than she did.

When I mentioned my feelings to Ben, he tried to put my mind at ease by explaining that American goods were more valuable to the Yaguas than they were to me, and just giving them things would turn them into beggars. Though I appreciated his comments, I still didn't feel right. For future trades, on both this trip and others, I'd do my best to rein in my natural instinct to negotiate.

Concerning the harmonicas, perhaps Ben had a point. They were definitely more valuable to the Yaguas than they were to me. A young boy offered a fishing spear for my second harmonica and immediately started playing. Then I noticed another boy, half hidden behind a post, too shy to approach me but obviously desiring one as well. I walked over to him, held out my third harmonica, and watched his eyes light up. He handed me his fishing bow and arrow in exchange and joined his friend in an impromptu jam session. Without a lesson, the boys played their harmonicas better than I ever could—and their beaming faces made the music perfect.

We left the village with our trades in hand. The Yaguas would no longer be able to paddle their dugouts or feed themselves, but they seemed happy with their T-shirts, batteries, and harmonicas.

I'm kidding. If they didn't already have replacement paddles, spears, and bows, they had plenty of materials around to make more. The only harm that could come from our trades would be if the dolphins saw the Yaguas in their No Newt T-shirts and began shape-shifting into Newt Gingrich.

Captain Rios piloted the *M/N Tucunare* to Madre Selva and maneuvered the boat so it ever so slightly kissed the dock. While the captain never failed to impress me with his deft steering, at that moment I had only one thing on my mind: *"Lance, lance, lance, fer-de-lance, lance, lance . . ."*

Accompanied by Ben, Cesar, and Segundo, I marched to the photography area carrying my prized possession. Next to the tent platform was a table with six-inch-high wooden sides, and it was partially filled with dirt and leaf litter. Although the table wasn't escape proof, it would give us an advantage over the snake.

As soon as I readied my camera, Ben released the fer-de-lance. The pit viper, which had been docile in the bag, raced to the side of the table and would have gone over the edge if Ben hadn't scooped her up with a stick and returned her to the center. She continued bolting for the side, and each time Ben redeposited her to the same spot. Once again, the doctor was in a battle of wills with a snake. This time, however, a battle ending with a bite wasn't an option. With a sigh of frustration, he turned the snake wrangling over to Cesar and walked away.

Cesar knew exactly what to do. He used the stick to maneuver the snake into a coiled position and then covered her with my baseball cap. After waiting a few minutes, he removed the cap to reveal a calm fer-de-lance, ready for her photo shoot.

How calm was she? I focused my camera lens within three inches of her head without a strike. In retrospect, moving so close was a careless thing to do. Though her relaxed posture made me confident she wasn't in a striking mood, it's a snake's prerogative to change its mind without warning—she could have easily tagged me.

As I looked through the viewfinder, I marveled at her collage of light- and dark-brown markings. She blended in so well with the leaf litter that I wondered how many fer-de-lances I had walked by and not seen.

Then a new thought entered my brain: "I should pick her up. I've seen Jeff Corwin and Steve Irwin handle numerous venomous snakes on TV. I could do what they do. No problem."

Soon familiar voices in my head joined in: "Come on, you can do it. Look how placid she is. This is the best chance you'll ever have to handle the deadliest snake in the Western Hemisphere."

Great, the travel gods had arrived. Having failed to get my fingers bitten off by a crocodile in Belize, they now hoped to convince me to get those same digits injected with venom in Peru.

The temptation was hard to resist. While I believed I could handle the fer-de-lance without a bite, I also knew the nearest hospital was far away. This wasn't a place to do something *really* stupid.

Oh, I picked up the snake all right—I couldn't pass that up. I just cheated a little. As I lifted the fer-de-lance's body, Cesar gently pinned her head to the ground with the stick. The travel gods were so disappointed.

Many people believe snakes—especially the venomous species—are worthless animals that should be eradicated. Since you're reading this book, I'm guessing you don't think in such a small-minded fashion. Still, in the event one of your less-than-enlightened relatives sits on the toilet and opens your copy of this book to this page, I'd like to make my case for snakes.

First, it's time for literalists to quit holding snakes responsible for what happened to Adam and Eve in the Bible. If the biblical God had a problem with snakes, he would have drowned every one of them in the great flood. Obviously, all of the 2,900 or so terrestrial species of snake were welcomed onto Noah's ark. Putting aside for a moment that the ark wasn't actually large enough to hold two of each unclean animal and fourteen of each clean animal on Earth, think of the 2,010 known rodent species and how rapidly they reproduce. If it weren't for snakes providing population control, rodents would have overrun the ark during the 378 days they were onboard—eating all the food and then proceeding to the actual wood of the boat. In fact, I submit that if it weren't for snakes, Noah's ark surely would have sunk.

Even today, snakes continue to provide the valuable service of rodent population control. But that's not all. As medical science advances, we're learning that snake venom can be a life *saver*. For instance, *Bothrops jararaca* (a close relative of the fer-de-lance) venom has been used in the development of effective drugs for people with diabetes, high blood pressure, and kidney disease.

Yes, snakes are animals with an undeserved bum rap. They're interesting, mysterious, often beautiful, and definitely not slimy. As for my fer-de-lance, she had provided me with a thrill I'd never forget, and now it was time to release her, so she could forget about me. Using the stick once again, Cesar carried the little viper to the edge of the rainforest and set her down. She froze for a moment, as if expecting to be scooped back up, then slithered under the leaf litter. Now, totally hidden, she was ready for an unsuspecting meal to scurry by.

Although no barefooted human would step on her here, I could see how such an accident could happen—especially near villages. Fer-de-lances don't seek out people to kill. When they meet humans, it's usually a surprise encounter for all involved.

For our final night at Madre Selva, we headed out on another skiff ride. This time Mary joined us. Although she hadn't totally recovered from her ailment, we were all glad to see her up and able to enjoy the idyllic Amazon evening.

We floated downriver under a cloudless sky. The stars were spectacular and the air just cool enough to feel refreshing. Overall, the ambiance overshadowed a relatively unproductive night of wildlife spotting. Our three notable finds were a nocturnal bird called a great potoo, a Boans tree frog that rode along on the gunwale, and a band of night monkeys high in the trees.

For me, the biggest surprise of the expedition was the lack of observable monkeys and other mammals. Deb had seen squirrel monkeys two days earlier, but at the time I was off photographing herps and insects with Ben. In fact, until this evening, dolphins had been the extent of my mammal sightings.

Night monkeys (also known as douroucouli) are the world's only nocturnal monkey species. They're small primates, weighing about two pounds, and look more like lorises (because of their round faces and oversized eyes) than monkeys. We spotted five individuals in all, but they were too high in the trees for good viewing.

I asked Devon why we saw so few monkeys, and he said, "Larger species, such as woolly monkeys, are hunted. The best chance to see them is inland, away from the river. As for smaller monkeys, they're here. Not spotting them has just been bad luck."

We returned to Madre Selva and retired to our tents. The expedition had been much too short. Although we still had a day and a half on the river and a day and a half in Iquitos, I had already vowed to revisit the Amazon.

As I lay awake, listening to a chorus of frogs, cicadas, and who knows what, I reflected on the trip. I had tried to keep up a species-count log, but with all the distractions I often forgot to make my entries. Even so, I had more than eighty animals on my list. I was thrilled. Sure, I would have loved to observe monkeys from close range, and not seeing an anaconda on an Amazon expedition was certainly a violation of the laws of nature, but how could I complain? I fell asleep with contented thoughts of a successful visit.

Deb and I awoke Thursday at sunrise to the faint sound of Devon's voice. He was talking to someone in the distance, but I couldn't make out his words. Suddenly Deb exclaimed, "Devon has an anaconda!"

I jerked out of bed and hurried down the platform steps. There I spotted Devon, heading toward me from the boat. "Is it true? Do you have an anaconda?"

"No, one of the Yagua boys just said he saw an anaconda in the river, but it's long gone."

I looked at Devon and tried to read his face. Was he messing with me again? My heart sank. His expression was serious—and besides, an anaconda showing up on the final morning was just a little too unbelievable. I trudged back to the tent and changed into a fresh set of clothes.

Deb also dressed. Then the two of us walked down to the *M/N Tucunare* for breakfast. I pride myself on not being gullible, but I guess everyone is entitled to an off week—Devon got me again!

Standing on the dock, posing for a picture, was an eight-year-old Yagua boy with a death grip on a three-foot-long anaconda.

"Look what we have for you, Marty," said Ben.

"I'd given up on seeing an anaconda—this is incredible!"

Before the trip, I had envisioned finding a thirty-footer, but I wasn't about to complain now. An anaconda of any size was an exciting sight.

"Breakfast is ready," announced Devon.

"Can I eat later?"

"We're having omelets."

"I guess not."

As with the Amazon tree boa and fer-de-lance, I'd have to put my curiosity on hold. Ben handed the boy an appropriate trade item and placed the snake in a cloth bag for safekeeping.

This time, at least, my wait was short. After inhaling breakfast, I excused myself from the table. "Sorry to eat and run, but the anaconda is waiting."

I glanced at Megan, so she could deliver one of her "all teeth" speeches, but instead she just stared at me blankly. I fetched the snake bag and jogged up the path to the photography area.

To take advantage of the morning sun, I selected a spot in the open, then adjusted my camera and checked my film supply. I was ready. I grabbed the bag with one hand and undid the knot with the other.

Whap! The anaconda struck.

As droplets of blood oozed from tiny holes in my finger, I looked around, half expecting to see Megan smirking at me from behind a tree.

My relationship with the anaconda was off to a rocky start. In fairness to the snake, he was just striking defensively, trying to bite whoever had put him in the bag in the first place—he had *obviously* mistaken me for Ben.

I wiped the blood off on my shorts, reached into the bag, and pulled out the anaconda. I expected to have to fend off more strikes, but once he was in the open, he became calm and cooperative. Images I had seen of anacondas in books and on television didn't do justice to how stunning this one looked in real life. His skin was bright olive green with large black spots, and it glistened in the sunlight. He was truly one of the most beautiful creatures I'd ever seen.

Once our photo shoot was complete, the time had come to give the last snake of the trip his freedom. A full-grown anaconda can weigh 550 pounds, qualifying it as the world's heaviest snake. No wonder they're objects of both legend and fear. I set the budding young Encantado next to a stream and watched him skim across the water, duck under some vegetation, and vanish.

Captain Rios started the *M/N Tucunare's* engine and blasted the horn to warn stragglers on land—like me—that the boat was departing. With last-second worries that I didn't have a good bullet ant photo, I had ventured out on my own to search for my old nemesis. At times during our visit, bullet ants seemed to be everywhere, but now that I actually wanted one, none was to be found. I shouted out in the most pained voice I could muster, "Damn you bullet ants! All you ever do is torment me! Why? Why?"

I ran down the path and jumped onto the boat. We headed downriver, short just one person.

Earlier in the day, Devon had motored ahead in the skiff to meet with someone who was going to build him a dugout. We would rendezvous with the doctor at the village of San José de Orosa, near where the Rio Orosa enters the Amazon River.

No map of the Amazon rainforest is accurate for long, as changing river conditions sometimes force entire villages to move. In the case of San José de Orosa, when an eroding riverbank backed the community against a swamp, they relocated three miles west of the spot indicated on the most recent quadrangle map.

We found Devon on the riverbank in front of the village. He was in the midst of a conversation with a small group of Yaguas. Though we had planned for only a brief stop, I was curious about the village and asked Devon if we could stay for a tour. He relayed my request, and a tour was warmly granted.

San José de Orosa was roughly the size of two typical city blocks, with paths instead of streets. When we started walking, an enthusiastic group of twenty-five children assigned themselves to us as our guides and led us from place to place.

Approximately twenty families resided in the village. Their stilted homes had thatched or wooden walls, uncovered rectangular openings for windows, and thatched roofs. Inside were hammocks, supplies, and perhaps a small table or two. Food was never far away, as pigs and chickens wandered about the grounds, and to prevent the spread of fire, the residents built their kitchens in separate huts.

At the far end of the village was a one-room schoolhouse built by the Peruvian government. Its blue concrete block exterior made it look out of place among the rustic buildings. When I stepped inside for a photo, the children promptly took their seats as if ready for a lesson.

Today's lesson was for me, not the children. The people in the village had no running water, no sanitation, and few possessions, yet they appeared to be healthy and happy. Although I wouldn't want to switch places with them, I admired their simple lifestyle and was glad to have the opportunity to witness how they lived.

As we walked about, no one seemed to care where we looked. I was struck by this difference between our cultures. If the Yaguas had showed up in an American town and proceeded to walk through yards and glance inside homes, they would have soon found themselves staring down the barrel of a gun.

We headed back toward the *M/N Tucunare* accompanied by our entourage of children. While the group meandered along, I jogged ahead to the boat and grabbed the sugar-free gum I had brought from the United States. I returned to the riverbank just as everyone caught up.

When I held out the gum for the children, they converged on me with squeals of delight. I felt as if I were a mother greater ani attempting to feed a brood of hungry chicks in a communal nest. The children closest to me grabbed onto my clothing with one hand while holding up the other for a stick of gum. If the drawstring on my shorts hadn't been tight, I'd have been pantsed.

What started in a frenzy turned into a touching situation. Although I had plenty of gum for everyone, the first children to get pieces promptly ripped them in half and turned around to share with the person behind them. I assumed they were sharing with a brother or sister but had no way of knowing for sure. Later, when I'd hand out gum in Iquitos, I'd see the same generosity between children.

We boarded the *M/N Tucunare,* and Captain Rios steered us toward Iquitos. The Amazon River was wide and calm, glowing in the setting sun. I couldn't decide which way to look. To the bow was the fiery sunset, to starboard birds hovered over the river, to port dolphins were feeding, and to the stern were the silhouettes of waving children. I glanced at Deb; she was also caught up in the moment. Without a word we passed through the moment together, wishing it would never end.

We motored west into the night with our captain somehow avoiding the many floating logs along the way. He eventually pulled to the riverbank for a few hours of sleep but had us moving again before sunrise. Despite periodic rainstorms, the Amazon had dropped by more than three feet since the beginning of our expedition. Because the river is so expansive, the change was virtually unnoticeable. The low water, however, necessitated our docking at a different port than the one we had embarked from.

Upon our arrival in Iquitos, Deb and I had thirty-four hours to explore the city before returning to Montana. We said good-bye to our wonderful Peruvian crew and shuttled with Devon, Ben, and the others to our hotel.

We stepped from the van onto the muddy street in front of the Amazon Gardens Hotel. Jack and Mary looked at each other, as if trying to decide whether to enter the seedy-looking, windowless, concrete-walled building. I must say, if it wasn't for the green awning with the hotel's name on it, I would have guessed the building was used for something in the adult entertainment business.

Walking through the front door was like entering a different world. Never had I seen such an extreme difference between the inside and outside of a hotel. The first thing I noticed was an open-air courtyard hidden from the street. Within it was a stylish swimming pool, surrounded by statues, palm trees, tropical plants, and umbrellaed tables. Next to the courtyard was a large formal dining area, and deep inside the building was our clean, comfortable room. Thinking about it now, the outside of the hotel was likely dressed down to blend in with the neighborhood.

Deb and I enjoyed our first hot shower in six days before heading out to do some shopping. Because shipping to Iquitos is expensive, three-wheeled vehicles called *motokars* were by far the most popular mode of transportation. Motokars are kind of like a horse and buggy with a motorcycle engine replacing the horse.

Hiring a motokar taxi was easy. All we had to do was walk to the street corner and raise a hand. Within seconds, several taxis raced toward us. We hopped into the back of the winning vehicle and roared into downtown.

In the center of the city was a large grass and concrete town square that served as the community's hub. While people rested on benches or played on the grass, motokars whizzed around, side-by-side, squeezing four lanes of traffic onto a road marked for two.

As Deb and I walked through downtown, the first thing we learned was to be extra careful when crossing the streets. Pedestrians didn't have the right of way, crosswalks were nonexistent, and if vehicles had a speed limit, it wasn't enforced. I flashed back to a sign I saw at the airport proclaiming, "Welcome to Iquitos, the Safest City in the World." Obviously, the sign referred to safety from crime, not traffic.

Also, this was one place where being six feet tall was potentially dangerous. Most of the storefronts had awnings with horizontal support bars at my chin level. I had to walk either hunched over or close to the curb. The few times I forgot, I nearly beheaded myself.

During the rubber boom of the early twentieth century, Iquitos was a prosperous city. We could still see remnants of the boom, as many of the buildings near the town square had colorful ceramic tile facades. Architecturally, two buildings from the era that stood out were the Iquitos Cathedral, which had a tall neo-Gothic-style steeple, and the Iron House, which was designed by Gustave-Alexandre Eiffel.

After an hour or so of shopping, Deb and I stopped for lunch at a popular open-air restaurant. We hadn't been sitting for more than five minutes when the boys we met the day we landed in Iquitos approached us. With photographic recall, they reminded us of our purchase promises. True to our word, Deb bought jewelry and various small items from Michael and two other boys, and I purchased some hand-painted postcards from Alfredo.

More of a young man than a boy, Alfredo had hardened facial features that belied his pleasant personality. Though his salesmanship may have been too persistent for some, I liked him.

"How long you in Iquitos?" he asked.

"We're here until tomorrow evening," I said.

"I rented motokar. I am learning to become guide. Would you and your wife like to be my first customers? I give you good tour."

While I suspected Alfredo had had other customers in the past, it wasn't an issue for me. I interrupted Deb's conversation with Michael to relay the offer.

"I'd love a tour," she said.

"Okay, Alfredo, you have your first two customers. How much do you charge?"

He shrugged. "That's up to you. Pay me what you think tour is worth."

"Sounds like a deal. Pick us up at our hotel tomorrow morning at nine."

"Amazon Gardens, right?"

"How did you?—never mind. We'll see you then."

I was impressed with the service we received from Margarita Tours. Once we reached Iquitos, no one would have thought any less of the organization if Devon and Ben had said good-bye and considered their job complete. Instead, they arranged for anything we needed and even hosted a farewell dinner at a fancy restaurant.

The theme for the family style dinner was "local delicacies." I love trying unfamiliar foods, but when our waiter brought out multiple courses of native animals, my stomach turned. I understand that caiman, capybara, and peccary are as normal to Peruvians as chicken and trout are to me. Even so, I could never enjoy eating a mammal or reptile from the rainforest. Just a few days earlier, I was excitedly photographing a caiman, and now a piece of one was on a plate before me. I took a few polite nibbles, then tried some plant-based dishes such as heart of palm salad and cassava, but I had lost my appetite. Deb and I excused ourselves to take a stroll through the streets.

Whether Iquitos truly is "the Safest City in the World" is debatable, but I will say I never felt in danger. The only time I had reservations about going anywhere was when we encountered a protest that evening in the town square. Several hundred people were chanting and thrusting their fists in the air. Although we were curious about the protest, being blond-haired, blue-eyed Americans, we couldn't very well blend in with the crowd and decided to keep our distance.

Saturday morning, at precisely nine, Alfredo pulled up in his motokar. Before we even got in, I asked him, "Do you know what that protest was about last night?"

"Corruption. Local leaders stealing money from people."

"We watched from across the street but didn't want to get too close."

"You would have been okay. No one bother you."

Deb and I slid in behind Alfredo, and we sped off down the street. My expectations for our tour were that it would be little more than just a way to pass time until we had to leave for the airport. Our young guide, however, had some surprises in mind.

First, he drove us to an area where he said the *really* poor people lived. To my outsider's eyes, the neighborhood, with its hodgepodge of thatched and rusty-tin-roofed shacks, looked dismal but not necessarily poorer than other parts of town.

Next on the tour was Alfredo's house. From the outside, it was typical of dwellings in the *less* poor areas of town. It was part of a long strip of interconnected buildings, and it had a painted plywood face, an unpainted tin roof, and a simple white awning.

We stepped inside to find little more than rough plywood walls, hammocks, and a kitchen. Alfredo shared his tiny home with fourteen other people. Though they had few possessions, what they did have was well cared for.

One of the reasons Alfredo brought us to his house was to show off paintings his brother was selling. I already had examples of his brother's work on the postcards I had purchased the day before.

"The paintings are beautiful," I said, "but they're too big to take back to the United States on the airplane."

"I understand," he said. "Do you like my house?"

"Yes, it's very nice," said Deb. "You should be proud."

"Thank you. I am very lucky."

We climbed back into the motokar for a short ride to the public school. When we arrived, Alfredo pulled up behind a crowd of about fifty students watching a boys soccer game. The majority of the students appeared to be sixteen or seventeen years old.

Alfredo waved to a group of girls partway down the sideline. "My girlfriend and her friends want to meet you," he said.

The girls, perhaps a dozen in all, came running. Many were very pretty, and most wore T-shirts and extremely short shorts.

The first girl to arrive was the most stunning of all. "This is my girlfriend, Maria," said Alfredo.

I reached out to shake her hand. "Glad to meet you," I said.

Alfredo looked at me with concern and whispered in my ear, "That is not how we do things in Peru. You must kiss her on each cheek."

"I'm sorry. I didn't know." I turned back to Maria and repeated my greeting—this time in the proper fashion.

When I looked up, the other teenaged girls were standing in line, waiting for their kisses. Oh, darn, now I had to kiss them all.

Of all the sacrifices I had to make to bring you this book, this was by far the biggest. I could feel their supple cheeks on my lips for hours—make that days—afterward. It was terrible. And to my wife, who will certainly read this—I was in agony. They were so young. Yet, if I didn't kiss every one of them, I most certainly would have started an international incident.

After I labored through each kiss, Maria requested I take some pictures of her with her girlfriends. I'm a *wildlife* photographer! What do I know about taking pictures of beautiful girls in short shorts? I did my best to dutifully comply, but it was grueling work.

Now, scarred for life, I joined Deb on the sideline to watch the game for a while. Though baseball, not soccer, is my sport, watching the players was a treat. Many were so talented that they handled the ball as if it were an extension of their bodies.

After we had seen enough of the game, we walked toward the motokar, passing through the crowd of students. When I felt a tug on my elbow, I turned to find a girl with big brown eyes looking up at me.

"It was nice to meet you, sir," she said. "Thank you for taking my picture."

Though I hadn't given her anything to thank me for, I would reward her politeness by mailing back copies of the photos once they were developed.

Alfredo pressed the starter, and the motokar engine roared to life. Everyone waved and smiled as we zoomed off to our next destination. Other stops on our tour included the public university, the cemetery, and the language school. Many of the young people in Iquitos spoke English in addition to Spanish. When Alfredo led us into one of the language school's tiny classrooms, he said, "Teachers only teach British English here. Most students would rather learn American English. Your slang words are better."

Our final stop was the Belen Marketplace. Here hundreds of vendors sold fruits, vegetables, meats, and traditional remedies. After a few minutes of walking the market's crowded streets, I began to feel nauseated. The heat was stifling, the sidewalks were slimy, and the smells were overpowering. Especially repulsive were the rows of unrefrigerated raw fish and chicken, buzzing with flies.

I felt as if I were in a giant petri dish of botulinum bacteria. My walking mantra was, "Don't trip, don't trip, do not trip, don't trip, don't trip, do *not* trip!"

Deb had the same walking mantra until she banged face-first into a hanging leg of smoked peccary. From then on her mantra was, "Don't trip, watch your head, don't trip, watch your head, don't trip, *watch your head!*"

The market sat atop a massive riverbank overlooking the settlements on the floodplain. While people could build on the floodplain for free, the rise and fall of the Amazon River made the land desirable for only the poorest of the poor. When I started photographing the jumble of tightly packed shanties, Alfredo suggested that I could get a better view from the roof of the house immediately to my right. "A friend of mine lived there before he died," he said. "We can go in anyway. His parents won't mind."

In we went, following a near stranger into the house of a dead stranger, whose parents we'd never met. Clearly the expectation of privacy in Peru is much different from what we have in the United States. Also, as this house demonstrated, not everyone in Iquitos is poor. Like our hotel, this house was far nicer on the inside than it was on the outside. I was surprised to see electric lights, ceramic tile floors, painted plaster walls, couches, a refrigerator, a china hutch, and even a television set.

The three of us climbed the stairs, stepped onto the roof, and looked out over the settlements. Alfredo was right. The view was much better.

Having had our fill of the market, we started back toward Alfredo's motokar. Another difference between the United States and Peru (at least in the Amazon region) is how children react to strangers. While most American children have been taught to be wary of strangers, here the opposite was the case. A touching example of this occurred moments before the end of our tour. An adorable girl, about six years old, approached me and said in perfect English, "Hello. How are you enjoying Peru so far?"

I had traveled to the Amazon looking forward to seeing the animals and exploring the rainforest. My expectations were realized—and then some. What I hadn't expected was to meet so many wonderful people. Whether we were in a remote Amazon village or the bustling city of Iquitos, Deb and I never met an unfriendly person. Often verbal communication was unnecessary. Sometimes people would just sit next to us and not say a word. Other times they'd lightly touch us or put their arms next to ours to compare skin color. I was going to miss Peru.

As the hotel van transported us to the airport, I waved to Alfredo going in the opposite direction in his motokar. He U-turned through traffic and caught up with us to say a proper good-bye. For someone who on our first meeting was a mild annoyance, he had turned out to be a person I felt privileged to know.

On the flight home, I thought about my new Peruvian animal and people friends and began to worry about their future. Though logging and oil companies were rapidly destroying rainforests in other parts of South America, so far they had left alone the areas we had visited. While I could only hope that enlightened leadership would find a way to protect this special region forever, greed dressed up to look like progress seems to always set its sights on the great wild places.

Now, however, high above the Andes Mountains, was not the time for such depressing thoughts. I closed my eyes to watch the smiling children and surfacing dolphins and tried to fall asleep.

3
G'day Down Under

Now that we had properly satisfied my dream of visiting the Amazon rainforest, Deb was eager to embark on her dream trip to Australia. Since I wouldn't decide to write this book until we were flying southwest over the Pacific Ocean, embarking on another exotic trip so soon after Belize and Peru seemed extravagant. Still, Deb's agreement to go with me to Peru was part of a two-trip deal, and now I needed to keep my end of the bargain—even if it would be a hardship.

Who am I kidding? I wanted to go to Australia just as much as my wife did. While she was eager to scuba dive, I couldn't wait to see all the unique wildlife.

Australia is home to great white sharks, giant crocodiles, the ten deadliest snakes in the world, the deadliest spider in the world, and the deadliest jellyfish in the world. All the dangerous Australian animals made me think of the grizzly bear reintroduction controversy in my home state. While Montana has a reputation for being a land of rugged, manly men, that image falls apart when a portion of the state's population trembles at the prospect of sharing the forest with grizzly bears. Imagine how the anti-grizzly crowd would react if they had to worry about Australia's wildlife.

Although not everyone travels to Australia hoping to view dangerous animals, the presence of such creatures has helped, not diminished, the country's tourist appeal. In fact, surveys consistently list Australia as the top place Americans would like to vacation, if they could go anywhere in the world regardless of cost.

Because Australia is approximately the same size as America's contiguous forty-eight states, properly exploring the world's only country/continent would take a lifetime. Since we only had thirteen days, we quickly narrowed our trip to Queensland (essentially the northeast quarter of the continent). There, Deb would have scuba diving access to the Great Barrier Reef, and I would have a chance to find a platypus, python, or perhaps something on the world's deadliest list.

Deciding where to go within Queensland took more thought, as the state is slightly larger than Alaska and Idaho combined. We eventually settled on a three-part itinerary, which included three days in the rainforest of Eungella National Park, three days in the arid Outback near Chillagoe, and four days in the Cape Tribulation section of the Wet Tropics of Queensland World Heritage Area. We'd also spend two days in the town of Cairns and one in Port Douglas.

Traveling from Montana to Brisbane, Queensland, took twenty-nine hours (including layovers in Los Angeles and New Zealand). Flying coach is always a sleepless experience for me, because for some reason I can't get comfortable in a near-upright position with my legs compressed in a vice. I considered business class, until I learned tickets cost $8,400 each. Suddenly flying coach, at $1,100 per person, didn't seem so bad. To save $14,600, I can stand to be uncomfortable for a *long* time.

We arrived in Brisbane at eight-thirty in the morning on Saturday, May 11, 2002. Even though I had been awake for roughly thirty-five hours, the day was just beginning. After enduring another airport layover, we hopped on a northbound flight, which touched down in the coastal city of Mackay at three-thirty. From Mackay, we still had to proceed by automobile fifty-two miles west to Eungella National Park.

Though I was now too tired to concentrate, I was somehow coherent enough to sign for the rental car. That I was able to locate the vehicle in a parking lot full of duplicates took a miracle.

"Marty, it's over here." Oh yeah—the miracle was Deb.

We tossed our luggage into the trunk and slid into our seats.

"Where's the steering wheel?" I asked.

"We're in Australia!" said Deb. "They drive on the left side of the road here."

"Are you sure the rental company didn't just give us a factory second?"

"Yes. Now switch sides with me."

I plopped into the bucket seat on the right-hand side, started the engine, and turned on the windshield wipers.

Deb tilted her head to look at me. "Why did you turn on the wipers? It's not raining."

"I was trying to signal my turn out of the parking lot. What happens if I push this stalk up?"

"Now the headlights are on."

"Okay, I'll try this one. . . . That worked."

Deb chuckled, nervously. "Are you *sure* you don't want me to drive?"

"No, I'll be fine." We proceeded down the road for a minute or two before I added, "Is that car in our lane?"

"Marty! You're in the wrong lane!" She grabbed the wheel and swerved us out of the way.

"I'm awake now."

"You better be! Or I'm taking over driving."

"What's that up ahead?"

"A roundabout. Just follow it. The road will continue on the opposite side."

Beeeeeeeep!

"Why is that truck—"

"Oh, my G—"

Screeeeech! Smashhhhh!

Okay, I made that entire driving sequence up. I wasn't *that* out of it. Still, anyone would have been challenged to go directly from a long flight, to a car where all the controls were on the opposite side of the steering column, to roads where everything was reversed. For me, turns at intersections took the most concentration, as I naturally wanted to enter the right-hand lane. I was thankful Mackay had a population of only 65,000. Had my initial left-side driving experience occurred in a major city, such as Sydney, my occasional lapses would have been tougher to recover from.

After successfully maneuvering beyond Mackay, we followed a lazy two-lane highway through a farm-filled valley and crossed abruptly into rainforest. Our destination, Broken River Mountain Retreat, sat just inside the rainforest, at the edge of Eungella National Park.

We had booked all our accommodations over the Internet, where we could view photos online. Nevertheless, each place we selected would surprise us in some way. In this instance, our accommodations were less rustic than we had expected. The retreat sat on a grass-covered hill overlooking the Broken River. Our cabin-style room was in a single-story building with a long front porch, and next door was a high-ceilinged lodge with a restaurant, lounge, and library. At that moment, however, our comfortable bed and quiet room were all that mattered. Sleep never felt so good.

Deb and I awoke early Sunday morning and walked down to the Broken River. The coffee-colored river varied in width from forty to seventy feet, and it appeared to be deep. But the reason we were here had nothing to do with how the river looked. We had come because of its reputation for being the best place in the world to view platypuses.

Reputation aside, we were anticipating a challenging search. Before finalizing our travel plans, we watched a documentary on platypuses, where the host spent more than a week trying to find the elusive little monotremes (egg-laying mammals). Either the host was looking in the wrong place or we were just lucky, because within minutes we had our first of several platypuses in sight.

Frankly, I was disappointed. We had allotted three days for our quest. How could I write about our search with any tension if the platypuses were literally waiting for us? Perhaps we should have booked accommodations near the *second*-best place in the world to view platypuses.

My disappointment didn't last long, however. Platypuses may have been easy to find, but they were challenging to photograph. Their brown fur blended in with the water, and since they were hunting for food (horsehair worms, tadpoles, freshwater shrimp, and insect larvae) they never popped up for air in the same place twice and seldom remained on the surface for more than a second or two. Since I could watch only a small percentage of the river through my camera's viewfinder, I had to guess where the next platypus would appear and rarely had time to recompose my shot if I was off target.

Traveling for this book was a great excuse to regularly update my photographic gear. To supplement my Canon Elan SLR (single lens reflex) film camera, I purchased my first digital camera, a Sony Mavica, the day before departing for Australia. The advantage of digital is that you can learn from your mistakes in the field and correct them on the spot. Unfortunately, the Sony had a low-power lens and shutter delay that made it inappropriate for fast-action wildlife photography. Since the

Canon was still my best option, I shot all my platypus photos on film. This wouldn't have been a problem, if I had done everything correctly. Without a digital camera screen to confirm the results of my work, I wouldn't know that none of my more than ninety shots would meet my expectations until the film was developed.

While I got a kick out of photographing the platypuses, once I had what I assumed were good shots, I put down my camera and just observed from the riverbank. The platypuses were cute and smaller than expected. Although some wildlife books claim these remarkable animals can reach two feet in length (from the tip of their ducklike bill to the tip of their beaverlike tail), the ones I saw were all about eighteen inches long. Since they rarely interacted with each other, and surfaced at different times, I'm not sure how many I was watching—maybe three or four.

Platypuses are classified as mammals, but they're really too unusual for such a simple description. They're warm-blooded (like a mammal or a bird), egg layers (birds, amphibians, many reptiles, and very few mammals), and they have fur (mammal), webbed feet (various species in all four classes), a cloaca (birds, reptiles, and amphibians), and injectable venom (some reptiles and very few mammals). I suggest a new scientific classification just for them: Mamreptabirphibian.

Only male platypuses are venomous. They have a hollow spur on each hind ankle for delivering their potent sting. While science still has much to learn about platypuses, the primary purpose of the spurs is thought to be for defending territory against other males. Of the few documented cases of platypuses stinging humans, none were fatal. The pain, however, is reportedly excruciating, resistant to morphine, and lasts for a week or more.

By late morning, the platypuses had disappeared. Deb and I would see them again during our stay, but from now on, they'd make us work a little harder to find them. We returned to the retreat for breakfast and prepared for an afternoon of rainforest hiking.

Eungella National Park encompasses 123,500 acres of rainforest-covered mountains punctuated by deep gorges. The rainforest here is unique because it's bounded by dry open forest. Since some of the park's flora and fauna species are incapable of crossing wide dry areas, they have evolved in isolation and may even differ in appearance from the same species located elsewhere. In addition, numerous plants and at least six animals—including orange-sided skinks, Eungella honeyeaters (a bird), and Eungella gastric brooding frogs—are endemic to the park.

There weren't many trails within the park, but the ones we found were well maintained. Some even had steps on the inclines. While the trails made the rainforest appear somewhat tame, they allowed us to explore without assistance from a guide.

What struck me on hikes during our first day were the things here that were similar to what I had seen in the Amazon rainforest: tall trees with wide buttress roots, strangler figs, ferns, and even butterflies resembling dead-leaf-mimic katydids.

By our second day, I became more aware of the differences between the two rainforests. For instance, in Eungella I saw Mackay tulip oaks, which are exclusive to the park, and spectacular fan palms (resembling large green pleated umbrellas), which I never saw in the Amazon. Also, since the forest floor here was less active with ants, I could sit or kneel more easily without becoming part of the "antformation superhighway."

Deb's goals when exploring Eungella were less specific than mine. She took equal pleasure in seeing pretty waterfalls, unusual fungi, colorful birds, and whatever else we happened upon. I, on the other hand, was determined to find either a python or one of the snakes on the top-ten deadliest list.

After the Amazon trip, perhaps I should have had enough of snakes for a while. Besides, Australia had so many other cool creatures to discover. Fortunately, choosing was unnecessary—reptiles, amphibians, birds, and mammals all shared the same rainforest. Having a specific goal in mind wouldn't lessen my enjoyment of other animals we encountered.

Even so, I had to ask myself, "Why am I preoccupied with finding snakes?"

The answer became clear when I remembered a discussion I had with a friend about hunting animals for food and sport. "You don't understand," he said, "men have been hunting since the beginning of time. We're preprogrammed to hunt—it's part of our makeup." If my friend was right, then I definitely missed out on the prehistoric programming, because I have no urge to kill animals. Consequently, the instinctive drive to partake in a blood sport has been replaced in me by a drive to search for and photograph snakes. As a man, I still must entertain my inner male.

Whether snake hunting in Eungella truly entertained my inner male is debatable. The searching part went just fine, but the photography opportunities were nonexistent. Snakes are world champion hiders, and though I likely walked past hundreds of them, none came out to say hello.

Lizards were another story. Not only did they come out to say hello, they spoke complete sentences:

"Move. You're blocking my sun!"

"As long as you're up, will you fetch me a fly?"

"How do you catch anything with such a short tongue? You can buy stuff on the Internet to fix that."

"Hey, baby! Under your rock or mine?"

Those obnoxious critters were, of course, lounge lizards. Eungella's true lizards were quieter but just as colorful. I spent a lot of time sitting alongside creeks, watching various specimens sunning themselves on the rocks—including a seven-inch-long beauty that was likely Eungella's own orange-sided skink.

Overall, our Eungella visit was a delightful introduction to Australia. Broken River Mountain Retreat's proprietors, Robert and Robyn Burns, were the first of many friendly Australians we'd meet, and the food they served was delectable. In fact, you don't need to read any further to learn where we ate the best food during our seven continents of travels. Their Thai shrimp and eggs Benedict earned first and second spots on my favorite-meals list.

Before we move on, I must mention what a great location Eungella National Park is for bird watching. Among the many birds we observed were Australian brush turkeys, Australian magpies, darters, egrets, little black cormorants, pelicans, spotted turtle doves, and white-gaped honeyeaters.

Three birds were particularly memorable:

Buff-breasted paradise-kingfishers were among the most beautiful birds I'd ever seen. They had large bright red beaks, pumpkin orange breasts, dazzling blue wings, and long blue tail feathers. Unfortunately, they were usually on the move when I saw them—whipping past me like a rainbow shot out of a cannon.

Almost as fetching were the sulphur-crested cockatoos. The large white birds had shocking-yellow crests, and like their close relatives parrots, they were extremely vocal. Deb and I had no need for an alarm clock to wake us up for platypus viewings, as each morning at daybreak a flock of fifty or more cockatoos jolted us out of bed with raucous screeching from the treetops.

Though not as stunning as the kingfishers or cockatoos, laughing kookaburras are handsome gray and white birds with a very famous call: *Oo-oo-oo-aw-aw-aw-oo-oo-oo-aw-aw-aw*. When motion picture soundtracks were in their infancy, someone used a kookaburra's laugh to represent the sounds of the rainforest, and ever since, directors of cheesy jungle flicks have been doing the same thing. Considering such movies are usually scripted to take place in Africa or South America, using the kookaburra's call is, well . . . laughable. The birds are endemic to Australia.

We departed Eungella on Tuesday morning. To reach the starting point for the second segment of our trip, we would have to fly 350 miles north to Cairns. Since takeoff wasn't until late afternoon, we had just enough time for a drive to the coast to check out the town of Seaforth and nearby Cape Hillsborough National Park.

The road to Seaforth made me glad I was fully awake. Instead of a two-lane highway, it was a car-width strip of bitumen (the preferred term in Australia for pavement). Vehicles would travel centered on the bitumen and veer to the gravel shoulder whenever necessary to avoid head-on collisions. This required extra concentration for me, as my inclination was to pull to the right.

Along the way, we stopped for anything that caught our attention. One such stop was to photograph Ulysses butterflies—the Australian equivalent to the blue morphos we saw in Belize. The wings on a Ulysses span four inches and are bright electric blue with a fringe of black. Butterflies may not be the most exciting creatures to come across on an overseas trip, but I challenge anyone who's feeling grumpy to maintain their mood while watching a Ulysses or blue morpho flutter about.

Leaving Eungella didn't mean giving up my search for snakes. Several times we parked near bridges so I could slide below to explore the riverbeds on foot. Since we were visiting during the dry season, the rivers were all shallow enough that I could walk between the banks or jump from rock to rock without getting wet. On one occasion, an old man slowed his car and shouted something through his open window. I couldn't make out his words, but in case I was trespassing, I climbed back up to the road and hurried to rejoin Deb at the car.

By the time we reached Seaforth, we were hungry for lunch. If the hamlet had a restaurant, we didn't see it, so we settled for a small grocery store instead.

I was perusing a shelf of junk food when a raspy voice startled me. "Did you find any gold?"

"Huh?" I said, looking over my shoulder at a wrinkled little man.

"I saw you looking for gold in the river."

"Oh! You're the man who yelled to me from the bridge. No, I wasn't looking for gold, I was looking for coastal taipans."

"Taipans! *Humph.* You're better off looking for gold."

I chuckled at the old man's reaction, though I can't say it surprised me. The snake is notorious for its potent venom.

At the beginning of this chapter, I stated that the ten deadliest snakes in the world all reside in Australia. I'd be negligent if I didn't also mention that membership on the deadliest snakes list is subject to debate. Some maverick herpetologists even include non-Australian snakes on their lists. While traveling for this book might qualify me to publish a list of the world's ten most annoying bugs, it doesn't qualify me to endorse any particular snake list. For indentification purposes, however, I carried with me color photos of Steve Irwin's all-Australian top ten. On his famous list, coastal taipans were number three.

After saying good-bye to the old man, Deb and I walked to the beach to see how Australians coped with what is considered—except by maverick marine biologists—to be the deadliest jellyfish in the world. Box jellyfish season officially runs from October through April, but local people warned us that we could still encounter "stingers" near shore through May. To make ocean access safe, Seaforth had erected a wide three-sided chicken wire fence that extended into the water. People were encouraged to swim or play within its confines. This was the only stinger fence we saw on our trip, but other towns and hotels along the coast use them as well.

Cape Hillsborough National Park was our final stop before the airport. The tiny park sat on the ocean, and it was supposed to have lots of kangaroos and reptiles. We had seen three eastern gray kangaroos near Broken River, but they were all semi-tame animals that had been relocated to the area years earlier. Here we hoped to see our first wild kangaroos—and perhaps a reptile or two.

Because we arrived with only an hour to spare, we were forced to speed explore. We covered a lot of ground, and exceeded the time we allotted ourselves, but didn't see any wildlife. The park was pretty, though, and much drier than Eungella.

We rushed to Mackay, boarded a small commuter plane, and headed north.

Deb and I spent the night at a hotel in Cairns, population 120,000. The city is the hub from where most people wishing to dive the Great Barrier Reef or explore the wilds of Cape York Peninsula begin their adventures. Despite being the region's major tourist town, it still felt laid-back and friendly—at least that's the impression we got from our observation post in the hotel lounge.

Early Wednesday morning we hopped a taxi to the train station and boarded the Savannahlander. The two-car train would take us on a seven-hour journey into the Outback and drop us at the village of Almaden. From there, we would travel twenty miles by van to our cabin in Chillagoe.

We could have rented a car and driven to Chillagoe, but the romance of traveling by rail was irresistible. The Savannahlander wasn't a luxury train. It had a stainless steel exterior and an early 1960s-style interior with aqua-blue padded bench seats. As we'd experience later, the entire train was reversible. Instead of the cars turning around on the track, we'd slide our seat backs to the opposite side of the bench and turn around in our seats. The engineer would also change positions. Only he'd make the switch by walking through the train and taking over identical controls on the opposite end.

Riding on the Savannahlander was lighthearted fun, and it allowed us to see breathtaking territory we would have missed from a car. Deb and I were the youngest people on the train—by at least twenty years—but we didn't feel out of place. The other passengers were personable, and we all took turns sitting up front with the engineer.

The train followed tracks that were one-quarter narrower than tracks in the United States. I couldn't tell the difference from the passenger seat, but when I took my turn next to the engineer, the frontal view accentuated the train's sway.

Our unhurried journey included a break for morning tea at a trackside café and stops at various points of interest along the way. About the only time we traveled fast was when dogs gave chase. The engineer would accelerate just enough to stay ahead, yet give each dog hope that today would be the day he or she finally caught the train.

The scenery changed dramatically as we proceeded west. From the verdant rainforest around Cairns, we crossed flat farmland, climbed over rocky forest-covered hills, and eventually entered the arid, sparsely vegetated Outback. Wildlife sightings were supposed to be common along our route, but this time the animals were hiding.

The train squeaked to a stop beside a white cabinlike building. We had reached Almaden. As we stepped to the ground, a trim man in his fifties greeted us. He wore blue jeans, a casual button-up shirt, and an Akubra (a traditional Australian wide-brimmed hat). I couldn't look at him without thinking, "Now *there's* an Australian."

We loaded our gear into the man's four-wheel-drive van and headed northwest on a rough gravel road. At first I thought the man was simply our shuttle driver, but as we engaged in small talk, I realized he was Gary Bondeson, our host. I felt embarrassed for not having paid closer attention when he introduced himself. We had exchanged several e-mails before the trip and were already somewhat familiar with each other.

"I've been keeping an eye out for Children's pythons for you," he said. "I saw one in a nearby cave a few weeks ago. We'll check out the spot tomorrow morning. It might still be there."

"That would be great," I said.

"Oh, there are keelback snakes living in the pond by your cabin."

"I bet you don't announce that to many of your guests," said Deb.

"This is definitely a first."

We arrived in Chillagoe forty minutes later. Had we arrived eighty-five years earlier, we would have found a booming mining (mostly copper and gold) town of 10,000 people. Once the mines closed, however, the town's population dwindled to 150. Although the area has recently regained some appeal to mining companies (marble, copper, and zinc), at least for now the local economy is tourism based, with the primary attraction being the region's six hundred limestone caves.

I was drawn to the area not for the caves per se, but for what lives inside them. Australia is the only continent in this book where television documentaries influenced our travel decisions. Our first decision, to search for platypuses, had turned out great—despite the unchallenging hunt. Now we were visiting Chillagoe, a decision influenced by a documentary about Children's pythons (named after zoologist J. G. Children) that waited near cave openings to catch bats that flew by. The biggest difference between the platypus and Children's python documentaries was that the pythons appeared to be plentiful and easy to photograph. In this case, since I had already had my share of challenging snake hunts, I *wanted* an easy reward.

Uh-oh.

Carolyn Bondeson greeted us with a big smile as we pulled up in front of Chillagoe Cabins. She was an attractive woman in her fifties, who wore her short salt-and-pepper hair parted on the side. As we exchanged introductions, I could tell we were going to get along splendidly. She had a welcoming, spunky personality and, like her husband, seemed genuinely interested in making sure we enjoyed our stay.

While Gary carried our gear to our room, Carolyn showed us around. Chillagoe Cabins sat at the edge of town, adjacent to the Bondesons' home. The facilities included three tastefully decorated cabins, a small swimming pool, an outdoor kitchen, and a large fenced patio for dining and socializing. Surrounding the grounds were thick trees and shrubs, and in front of Deb's and my cabin was a tiny pond that couldn't have accommodated more than eight ducks. In all, this would be our base for the next three days.

Deb and I settled into our cabin and checked out the pond before joining our hosts on the patio.

"Did you find any keelbacks, Marty?" asked Gary.

"No," I replied while pulling a chair out from the table.

"I usually see them just after sunrise or just before sunset," said Carolyn. "Try then."

"Thanks, I'll do that."

"We had a king brown snake around here for a while, but I haven't seen him for several weeks," said Carolyn. (King brown snakes are number two on Steve Irwin's deadliest snake list.)

"Oh, I'd love to photograph a king brown. Where did you see him?"

"Over there," she said, pointing. "The last time I saw him, he was stretched out on top of the fence. His sense of balance was amazing."

"*Yowwwww!*" Deb jerked in her chair. When she looked down, her shocked expression melted into a smile—a tan two-foot-tall kangaroo was licking the back of her knee. "You startled me. Who are you?"

"That's Herbie," said Carolyn. "He's an agile wallaby."

"What a cutie!" said Deb. "How old is he?"

"Eleven months," replied Carolyn. "Almost old enough to be released into the wild."

"We're wildlife rehabilitators," added Gary.

"See that cloth bag, hanging next to the gate?" asked Carolyn. "That's an artificial pouch. Bonnie, our latest project, is sleeping inside it. If you'd like, I can warm up a bottle, so you two can feed her."

"That would be wonderful," said Deb.

Gary poured us each a glass of homemade beer, while Carolyn prepared the formula and extracted Bonnie from her pouch.

"Okay, Deb. Hold out your arms," said Carolyn. She handed over a fuzzy light-gray marsupial that was a bit smaller than a cottontail rabbit.

"Oh . . . she's adorable! Look at those big brown eyes and long eyelashes!"

"She's gorgeous. How old is she?" I asked.

"Six months," said Carolyn.

"Is she a wallaby, like Herbie?" asked Deb.

"No. She's a silver wallaroo," replied Gary. "After Bonnie's mother was killed by a car, we found her alive inside the pouch."

Wallaroos and wallabies are types of kangaroos—members of the Macropodidae family. In general, wallabies are small-to-medium-sized kangaroos and wallaroos are large muscular kangaroos.

While Deb fed Bonnie, I played with Herbie. One of the signs that Herbie was ready to be released was his desire to spar with people as he would have sparred with wallabies in the wild. Sometimes he'd let me hold or pet him; other times he'd slap my hands or grab them with his sharp nails. Though he scratched me several times, the temporary discomfort was a small price to pay for the unique experience of sparring with a wallaby.

"Can I hold Bonnie now?" I asked.

"No, I'm not done yet," said Deb in a playful voice.

I stuck out my lower lip and pretended to pout.

"All right . . . I *suppose* you can have her."

I cradled Bonnie in the crook of my arm while she suckled her bottle—steadying it with her hands as a human baby would. Her dainty features and fawnlike face made her look more like a stuffed toy than a live wallaroo. Before I knew it, I was prattling to her in baby talk. If I could have, I would have happily carried her around for the rest of our visit. Bonnie, however, had other ideas. After finishing her bottle, she squirmed until I let her down to explore the patio.

"Would you like to see the rest of our menagerie?" asked Carolyn.

"Of course we would," I said. "Lead the way."

Deb and I followed Carolyn to a large walk-in cage next to the house. Inside were sulphur-crested cockatoos, red-tailed black cockatoos, channel-billed cuckoos, and other birds being readied for release.

A tawny frogmouth, named Frog, was Carolyn's favorite. He was a stocky medium-sized bird with an extra-wide beak and a cartoonish face that exuded personality. Imagine an owl crossed with a bullfrog and you'll have a good idea of what he looked like.

Carolyn placed Frog onto my shoulder for a photo. "You should make this quick," she said with wry smile.

"Why? . . . Oh!"

I handed my new digital camera to Deb and gave her instructions on how to use it. She clicked a shot and showed me the screen. The photo looked fine, though Frog's oversized mouth was precariously close to my ear.

"Do you want me to take another one?"

"Please. Take another two. I'll want a variety to choose from if this becomes the author photo for the newspaper story I'm writing."

Deb clicked off two shots. "Okay, I think I got it."

"Thanks. . . . You know . . . I'm never happy with photos of myself. Let's do one m—*Ohhhh!*"

Deb and Carolyn broke into laugher.

A frogmouth's diet consists of insects and small rodents. Its excrement is worthy of inclusion on the top-ten list of the world's worst-smelling natural substances. And I swear, Frog had been holding his for days, just waiting for the proper moment.

"I can feel it running down my back," I said.

"*Ewwww!* You should go change your shirt," said Deb.

"I will. Just one more picture first."

When I opened my eyes the next morning, a shaft of sunlight was peeking between the curtains, bathing Deb's delicate face in an amber glow. As I watched my wife sleep, I contemplated kissing her awake and—

"Pythons!" I remembered. "This is no time to fool around. Gary is gonna take us to the caves to find bat-catching snakes!"

I showered, dressed, searched the pond for keelbacks, and ate breakfast—though not necessarily in that order—before Deb even got out of bed. Of course, since she'd be going to the caves as well, now I'd have to wait for her. But that was okay. Finding things to do was never a problem at Chillagoe Cabins.

Though Bonnie was still asleep, Herbie was up and about, and so were the galahs and apostlebirds.

Galahs are Australia's most common parrot. They have bright-pink breasts, light-pink heads, and medium-gray wings. Thirty or so galahs occupied the trees next to the patio. When I tossed food into the air for them, they hovered above me in a massive pink cloud. Nothing edible ever hit the ground.

Apostlebirds were equally adept at midair feedings. As members of the two-species family of Australian mudnesters, they weren't colorful, but their disheveled light- and dark-brown feathers gave them character. According to Gary, their name comes from their propensity to congregate in flocks of twelve. On this morning, eight apostlebirds—four short of an avian Last Supper scene—sat perched on the fence, waiting for their next airborne snack.

Eventually Deb emerged from our cabin, yawning. While Gary cooked her breakfast, I inspected the grounds for the king brown snake. Although my search was unsuccessful, I appreciated the Bondesons' nonchalant attitude toward living with the world's second-deadliest snake. The king brown likely crossed their property often, yet they didn't try to kill it.

By midmorning, we were on our way to the first of many caves we would explore. The cave system around Chillagoe is extensive. In fact, spelunkers have followed a series of underground passageways for approximately four miles.

The Queensland Parks and Wildlife Service leads tours through the area's three most popular caves, but we didn't visit them. Instead, Gary took us to the caves he deemed most promising for pythons.

In many ways, the caves here were similar to the one Deb and I had explored in Belize. Most had multiple chambers with various-sized stalactites and stalagmites. Caves, however, are seldom as spectacular as I anticipate they'll be. Sure, I've been inside stunning caves before, but I can't think of one that hasn't already been developed for tourists. Chillagoe's caves had an inconsistent beauty. While occasionally we'd come across smooth and colorful formations, the majority were rough and dull. Nevertheless, I'd much rather explore untouched caves than those rigged with electric lights, stairs, and platforms—the best part of caving is the adventure.

For instance, in a tourist cave, you'd never have to suck in your breath to squeeze through a passage leading to an unseen chamber below.

Okay, I didn't like that part. Admittedly, several tight places forced me to repress waves of claustrophobia. Once I popped out on the other side, however, and realized I wouldn't have to live out the remainder of my life wedged between slabs of rock, I felt exhilarated for having survived the experience.

The cave-dwelling wildlife in Chillagoe was also comparable to what we had seen in Belize. Bats were common in both locations, only in Belize we saw mostly vampire bats, and here we saw mostly bentwing bats. The same held true with lizards, moths, and spiders. Though they weren't the same species, many were similar in size, appearance, and biological function.

The other consistency between the cave systems was the absolute lack of bat-catching snakes. Now I suppose they could have been on vacation, just like we were, but we should have at least seen a shed snakeskin or some scat. Gary, Deb, and I painstakingly scoured the caves until we had to return to the cabins for dinner. Then, while Deb relaxed on the patio with a book, Gary and I headed back out to search some more.

By Friday, even I had had enough of combing through caves for pythons. When Deb suggested spending the day exploring aboveground, I readily agreed. The two of us packed plenty of water and followed a route that would lead us out of town, past an old marble mine, and into the untamed hills.

We were hiking along a sandy two-track road when I spotted a small legless animal. I pointed and whispered, "Deb, look!"

"Hey, you finally found a snake!"

"I don't think it's a snake."

When I moved closer, the creature spotted me and wiggled toward a patch of tall dry grass. The reptile was about seven inches long, and despite its fast-moving body, it was too small to make significant forward progress. I dropped to my hands and knees to confirm my hunch. "It's a legless lizard."

I had to laugh. What were the odds of spending days searching for snakes and having a lizard be my first legless find? As I'd verify in a book later that afternoon, I had found a Burton's legless lizard (sometimes called a snake-lizard). The species comes in several color variations and can reach two feet in length. The little guy I found was medium gray with a line of dark-gray spots down his side.

The differences between a Burton's legless lizard and a snake are subtle. What tipped me off were the lizard's wedge-shaped head and extra-long tail. Other differences, which I hadn't noticed at the time, include external ear openings, a wide tongue, and a breakaway tail (snakes have no external ear openings, a narrow forked tongue, and a fixed tail).

If I were to give this chapter a subtitle, it would be *The Proof of Evolution Tour.* We had come from Eungella National Park, where many animals had evolved separately from the rest of Australia, we have the legless lizard we're discussing now, and later I'll introduce you to a bizarre creature that will eliminate all reasonable doubts about the validity of evolution.

What does a Burton's legless lizard tell us about evolution? If you were to look carefully at one, you'd see scaly flaps where their ancestors used to have hind legs. As humans, we'd have a difficult time without our limbs. But if we were two feet long and regularly pursued our food through sand, leaf litter, and burrows, we'd find our limbs got in the way. I could relate to this after my previous day in the caves—if my body were more snakelike, sliding through tight passages would have been much easier.

After the lizard took cover, we proceeded to the old marble mine. The site wasn't pretty, but it was interesting. Blocks of pinkish marble—the size of sport utility vehicles—had been carved out of the earth, leaving a deep flat-sided pit. Much of the marble had been hauled away, but numerous flawed blocks were scattered about the ground. Because no equipment or people were in sight, walking among the blocks felt a little strange, almost as if we were touring a disorderly Stonehenge.

The temperature was a sweltering ninety-five degrees Fahrenheit, and the nearby riverbed was dry. Cooling off was still possible, however. All Deb and I needed to do was go to the shady side of a large slab of marble and press our backs against its smooth cool surface. Within minutes, we were refreshed and ready to continue our hike.

We followed a faint path through acres of dry grass, scrub, and deciduous trees (mostly kurrajong and helicopter). As we climbed into the hills, the terrain became a crust of smoothish rock with various-sized cavities below us. Sometimes we could look down through cracks into caves, and other times we could only hear the hollow sound beneath our footsteps.

A few of the caves had entrances large enough for a human to squeeze through. Reaching the small chambers, however, would have required dropping through layers of spider webs and risking getting stuck. Rather than do that, we continued exploring aboveground and eventually looped down to the Chillagoe Golf Course.

I'm not a fan of golf, because most courses represent a tremendous waste of land and water. Even worse are the chemicals many groundskeepers use to keep their grass "healthy." Consequently, if I ever had to find a deformed frog, a golf course would be the first place I'd look.

On the other hand, if all golf courses were like Chillagoe's I'd change my mind about the game. No water was wasted here—everything was bone-dry. The greens were packed sand, the fairways were rarely mowed spear grass, and the rough was never-mowed spear grass.

People often refer to golf as a "sport." In my mind, for a game to be considered a sport, at some point you have to run. The Chillagoe course could elevate golf to sport status. I can see Tiger Woods now, wading though the tall grass, hitting his ball, and disturbing a large king brown snake. I bet he'd run.

Incidentally, play at the Chillagoe Golf Course was free. I saw no evidence of recent use, however. Who could afford to replace all the lost balls?

We returned to the cabins for lunch. Gary served us an excellent meal while Herbie provided tableside entertainment. During our stay, the first two meals of the day were always basic American-style fare, and the evening meals were bigger productions featuring tasty selections off the barbecue.

When Gary pulled out a chair to join us, I asked him, "Do you do all the cooking, or does Carolyn cook as well?"

"If Carolyn cooked, we'd have to *pay* people to stay with us."

We all laughed and continued our conversation in a lighthearted fashion.

I was just about to get up from the table when Carolyn called out from behind me, "Marty, am I your friend?"

"Did you find me a snake?"

"Come here."

Carolyn was crouched on the little wooden bridge that crossed the pond. I hurried over to join her.

"Look between the reeds," she said with a grin.

"I don't see anything."

"It's a keelback. You're staring right at him."

"Oh! There he is."

Only the keelback's snout protruded from the surface of the pond. The rest of him wound underwater through the reeds. He was about two feet long, and he had stunning golden ridged scales. I snapped a photo before attempting—unsuccessfully—to capture him for a closer look.

Keelbacks are notable because they mimic the deadly rough-scaled snake. In fact, when I compared the image on my digital camera screen with a photo of a rough-scaled snake in a book, I was amazed by how similar the two species appeared. Since the Bondesons had handled keelbacks in the past—and lived to tell about it—I trusted Carolyn's identification. Of course, venomous snakes don't *always* bite when they're handled.

Also interesting is that keelbacks are one of the few animals that can eat cane toads—and live to tell about it. When Deb and I were exploring the Amazon rainforest, I was excited to find a marine toad. Here, on the other side of the world, marine toads are called cane toads, and they're considered pests. As usual, when humans try to improve on nature they screw things up.

The toads were introduced to Australia in 1935 to control the cane beetle population. The beetles, however, turned out to be one of the least favorite foods of an animal that will eat virtually anything it can fit in its mouth. To make matters worse, the toads have potent venom glands on their shoulders that are capable of killing most predators. Consequently, the cane toad population has exploded while the populations of many carnivorous birds, reptiles, and mammals have crashed.

As time passes, some animals are learning either not to eat the toads or to flip them over to avoid the venom glands. A few species may even be developing immunity to the poison. Such is the case with keelbacks. They can eat small cane toads but are still overwhelmed by the amount of poison produced by large specimens.

In legend, Saint Patrick was a hero for ridding Ireland of snakes. Here, in real life, the heroes are the keelback snakes for helping rid Australia of cane toads.

Deb and I set off on our own shortly before sunset. The biggest surprise of our trip, so far, was the lack of kangaroos, wallabies, and wallaroos. Sure, we had Bonnie and Herbie to admire, but we wanted to see some roos in the wild. Though we weren't within the territory of Australia's famous red kangaroo, other species were a possibility.

We decided to make spotting a rock wallaby our goal for the evening. According to Gary, perching ourselves atop Lookout Hill at the edge of town would give us the best chance for success. The numerous trees, boulders, and crevices dotting the hill's eastern slope were ideal wallaby habitat.

We reached the hilltop from the west. Once we found a good vantage point, we sat and scanned the terrain for wallabies. Nothing seemed to be moving except the sun, which was dropping into a dusty haze. As the sunset grew in intensity, Deb gave up on the wallabies and turned around to watch nature's sure thing.

I wasn't as easily distracted, but since I couldn't see any wallabies from my position, I decided to explore the hillside. I wound my way past bushes and boulders, heading down and around simultaneously. Now that the hill was blocking the sun, darkness came swiftly. I reached for my flashlight before remembering—Deb had it in her fanny pack.

Suddenly every stick looked like a taipan or king brown snake. Though I love snakes, this wasn't the time to find one. I held my breath each time I stepped over a dead branch or squeezed through a blind crevice.

Sticks weren't the only things that looked alive. Near the bottom of the hill was a kangaroolike shape. I crept toward it, closing to within thirty feet. When the shadowy figure didn't move, I concluded it was a stump and resumed my concentration on avoiding "venomous sticks."

I took several steps while staring at my feet. When I looked up, I jumped back in surprise—a four-foot-tall animal was hopping across my path! I forgot about the snakes and took off in pursuit. I lost the animal briefly but soon spotted her again. She was standing in a clearing, illuminated by the last shaft of sunlight—an adult silver wallaroo. I was briefly disappointed, still thinking—inflexibly—about my rock wallaby goal. Then I realized what a ridiculous thought that was. Seeing *any* roo in the wild was a great experience.

Since the wallaroo seemed content where she was, I backed off and went to find Deb. Locating a quick route up through the rocks and trees soon proved frustrating, so I yelled for her to come down with our flashlights. Once we met up, we hurried to the clearing, but both the sunlight and the wallaroo were gone.

We returned to Chillagoe Cabins, where music filled the air and beer instantly filled our glasses. Gary and Carolyn had decked out the patio in tropical-themed decorations, including a long candlelit dinner table with fresh palm leaves for a tablecloth and hundreds of fuchsia bougainvillea flowers for a runner.

Deb and I weren't the Bondesons' only guests. Also renting cabins were Carol and Les, a couple from New South Wales, and Hanne and Tommy, the owners of a graphic arts firm from the Brisbane area. Hanne, Tommy, and their staff of three were living in Chillagoe temporarily while they erected displays in the town's new visitor center.

The evening's festivities were in honor of Hanne's fiftieth birthday. This, however, was no ordinary birthday party.

In addition to the eleven humans, a wallaroo, wallaby, miniature horse, dog, and galah all took part in the celebration. The horse had a particularly good time. First he drank someone's beer, then he ate the tablecloth—now that's a true party animal.

We humans also enjoyed ourselves. First we drained Gary's supply of home brew, then we moved on to a strong Danish bitter called Gammel Dansk (a favorite of several from the graphic arts firm, who had immigrated to Australia from Denmark). As royalty for the night, all the women wore tiaras, and everyone danced to the King, Elvis Presley.

Dinner arrived with a flash of fireworks! Gary had stuck sparklers into the barbecued pork before carrying the platter to the table. We all howled in laughter—partly because it was funny and partly because at that moment we would have laughed at anything.

What more could we have asked for than great company, good food, and fantastic hosts with a flair for the dramatic. Such was our final night in the Outback.

On Saturday morning, we reluctantly parted ways with our new Chillagoe friends and boarded the Savannahlander for Cairns.

For me, obtaining tidbits of local knowledge through observation and conversation is one of the joys of visiting different countries. Sometimes these tidbits are important, and other times they're just amusing. While the train chugs through the Outback, I'd like to share with you some of the things I learned during this trip:

• Australians are more conservation oriented than Americans. Solar panels, hybrid cars, and dual-flush toilets were frequent sights.

• Tipping is not customary in Australia. The first time I inquired about tips, I was asked, "Don't restaurants in America pay their employees a fair wage?"

• Never ask an Australian if rugby and Aussie Rules football are the same thing—unless you want an emphatic, drawn-out answer describing *exactly* why one sport is better than the other.

• Steve Irwin is apparently more popular in America than he is in his own country. Every Australian I asked thought he was too over-the-top and destined for a fatal encounter with a snake or a crocodile.

• Australians generally like Americans but feel the U.S. government is too pushy in the way it treats other countries.

• Australia provides its residents with free universal health care. Unlike in America, where puppet pundits spew horror stories about universal health care, everyone I asked here was happy with their coverage.

• Voting is required in Australia, and those who do not participate can be fined. Since voters rank candidates in preferential order on their ballots, they can vote simultaneously for the minor party candidate of their conscience and the major party candidate who is least objectionable.

• Australians have their own version of English, called *Strine*. Here are some common words and phrases that differ from American English: *g'day* (hello), *bloke* (man), *sheila* (woman), *mate* (friend), *biscuits* (cookies), *stubby* (beer in a bottle), *tinnie* (beer in a can), *tomato sauce* (ketchup), *chips* (French fries), *crisps* (potato chips), *hire* (rent), *morning tea* (late light breakfast), *on holiday* (on vacation), *take away* (take-out food), and—my favorite—*no worries* (no problem/you're welcome).

Upon reaching Cairns, we hired a car and drove forty miles north to the town of Port Douglas. We had scheduled a one-night stay at the Wildwood Lodge—a cottage next to the home of John and Oriel Wild.

Because our drive took longer than expected, we didn't reach town until dusk. Since the Wilds had already broken their three-day minimum stay requirement to accommodate us, I worried our late arrival might push their generosity too far. When the elderly couple greeted us at the curb with smiles, my concern dissipated.

"Welcome!" said John.

"Did you find us okay?" asked Oriel.

"No problem," said Deb. "Your driving instructions were perfect."

"I hope you two aren't light sleepers," said Oriel. "The mango tree above your car is full of flying foxes. They can be quite noisy."

My face lit up. "Bats? No—they could never be too noisy for us!"

"That's good, because some people complain about them," said Oriel.

We followed the couple inside for a tour of our spotless, elegantly decorated accommodations. Oriel graciously showed us every feature—in detail.

Once our hosts said good night, Deb and I grabbed our flashlights and beelined for the tree. When we looked up, eight feet above us were four flying foxes licking nectar from clumps of white flowers. Many more bats were rustling high in the tree.

Because the sky was now dark, I enlisted Deb to help me take some pictures. While she aimed her flashlight on the bats, I captured their images. This was a low-skill operation. I set my camera on auto, shot two rolls of film, and hoped for the best.

I didn't need to see the results of my successful photo shoot to be amazed by the bats' three-and-a-half-foot wingspans or to admire their handsome foxlike faces. Australia is home to numerous flying fox species. These were spectacled flying foxes—a mostly black species with brown fur around their eyes, on their nose, and partway down their back.

As for the noises Oriel had warned us about, the bats' repertoire of chirps, trills, and twitters sounded joyfully funny and surprisingly birdlike. Since the cottage bedroom had shutters, instead of glass windows, I could understand why the vocalizations might have kept some guests awake. For us, however, they had the opposite effect. We left the shutters open and let the chatter lull us to sleep.

Deb was up early, readying for the first of her two dive days. Exploring the Great Barrier Reef (a 1,250-mile-long collection of three thousand individual reefs) would be the realization of a longtime dream of hers. Although she had scuba dived several of the world's top locations, she, like many other diving enthusiasts, considered the Great Barrier Reef to be the ultimate destination. As she kissed me good-bye and headed out the door, I imagined the same enchanted feelings that went through me, when I first experienced the Amazon River, would be going through her as soon as she hit the water.

My day, on the other hand, was destined to become the most mundane of our seven continents of travels—someone had to do laundry.

Deb and I met up late in the afternoon. Since we had a two-hour drive to Cape Tribulation, and wanted to arrive before dark, we thanked John and Oriel for their hospitality and promptly headed north.

"So, how was the Great Barrier Reef?" I asked.

"I went through an entire range of emotions today," she said. "I had selected the *Poseidon* in part because a maximum of twenty-five divers would be on the boat. When I showed up and learned ninety snorkelers were *also* coming along, my hopes for an intimate experience were shattered. Turn left here."

"That's too bad."

"It gets worse. Dive boats lease specific sites, where they anchor to large concrete fixtures. The idea is to prevent damage to the reef, but in reality, all it does is contain the damage to a particular area. The first of my three dives was so disappointing, it made me angry."

"Why?"

"Well, as you know, ocean coral is sensitive to touch. With all the inexperienced tourists diving on the reef, the coral takes a beating. In fact, much of it was dead and broken. I also saw a phenomenon I'd never seen before. When I looked around, all the coral was bleached."

"From what?"

"Global warming. Bleaching is a stress response caused by water that is too warm."

"Okay, now I'm depressed."

"My second dive was better. We moved to a location where the coral wasn't so abused. There I saw all kinds of fish, and the anemones, sponges, and soft corals were impressively large. Turn right."

"How was your third dive?"

"The crew *definitely* saved the best for last. We were headed to one of the regular spots, when the dive master announced that since the water was unusually calm our destination had been changed to the outer reef wall. He was very excited. He said he'd been working on the *Poseidon* for nine months, and this was only the third time he'd been able to take clients—Wrong way!"

"Sorry! I'll have roundabouts figured out by the time the trip is over—I promise."

"If you don't get us killed first. Anyway, as I was saying. . . . The outer reef wall is where relatively shallow water drops off sharply to the ocean floor—hundreds of feet down. We were sternly warned to pay attention to our depth gauges, because it would be easy to follow the wall and move deeper than we should. The dive was *amazing!* Brightly colored fish were everywhere; the coral was brilliant, and the sponges, vivid. For me, this dive typified why it's called the *Grrrrreat Barrier Reef.*"

"That's so cool. Tell me more about the sea life. Did you see any sharks?"

"Yes, I saw several whitetip sharks. I also saw stingrays, clown fish, gobies, parrot fish, triggerfish, nudibranchs, blue starfish, sea cucumbers, giant clams, and . . . How was your day?"

"Well, my biggest adventure was getting enough change for the laundromat. I swear. No one in town had any coins. Then, the dryers didn't have any heat. I tell ya—you women think us guys have it so easy. Just try slaving over a *cold* dryer all day."

Cape Tribulation is located fifty miles north of Port Douglas. Captain James Cook named the spot in 1770 after his ship, the *Endeavour,* struck a reef there. While Cook was able to save his ship and continue his voyage, the area obviously made him grumpy. Other local landmarks named by him include Mount Sorrow, Mount Misery, and Weary Bay.

We would be staying at the Cape Trib Beach House, located in Cape Tribulation National Park, now part of Daintree National Park, which in turn is encompassed by a 3,453-square-mile region known as the Wet Tropics of Queensland World Heritage Area.

The final hour of our northbound journey consisted of a ferry crossing at the Daintree River and an eighteen-mile drive along the coast. The Cape Trib Beach House is nestled between the Cape Tribulation Road and the Coral Sea. Just before our accommodations, the road's surface changed from pavement to gravel. Shortly beyond our accommodations, the road's name would change from the Cape Tribulation Road to the Bloomfield Track—for about fifteen miles. Then it would become the Bloomfield Cooktown Road—at least according to some. Geographical names in this region are so variable that even maps disagree with one another.

One thing was certain: we were visiting a biologically important region. The rainforest here is not only considered the oldest in the world, it's also home to at least eighty-five endemic vertebrates and seven hundred endemic plants.

After all the wonderful, friendly service we had enjoyed up to this point, the Cape Trib Beach House seemed impersonal. Part of the reason was that it was a relatively large facility with thirteen cabins, including some dormitory style. Also, instead of dealing directly with the owners, we were served by employees who hadn't yet figured out that the customers standing in front of them were more important than the long conversations they were having on the telephone.

Aside from the occasionally aggravating service, we would have no regrets about our lodging choice. We had reserved the farthest cabin from the reception office, so we had privacy, and the beach was only seventy feet away.

Typical of oceanfront property we saw elsewhere in rural Queensland, our cabin (a simple, stilted, wooden structure with a small front porch) wasn't visible from the water. Instead, it was hidden behind a buffer zone of rainforest. While an ocean view would have been pleasant, I admired the Australians for having the foresight to keep their shorelines natural.

Because the sun had set by the time we finished checking in, we hiked the quarter-mile-long concrete path to our cabin in twilight. As I climbed the porch stairs, something floating between the roof and railing startled me.

I flicked on my flashlight. "Deb! It's a Belizean fangs-o-death!"

"Let me see. Wow, it's amazingly similar to the orb weaver spiders in Belize. But its body isn't as colorful or shiny."

I had to agree. It wasn't quite a Belizean fangs-o-death, but it was definitely in the same family. I reached for the door. "Whoa! There's another one!"

The second spider's web stretched between the top of the doorframe and the porch ceiling. Though I could open the door without destroying the web, I hoped the *Aussie fangs-o-death* wouldn't decide to build on a mother-in-law apartment overnight.

I turned on the lights and lugged our gear inside. While Deb unpacked, I paged through the *Wildlife of Tropical North Queensland* book I had purchased earlier in the trip. Soon I found a matching picture. Like the spiders in Belize, the Aussie fangs-o-death was a golden orb weaver subspecies. I scanned the text to learn the human reaction to their bite. "None to severe," it said. Well, that about covers it!

I grabbed my camera, stepped outside, and snapped a photo. When I looked at the image on the digital screen, the spider's size was indeterminable.

"Deb, come here. I need you."

"For what?"

"Slip your hand behind the web so I have something for size comparison."

Deb looked at me and grinned. "You're gonna make me do this, aren't you?"

"As long as the Aussie fangs-o-death stays on her side of the web, you'll be fine."

"Okay, how's this?" The span of the spider's legs equaled Deb's hand from wrist to fingertips.

"A little closer."

"I'm practically touching it!"

I pushed the button and checked the image. "No, I still need you closer."

"You owe me, big time!"

Now, the spider looked as if it were resting on her hand. I pressed the button again. "Don't move. That one was out of focus."

Deb frowned. "You've got fifteen seconds."

"Okay, just one more. . . . Got it! Thanks, Hon."

"No worries."

"I suppose I should feed them now."

"What, are they gonna be like Spike at Black Rock Lodge?"

"Yeah. We'll make it a travel tradition. They'll need names."

"How 'bout Ozzie and Harriet?"

"Sure. But since both spiders are female, we'll have to let Ozzie think she's really Harriet. The last thing we need is a pissed off fangs-o-death."

Our first day in Daintree National Park would be a long one—but that was good. After breakfast in the Cape Trib Beach House outdoor cafeteria, we set off on a six-mile-long hike. Heading north, we'd walk along sandy beaches, around tide pools, over jagged outcrops, and into the rainforest. Much of our route was above water only at low tide—something we'd have to keep in mind each time we got distracted.

And the distractions were many. Dazzling blue triangle butterflies (a type of swallowtail) fluttered by, challenging me to capture them on film, and yellow-banded Saint Andrew's cross spiders clung to the braided white X on their webs, hoping to blend in. I could have easily spent an hour at each tide pool, watching colorful little fish and stalking shy psychedelic green crabs.

Earlier in this chapter, I promised to introduce you to a bizarre creature that would eliminate all reasonable doubts of evolution. I found such a creature—in fact, oodles of them—when I walked up a shallow stream that emptied into the ocean. I might not have noticed them if they weren't jumping *out* of the water and climbing onto logs and fallen branches.

What were they? Mudskippers—a fish that spends more time out of water than in it. They breathe on land by absorbing oxygen through their moist skin, they propel themselves by using their fins as legs, and since fish don't have eyelids, they keep their eyeballs moist by periodically retracting them into their sockets. These unique adaptations give mudskippers the ability to remain on land for a day or more.

The six-inch-long fish were comical in appearance. They had bright-blue protuberant eyes atop their heads, pointed tails, and golden bodies with blotchy dark-brown bands.

What do mudskippers have to do with evolution? They're a species in transition—evolving from fish to terrestrial animal. If we could sit by the stream for thousands of years, we could watch them change. Hmmm, what if in addition to developing legs, their eyes grew even farther out of their heads? Then, they'd look like little *extra*terrestrial animals.

Emmagen Creek was our last stop before we'd cut through the rainforest and walk back to our cabin via the Bloomfield Track. We wanted to catch a glimpse of the estuarine crocodiles inhabiting the mouth of the creek. Reaching twenty-three feet in length, they're the world's largest crocodile species (for comparison, a typical full-size pickup truck is eighteen feet long). Unfortunately, none were visible. Though I was disappointed, how could I make the crocs show themselves if they didn't want to be seen? If I only had a "stunt author" to wade into the river and thrash around like a wounded animal for me. . . .

We returned to the Beach House with just enough time to eat dinner and prepare for our evening adventure. Before leaving the United States, I had e-mailed Mason's Tours and General Store to arrange a night walk with local guide and snake expert Chris Leach. Mason's is Cape Tribulation's primary source for food, gas, information, and almost everything else (the family-owned business has a history going back to 1932, when Andrew Mason became the region's first white settler). Even though a private night walk devoted entirely to snake hunting wasn't on their activity menu, they were flexible enough to accommodate me.

Chris met us at the reception office at dusk. He was in his midthirties and wore a long-sleeved plaid flannel shirt. His neatly trimmed hairstyle contrasted with his chest-length, somewhat disheveled beard. He reminded me of lumberjacks I used to see in northern Minnesota when I was growing up.

After introductions, we climbed into a Mason's Tours Toyota Land Cruiser. Deb sat in back; I sat in front. As Chris started the vehicle, he looked over at me and grinned. "I have a present for you," he said.

I followed his eyes to a cloth bag between our seats, lifted it, and smiled. "You brought me a snake!"

"Actually two. They're brown tree snakes."

"Aren't they venomous?" I asked.

"They're rear fanged, mildly venomous."

"Cool! I can't wait to see them."

Deb leaned forward. "I want you to know, Chris, you just made Marty's trip."

"My pleasure. They were easy to find."

On a normal night, Chris would have been leading a group on a very general tour. I could tell he relished the opportunity to set out with people who had rainforest experience and a definite goal in mind. Not only had he found the brown tree snakes, but he had also scouted out specific locations for us to explore—work that would pay off when we made our first stop.

After following a dirt road into a section of rainforest owned by Mason's, we stepped out of the truck and proceeded on foot. We hadn't walked far before Chris shined his spotlight on a bush and announced, "There's another brown tree snake."

I turned to Deb and whispered, "He's goooood!"

Rather than attempt to capture the snake, we watched it until it disappeared into the foliage. Now, of course, my confidence was soaring. Surely, with such a talented guide, we'd find more snakes on this night than we knew what to do with.

Though my goals for the trip fluctuated from time to time, the ultimate for me would be to find an amethystine python. Capable of reaching twenty-six feet in length, it's Australia's largest snake.

Before looking for giant pythons, however, we still had the brown tree snakes in the bag to examine. When Chris found a suitable open area, he took the first one out and set it on the ground. Sometimes when a snake is released, it will freeze for several minutes before gradually slithering away. In this instance, the snake had no interest in sticking around and headed directly for the nearest thicket. I snapped two photos before it slipped out of sight.

"Can I hold the next one?" I asked.

Because Chris's primary job, as a guide, was to protect his clients, I wasn't sure if he'd let me handle anything venomous. Although brown tree snakes wouldn't make any herpetologist's top one hundred list for danger, even mild venom can lead to a bad reaction.

After a moment of hesitation, he answered, "Sure."

I grasped the three-foot-long snake by the head and midbody and held her in the beam from Chris's spotlight. She wasn't drab brown, as you might surmise from the species' name. Instead, she was bright reddish brown with a touch of gray.

Holding a venomous snake for the first time in my life—without assistance—was exciting. Especially when she anchored herself to my arm with her tail and attempted to free her head by pulling backward. I had to concentrate on gripping her firmly enough that she couldn't twist loose, yet not so firmly that I'd injure her.

After Deb took some photos, Chris pointed to a drop glistening on the snake's lower jaw. "That's venom," he said.

"Really? I wouldn't have noticed it. I guess I should set her free."

"The tree over there looks good," said Chris, illuminating the way with his spotlight.

I walked over, set the snake on one of the low branches, and jerked back—just in case she struck. Biting, however, was no longer on this snake's mind. Instead, she climbed from one branch to another until safely out of reach.

"That was great!" I said. "Thank you! Are amethystine pythons as common around here as brown tree snakes?"

"It depends on the time of year. I frequently find them during the rainy summer season, but now that it's fall they're less active and harder to find."

"What other kinds of pythons live in the area?"

"I see spotted pythons around here quite often."

"How big do they get?"

"They stay pretty small. Usually less than a meter."

"What about the amethystines?"

"I've seen them as long as six meters. But three meters is a more common size."

"Wow! When Deb and I visited the Amazon, our expedition leader told us not to expect anything large—and his prediction came true. I'd be thrilled to find any python longer than two meters."

"We have a good chance of doing that."

The three of us returned to the truck to check out several areas accessible by vehicle. When none produced pythons, we set off on foot again.

As we followed a narrow path through the darkness, I was glad to be with a knowledgeable guide. Not only could Chris identify wildlife and keep us from getting lost, but he could also steer us around two extremely nasty plants.

At night, tropical rainforests are virtually indistinguishable from one another. Since I was concentrating on spotting snakes, I barely noticed the trees with their widespread buttress roots, and the many ferns, mosses, and vines. In Australia, however, you *always* want to notice the wait-a-whiles and stinging trees.

The appropriately named wait-a-whiles (also known as lawyer vines) are the lesser of the two nasties. They're a type of climbing palm, with long stems that can extend for hundreds of feet. Backward-facing barbs cover each stem, and though not poisonous, they are annoying. A person caught in the palm's grasp must stop and "wait-a-while" to detach each barb or face the consequences of ripped skin or clothing.

As for stinging trees (also known as gympie-gympies), they're ordinary-looking plants with green heart-shaped leaves. What makes them dangerous are the tiny stiff, hollow hairs covering each leaf and the poison stored at the base of each hair. Think of the hairs as mini-syringes. If you were to brush against a leaf, the hairs would break off and embed themselves in your skin, carrying the poison with them.

During our visit, I spoke with several Australians who had had run-ins with stinging trees. They all stressed they'd never make the same mistake again. Typically, a stinging tree encounter causes blistering with several hours of intense pain, followed by weeks of recurring pain, as the hairs release additional toxins. In severe cases, hospitalization may be necessary.

What began as a promising night eventually became a frustrating night—at least regarding our python search. We did see other animals, however, including a bush rat, a praying mantis, a white-lipped tree frog, and an Australian lace-lid frog. The two frogs were especially good finds.

Australian lace-lid frogs are classified as "endangered" by the IUCN. They reach two and a half inches in length and have tan skin with white spots. At first glance, our lace-lid frog didn't appear to be unusual. That changed when she closed her eyes to reveal eyelid veins in a distinct lacelike design—almost as if she were wearing a veil.

White-lipped tree frogs are large, green, and fairly common. What made our frog special was his willingness to patiently balance on a stringlike horizontal vine for what would become one of my all-time favorite photos.

"I'm ready for bed," said Deb.

"Oh, come on," I whined. "We just got started."

"We've been out here more than three hours! I'm sweaty and exhausted."

"I suppose. . . . It's just that tonight was my best chance to find a python."

"You still have two more days."

"But this was the only night walk I had scheduled."

"Maybe you can ask—"

"Hey, Chris, are you available tomorrow night?"

"Sorry, mate, I'm booked. But I think I'm free after that. If you stop by Mason's tomorrow, they'll have my schedule."

"Okay then. Let's call it a night."

Though I didn't want to admit it, I too was exhausted. We had had a long and eventful day. Collapsing in our cozy cabin bed—after a cool shower—was a grand idea.

Tuesday morning Deb was up early for another day of scuba diving the Great Barrier Reef. This time she had scheduled two dives off a catamaran called the *Rum Runner*.

While Deb's previous dive day had definitely surpassed my laundry day, our second time apart would produce adventures that were more comparable. In fact, my next eight hours were going to be nearly perfect.

After driving two miles south to Mason's, to schedule another evening with Chris, I headed north along the Cape Tribulation Road/Bloomfield Track. My goal was to walk up Mason, Rykers, Blockade, and Emmagen creeks. All four creeks ran west to east, from the nearby mountains to the Coral Sea. Traveling a specific distance up each creek wasn't part of my plan. Instead, I would just walk until I felt like turning around.

One of my favorite activities is to thoroughly explore small sections of terrain. While Deb enjoys exploring underwater in a similar manner, being with me on this day would have driven her crazy. At one point, I spent an hour on my hands and knees watching and photographing all the tiny frogs and insects within a ten-foot radius.

While I generally stayed in or near the creeks, if I saw something interesting, I'd head off into the rainforest for a closer look. From there, I'd often see something else in the distance, walk to it, and so on. Without a map or compass, I was unprepared for jungle trekking, and sometimes my heart fluttered when I'd look back and realize I had traveled much farther than expected.

The mountains would keep me from getting totally lost, but at the same time, no one knew where I was. If the wrong creature bit me, or I became injured in some other way, help wouldn't arrive until Deb returned from diving and became concerned enough to dispatch a search party.

Often I had to maneuver around large, colorful spiders—which I temporarily named "Aussie fangs-o-*painful*-death"—and extricate myself from wait-a-whiles. One climb alongside a fifteen-foot-high waterfall took almost ten minutes, as I worked my way through a thicket of wait-a-whiles and contorted past clusters of spider webs. I was having fun—really.

I reached Emmagen Creek by late afternoon. At roughly twenty-five feet wide, it was the biggest of the four creeks. Before heading upriver, I hiked to the mouth to check for crocodiles. When none were in sight, I reversed course and strolled along the riverbank. I hadn't gone far when I heard something large rustling across the leaf litter—it was heading toward me. Crocodile? The last place I wanted to be was between a croc and the river!

I froze and listened. Whatever it was, it was low to the ground and about fifty feet into the rainforest. I could hear what sounded like a tail sweeping and see ferns moving, ever so slightly. Then I caught a glimpse of its tapered snout. It wasn't a croc. But what was it?

When the five-foot-long animal stepped into the open, I could see dark-gray beady scales, cream-colored spots, and raptorlike claws. Folds in her thick skin gave her an armored dinosaurlike appearance. Now I recognized her. She was a lace monitor—a lizard closely related to the Komodo dragon.

Though I knew what she was, I knew nothing about her natural history or temperament. If I startled her, would she fight or flee? I got down on my hands and knees, so as not to appear threatening, and snapped some photos.

I expected her to turn away at any moment, but instead she continued toward me. Her movements were slow, and she stopped often to search for food in holes and hollow logs. I decided to mimic her movements and crawl toward her.

As the gap closed between us, our eyes met several times. Soon we were less than twenty feet apart. I was excited and a bit nervous. Never before had a wild animal reacted to me in such a way. At ten feet, I stopped crawling to let the monitor decide how close we'd get. I was too big for her to consider me prey. She wasn't confusing me for another monitor, was she? If so, did she think of me as competition—or a prospective mate? I quickly purged the last possibility from my mind. That a large lizard might consider me attractive wasn't exactly an ego boost.

When only three feet separated us, the monitor paused, flicked her tongue, decided I was the most pathetic-looking lizard she'd ever seen, and headed west along the riverbank.

Our encounter could have ended there, but since neither of us was in a hurry, I decided to follow. For the next fifteen minutes, the monitor let me share her world. While she methodically searched every depression that could contain a meal, I sporadically whistled to get her attention. She popped her head up to look at me the first few times I whistled but soon caught on and ignored me.

She had an aura of intelligence that I'd never sensed in a lizard before. In fact, if I were able to follow her long enough, I could have watched her do something truly amazing: manipulate another species into protecting her eggs.

She'd accomplish this by ripping open a termite mound with her claws and then depositing her eggs in the hole. When the termites repaired the damage, they'd seal her eggs inside, creating the perfect incubator. Later—and this part is speculative—she'd return to extract her hatchlings.

Some people may call the monitor's maternal behavior "instinct," but if humans could do something comparable—perhaps convince another species to provide free, reliable daycare for our children during the terrible twos stage—we'd think we were pretty smart.

My time with the lace monitor concluded after she stopped for a drink at the creek and proceeded into a thorny thicket. I already had dozens of wait-a-while scratches on my legs and didn't want them on my face as well. Besides, *my* mate was due back from her dive day, and I was eager to exchange adventure stories with her.

When I returned to the cabin, Deb was waiting for me—smiling. She had had a delightful time diving with a small group on the *Rum Runner.* While she told me about swarms of fish, ancient reef formations, and giant clams, I told her—simultaneously—about clusters of spiders, cool little frogs, and the lace monitor.

We continued our volley of stories over dinner, and—once we were talked out—strolled along the beach, watching the sunset. In all, we had a wonderful day apart and a pleasant evening together.

When I shared with you the story of the lace monitor, I discussed lizard intelligence. Now, I'd like to share with you a story about human stupidity—my stupidity.

I awoke at three in the morning thinking, *again,* about pythons. When Deb and I were out with Chris, he mentioned that the snakes often hunted in the trees along the edge of the beach. Though my previous seaside searches hadn't produced anything, perhaps I was just looking at the wrong time. Until I at least checked, I knew I couldn't fall back asleep.

Being careful not to wake Deb, I slipped out of bed, grabbed my camera, and tiptoed out the door. A short path led me through the rainforest to the beach. The stars were out, but with no moon in sight the night was extraordinarily dark. A spotlight, such as the one Chris had, would have been great. Instead, I'd have to get by with my woefully inadequate flashlight.

The beach was expansive at low tide. But now, at high tide, it was maybe fifteen feet wide. The tide didn't concern me much, however, as my interest was in the wall of trees where the rainforest met the beach. In fact, as I walked south on the sand, painting branches with my flashlight, my only concern was inadvertently stumbling over people having sex. If such an accident were to occur, an apology of, "Sorry, I'm just out looking for snakes," would have likely been misinterpreted. Fortunately, I was the only human on the beach.

As for the pythons, if they were having sex on the beach, they were certainly being discreet. I walked for forty-five minutes, inspected countless trees, and saw only an orgy of flying insects. I turned back in frustration.

"What happened to the beach!" I shouted, knowing no one could hear me.

I had been concentrating so hard on the hunt that I hadn't realized the tide was still coming in. Everything looked different now. I couldn't even tell how far I had walked. My stomach churned.

The border where the beach met the rainforest was uneven. Initially I still had room to maneuver, but as I hurried north, I came upon a spot where a huge tree and a spit of steep rock blocked my way. My choices were to cut through the jungle or wade through the water.

"Hmmm," I thought. "Box jellyfish or stinging trees—pick your poison."

Had it been light out, or had I not irrationally convinced myself I'd get lost, the choice would have been obvious. At that moment, however, I was obsessed with returning to the cabin in the quickest possible manner.

I leaped into the knee-high water and ran through the waves—as if speed would have lessened any jellyfish stings. Luckily, no jellyfish—or crocodiles for that matter—were in my way.

Once past the obstructions, all I had to do was find the path to the cabin. The marker for the path was . . . underwater. Nothing was distinct. I jogged down a skinny strip of smooth sand searching for a break in a solid wall of rainforest.

Thinking I had gone too far, I jogged back to the big tree. When I still couldn't find the path, I concluded it had to be on the opposite side—I had risked jellyfish stings for nothing!

I tried to suppress feelings of panic: "Perhaps I should just stay put until sunrise. . . . No, if Deb wakes up, she'll worry. . . . The path couldn't be on the other side of the tree. I'm already too far south. . . . It has to be to the north; I just didn't walk far enough. . . . How could I get lost on a beach!"

I jogged north again, this time much farther than before. "Damn! I know it's not this far," I muttered. Breathing heavily, I turned and slowly walked back. "There it is!"

I shook my head in disbelief. I had passed the opening two, maybe three times. Now it looked so obvious. I hurried back to the cabin and crawled into bed.

Deb was still asleep.

Wednesday was our last day in Daintree National Park, and we had every moment planned. We'd begin with a half-day four-wheel-drive trip up the Bloomfield Track, then we'd stop at the Bat House, and finally we'd embark on another snake hunt with Chris Leach.

Before I get to the events of our day, I'd like to share with you the history of the Bloomfield Track. It's one of my favorite conservation stories, because it recounts a lost environmental battle that resulted in the winning of a much larger environmental war:

The coastal community of Cooktown is located roughly forty-five miles north of the Cape Trib Beach House. When the controversy began, the only road from Cooktown to Cairns was a rough inland track called the Peninsula Development Road. Two roads existed on the coast, but they didn't meet. The Bloomfield Cooktown Road ran south from Cooktown to the Bloomfield River, and the Cape Tribulation Road ran from the Daintree River Ferry to just north of the Cape Trib Beach House. Between the two roads were fifteen miles of virgin rainforest.

The Douglas Shire Council (which is similar to a county commissioners board in the U.S.) and the Queensland government backed a plan to link the two coastal roads, and conservationists opposed the plan. While both sides stated multiple reasons for their positions, logging and development were the two primary issues.

In December 1983 the bulldozers arrived, triggering the Daintree Blockade. Conservationists attempted to stop the construction by chaining themselves to trees and burying themselves in front of the bulldozers. Despite their resistance, the two roads were linked within three weeks. The Douglas Shire Council and Queensland government had won the battle.

From that moment on, the tide turned in favor of the environment. Mother Nature promptly sent rain and landslides, which closed the road for many months. The Bloomfield Track finally officially opened during the following dry season (October 1984) with a ceremony and motorcade. Once again, Mother Nature expressed her displeasure. This time she sent heavy rains, which caused the motorcade to become hopelessly stuck in the mud.

The Bloomfield Track didn't go away, but the elements and hasty construction have prevented it from becoming the quick route between Cooktown and Cairns some had hoped for. In fact, four-wheel-drive vehicles are still recommended for travel north of Emmagen Creek.

Now, here's where the story gets really good. Conservationists, with the support of the Australian Commonwealth government, fought back by applying to have the Wet Tropics of Queensland protected as a World Heritage Area. The Douglas Shire Council and Queensland government opposed the plan, but this was the war they were going to lose. In December 1988, the Wet Tropics of Queensland, including Daintree National Park, officially became a World Heritage Area—joining the Great Barrier Reef, which was declared a World Heritage Area in 1981.

Have the local people been pleased with what the conservationists accomplished? Here's a hint: Mike Berwick, the spokesperson for the blockade protesters, was elected mayor of the Douglas Shire Council in 1991. He has subsequently been reelected multiple times and was still mayor as of January 2006.

Deb and I met up with Allen Sheather at Mason's Store. While today Allen would be our Bloomfield Track guide, he was also a botanist and the director of the Daintree Rainforest Foundation. After introductions, we hopped into one of Mason's Land Cruisers and headed north, literally driving through Emmagen Creek.

Seeing the rainforest beyond the creek helped me to better appreciate why the conservationists had been so passionate for their cause. We wound through pristine wilderness that certainly would have been logged, farmed, or developed for mega-resorts if the World Heritage listing hadn't been achieved.

The Bloomfield Track wasn't as rough as I had expected. With the exception of a few bridgeless river crossings, most of the road could have been navigated with an ordinary two-wheel-drive vehicle. Of course, this was the dry season. A wet season journey would have been much more hazardous. In fact, our truck was equipped with a snorkel to keep the engine running on high-water river crossings.

We spent much of the morning watching the scenery go by. When we stopped for short walks, Allen would point out plant and bird species in rapid-fire succession. Some of the birds we saw included rainbow bee-eaters, metallic starlings, and great-billed herons. Unfortunately the bird we most wanted to see, the southern cassowary, eluded us.

A cassowary is a flightless bird that stands up to six feet tall and weighs nearly 175 pounds. It has a hard casque atop its head and dagger-sharp claws capable of inflicting a fatal wound. The IUCN classifies the bird as a "vulnerable species." It's in trouble primarily because of competition from feral pigs, which eat its eggs and food. For example, in the eighteen-mile stretch of rainforest between the Daintree River and the Cape Trib Beach House, an estimated fifty-four cassowaries must contend with ten thousand feral pigs. Sighting such a rare and impressive bird would have been a momentous event.

More than three thousand plant species have been identified within the Wet Tropics of Queensland World Heritage Area. Of all the plant life Allen showed us, the most memorable for me were the orchids and cauliflory.

Although Deb and I would see orchids in every rainforest we'd visit for this book, my animal interests often kept me from giving the flowering plants much attention. I enjoyed watching our botanist-guide get excited when he spotted a particularly unusual orchid. Even if I couldn't share his level of excitement, it illustrated for me how individual people can enjoy the same rainforest for different reasons.

Cauliflorous trees produce flowers and fruit directly from their trunks instead of (or in addition to) their branches. This phenomenon is rare, except in tropical rainforests. Early botanists believed cauliflory were parasitic plants—not part of the trees—and until I learned differently, I assumed the same thing. Theories for the existence of rainforest cauliflory include the close proximity to other trees and the ability to support larger fruits. Another likely reason is that trunk-based flowers are more easily accessible to pollinators such as moths and bats.

The turnaround spot for our four-wheel-drive journey was where the 130-foot-high Bloomfield Falls dropped into an idyllic swimming hole—for crocodiles. The water was clear, yet deep enough that we couldn't see bottom. This was a frustrating place to be on a hot, sunny day. A swim would have felt great, but we couldn't go in the water because of the crocodiles. That would have been okay, if we could have actually seen the crocodiles. Since the crocs were hiding, all we could do was look at the cool water as it taunted us. Yes, this would have been another handy time to have a stunt author along—someone who could serve as bait while the rest of us swam. Lacking such a person, we piled back into the Land Cruiser and returned to Mason's Store.

Deb and I said good-bye to Allen and headed back up the road. After our Port Douglas flying fox experience, we were eager for another, even closer, bat encounter. We soon arrived at the Bat House, the visitor center of the Cape Tribulation Tropical Research Station. Here volunteers and researchers conduct conservation and educational activities as well as rehabilitate flying foxes that have been injured, orphaned, or overcome with scrub-tick paralysis.

We stepped inside the light-filled one-room building and were surprised to be the only visitors. Informational displays lined the walls, and a flying fox hung on a net suspended from the ceiling in the middle of the room. A college-aged researcher greeted us as we approached the bat.

"Would you like to hold Annie?" she asked.

"Sure," I said, looking at the woman for further instructions.

"Just stand next to her, and she'll climb up the front of your shirt."

"Ouch!" The ten-inch-long bat had grabbed onto my sleeveless T-shirt with one sharp thumb and nearly pierced the bare skin under my arm with the other. "I'm wearing the wrong shirt for this."

To understand what happened, you need to know a little bat anatomy. Stretch your arm straight out from your side with your thumb pointing up and your fingers splayed out. Imagine your fingers are about seven times longer and that a wing membrane (a double layer of skin) stretches between your fingers and attaches to the bottom of your arm, side of your body, and corresponding leg. Notice how your fingers support the membrane and that your thumb is free. Next, imagine your thumb is bone skinny, twice as long, and ends in a claw. Finally, add a matching wing to your other side and shrink your legs—now you're ready to fly.

Since Annie was climbing, not flying, she resembled a mountaineer ascending a precipitous glacier using two ice axes. Her thumbs were the axes and my chest was the glacier. Her technique was effortless, and painless for me—as long as she was climbing T-shirt instead of bare skin.

"How old is Annie?" asked Deb.

"Sixteen years old," replied the woman.

"How long do flying foxes live?" asked Deb.

"About thirty years in captivity."

"Annie looks uninjured. Can she fly?" I asked.

"Physically she's perfectly capable of doing so. She just doesn't know how. Mother flying foxes teach their pups to fly, and Annie was an orphan. By the time we got her she was too old to train."

"What kind of flying fox is she?" asked Deb.

"She's a black flying fox."

"She's adorable," I said. "Look at that face!"

"Okay, it's my turn to hold Annie," said Deb.

"All right . . . I *suppose* you can have her."

When I moved close, Annie climbed onto Deb's T-shirt and hung upside down from her collar. "Oh, she's such a sweetheart!" said Deb.

Bats are another remarkable example of evolution. When they evolved, their legs diminished in size and rotated 180 degrees. Smaller legs keep them balanced during flight, and because their knees and feet bend the opposite way of other mammals, it's easy for them to grab onto branches and other surfaces with their claws when landing.

Sleeping while hanging upside down is effortless for bats. Their claws have evolved to lock closed, making the position extremely energy efficient. Hanging in such a manner doesn't mean bats prefer to view the world upside down, however. In fact, they will turn their heads upright to look at something particularly interesting.

Bats are classified in two major groups. Most (including all species in North and South America) belong to the suborder Microchiroptera. "Microbats" are generally small, navigate by echolocation, and eat insects (some species, such as vampire bats and fisherman bats, have specialized diets). Flying foxes are found only in tropical regions of the Eastern Hemisphere, and they belong to the suborder Megachiroptera. "Megabats" are generally large, navigate by eyesight, and eat fruit. Some maverick biologists, incidentally, contend that flying foxes should actually be classified as primates.

What do bats have in common with snakes and wolves? They make my top-three list of the most unfairly persecuted animals on earth. While I've previously addressed human attitudes toward snakes, similar small-minded thinking also affects wolves in the United States and flying foxes in Australia. Even though both countries have enacted laws to prevent extinction, Americans still kill wolves that can't tell the difference between natural prey and livestock, and Australians still kill bats that can't tell the difference between wild and domestic fruit trees. In both cases, humans, who could be using their big brains to implement or develop nonlethal methods of protecting their interests, have chosen to use violence instead.

"My shift is over," said the woman. "If you'd like, I can take you to see the rest of the bats."

"That would be great!" I said.

Deb and I followed the woman down a path to a large wire pen. Inside was a mix of approximately ten black and spectacled flying foxes. Because of the time of day, most were asleep—hanging from the wire ceiling, wrapped in their brown leathery wings. The bats in this colony couldn't return to the wild. Even so, they lived active lives, greeting guests at the Bat House and raising pups. In fact, Annie was already the mother of eight pups that had been released into the wild (flying foxes usually give birth to one pup at a time).

After thanking the woman for the tour, we reluctantly parted ways with the bats. You have no idea how tempted I was to slip a flying fox under my shirt and carry it back with me to Montana. Of course, my squeals of pain whenever a thumb scraped across my chest would have probably given me away to airport security officials. No, the bats belong in Australia—preferably flying free. They sure did steal my heart though.

Deb and I returned to the Cape Trib Beach House. Since sunset was still an hour away, we took a leisurely stroll along the beach and couldn't resist wading in the warm water. Although no jellyfish were in sight, we did find dozens of amazing little crabs, which buried themselves instantly whenever we approached them. The evening was so glorious we stayed on the beach until darkness threatened to hide the path to our cabin.

My day was just getting rolling. Deb, on the other hand, decided a little relaxation was in order and begged off traipsing through the sweltering jungle in favor of the cool breeze on our cabin porch. While part of me envied her, I still had a goal to accomplish—tonight was my last chance to find a python.

Chris picked me up by the Beach House reception office. As I climbed into the Land Cruiser, I noticed his smile was a bit broader than normal.

"G'day, or should I say 'G'evening'?" I asked.

"It's a *great* evening," said Chris. "How are you, Marty?"

"I'm doing terrific. Tonight's gonna b—what's in the bag?"

"It's a surprise."

"Did you find a python?"

"*Maybe.*"

"You found a python!"

"Just a little one."

"When did you find it?"

"This evening. I spotted it in my driveway as I was leaving to pick you up."

"*What!* Let me get this straight. I've been looking for pythons—*unsuccessfully*—for almost two weeks, and *you* found one in your *driveway!*"

"Sorry."

"You know it doesn't count."

"What do you mean?"

"I need to spot the snake, or at least take part in the search, to 'officially' say I saw a python in Australia."

"I understand."

"Of course, that doesn't mean I'm not excited about seeing the python you found."

"Of course—that goes without saying."

We both laughed.

When we reached the location from where we would proceed on foot, I stepped out of the truck and removed the three-foot-long amethystine python from the bag. She was a mellow snake who showed no inclination to bite.

Amethystine pythons are gold with brown geometric markings—they're handsome but not stunning. Lighting makes a big difference, however. When Chris aimed his spotlight on the snake, her skin glowed with a hint of purple, justifying the amethystine name.

We gave the young snake her freedom and headed into the rainforest in search of her mother, father, grandmother, or, if we were really lucky, great-grandfather.

Though the weather had been consistently warm during our stay, this night felt particularly hot. Sweat poured off my body, and I could have wrung out my baseball cap. I longed for just a whiff of air to move the mugginess. I followed Chris, who was once again wearing a long-sleeved flannel shirt, and wondered what kept him from fainting.

The first hour passed without any notable animal sightings. The next hour produced only one sighting—a bird with lime-green wings and a lemon-yellow breast called a noisy pitta. Nights in the rainforest aren't only for finding reptiles, amphibians, and invertebrates. Most night walks during my travels for this book produced at least one bird sighting. Since diurnal bird species are often reluctant to fly in the dark, getting close to them for photos is easy. To be courteous, I work fast and limit the number of flashes they have to endure from my camera.

I had paid for a two-and-a-half-hour night walk, but neither Chris nor I were concerned about sticking to what we had scheduled. For Chris, finding a python was now a matter of professional pride. For me—well, you know how I felt.

Eventually we gave up on following trails and cut directly through the rainforest. We were well into our third hour when Chris shouted in a hushed voice, "Marty! Look over there. On the tree."

My heart pounded as my eyes shifted to where he was shining his light. "Wowwww! Is he cool!"

I was now at the point where any sighting that wasn't a python would be a disappointment—with one exception. The first time I stopped at Mason's Store, I saw a postcard with a photo of the most spectacular lizard I'd ever seen. I remember thinking, skeptically, "Yeah, I bet even guides don't see this lizard more than once in a lifetime."

Chris had found a Boyd's forest dragon—an eighteen-inch-long greenish-gray lizard with large spikes atop its head and smaller spikes along its backbone. If Boyd's forest dragons could sing, every punk rock band would want one for its lead singer. Despite their outlandish appearance, they're surprisingly well camouflaged. Consequently, the one we were watching was easy to photograph, because he was convinced we couldn't see him as long as he stayed clutched to the tree trunk.

Boyd's forest dragons, incidentally, weren't the rare find I assumed they were. Although they're exclusive to tropical north Queensland, they're locally common. In retrospect, I should have known I'd see one. Once lizards learn I'm in the area, they literally jump out of the forest to be found. Without even trying, I had now seen all five major kinds of Australian lizards (dragons, geckos, goannas, legless lizards, and skinks) and roughly a dozen species in all.

As for giant pythons, the futility of our quest was becoming the difficult reality. Nearing the end of our fourth hour, I noticed Chris glancing at his watch. I thought about Steve Irwin and the large pythons I'd seen him catch on his television show. I decided upon returning to the United States, I'd petition the FCC to require a disclaimer before each episode of *The Crocodile Hunter.* The disclaimer would say, "Only one small python actually exists in Australia, and it's shared by Steve Irwin and various guides. Any python appearing longer than three feet has been digitally enhanced for dramatic effect."

Eventually Chris uttered the words I didn't want to hear: "Marty, I'm sorry, but we have to head back to the truck. My family expected me home a long time ago. If I don't return soon, they'll think something happened to us."

"I understand. I'm bummed—but it just wasn't meant to be."

"Come back during the rainy season. I guarantee we'll find a python then."

"You have a deal. And thanks for trying. I know you stayed out much longer than scheduled."

"No worries. I *wanted* to stay out. I'm just as frustrated as you are."

"I'm totally lost. How far are we from the truck?"

"We're about five minutes away. It's just up this trail."

Suddenly I felt exhausted. The intensity of the hunt had kept me going. Now, I trudged along behind Chris—beat.

What happened next is still a blur to me. If we were watching ancient Greek theater, we'd call it *"deus ex machina,"* if we were watching a football game, we'd call it "a completed Hail Mary pass," if we were watching *The Crocodile Hunter,* we'd call it "a typical show ending." All I know is that I was sweeping my flashlight alongside the path, hoping for a miracle, when Chris bobbed behind a fallen tree and emerged with an amethystine python!

"Marty! Look what I found!"

"Oh . . . my . . . God! He's *huge!*"

Chris stood with the snake's head clutched in his hand, its body wrapped several times around his arm, and its tail looped over his shoulders.

"Several months ago I saw a python behind the same tree. I had a hunch he might be back—and there he was."

"Do you really think it's the same snake?"

"He's about the same size, but there's no way to know for sure."

"How long do you think he is?"

"A little over two meters. Do you wanna hold him?"

"You know I do. But first let me take some pictures of you with the snake."

Up until now, shooting photos in the dark had been a two-person operation. Without Chris to shine his spotlight where I wanted to focus the camera, I had to aim my flashlight with one hand and my camera with the other. The process was awkward, but it worked.

The next maneuver, however, would be significantly more difficult. To transfer the python, I'd have to grasp its head while Chris simultaneously released it, and then we'd have to work together to uncoil its body and tail.

"Whatever you do," said Chris, "don't let the snake bite you. A python this large won't let go—we'd be here all night trying to dislodge it."

As we positioned ourselves for the handoff, we realized our predicament and laughed. We needed all our hands for the python, but unless one of us held a light, we couldn't see what we were doing. Ultimately we completed the transfer with moves worthy of a contortionist and my flashlight wedged between my feet.

Once I had control of the python, I was surprised how strong he was. He had wrapped himself so tightly around my arm that my fingers began to tingle from lack of circulation.

"Look how purple your hand is!" said Chris.

"I know. Imagine what it would look like if he *really* wanted to squeeze."

Pythons are constrictors closely related to boas. The main difference is that pythons lay eggs, and boas (with one disputed exception) bear live young. The python I was holding wasn't squeezing me as if I were prey, however; he was just tense from the abrupt change of circumstances and likely waiting for an opportunity to sink his teeth into me.

He began to relax once he realized I wasn't going to hurt him. In fact, while Chris snapped photos with my camera, I was able to release the snake's head without having to fend off a bite attempt.

"Well, mate, we better go."

"Thank you, Chris. This has been a fantastic night."

"No worries. I'm just glad we had success."

I set the python down and watched him glide along the forest floor. "Now that he's stretched out, I'd guess he's seven feet long. What do you think?"

"I'd say seven and a half feet."

"Okay, we'll go with that. Now, if I come back in the rainy season, you'll show me where the twenty-footers are hiding—right?"

"I can't guarantee a specific size. But we will find some big ones."

"You know, in retrospect, I think tonight's python was closer to twelve feet long."

"Oh, I'd say at least fifteen. . . ."

Thursday morning, after Deb listened to me ramble on about the python, we packed our bags and departed for Cairns.

As we headed toward the city, we relived highlights of our trip and filled each other in on missed details from our solo adventures. When we were all talked out, I turned on the car radio. "Hey, they're playing 'Copperhead Road' again. I swear Steve Earle gets more airplay in Australia than he does at home."

Every trip in this book has at least one song that triggers happy travel memories for me. In this case, it was "Copperhead Road." Though Earle's lyrics had nothing to do with the trip, and try as I might, I couldn't sing the chorus as "Amethystine Python Road," I heard the song virtually every time I turned on the radio.

Although the kind of travel Deb and I do usually keeps us away from electronic entertainment, I enjoy listening to radio stations in foreign countries. Based on what I heard on this trip, American music is popular in Australia, but the songs and artists the stations play often differ from what is aired commercially in the United States. I found the change of pace refreshing.

Radio, however, was perhaps the smallest part of a trip that had exceeded both Deb's and my expectations. Even though our flight to Montana wouldn't leave until the following morning, I was already homesick—for Australia. I knew once we completed our seven continent journey the Land Down Under would be one of the first places we'd revisit.

In fact, Deb and I were already discussing future locations to explore. Western Australia, Victoria, and Tasmania were all on our must-visit list. On the other hand, how could I return to Australia without stopping in Chillagoe to see the Bondesons and their latest rehabilitation projects or traveling to Cape Tribulation to search for twenty-foot pythons with Chris Leach? And need I say anything about Deb wanting to squeeze in a few days of Great Barrier Reef diving? Decisions, decisions. One thing was certain: our next visit would have to be longer.

For our farewell dinner, we dined at a sidewalk café in downtown Cairns. As I perused the menu, another colorful but unfamiliar Australian term jumped out at me. When the waiter asked for my order, I seized the opportunity for a final adventure. "I'll have the *bugs*, please."

4
Ooooo Canada

Our dogs were starting to complain. Until Deb and I began traveling for this book, they had never stayed in a kennel. Now they
were feeling as if it were their second home. If you've ever left a dog at
a kennel, you know what a heartwrenching experience it can be. I swear,
dogs sit in front of mirrors and practice their "you don't love me anymore" look for just such occasions.

We have two dogs: Kate and Annie. Kate, our golden retriever, had
her eighth birthday in 2002. When she was a puppy, I registered her
with the American Kennel Club as Kate Trouble Essen, and ever since
she's done her best to live up to her middle name. Her hobbies include
rolling in dead things (the stinkier the better), carrying rocks (the bigger the better), and swimming in swamps (the muddier the better).

Annie is our mostly white, not quite purebred, Labrador retriever.
We're not sure how old she is, because we adopted her from an animal
shelter, but she's probably a year younger than Kate. Annie is a sweetheart who loves to make friends with everyone. The only problem is that
there are actually two Annies: the "good Annie" and the "bad Annie."

If you've ever watched *Star Trek* or read science fiction books, you're
probably familiar with the concept of alternate universes and know that
hidden portals usually provide shortcuts from one universe to another.
What you don't know is that similar portals exist here on Earth—and
they all lead to Idaho.

I learned of the portals upon discovering that Annie's naughty but
physically identical counterpart lives just across the border in Idaho.
Life is fine when each Annie remains in her proper state. Unfortunately,

our dog—the good Annie—can sniff out the hidden portals in almost any wooded area. She usually resists the portals, but sometimes the bad Annie tempts her from the other side. And as any physics student knows, two Annies can't occupy the same state at the same time. Therefore, when the good Annie goes to Idaho, the bad Annie joins us here in Montana. The exchanges are usually brief, and if the bad Annie overextends her stay, we've found that threatening to give her a bath sends her hightailing it back to Idaho.

After three straight overseas trips, Deb and I couldn't bear leaving Kate and Annie in a kennel again. The time was right for our North American adventure, and we'd make it a road trip. Since dogs, both good and bad, love to ride in cars, we'd have to make sure the correct Annie was with us when we departed. If not, well . . .

Deciding where to go in North America took some deliberation. Deb suggested driving the Alaska Highway to Fairbanks, but when I checked with the American Automobile Association (AAA), they projected an eighteen-day round-trip, averaging seven hours of driving per day. The biggest obstacle was time. Because of some recent employee turnover, my office staff was inexperienced, and leaving my business for more than two weeks would give me night sweats.

As we looked into other options, I kept returning to the Arctic Circle in Canada's Yukon Territory. The mileage savings versus Fairbanks was only one hundred miles, and I knew once we reached the Arctic Circle I'd want to continue all the way to the town of Inuvik, Northwest Territories, at the top of Canada. According to the AAA, a round-trip between my home and Inuvik would log 5,344 miles and take twenty days. While adding two more travel days should have eliminated the trip as a possibility, once the idea was planted in my brain nothing else interested me. The AAA's travel times did seem conservative. How conservative, I didn't know—but we were going to find out. If the trip took longer than two weeks, I'd just deal with the night sweats.

Our mode of transportation for the trip would be my 1999 Ford F-150 pickup. Owning a full-sized truck isn't something an environmentalist like me is proud to admit, but after spending a few winters in Montana, I grew tired of becoming stranded at the bottom of the steep, unmaintained road to our house and gave in to the practicality of a high-clearance four-wheel drive. The way a vehicle is driven, however, can be just as important as the gas mileage it gets. By consolidating my excursions to town and riding my bicycle when possible, I consume less gas annually than a typical city dweller with a hybrid vehicle. In fact, I would drive more miles on this trip than I usually drive in a year.

I cringe when I see people transporting their dogs in the open box of a pickup. The unprotected animals can get frostbite, eye injuries, broken bones, or worse. A dog's place is in the cab with its owner. Consequently, when I purchased my truck I specifically selected an extended cab model with rear seats that folded flat to the floor for an even surface. At the time, I was thinking of Kate and Annie's comfort on our usual short trips. Now, as we embarked on a long journey, I wouldn't have to worry about them becoming crowded, stiff, or sore.

From the dogs' point of view, this would be the ultimate trip: ride in the truck, get out and swim, ride in the truck, get out and explore, ride in the truck, get out and roll, ride in the truck. . . . Actually, from a human's point of view, the dogs' activities looked equally appealing— except for the rolling part. We all know what they roll in.

Preparation for our trip was minimal. I put new tires on the truck and made sure it was in tip-top operating condition. Deb packed the food and camping gear, and the dogs packed their all-weather coats and swimsuits. We'd bring maps and lodging information with us but have no reservations or fixed route. We'd decide where to stay each night, on the fly, and unlike our previous trips, we'd have no firm return date.

Deb and I left home Saturday morning, September 7, 2002. Our goal for the first few days was to put as many miles behind us as possible. Still, a slight detour through Glacier National Park was irresistible. Although we had lived in Montana for six years, we had never visited the park and were beginning to feel like New Yorkers who had never been inside the Statue of Liberty.

We reached Glacier National Park by noon and turned onto the Going to the Sun Road. The scenic fifty-two-mile-long mountain road snaked toward the northeast with numerous steep climbs, sharp turns, and sheer drop-offs. The road has long been famous for the dangerous job snowplow drivers have clearing it before the start of each tourist season. Earlier this year it became even more famous when Montana's Republican senator, Conrad Burns, complained the plowing wasn't proceeding fast enough. The senator, who in the past had called Arabs "ragheads" and told lobbyists—after a vote on civil rights legislation—that he was going to a "slave auction," had stuck his foot in his mouth again. The unofficial local response to the senator's latest gaffe was, "Grab a shovel, Conrad."

One of the reasons we hadn't visited Glacier National Park was because I expected it to be crowded. Passing through on this cold, rainy off-season day confirmed my assumption. Scores of cars packed the Going to the Sun Road, at times slowing traffic to a crawl. While solitude could have been found by hiking into the backcountry, I wondered if the effort would be worth it during the peak season, when throngs of tourists descend upon the park.

On the other hand, I mustn't be too critical of any place where people go to enjoy nature. The crowds show how much we value our wildlands and demonstrate the need to protect additional areas from extractive industries. Sadly, the park's melting glaciers need more than just protection from development to survive. At the time of our visit, U.S. Geological Survey computer models were projecting that all the glaciers within the park could disappear by 2030, unless global warming is stopped.

We traversed Glacier National Park without pausing to explore, and when we popped out on the eastern side, the Canadian border was only twenty-five miles away. Crossing into Alberta was easy. Because the truck's topper-covered rear end was full of food and supplies, I thought for sure customs agents would want to look inside. Instead, they asked a few questions, checked our passports and dog vaccination records, and sent us on our way.

We proceeded north on Highway 2, passing through Calgary and into Edmonton. Fuel for the trip seemed expensive at the time, but considering gas prices have increased steadily since oilman George W. Bush became president, the price we paid will probably seem like a bargain to you now. Computing the cost of a gallon of gas in Canada was tricky, because we had to convert liters to gallons and Canadian dollars to American dollars. When we departed Montana, regular gas was $1.35 per gallon, and when we arrived in Edmonton, it was $1.40 per gallon. The price would continue to rise as we traveled north, ultimately reaching $2.50 per gallon.

Deb and I planned to sleep in our tent for as many nights as possible. We'd limit our hotel stays to times when we needed to dry out gear or absolutely had to take a shower. When we did stay in hotels, having Kate and Annie with us would seldom be a problem. Sometimes we'd have to pay a surcharge and/or stay in a smoking room, but as long as the bad Annie didn't show up thinking the room was an invitation to light a cigarette, we were happy.

For our first night, we checked into a hotel on the western side of Edmonton. Since pounding tent stakes into a Wal-Mart parking lot only works after hot sunny days, camping in the city wasn't practical. We'd wait until the following night before commencing our outdoor sleeping routine.

Miles traveled so far: 673

We began our second day by driving northwest on Highway 43. Although once again our goal was to eat up miles, we occasionally paused to enjoy the wildlife. The surrounding terrain was rolling farmland interspersed with small patches of forest. It was ideal territory for red-tailed hawks and other birds of prey. In fact, during the first two hours of our drive we spotted more than fifty raptors.

"Moose!" yelled Deb. "Watch out!"

I hit the brakes as the bull moose loped across the highway in front of us. His long legs carried him swiftly, and by the time I pulled to the shoulder, he had already slipped through a line of alder trees on the far side of the road. I turned off the engine, grabbed my camera, and jogged across the highway. At first I thought the moose had continued on his way, but when I leaned a little to my left and squinted just right, I could see a swatch of brown fur in a gap between the foliage. He had stopped in a meadow to graze.

To capture a quality image of the moose I'd need to use my film camera with a zoom lens. Of course thinking of such a thing before reaching the trees would have been prudent. Now, carrying my weak-lensed digital camera, I'd have to sneak in close.

Although moose are legendary for their quick tempers and defensive aggression, my personal experience with them has been that they'd rather flee than fight. Back in Montana, moose walk across my property often, and only once have I seen an individual act with hostility. In that instance, Kate got too close to a bull, and he responded by emptying his bladder in my driveway. If you've never seen a moose empty its bladder, you should add it to your list of things to do before dying—I thought my entire gravel driveway was going to wash away. Kate, naturally, had her own interpretation of the moose's actions. She thought he was presenting her with a gift—a prime rolling spot within easy access of our back door.

Despite my previous observations, I'm always keenly aware that underestimating wild animals is a sure way to get hurt. An adult moose is a formidable mammal, capable of killing a wolf with a single kick—and you never know if one is having a bad antler day.

On this day, the bull moose spotted me as soon as I cleared the trees and traversed to the far side of the three-acre meadow in a series of long strides. Now I had to choose between an unexciting long-distance photo and an exposed meadow crossing. I took a deep breath and crept forward.

For a moment, I thought the moose would take off again, but instead he returned to his grazing. He was a beautiful animal. I estimated his shoulder height at five and a half feet and his antler spread at four feet. Though close to full grown, he had the gangly look of adolescence.

Upon reaching the center of the meadow, I switched on my camera and looked at the screen. Ten more steps would get me close enough for a breathtaking portrait. The moose, however, decided three steps was sufficient and raised his head to glare down at me. I pushed the shutter button an instant before he charged away through the trees bordering the meadow.

I didn't want to harass the moose, but the narrow grove of alder would provide good cover; perhaps this time he wouldn't see me. I jogged to the edge of the meadow, slipped through the trees, and peeked out the other side. Before my eyes was a wide expanse of gently rolling grassland, thirty times larger than the meadow behind me.

Where was the moose? No animal so big could have run out of sight that fast. I felt a rock in my stomach. Was he in the grove with me? I looked left and right—nothing. Had he circled around behind me? I held my breath and turned—nothing. I stepped into the large field and scanned the landscape. He had nowhere to hide.

Since I had taken a photo, I hit the review button on my camera to check it out—not bad, considering the situation. Then I realized almost thirty minutes had passed since I started pursuing the moose. Deb, Kate, and Annie were waiting for me back in the truck. Annie? That was it!—the moose had discovered a portal to Idaho.

We continued down the highway until lunchtime. Because Deb is prone to mood swings if she gets too hungry, I'm really married to two wives—and they don't even need a portal to make a switch. The bad wife automatically shows up whenever the good wife's blood sugar drops below a certain level.

For safety's sake, each time Deb announced she was ready to eat, I'd immediately search for a suitable spot to pull over. An ideal location would be off the main road, where the dogs could run and swim. The farther north we'd travel, the easier that objective would become. In the meantime, I did my best to find a place with at least a modicum of ambiance. Being picky was risky, however, as sometimes Deb's head would start to rotate and her voice would deepen. In those instances, the only way to escape the imminent wrath of the bad wife was to keep a supply of chocolate between us and swerve off at the next opportunity.

This time we parked on a gravel road between two tracts of farmland. While Deb and I enjoyed a tailgate picnic, the dogs sniffed their kibble banquet and decided it wasn't nearly as appetizing as what we were eating. Then, moments before we finished, a farmer rumbled by on his tractor and shot us a look of suspicion. I felt embarrassed, but what could I say? "Don't mind us. We're just warding off the bad wife."

An hour or so later we reached the town of Dawson Creek, British Columbia, and the official start of the Alaska Highway. The image that comes to mind when I think of the Alaska Highway is a dirt road littered with broken down automobiles and dotted with potholes that could hide a pumpkin. That image may have been true years ago, but now the road is paved, and stalled vehicles are an anomaly.

Construction on the highway commenced in 1942, after the Japanese bombed Pearl Harbor. Because Alaska was isolated and vulnerable to attack, an overland military supply route and a linkage to airfields were crucial. This led to the building of the 1,422-mile road in an amazing eight and a half months. The United States built and paid for the project, while Canada provided the right-of-way and waived duties and taxes. After the war, each country took responsibility for maintaining the road within its respective boundaries.

While the achievement of building the highway in the extreme conditions of the far north impressed me, the continued improvements disappointed me. Don't get me wrong. I understand the need for a smooth, well-maintained road. I just wish I had had the foresight to drive the Alaska Highway before it lost its ruggedness.

When evening arrived we decided to camp at Charlie Lake Provincial Park, just north of the community of Fort Saint John. Canadian provincial park rules require that dogs be leashed or tied at all times. We don't restrain Kate and Annie at home, because they stay close and don't chase wildlife. Now, tied for the first time, both dogs thought they were being punished and gave us their best "we're really sorry for whatever we did" look. To make amends, we took them for a walk along the Charlie Lake shoreline until we found a secluded spot where they could swim. The lake was big with no memorable features—the dogs loved it.

The weather grew cold and windy after sunset. We dried the dogs the best we could and crawled into our tent for the night. Our three-person backpacking tent was the ideal size for two people and two dogs. Bushmen in Australia use dogs as a measurement for coldness—the chillier the night, the more dogs they need to sleep with to stay warm. In our case, this was definitely a two-dog night. Without the added warmth of Kate and Annie, we would have frozen our buns off.

Miles traveled so far: 1,097

Our journey resumed early Monday morning. Though we still had a long way to go on the Alaska Highway, I was already tired of seeing tourists in their recreational vehicle (RV) campers. Technically, I was also a tourist, but a vast difference exists between someone who is using a vehicle as transportation to reach wild areas and someone whose vehicle *is* the vacation.

Worse than the RVs was that the Alaska Highway was a magnet for traveling slobs. The quickest way to ruin any special place is to make it popular with the masses. While slobs have undoubtedly driven the highway since the day it opened, as word has spread about the ease of crossing to Alaska, the number of people who are destructive or too lazy to clean up after themselves has increased accordingly.

Similarly, while creating this book, I've worried that publicizing the special places Deb and I have visited will contribute to their degradation. After all, many readers will want to personally experience some of the locations I've described. Therefore, let's solve my dilemma right now, before you read another page. Please raise your right hand and repeat after me:

> I, the enlightened reader who had the good taste to buy this book and recommend it to all my friends, hereby promise that I will treat with the utmost respect every place I visit that is described within these pages. I will not harm any of the animals, and I will leave no trace of my presence when I depart.

Good, I feel better. Now, where were we? Oh yes, I was bitching about slob tourists on the Alaska Highway. I don't understand why some tourists insist on turning the very places they came to admire into their personal trash receptacles. Deb and I saw a prime example of this when we stopped at a river for lunch. Previous travelers had spotted the same turnoff and thought it would be a grand place for a bowel movement. Rather than walking thirty feet into the woods and digging a hole, they went right beside their cars—leaving piles of feces and toilet paper scattered about.

Okay, now that I have that out of my system, let's move on to Canada's amusing road signs. Since French and English are both official languages in the country, most of the signs used graphics instead of words. I only mention this because apparently Canada hired its national sign artist directly from a remedial seventh-grade art class. Many of the illustrations were so crudely drawn that they implied an unintended meaning if taken literally. For instance, "Elk Crossing" signs showed the outline of an elk with a big orange reflector for an eye. Were we supposed to be on the lookout for possessed elk? The "Moose Crossing" signs, depicting a grotesquely muscle-bound bull moose, weren't any better. How long had moose on steroids been a problem in Canada?

After Deb and I saw the first few signs, pretending to be literalist travelers became a game. Other signs that almost sent us racing back to America included "Beware of Driverless Cars" (an illustration of a car going straight when the road curved), "Trucks Falling from the Sky" (an illustration of a truck bouncing on pavement), "Stunt Trucks Approaching" (an illustration of a truck with its right wheels on the ground and its left wheels in the air), "No Stop Signs Allowed" (an illustration of a stop sign with a line through it), "Suicidal Truck Drivers Ahead" (an illustration of a truck speeding toward our road at a right angle), and "Acid Showers Next Exit" (an illustration of a man under a showerhead with his arms positioned above his head as if trying to deflect the spray of burning acid).

We were far ahead of schedule and by midday were already halfway to Inuvik. In fairness to the AAA, their travel time estimates would have been accurate had we been driving an RV and limited our travel time to seven hours per day. Instead, we were passing RVs and driving ten hours per day.

Our Monday wildlife sightings included a small black bear and six caribou. We were driving through a provincial park when we saw the caribou. Known as reindeer in Europe and Asia, caribou shared the top of my animal-viewing wish list with wolves. Specifically, I hoped to witness the migration of the great Porcupine caribou herd. If we were lucky, very lucky, we'd catch their migration sometime within next the week.

Before humans decimated them, caribou roamed the northern United States from Washington to Maine. Now all that's left is a herd of fewer than fifty woodland caribou in the Selkirk Mountains of northern Idaho and northeast Washington. What a shame that Deb and I had to travel to another country to see an animal that once grazed in our own backyard.

The caribou in the park didn't excite me, however. They weren't part of the Porcupine herd and were obviously habituated to humans. In fact, they calmly walked within a few feet of my truck and looked right at me. For as long as I can remember, I've maintained strict criteria for counting my wildlife sightings. My main rules are that I must personally see the animal long enough to recognize it, and it must not be caged, tame, or display noticeable effects of human contact. In this instance, some of the caribou even had ear tags. Now that I think about it, just forget I mentioned seeing them—they didn't count. Besides, we had a long way to go, and I was feeling lucky.

Despite occasional parades of RVs, traffic on the Alaska Highway was moderate. If I had to pick one word to describe the difference between the successes and failures on this trip it would be *timing*. Had we traveled during the summer, the weather would have been warm and all the parks, hotels, and gas stations would have been open. On the other hand, we also would have had to endure crowds of people and clouds of insects. Choosing to travel in September, the off-season, meant avoiding most of the people and all of the insects. From here on up, however, life would become unpredictable. Severe weather could strand us at any time, and parks, hotels, and gas stations were closing for the season at a rapid rate. We'd have to be flexible enough to change plans, or even turn back if necessary.

Our first exercise in flexibility occurred when the place where we hoped to camp was closed and we had to stay at Laird River Hot Springs

Provincial Park instead. When camping, we'd stay in either provincial parks or government campgrounds. Literature and maps we picked up along the way helped us determine where to go to avoid crowds. If a park was big or near an attraction, we knew a night of seclusion wouldn't be on the itinerary. Since Laird River had fifty-three campsites *and* a hot springs, I lobbied to keep driving. Deb, however, was tired and insisted on stopping.

We pulled into the soon-to-be-full park an hour before sunset and erected our tent. Because huge RVs with yard lights and satellite dishes occupied the majority of the spots, we were fortunate to find a site on the outer ring where we wouldn't feel quite so overwhelmed.

At Kate and Annie's suggestion, we toured the grounds. Though the dogs were just happy to get some exercise and new sniffs, our stroll along the park's network of gravel driveways was anything but a nature walk. Stereos, televisions, and generators blared simultaneously. I felt as if we were in a giant open-air arcade.

"Do you think anyone would hear if I screamed?" I asked.

"I doubt it," said Deb.

"Okay, here I go. One, two, thr—"

"Don't you dare!"

One thing I noticed while driving the Alaska Highway was that RV parks outnumbered campgrounds. To me, camping, by definition, is electricity free. When I camp, I'd rather gaze at twinkling stars instead of glaring lights, and listen to howling wolves instead of humming generators. With all the RV parks available for people who prefer the conveniences of home, is it too much to ask that campgrounds be left for those who prefer the inconveniences of nature? I'm not saying RVs should be banned from campgrounds, just their sounds and lights.

Miles traveled so far: 1,503

After breaking camp on Tuesday morning, we hiked the half-mile trail to the hot springs. Part of the trail was a wooden walkway crossing a marsh of geothermally heated water. The temperature difference between the air and water produced an eerie fog that weaved through the tall grass and trees. I expected to find the actual tourist soaking area walled off with concrete, but other than a fence and some changing rooms, the springs had been left in their natural condition.

The water looked inviting, and since our last shower had been in Edmonton, we contemplated walking back to the truck to get our swimsuits. We ditched that thought when a large group of people arrived. Instead of swimming with the crowd, we decided to get back on the road. Besides, the dogs were thrilled—we were finally beginning to smell like respectable canines.

A short distance beyond the park, we spotted a herd of twenty-one American bison (buffalo). We stopped to watch them graze along the roadside. Whether I could count these bison as an official animal sighting was debatable. Though they weren't fenced, their lackadaisical demeanor toward our presence gave away the fact they were a managed herd.

In one of the more shameful episodes of American history, white men slaughtered bison to starve the Plains Indians and drive them onto reservations. By the late 1800s, fewer than one thousand bison remained in North America. Conservation efforts ultimately saved the animals, and their numbers have since increased to two hundred thousand. Still, almost all wild bison live within Yellowstone National Park in the United States and Wood Buffalo National Park in Canada. The days of enormous herds roaming free across the Great Plains are over.

That being the case, I decided to count the bison. Although I was bending my rules, I couldn't fault an entire species for what humans had done to them. As I admired the herd, I wondered how anyone could shoot such magnificent animals with anything except a camera. I stood beside the truck and photographed them all, from the adorable little babies to the massive two-thousand-pound bulls. Once I had my shots, we left the herd undisturbed and continued on our journey.

We experienced our first gas scare when we tried to fill our tank in Laird River. Of the two filling stations in the village, one was closed for the season and the other had a broken pump. The next town of any size was Watson Lake, 139 miles down the road. We didn't have enough fuel to drive that far and had to hope one of the tiny communities along the way would have an open station. This time we were lucky. Coal River, thirty-seven miles to the northwest, had one open station, and it too was closing for the season within the next few days.

Having to hunt for gas on the Alaska Highway, the busiest road in the region, was a bit unnerving. Open stations would only become scarcer when we headed north on quieter roads. We vowed never to pass another refueling opportunity, unless our tank was at least three-quarters full.

We crossed into Yukon Territory and stopped in Watson Lake for information and supplies. The town is famous for its Sign Post Forest of nearly fifty thousand pilfered street and city limit signs. Deb and I toured the forest before stepping inside the adjacent Yukon Visitor Reception Centre to find out where we could buy a hammer for pounding in tent stakes (we had been using a rock).

The woman behind the desk assumed I wanted the hammer to put up a sign and said, "Here, use ours. People borrow it all the time."

"Don't government officials from other towns complain about you posting their signs?" I asked.

"Officials from Haines, Alaska, are the only ones who've ever complained. They've sent representatives over to retrieve their sign on several occasions, but last time we didn't have it."

I had to laugh at the prospect of a Yukon Department of Tourism employee being happy to assist me in putting up whatever I had stolen for the forest. Even more amusing was an advertisement the town of Watson Lake had placed in the local tourism guide. "Bring a sign from your hometown," it said.

Since Watson Lake was essentially encouraging me to commit an act of theft, I wondered what would happen in reverse. Would the local police arrest me if I stole a Watson Lake city limit sign in broad daylight? After all, a write-up in the same tourism guide states that the forest is "mimicked around the world." Surely no copycat forest would be complete without a Watson Lake sign, and how could the police justifiably arrest me for doing what their own city was requesting I do elsewhere? Though I didn't act on my curiosity, I now had something new to ponder on the next long stretch of road.

I don't know if it was the pavement or the retirees in their RVs, but something about the Alaska Highway made me feel old for the first time in my life. I needed a change. Our original plan was to stay on the Alaska Highway until the turnoff for Dawson City, 282 miles away. Then Deb discovered we could also get to Dawson City via the Campbell Highway.

From this point on, we need to keep in mind that calling a road a *highway* doesn't necessarily mean it's paved. The Campbell Highway, for instance, was a 362-mile-long, well-maintained gravel road. We planned to follow the Campbell for its entire length. While our original route would have gone west and then north, this new route would arc to the northwest, saving us twenty miles of travel.

The mileage reduction, however, was unimportant. When I realized we'd have the highway virtually to ourselves, and the scenery would be stunning, I immediately felt young again. When we departed Montana, the leaves on the trees were all green; when we reached Dawson Creek, they were beginning to change; and now in the Yukon, they were bursting with color. We had left the pavement and driven into fall.

We wound through a forest-covered valley with rolling hills. Each time we reached a hillcrest we could see for miles. The aspen and alder were bright yellow with a smattering of red, and mixed in were stands of dark green pines. Seemingly around every corner and below every hill was a lake or river, sparkling sky blue in the sunshine. The elevation of the valley floor was about three thousand feet, and surrounding us were partially treed mountains at six thousand feet. A thin line of clouds hugged the mountainsides, halfway up, creating the illusion of a much higher altitude.

The Campbell Highway was worth savoring. We slowed our pace considerably and stopped often to take pictures and watch birds. We also enjoyed a picnic without enduring suspicious glances from farmers or stepping gingerly around piles of—yuck, I don't even want to think about it.

Kate's and my favorite stop was a narrow mountain stream bordered by bright-yellow shrubs. I loved the stream because it was photogenic, and Kate loved it because she could finally change into her alter ego, Fox Dog.

Whenever Kate sees a river, lake, or pond, she sprints into it and lies down. If the body of water happens to have a muddy bottom, her transformation takes place. The mud turns her legs and chest black, while the rest of her coat stays red, making her look like a large red fox (we don't tell her that red foxes have white chests). She loves being Fox Dog and will strut about showing off her accomplishment. If she's found the perfect location, the mud will contain decomposing matter, making her smell as good as she looks. Like all superheroes, Fox Dog has a special power to use against her archenemies—in this case, Mr. Shower and Ms. Bath. Before her nemeses can make a move, she'll sneak up beside them and shake, covering them with doggie slime!

Kate has another alter ego, who only appears when we hike in areas populated with free-range cattle. I'll let you guess her name (hint: it starts with an S).

Despite the many scenic diversions, we reached Lapie River Canyon Campground well before dark. The ride had been so pleasant I was surprised to learn we were already 225 miles beyond Watson Lake. The wooded campground was wilder than the places we had stayed at previously. We shared it with just one other person, and he was on the opposite side of a dense stand of pine trees.

After erecting our tent atop a hill overlooking the Lapie River, we built a campfire and sipped mugs of hot chocolate. Aah, no generators, no stereos, and no televisions. Even the dogs appreciated the difference.

The last time I had seen northern lights (aurora borealis) was fifteen years earlier at our family cabin in northern Minnesota. I hoped to see them again on this trip, but so far every night had been cloudy. I scanned the sky before going to sleep. Though we finally had a cloudless evening, the northern lights weren't out yet. I drank a third cup of hot chocolate to ensure a second chance of seeing them later that night.

I awoke at three-thirty and checked the thermometer on my compass. The temperature inside the tent was twenty-eight degrees; outside would be several degrees colder. I was prepared for the cool weather but still needed motivation to leave my toasty sleeping bag—the extra mug of cocoa did the trick.

I crawled outside and looked up to see bright lights flashing across the sky. My memory of previous northern light sightings included shimmering reds and greens. Tonight's show mimicked colorless horizontal sunbeams. The lights would glow steadily for a moment before widening and narrowing as if multiple suns were shining through giant lenses, which were rapidly changing focus. The sky would suddenly go dark, and then, just when I'd think the show was over, another round would start. I considered waking Deb but knew luring her out of her sleeping bag would have required at least four cups of hot chocolate at bedtime and one color in the sky never before seen in nature. I crawled back into the tent and fell asleep.

Miles traveled so far: 1,905

We began our day at seven o'clock. Clouds had moved in, but they weren't threatening. The only problem with squeezing two dogs and two people into our tent was that condensation would build up overnight, and something always needed to be dried out. On this morning, Deb removed the tent's wet rain fly and hung it on a tree branch.

I was going to pull our gear from inside the tent and pack it in the truck but got distracted when several gray jays began stealing food from the dog bowls. While Kate had no interest in eating her food, she didn't want the birds eating it either. The harmless confrontation between Kate and the jays had potential for some great action photos—if I could push the shutter button at the proper moment.

Once breakfast was ready, Kate focused her attention on what I was eating, and the birds took advantage of the unguarded dog bowls. Midway through our meal, the clouds, which had been too polite to threaten us, opened into a downpour. A degree or two colder and we would have been enjoying a picturesque Yukon snowfall. Instead, we ended up racing to tear down camp and tossing our gear haphazardly into the back of the truck. We finished with our teeth chattering and our clothes soaked to the skin.

The villages of Ross River and Faro were the only places to get fuel along our route, and both were located several miles off the Campbell Highway. We were closer to Ross River, but since going there would require backtracking seven miles, we decided to drive forward forty miles to Faro. We had enough gas to reach our destination, but if our quest was unsuccessful, driving back to Ross River would have us running on empty—or worse.

"How bad could spending the winter camping in the Yukon be anyway?" I said.

Deb just stared at me.

The Campbell Highway was particularly stunning on this morning. The rain had moved on, and where the sun broke through the clouds wet trees glistened in shafts of light. We snaked west through a corridor of yellow, orange, and green until turning north onto the road to Faro.

Soon we reached the Pelly River, where we stopped to enjoy the view. I could see Faro atop the next foothill, tucked among colorful trees, and framed by low clouds and the wide river. The village looked mystical, as if it were hiding from time. I half expected that when we arrived, we'd find the community still living in the eighteenth century.

Instead, Faro was relatively conventional and not nearly as mysterious or out-of-date as it looked from a distance. We promptly found the village's only gas station and pulled up to the pump. The lights inside the station were off, and no one was around.

I turned to Deb and smiled. "Oops!"

She smiled back. "It's still early. I don't see a sign on the door, but they probably open at nine. What do you wanna do?"

"Well, we can hang around here, drive to Ross River and hope we have enough gas—" I started.

"—or we can try to find the Fannin sheep," Deb finished.

"I vote for the sheep. But if we drive out to see them, we blow any chance of reaching Ross River later."

"I vote for the sheep too."

"Annie, Kate, what's your vote?" I glanced at the two eager faces behind me. "Dogs always vote 'yes.'"

Fannin sheep were the other reason we hadn't originally headed for Ross River. Deb and I had read about them in a tourism booklet we picked up in Watson Lake. Only three thousand Fannins exist on Earth, and the best place to view them was supposed to be outside Faro.

We followed a gravel road into the craggy hills behind town, scanning the rocks and cliffs along the way. When we came upon a sign proclaiming "Sheep Viewing Area," we stopped to explore on foot. I'm sure the sheep enjoyed their opportunity to view us, but they weren't in a reciprocal mood.

Based on the tourism booklet, I had assumed Fannins were an endangered animal, but later, when I searched the *IUCN Red List of Threatened Species,* I was surprised to find them missing. The reason is because Fannins aren't recognized as a distinct species. Canada's thinhorn sheep (lightweight relatives of bighorn sheep) are currently divided into two subspecies: Dall and Stone. Dall sheep have all-white coats and live in the far north, and Stone sheep have gray or brown coats and live to the south. Where their territories meet, they are believed to interbreed to form Fannin sheep, which have white coats with a dark saddle. The status of Fannins as "mongrels" isn't without controversy, however, as some people contend that the sheep aren't a product of interbreeding but are actually a separate subspecies.

As for our endangered fuel supply, we had taken the proper gamble. After giving up on finding the sheep, we returned to the gas station, where a man greeted us with a smile and offered to fill our tank.

We continued west and once again had the Campbell Highway to ourselves. I was enjoying the fall colors on a long straightaway when I noticed an animal standing in the middle of the road. "Is that a dog?" I asked.

"How could a dog get out here?" said Deb.

"Maybe someone dumped it."

"No, I think it's a bear."

I slowed the truck as we neared. The animal dashed into the woods!

"It's a wolf!" we yelled in unison.

What threw us off was that this wolf didn't have the familiar salt-and-pepper fur with a hint of brown. Instead, he was black.

Wolves are one of my favorite animals. They're highly intelligent, mysteriously secretive, and greatly misunderstood. When we were leaving Montana, I mentioned to Deb that seeing wolves up close during the day and hearing them howl near our tent at night were among the experiences I most desired on our trip. She felt the same way. She loves wolves as much as I do.

I pulled the truck even with where the wolf had entered the woods, hoping to catch another glimpse—nothing. The forest on both sides of the road was thick. The wolf could have been watching us from ten feet away and we wouldn't have seen him. My heart sank. While I had technically achieved my desired wolf sighting, I had envisioned the experience lasting longer.

Since wolves travel in packs, I eased the truck forward while watching the road in my rearview mirror. "There's another wolf!" I shouted.

"Where?" asked Deb.

"She crossed right behind us—a gray one."

"Ah, I missed her!"

"If there are two, there should be more. I'm gonna drive down the road a bit and park."

I proceeded about a hundred feet and U-turned to face where the wolves had been. "Where's my camera?" I asked.

"Right here," said Deb, handing it to me.

"Damn! Wrong lens." I sifted through my daypack until finding my largest zoom lens. When not in a hurry, I can switch lenses instantly. Now, I fumbled about, nearly breaking my camera in the process.

Finally successful, I turned to my wife. "Are you coming?"

"No, I'll wait for you here."

"Okay, keep the dogs from barking if you can."

I opened the door as quietly as possible—*Ding! Ding! Ding! Ding!*

I snatched the keys from the ignition and stuffed them into my pocket.

Between the ignition alarm and the time lost changing lenses, my klutziness had likely cost me the opportunity to see another wolf. Still, on the slim chance the pack wasn't already halfway to the Arctic Circle, I carefully shut the door and tiptoed down the center of the road.

With each step, I scanned the forest for movement and listened for a crackle or a snap. Stillness and silence prevailed. I knew wolf attacks on people were grossly blown out of proportion, but at 130 feet from the truck I began to wonder, "Should I feel uneasy?"

Ooooooooooooo. A wolf howled! I spun toward the sound but saw only a wall of trees. Wherever the wolf was, it was close, very close.

Ooooooooooooo. The second howl came from the opposite direction. I spun again and gazed into the shadowy forest.

Ooooooooooooo. Ooooooooooooo. Ooooooooooooo. The rest of the pack joined in.

I was surrounded!

When I turned to face Deb, sunlight glared back at me from the windshield. While I couldn't see either my wife or the wolves, I knew they could see me just fine. Whether I should feel uneasy was no longer a question. I felt exhilarated!

Ooooooooooooo. I cupped my hand to my left ear and leaned toward the howl.

Ooooooooooooo. I cupped my hand to my right ear and leaned again.

Suddenly I was the conductor of an all-wolf opera, leaning with each successive howl. Left, right, together! At least six wolves sang solos, and when they sang as a chorus, their howls blended into an eerie song.

Thoughts whisked through my head as I conducted: Right! "This is so cool!" Forward! "I can't believe how loud they are." Left! "Why hasn't Deb come out to join me?" Together!—

The truck door popped open. "Behind you!" yelled Deb.

I pivoted just in time to see the black wolf dart down the road and cut left toward the forest. I lifted my camera to locate him in the viewfinder—nothing.

I lowered my camera and spotted him again. Instead of disappearing into the woods, he had changed his course and was running along the inner edge of the forest—toward me!

I raised my camera. He was at 120 feet and closing fast! Each time I glimpsed him in the viewfinder a tree promptly obstructed my shot. I chanced a look to the side. He was headed toward an opening. I'd have the perfect shot! My finger tensed on the shutter button. . . .

He was gone!

Though I'd lost the photo opportunity to another Idaho portal, it was a minor disappointment compared to the thrill of being so close to the pack. I jogged back to the truck to share the experience with Deb.

"Couldn't you see me?" she asked as I climbed into the cab.

"No, all I could see was sunshine reflecting off the windshield."

"The wolf was standing *directly* behind you! I kept waving to get your attention. I knew if I opened the door I'd frighten the wolf, and I couldn't roll down the [electric] windows because the truck was off and you had the keys."

"How close was he?"

"Oh, he was close—about fifteen feet."

"Wowwww! How long was he there?"

"At least twenty seconds. He stood with his tail held low, staring at you curiously."

Now my feelings were truly mixed. Although I had just enjoyed a once in a lifetime experience, I had not only failed to get a wolf on film, but I had also missed out on a possible extended close-range encounter. What would the wolf have done if I had slowly turned around before Deb's shout frightened him? He wasn't being aggressive.

In less than fifteen minutes I had seen either two or three wolves, depending on if I had seen two individual black wolves or the same one twice. Though the howling had ceased, and the chances of seeing another wolf were slim, I felt like an addict. Just one more hit of *Canis lupus* and I'd have my fix.

Since the last howl came from behind the truck, I walked in that direction. Fifty feet later, I stopped and waited. The forest was silent. Eventually I gave up and turned to walk back toward—another wolf! The gray and white beauty was crossing the road near where I had been conducting the opera of howls. I snapped a quick photo before she vanished. Because of distance and camera shake, I knew my shot would be blurry, but at least I had something.

Now, if I could just get a *close up* wolf photo, I'd have my fix. . . .

Before we move on, I'd like to step away from our story to address wolves' undeserved bad reputation. Throughout history, wolves have been victimized by both inaccurate human interpretations of their behavior and outright lies.

Few things upset me more than when anti-wolf groups use the media to stir up fear with comments such as, "Our children won't be safe as long as wolves are in the area." What they're doing is resurrecting the big bad wolf from the bedtime stories most of us grew up with. Unfortunately, when these groups spew forth their disinformation, a large unquestioning segment of the populace is all too willing to believe.

In truth, research has shown that wolf attacks on humans are extremely rare. To find a documented fatal attack in North America you'd have to go back more than one hundred years. Even those who dispute that claim must admit that the chances of being killed by a wolf are substantially less than being killed by lightning, horses, hunters, or bees.

One of the reasons I felt exhilarated standing in the midst of the pack was because I was personally demonstrating that healthy wild wolves are not a threat to humans. I wasn't carrying a weapon or pepper spray (I also wasn't stupidly waving a slab of bloody meat). If they had wanted to kill me, they could have done so easily.

What people need to recognize is that individuals and groups who demonize wolves usually have an ulterior motive. They may say they're concerned about wolf attacks on humans, but what really concerns them is that wolves might make them work a little harder. For instance, some ranchers want to run their cattle on public lands—our lands—without having to watch over their herds, and some hunters don't want anything competing with their chance for an easy kill during deer- or elk-hunting season. Regarding the ranchers, the thought that a domestic cow grazing on public wildlands should take precedence over a wolf is preposterous. As for the hunters, they needn't worry about wolves. While most hunters prefer killing the big and healthy animals, wolves prefer to subsist on the weak.

Wolves, sadly, won't overcome their long history of human prejudice until more people remove their emotional blinders and look at the facts. What does it say about us as a society when George W. Bush can run an atrocious television commercial using wolves as symbols for terrorists and have it turn out to be one of the most effective ads of his reelection campaign?

Our Campbell Highway drive concluded at the Klondike Highway, near the village of Carmacks. Since ample daylight remained, we decided to head for Dawson City, 220 miles to the northwest. Now back on pavement, we proceeded uneventfully until thirty miles before our destination. "What was that!" I shouted.

"I didn't see anything," said Deb.

"By the side of the road. I think it was either a wolverine or a porcupine. I'm going back to investigate."

I U-turned twice and stopped the truck where the animal had ambled into the forest. Kate, who saw what I saw, wagged her tail and shuffled her feet with more enthusiasm than usual. I had hoped to see a wolverine, but based on Kate's reaction, I guessed it was a porcupine—*her* favorite animal.

Although Kate is a smart dog, her goal in life is to make friends with a porcupine. If one is nearby, she'll find it—the hard way. In fact, she was currently on a four-year streak of annual finds.

Once, on a backpacking trip, she got porcupine quills embedded so deeply into her front legs that I had to carry her—ninety pounds of wet dog—on my shoulders until she recovered enough to walk on her own. Deb and I always extract the quills on-site to minimize tissue damage. We usually carry tools to assist us, but Kate has a knack for getting into trouble when we've forgotten them. The short and deep quills are particularly difficult to grip by hand, and for the sake of the dog, each pull must be successful. By Kate's third porcupine encounter, I discovered I could use my teeth to efficiently jerk out the quills. The process feels primeval and can be a little gross, but nothing works better.

Today, Kate wouldn't have an opportunity for encounter number five. As I trotted into the woods, I could hear her behind me, barking her displeasure about being left in the truck with Deb and Annie: "Come on, Dad, let me go with you. Five times is a charm! I just wanna smell its butt! We'll be good friends, I promise. Come back! Daaaaaaaaaaaad!"

Ahead of me, I spotted something waddling through the undergrowth. Yes, it was a porcupine. I followed the rodent until she stopped with her nose near the trunk of a large pine tree and fanned her quills. Since porcupines can't throw their quills, I was okay, as long as I didn't touch her. I snapped some photos from Kate's customary rear end view, then ducked under some tree branches and came around to the far side.

The porcupine shifted, so she could see me, and when I dropped to my hands and knees we looked into each other's eyes. She had the cutest face I'd ever seen—and I thought nothing could beat the face of a Labrador retriever puppy.

I contemplated reaching out to pet her furry brown head—the part without the quills. I hadn't heard of anyone petting a porcupine before and wondered if she'd try to bite me or swing her tail around to nail me.

Wait a minute! Wasn't trying to make friends how Kate got into trouble? I decided to keep my hands to myself.

Porcupines are vocal animals capable of a variety of sounds, including grunts, snorts, and squeaks. In this instance, when Deb walked over to join me, the porcupine whined like a lonely puppy in response to the stress of being admired by two people.

I wanted to take her into my arms, hug her, and tell her everything would be okay. In lieu of an embrace, Deb and I backed off and let the prickly beauty continue on her way.

We pulled into Dawson City, population 1,818, thirty minutes later. The tourist town had been restored to resemble its appearance during the gold rush of the late 1800s, and as a nice touch, several buildings had been left unrestored for comparison.

Finding a place to spend the night wasn't easy. We had hoped to rent a cabin at Klondike Kate's, but they didn't have a vacancy. Other places we checked were either closed for the season or reeked of stale beer. We finally ended up just outside of town at the Bonanza Gold Motel. Our room was pricey for being so basic, but since it didn't smell like a tavern and dogs were welcome, we were pleased with the accommodations.

I backed the truck to the door and transferred our wet gear to the room. We hung our tent over the shower curtain rod, draped our sleeping bags over the doors, and laid our clothes wherever we could find a suitable spot. By the time we finished, our room looked like a tornado had passed through it. As Deb and I admired our handiwork, we couldn't help flashing back to our respective college living quarters and laughing—we still had the touch.

Neither of us had showered since Edmonton. I didn't think we smelled, but when I lay on the floor next to Kate she tried to roll on me. Perhaps my wife and I had become accustomed to each other's odor. As for my appearance, when I looked in the mirror I hardly recognized myself. My beard was so scruffy I would have fit right in with the gold rush miners. My hair, on the other hand, was awesome. I could put it in any position I wanted, and it wouldn't move. I spiked it in honor of my new porcupine friend.

I yearned for a shower, but dinnertime had arrived, and the bad wife was threatening to make a visit. One of the joys of foreign travel is being anonymous. No matter how dreadful we appeared, our names would be unattached to any subsequent local gossip. We headed out in search of Dawson City's best restaurant.

Miles traveled so far: 2,285

On the morning of September 12, we decided to brave the C$2.99 ($1.88 U.S.) breakfast special at the Triple J Hotel. The food—eggs, toast, hash browns, and coffee—turned out to be a pleasant surprise and would have been a bargain at thrice the price.

Our waitress was a sturdy dark-haired woman whose hardened facial features bore witness to the difficulty of life in a far-flung Yukon town. Since Deb and I were the only customers in the café, I took the opportunity to chat with the woman.

"We were glad to find you open this morning," I said.

"You're just in time," she replied. "We close for the season tomorrow."

"Does anyone in town stay open all year?"

"There're a few places that cater to locals, but everyone else closes."

"What do the locals do for work in the winter?"

"Most of the men head north to the oil fields."

"What about the women?"

"Many are unemployed. As for me, I work three part-time jobs and barely scrape by."

"We're driving up the Dempster Highway today. Does it take one or two days to reach Inuvik?"

"Some people do it in a day, but you really have to rush. You're better off taking your time and allowing for two days."

"Good, we planned correctly then. Has the Porcupine caribou migration started yet?"

"No, it's at least a week away, but you might see a few stragglers that have wandered off from the herd."

"That's too bad. The migration is something I've wanted to see for years. We've been traveling a lot lately and have had great luck with our timing. I guess we were due to hit something wrong."

"Now you'll have an excuse to visit us again."
"There you go. I like that idea."

An hour after breakfast we turned onto the 456-mile-long gravel road known as the Dempster Highway. A sign posted at the entrance proclaimed the Dempster to be the only public highway in North America crossing the Arctic Circle. Though the sign looked new, it was dispensing old information. The Dalton Highway in Alaska has been public since 1994, and it too crosses the Arctic Circle. The discrepancy was confusing until I remembered we were in the same country that erected signs warning us of possessed elk and moose on steroids. But, hey, if road signs are the only things I can find to pick on Canada about, then the country must have a lot going for itself.

The Dempster Highway was fun to drive. It felt primitive because of its gravel surface, yet it was in such good shape that some sections were pavement smooth. The scenic road would lead us first through the Ogilvie Mountains and then the Richardson Mountains. Knowing this, I expected lots of climbs, narrow passes, and sharp turns. Instead, I was surprised to encounter rolling hills, wide-open spaces, and gentle curves.

The flora was never boring, often alternating from pine forests to waves of bright-yellow shrubs to fields of tiny multicolored plants. The tree line in Canada (where trees can no longer grow) isn't determined solely by distance to the north. Instead, it starts at the mouth of the Mackenzie River (near Inuvik) and heads in a southeasterly direction toward Hudson Bay, just north of Manitoba. The tree line often seemed farther south than it actually was. As we traveled along the Dempster, we'd cross miles of treeless landscape. Then, just when we'd think all the trees were behind us, we'd pass through a stunted forest.

I was eager to get out and hike the tundra. When we came upon a shallow valley pointing to the west, I stopped the truck, and we all piled out. The dogs thought this was the best idea I'd had in days. With Annie in the lead, we crossed the highway, followed an old animal trail through a line of shrubs, and proceeded down the valley.

We hadn't walked far when the trail petered out and we found ourselves crossing a blanket of plant life. The tundra floor was covered with "cushion plants," so-called because they feel like pillows underfoot.

The flora around us included lichens, mosses, grasses, and sedges—collectively very cool stuff. To survive the extreme weather and absorb heat, most were dark in color and low to the ground.

I spent a lot of time on my hands and knees photographing the tiny plants. My favorites were alpine bearberries, which had berries almost as big as their deep-red leaves, and mountain cranberries, which had berries almost as big as their rubbery green leaves. Though tundra in general doesn't support a wide variety of plants, when I took photos of four-inch-square patches of the cushiony ground, I was able to count up to five separate species—all arranged in a dazzling natural bouquet.

The four of us returned to the truck and continued north. We had traveled 175 miles since breakfast and were thoroughly enjoying the scenery. Yes, even the dogs appreciated the view. Since they each had a side window in the back compartment of the extended cab, they'd stare outside—making mental notes of the prime rolling and swimming locations—until growing tired. Usually they'd fall asleep while sitting, melt to the floor for a short nap, then pop up and repeat the process.

So far, we hadn't seen any wildlife along the Dempster other than birds. In fact, Deb and I were discussing just that, seconds before I spotted something up ahead.

"Look! There! On the mountainside," I said, pointing.

"You mean those white rocks?" said Deb.

"No, those are sheep."

"Or rocks."

"No, really, they're sheep." I slowed the truck, as we approached the—

"Dall sheep! You're right!"

Like most husbands, I would have loved to have had a tape recorder running at that moment: "You're right!" Rewind. "You're right!" Rewind. "You're right!" Rewind. . . .

Dwelling on such juvenile thoughts, however, would have to wait. I pulled the truck to the shoulder and stepped outside.

"Whoa! What an awful smell. Deb, come out here."

"What? *Ewwww,* sulfur!"

Between us and the sheep flowed Engineer Creek, a forty-foot-wide river, fed in part by a sulfur spring. The pungent smell was overpowering at first, but I soon got used to it—or at least became too distracted to notice anymore.

The Dall sheep, of course, were the distraction. The herd of five females and their young had white coats with just a hint of gold (an exact color match for Annie), and the adults had seven- to nine-inch-long horns that extended just past the point where they started to curl. They were all partway up the steep mountainside, in the midst of a descent to the river.

Once they reached the water, I slid down the high riverbank opposite them and balanced on a partially submerged rock. As I observed the herd, the two largest members crossed to a long sandbar island to nibble on some plants. Though less than twenty feet separated us, they seemed unconcerned by my presence.

I immersed myself in *sheepscape* photography until Deb informed me that Kate and Annie were complaining in the truck. The dogs, which had been fine until I slid out of sight, wanted to get out to make sure I was okay. If Deb released them, they wouldn't chase the sheep, but they'd probably bark at them. For the benefit of all, I returned to the truck so we could continue on our way.

As the day grew late, we had to decide where to spend the night. Our options were the hotel in Eagle Plain or our tent at the Rock River Campground. Eagle Plain, population seven, marked the Dempster's approximate halfway point, and the campground was another fifty miles north. Since traveling the extra distance would also mean crossing the Arctic Circle, the choice was easy for me—I wanted to camp above the parallel of latitude at 66°33' north. Deb, on the other hand, wasn't enthusiastic about the idea. The temperature was already chilly, and it would only get colder after sunset.

Since we planned to fill the gas tank in Eagle Plain anyway, we agreed to hold off on deciding where to stay until finding out what to expect for nighttime temperatures.

Eagle Plain existed solely because of its location. At 231 miles from the beginning of the highway, it was the first place to get gas. If we didn't stop there, the next fueling possibility was in the village of Fort McPherson, 110 miles to the north. While we could have made it that far, we would have been driving on fumes. And as we'd already learned, gas stations in northern Canada do not come with an open for business guarantee.

We pulled up to the pump expecting to get gouged. When Deb calculated the price at $2.50 (U.S.) per gallon, I wasn't sure how to feel. I'd never spent that much on gas before but was surprised the price wasn't higher. If a more important gas station exists in North America, I'm unaware of it. During the tourist season, countless people would be stranded if the Eagle Plain station closed unexpectedly or suffered a fuel pump malfunction.

Once our tank was filled, I stepped into the station to pay the bill. When the attendant handed me my receipt, I asked him, "How cold has it been getting here at night?"

"Very cold," he said scrunching up his weathered face. "About zero to seven below."

"Brrrrrrrr. My wife and I are sleeping in a tent tonight."

"Ha-ha! Have fun." He pointed across the parking lot to a building that reminded me of a boarding school dormitory. "If you change your mind, the hotel is right there."

"Thank you. But that won't be necessary."

When Deb and I have disagreements, she gets her way nine out of ten times. This was my one time. I don't know why I even bothered to ask the attendant. I didn't care how low the temperature was going to drop or that our sleeping bags were only rated for twenty degrees minimum. Our travels were all about taking chances and doing things for the first time—and I had definitely never camped north of the Arctic Circle before.

I returned to the truck and cranked the ignition. As we veered onto the Dempster, Deb asked, "Well, did you find out how cold it's supposed to get tonight?"

"We'll be just fine."

"Marty, how cold did he say it would get?"

"Um . . . zhrm ts sbbhnnn bnow," I mumbled.

"Zero to seven below!"

"But there's no humidity. It'll be a *waaaarm* zero to seven below."

"That's too cold. We'll freeze our asses off!"

I drove in silence for a moment—partly to think, and partly to get us farther away from the hotel. "Wait a minute . . . we're in Canada. How stupid! He was talking *Celsius* not Fahrenheit! Let's see, zero Celsius equals thirty-two Fahrenheit. What's minus seven?"

Deb checked a conversion table before answering, "Nineteen degrees."

"Perfect! It'll be downright balmy."

"Okay. You win this one."

A long straightaway allowed me to turn my head to the back. "Guess what, girls. We're camping north of the Arctic Circle tonight!" The dogs wagged their tails in approval. "See, Deb, you would have been outvoted three to one anyway."

A half hour later, we spotted the sign marking the Arctic Circle. I turned into the pullout and stopped several truck lengths short of the invisible line. Our timing was ideal. The few vehicles we saw earlier in the day were long gone, and now we could hike to the Arctic Circle in solitude.

Our trek was exhausting. Complete with stops to rest and reorient ourselves with readings from my GPS receiver, it took eight—maybe ten—seconds to reach our goal. Each of us crossed the line in our own way: Deb walked over it, Kate and Annie wrestled over it, and I jumped over it.

The snowless ground was deceiving: the temperature was a hair above freezing and wind was whipping across the mountains. This was no time for maturity! I mounted my camera on a tripod, set the timer, pulled off my shirt, and posed with Deb and the dogs in front of the Arctic Circle sign. I tried, of course, to talk Deb into posing topless with me, but she declined. We had been married almost eighteen years, and I still didn't understand her. Who wouldn't want to pose topless when the windchill factor was plunging the temperature into the single digits? I guess it's just a guy thing. I will admit, however, that after resetting my camera for the fourth photo, I was eager to slip back into my shirt.

Why is the Arctic Circle significant? It marks the southernmost line where the sun does not set on the first day of summer or rise on the first day of winter. Coinciding with this phenomenon was that the days grew noticeably longer the farther north we traveled. Had we attempted this trip between the first day of fall and the last day of winter, we would have experienced the opposite effect.

We returned to the truck and continued on our way. A few miles past the Arctic Circle, my eyes locked onto the surprise sight of the day. "Carabiners!" I shouted.

No, I wasn't announcing the discovery of mountain climbing equipment on the road. Carabiners was my pet name for caribou.

The Porcupine caribou herd consists of 123,000 barren ground caribou, named for the Porcupine River they cross during their migration. The journey between their summer and winter range is the longest of any terrestrial animal on earth. Herd members typically travel eight hundred straight-line miles per year, but since they don't follow a direct route, their actual mileage can more than triple.

The herd's winter range is large—stretching from the Arctic Ocean to Dawson City and from eastern Alaska to western Northwest Territories. In the spring, they migrate to the Arctic coastal plain to give birth. Calving takes place along a two-hundred-mile stretch of land, with seventy-five of those miles being in Canada's Ivvavik National Park and the remainder in Alaska's Arctic National Wildlife Refuge (ANWR).

The caribou do fine in Canada. It's when they move into Alaska—their preferred calving area—that concerns arise. Of Alaska's Arctic coastal plain, 95 percent is already open to oil exploration. That, of course, isn't enough for George W. Bush and the oil companies. They want the "1002 Area," a one-hundred-mile stretch of ANWR coast. Oil companies claim they have the technology to drill in ANWR without disturbing the caribou, but their technology obviously doesn't work in nearby Prudhoe Bay, where they emit more air pollutants than Washington, D.C.

Also, based on recent history, oil spills in ANWR would be inevitable. According to the Alaska Department of Environmental Conservation, regulated facilities within the state had 413 reportable oil/chemical spills during the year of our trip and from 280 to 487 spills annually during the five years preceding it. If the president and Congress open up the 1002 Area for the oil companies, all parties involved must be held accountable for the environmental damage that follows.

George Bush and his oil buddies were the last thing on my mind as I gazed upon my first three countable Porcupine caribou. As the waitress at the Triple J Hotel had speculated, a few stragglers had wandered off from the main herd.

"There's more ahead! On the left," said Deb. "One, two, three . . . about ten of them."

"Look at that beautiful bull! His antlers must be three feet tall."

The caribou were walking parallel to the road, eighty feet out on the tundra. We slowed to watch them until spotting another group in the distance. Comprising the second herd were a dozen young bulls and cows. We slowed for them as well and would have stopped, but we needed to keep moving if we were going set up camp before dark. Besides, we were both confident more caribou would be in our future.

When we came upon a third herd—a group of eight, to our right, grazing beside a rocky butte—my resistance was futile. I pulled to the shoulder, cut the engine, and said in a deep monotone voice, "I'll be back."

Deb smiled. "Okay, but don't take too long."

I walked out on the tundra. Since the caribou were between the butte and me, I gave them space so they wouldn't feel trapped or become spooked. I took a few photographs and spent a moment admiring my subjects. They were handsome animals, mostly brown, except for white fur around their necks, under their tails, and on their bellies. Caribou are members of the deer family, but something in their big brown eyes made them seem more intelligent than other species in their family. Perhaps it was because as a child I associated them with Rudolph the Red-Nosed Reindeer. Whatever the reason, observing them in the wild was a special experience and a great way to end an outstanding day.

I returned to the truck and was just about to veer back onto the road when I noticed a sport utility vehicle speeding toward us from the north. I expected the vehicle to pass us by, but instead it swerved to the opposite shoulder and stopped.

"That's strange," I said. "I wonder what they want?"

"They probably wanna watch the caribou, just like us," said Deb.

Three burly men stepped out of the vehicle—each carrying a high-powered rifle.

"Oh, my god!" I screamed. "They're going to kill the caribou!"

"Damn!" shouted Deb.

"They have nowhere to run! They're dead ducks!"

My first instinct was to lay on the horn to alert the caribou. Then it occurred to me that Canada might have a hunter harassment law. Also, enraging armed men on the only road in the region was asking for trouble—we'd have nowhere to run.

I'm sympathetic to native people who hunt caribou for subsistence, but I've never understood hunting any species for trophy or sport. Since successfully shooting an animal with a camera often takes more skill than successfully shooting an animal with a gun, I don't need to kill for a thrill. I also don't need to mount a head on my wall to commemorate the event.

The other problem with trophy and sport hunting is that it works against natural selection. Since the biggest and healthiest animals are usually the targets, over time the affected species become genetically inferior to their forebears. This was confirmed when a recent study, led by Dr. David Coltman of the University of Sheffield, concluded that trophy hunting had significantly reduced both the horn size and body weight of bighorn sheep in Alberta. Similarly, trophy/sport hunting has been tied to smaller antlers in moose, and poaching has dramatically increased the number of elephants born without tusks.

My friends who hunt often speak of a "fair chase." Though we seldom agree on the definition of *fair*, in this case I think they'd agree with me that the Dempster Highway hunters had an unfair advantage over the caribou pinned against the rock face. What the three men were about to do was unethical but most likely legal. I shot them a look of disapproval and accelerated down the road before the carnage began.

One of the idiosyncrasies of my personality is that I often internally rehash upsetting situations for days. As Deb and I stared ahead in silence, questions rumbled through my brain: "Should I have said something to the men? Were they subsistence or trophy hunters?—what they were doing *certainly* wasn't sporting. Should I have honked the horn? What if I'd stepped out of the truck for more pictures and stood in their line of fire? Since I was there first, would my photography rights have superseded their shooting rights? Did the men kill one, several, or all of the caribou? Could any have? . . ."

Fortunately, I dwelt on the situation only until we reached the Rock River Campground. From then on, all I could think about was how much I looked forward to my first night north of the Arctic Circle.

The campground sat at the edge of Rock River in a forest of normal-sized pine trees. We shared the place with a courteous couple who, despite their RV, didn't disturb us with electronic devices or generator noise. Since the couple already had the riverside site, Deb and I erected our tent away from both the water and the RV. On a cold night, keeping the river out of Kate's sight was just as important as the solitude. Though we had let her swim earlier, we wanted her at least semidry before she joined us in the tent. If she could see the river, she'd lobby for a bedtime dip.

Deb had packed a bottle of wine in the back of the truck before leaving Montana. We had been waiting, patiently, for it to reach the perfect temperature, and now it was finally ready to drink. We toasted to the Arctic Circle and roasted marshmallows over a fire for s'mores.

The cool air eventually coaxed us into our tent and the relative warmth of our sleeping bags. While the temperature plummeted to eighteen degrees, we made it through the night without freezing off anything vital.

Miles traveled so far: 2,570

We crossed into the Northwest Territories on Friday morning and spent much of the day driving northeast through a forest of stunted evergreen trees. When I spotted a small sign listing the frequency for the Fort McPherson radio station, I tuned in. The announcer on the community station was in the midst of a long list of personal messages: "Hope you have a good day, Jake, from Donna. Bill, please call Mary at the office. Students in Mrs. Johansson's class need to bring their indoor shoes and dental forms tomorrow. Wanda, please meet Belva in the library at noon. . . ."

Eventually the announcer delivered a message for me: "The Porcupine caribou migration has started. Beginning tomorrow there will be a one-week hunting ban to protect the leaders of the herd. The ban applies to all hunting within five kilometers of the Dempster Highway."

"Yesssssss!" I gleefully pumped my fist. Now, not only could the caribou cross the road without becoming targets, but also Deb and I would have a chance to witness the migration.

The final leg of the Dempster Highway required two ferry crossings. Though the ferries were free, they would have been frustrating to use had we been in a hurry. The first ferry was a direct crossing of the Peel River that took fifteen minutes. The second ferry crossed just north of where the Tsiigehtchic River flowed into the Mackenzie River, and it took an hour. The reason for the extra time was that the ferry ran a triangle-shaped route, stopping on the east and west banks of the Mackenzie River and at the village of Tsiigehtchic, a short distance to the south. We had arrived seconds after the ferry departed the east bank and had to wait for it to make its complete cycle.

In terms of isolation, Inuvik is similar to Iquitos, Peru. Since each ferry has a capacity of about eight vehicles, only a small percentage of the town's 3,451 residents can leave at once. Complicating the situation is that the ferries can't run when the rivers are frozen, and vehicles can't drive over the ice during periods of freeze or thaw. As a result, automobile travel between Inuvik and the rest of the world is impossible from the approximate dates of October 15 to December 14 and May 1 to June 9. Inuvik does have an airport for those who wish to fly.

After crossing the Mackenzie River, we drove straight north for seventy-eight miles. We would have gone farther, but we had reached Inuvik.

Our satisfaction with successfully driving to the top of Canada was short-lived. When we stopped at the visitors' center to inquire about a dog-friendly place to stay, we were directed to the Eskimo Inn. Although the hotel's rates seemed high, we didn't fret over the price at check-in, because the lobby and exterior were in good shape. Stepping into our room, however, was like entering a different hotel. The carpet was dirty, the bathroom smelled of urine, the tile had cigarette burns, and a section of paneling was falling down. We considered asking for a refund but decided finding another place wouldn't be worth the hassle.

Inuvik was established in 1958 as a planned community to replace the flood-prone hamlet of Aklavik. It became an official town in 1970. Despite being young, the town was rundown and depressing, and though not literally colorless, it felt that way. Life north of the Arctic Circle can be hard—I'm sure the thirty days in the winter without sunlight were draining. Still, only so much can be blamed on location. Trash and broken glass littered the streets, and the local people were standoffish.

When Deb and I strolled through downtown, I tried to make eye contact with the locals, and say "hello." Except for a few children, everyone looked down and walked by as if we were invisible. Even Annie's "Hi, I'm the cutest, friendliest dog in the world. Let's be friends" routine fell flat.

Deb surmised the cold behavior was due to cultural differences, and she would have been right had we encountered only the Inuit (a people whose tradition of quietness can be easily misconstrued). Inuvik's population, however, was comprised of 60 percent nonnative people, 25 percent Inuit, and 15 percent Dene/Métis. No single group had a monopoly on unfriendliness, and we didn't find similar frostiness in other Canadian towns.

Inuvik's visible alcoholism problem also added to the unattractiveness of the town. I've never seen so many fall-down-drunk people in my life. In this case, culture most likely was involved. In the 1950s, the Canadian government pressured the Inuit to give up their nomadic lifestyle and relocate to permanent settlements. The loss of their traditional ways has led to increased alcoholism and suicides. In 1999, the Canadian government attempted to rectify the situation by dividing the Northwest Territories to establish the new Inuit territory of Nunavut. The creation of a new homeland, bigger than any other Canadian province or territory, won't help the Inuit of Inuvik, but at least now native people have a place to call their own and an opportunity to reclaim their traditions.

Even though Inuvik was now the leading candidate to hold the title of "least favorite town visited" during our travels, Deb and I still wanted to support the local artisans by buying something handmade. This was a difficult task because most of the crafts contained fur, bones, or teeth, and I refuse to decorate my house with dead-animal parts. We eventually found a shop that served as a direct outlet for the artists and bought an Inuit soapstone carving of a bear.

The first half of our trip was complete.

Miles traveled so far: 2,741

With no reason to linger, we departed Inuvik Saturday morning and began the southbound portion of our journey. If we had known what was in store for us, we would have been giggly with excitement. We were making good time, hit both ferries without waiting, and had already traveled nearly two hundred miles. The Dempster was heading in a southwesterly direction through a series of treeless, rolling hills. When the road curved south, the hills to our right gave way to a wide, deep valley lined with miles of golden tundra. The view was stunning, and far out on the valley floor I could see hundreds of rocks—they were moving.

I swerved to the shoulder, shouting, "Carabiners! It's the great herd!"

"Really! Are you sure?"

"Grab the binoculars. See for yourself."

Deb fumbled through the pile of maps, brochures, and snacks at her feet, found the binoculars, hopped out her door, and peered over the valley. "Wowww! There are *hundreds* of them."

I grabbed my camera and zoom lens before joining my wife. When I squinted through the viewfinder, I could just make them out. "Wowww! They're bigger than the caribou from two days ago."

"You should see them through my binoculars. Some of the bulls have *huge* racks."

"Let's hike out to them."

"They're much farther away than they appear. It would take us at least an hour to reach them, and we'd have to leave the dogs in the truck."

"The dogs will be fine. They'll protest, but the weather is cool, and there's enough cloud cover that we won't have to worry about them overheating in the sun. Come on. This will be a once-in-a-lifetime experience."

Deb tilted her head skeptically. "Just so you know, we're coming up on a long section of road without campgrounds. If we stay here all day, we'll be setting up the tent in the dark."

The valley paralleled the Dempster for a quarter mile, before cutting west around a hill and heading off in a south-southwesterly direction. Since we were on a high spot, I could see a faint gravel clearing to the right of where the road crossed the eastern edge of the hill. I pointed to the clearing and said, "If we park down there, the dogs will be off the road, and we'll cut a few minutes off our hike."

"Okay, let's go for it."

I drove to the clearing, which turned out to be a makeshift campsite, and found a spot where a rise in the terrain shielded the truck from the road.

Kate and Annie looked out their windows, couldn't believe their good fortune, and began their adventure dance. "Oh boy! Oh boy! Oh boy! We're gonna run with the caribou, just like our ancestors! New sniffs! And we're gonna pee there and there and there and there!"

"Sorry girls," I said. "You two have to stay here and guard the truck."

"Noooooooo! You can't leave without us, Dad. We've been good dogs."

"Sorry, girls," said Deb.

We locked the doors and walked away.

"Wait! Mom! Dad! You forgot the dogs! Hey! This isn't fair. Wait! The Golden Retriever Union is gonna be very upset about this. Come back! Daaaaaaaaaaad!"

Deb and I decided our best strategy was to hike west along the hill's northern slope. If you put your right hand palm side down on a flat surface, bring your fingers in tight, and slide your thumb under your forefinger, you'll have the general shape of the mile-long hill. We left the dogs on top of your wrist and proceeded along your pinkie.

Walking was challenging because the landscape was uneven, and we had to scramble over boulders and rock formations. The obstructions, however, scarcely slowed us down, as the excitement of catching the herd kept us moving. Twice we surprised stray caribou grazing in low spots. In both instances, we reached the top of a rise and looked down into startled eyes.

Deb and I communicated with gestures to stay as quiet as possible. When we reached the nail on your pinkie, I pointed to the tip of your middle finger. Once that far, we could drop down alongside the herd. Now hold your fingers together; we're coming across.

Upon reaching the nail of your middle finger, we paused to watch the migration and burst into wide grins, mouthing, "Wowwwwwwwwwwwwww!"

We descended to the valley floor. Since the caribou were walking down the center of the three-quarter-mile-wide valley, we still had a ways to go. Our goal was to get as close as possible without spooking them. We'd slink forward a bit, stop, take some photos, sneak forward some more, stop, and so on.

We weren't watching all 123,000 herd members at once. The pace and concentration of the fall migration is influenced by weather conditions. Caribou could continue passing by where Deb and I were standing for days or weeks. In fact, if the weather warmed up, the migration might even temporarily reverse. The number of animals within our field of vision changed continually but averaged several hundred. You might expect so many caribou to be noisy, yet they flowed past us in a silent parade.

Calves and cows comprised more than half of the herd, and while they were fun to watch, the bulls were by far the most unforgettable sights. The antlers on some were so tall they appeared out of proportion to their bodies. According to various reference sources, a full-grown bull can weigh 660 pounds, stand 4'7" at the shoulder, grow antlers 5'2" tall, and run fifty miles per hour. Although I couldn't confidently judge their weight, and I didn't see them run faster than a trot, from my vantage point several bulls exceeded the stated maximum shoulder and antler height specifications.

Because the caribou in this leading group were so large, I presumed the reason for the one-week hunting ban was to protect the genetic lines of the biggest and strongest members. While my presumption was logical, the actual reason for the ban was to avoid scattering the herd and to preserve traditional migration routes. Migration leadership changes from season to season and isn't dependent on size. This time, however, it was the big boys' turn to lead.

Jutting out from the opposite side of the valley, three hundred feet north of us, was another long hill. A trio of huge bulls, whom I dubbed the Three Kings, stood atop the hill keeping a close eye on their subjects and Deb and me as well. Though I'm speculating, the Three Kings appeared to be taking responsibility for the security of the current migration wave. Once their subjects were safely beyond us, they descended to the valley floor and trotted on by.

Excuse me while I catch my breath. . . .

During my travels for this book, I enjoyed several experiences that felt spiritual: my first moments on the Amazon River, the wolves howling around me, and a few surprises yet to come. Watching the procession of the great herd, while three majestic bulls watched me, was another such experience. Thirty years from now thoughts of the moment will still send tingles up my spine.

The departure of the Three Kings wasn't the end of our migration adventure. We were still working our way toward the center of the valley when a scene from *Never Cry Wolf* flashed through my brain. I whispered to Deb, "Did you ever see the movie where the guy ran naked with the caribou?"

"No."

"If we can get close enough, I'm going to reenact the scene."

"Okay, I'll be ready with my camera."

Tyler, the main character in the movie, wore boots when he ran, but I decided to go barefoot if I ran. While I couldn't be sure until I tried, running barefoot on a blanket of cushion plants seemed as if it would feel great—like crossing a field of feathers. I scanned the terrain and contemplated stripping. Our trek had taken us beyond all signs of people. Being seen wouldn't be a problem.

Even though the herd didn't object to our presence, we soon discovered they had a precise line of comfort we couldn't cross. Had we been primitive hunters, the line would have been just beyond the distance I could have effectively thrown a spear. The few times we pushed their limit, the caribou picked up their pace and arced around us. I wasn't about to ruin a tranquil scene by frightening the very animals I'd come to admire. There'd be no running naked with the bulls today.

Deb and I would have loved to hang with the herd all day, but more than two hours had whisked by, and we didn't feel comfortable leaving the dogs alone any longer. As we headed back, I was surprised to see how far we had hiked. Just reaching your middle finger was a respiration-raising hoof, and now that we were devoid of adrenaline, the climb over your knuckles was a grind. By the time we reached your wrist, I was dripping with sweat.

When we opened the truck doors, Annie was excited to see us and immediately forgave us for leaving her behind. Kate, however, refused to say a word. Since both dogs had been cooped up, we let them out to—Oh! Quick! Take your hand back!

Whew. Sorry about that. They *really* had to pee.

The rest of our afternoon was uneventful—if you can call driving through spectacular scenery uneventful. The first established place to pitch our tent south of the Arctic Circle was at Engineer Creek Campground, 150 miles past the caribou. I had low expectations for the spot. If you recall, Engineer Creek was the river that reeked of sulfur. Also, for me, nothing with the word "engineer" in it inspires thoughts of communing with nature.

This day, though, was one of those few magical days each person gets in a lifetime where *everything* exceeds expectations. The campground turned out to be wooded, rustic, and, best of all, uninhabited. We had our choice of fifteen campsites and selected the one at the edge of the river.

As a reward for spending the afternoon in the truck, we let Kate swim as often as she desired—now even her day exceeded expectations. I sniffed the air. No sulfur. The river flowed north toward where we had observed the Dall sheep, and the sulfur springs had yet to taint the water.

Deb and I finished setting up camp just in time to watch the sunset. Our tent sat on the western riverbank. Opposite us was a stony beach, fringed by a forest of dark-green pine and vibrant-yellow alder abutting the base of a towering craggy butte. In the west, the sun painted the clouds, creating a fiery canvas of blaze orange and molten red, and in the east, the butte reflected the sunset, glowing as if made of burnished gold. Both views, west and east, were equally intoxicating.

Having savored the Porcupine caribou migration, enjoyed the brilliant fall colors, and relished the intense sunset, we retired to our tent. Once cocooned in our sleeping bags, we flicked on our headlamps and relaxed with our books. While we read, the river's gentle gurgle accompanied us. Soon we grew drowsy and opted for darkness.

As the two of us drifted toward dreamland, something to the west began whimpering. We were barely conscious of the sound until it crescendoed into a howl.

A wolf was next to our tent!

Almost immediately a wolf from across the river answered the howl, and another to the north added harmony. I braced myself up on my elbows so I could hear better but kept my headlamp off. Though I couldn't see Deb, I sensed her smile. As for the dogs, they surprised me by listening without barking or growling.

An opera of howls echoed around us as the rest of the pack joined in. Their music—in true surround sound—was especially haunting at night.

At the beginning of the trip, when I mentioned to Deb my wish to hear wolves howling around our tent, I was thinking they'd be far off in the woods. Judging distance based solely on sound is subjective, but my guess is that the first wolf was fifteen feet from our tent and the others were spaced from fifty to two hundred feet away.

The opera ceased after a few minutes. A single wolf howled near the butte an hour later, and solo performances serenaded us from time to time throughout the night. Though we never heard the pack as a chorus again, for the first time in my life wake-up calls were something I looked forward to.

Deb had a theory about the wolves that made perfect sense. When we were reading, the light from our headlamps made our nylon tent glow, and the glowing caught the wolves' attention. The whimpering we heard was from a wolf who had been sent to scout us out, and his first howl was a message to the pack on the status of our tent: "No, the mother ship hasn't returned for us yet. It's just more of those stinky humans." The entire pack then howled to acknowledge the message, and the subsequent solo howls were periodic announcements that we were still in the area.

Miles traveled so far: 3,071

When we awoke on September 15, the temperature was seventeen degrees—the coldest morning so far. The arctic weather hadn't kept us from sleeping, but we did have some chilly body parts. Later we'd discover the water in the dog bowl had turned to ice, the tent poles had frozen together, and the toilet seat in the outhouse—well, let's just say neither of us wanted to be the first to sit on it.

Deb and I both use mummy-style sleeping bags. Even on the coldest nights, I never made full use of my bag's design, as I can't sleep unless my arms are free to move. Deb, on the other hand, usually slept with her hood cinched tight around her head and only her nose exposed to the elements.

On any other morning, the sight of my wife in her puffy yellow cocoon would have been my cue to give her a hard time with a comment such as, "Only someone with a snorkel like yours could breathe cinched up like that." On this morning, while Deb snuggled in her bag working up the nerve to emerge and face the cold air, I resisted the obligatory schnoz joke. Instead, I leaned over—though not too far—and kissed the tip of her nose. "Happy eighteenth anniversary, Honey!" I said.

I had married a truly amazing woman—and not just because she had willingly put up with me for eighteen years. While Deb can be tough and downright nasty when she needs to be, she's also beautiful, intelligent, and the most likable person I've ever known. She'd make a great therapist, because people love to talk to her. Even strangers open up to her with unsolicited personal stories. Come to think of it, she'd make a good police detective, as criminals would confess to her before even realizing what they'd said. Frankly, Deb is the kind of person who can excel at anything she desires.

Now, about her nose. . . .

We decided to take a different route home. Instead of revisiting the Campbell Highway, we planned to follow the Klondike Highway south to the town of Whitehorse. From there we'd catch the Alaska Highway going east; turn south onto the Cassiar Highway; take a side trip west into Hyder, Alaska; travel east across British Columbia on Highway 16; head southeast on Highway 93 through Jasper, Banff, and Kootenay national parks; and finally proceed south into Montana.

Since our tent and sleeping bags needed to be dried out again, we took a day off from adventuring and headed directly to Whitehorse. For our anniversary night, we hoped to find someplace nice to stay that would still accept dogs. We lucked out when the Westmark Hotel said they'd be happy to accommodate us.

The last time we had dried our gear we were at the Bonanza Gold Motel, where we could toss everything directly from the back of the truck into our room. This time I had to carry our wet stuff past the reception area and down a long hallway. The young woman behind the front desk smiled at me pleasantly, but by my second trip down the hall—this time carrying the tent on one shoulder and an unrolled sleeping bag on the other—her eyes gave away her suspicion. Either that, or she was jealous of the porcupine hairdo I'd acquired during the previous night.

Deb and I showered and walked down the street to Giorgio's Cuccina for dinner. Crowded restaurants typically have good food, and on this Sunday night, we had to wait in line a half hour just to get a table. The fashionable Italian restaurant lived up to our expectations and served us a great dinner with great wine and a great dessert. We then walked back to the hotel for great . . . well, it was our anniversary. The dogs covered their eyes.

Miles traveled so far: 3,510

We spent the morning in Whitehorse exploring and shopping. Though Yukon Territory is roughly twice the size of the state of Oregon, it has a population of only 29,960 people, 22,131 of whom live in Whitehorse. Unlike Inuvik, this town was easy to fall in love with. It sat on the scenic west bank of the Yukon River, surrounded by tree-covered mountains, and lining its spotless streets were brightly painted shops frequented by friendly residents.

An example of the friendly townsfolk arose during my search to satisfy my craving for smoked fish. I had seen several smokehouses during our journey but couldn't find any place that actually sold the fish. When a clerk in a large Whitehorse supermarket told me he didn't know of any store that could help me, I was about to give up. My luck changed when a shopper overheard my request and provided detailed driving instructions to a tiny out-of-the-way shop where I gleefully acquired enough fish for several tailgate picnics.

Like the previous day, this one was pleasant but adventure free. We followed the Alaska Highway almost to Watson Lake, turned onto the Cassiar Highway, crossed into British Columbia, and camped at Boya Lake Provincial Park. There we spent an unexciting night at an ordinary campsite in a moderately full park and had average . . .

I'll let you fill in the last word in the previous sentence, but believe me, it wasn't *sex*. After being married for eighteen years and a day, we could wait for the next hotel—the ground was way too hard and the dogs were much too close.

Miles traveled so far: 3,839

The surface of the Cassiar Highway alternated between pavement and gravel. Perhaps I was imagining it, but the scenery always seemed better when we were on gravel sections of road. For much of the morning we would cut through a valley with towering mountains on each side. Along the way we would pass numerous small aquamarine lakes nestled between the road and the mountains. Forests of fresh autumn colors bordered each lake, and the glassy water mirrored the foliage like an abstract painting.

When we departed from camp, I had no idea that beautiful intensely colored lakes would become a common sight. Therefore, I stopped at the first lake I saw, which was down a hill on the left side of the road, partially blocked by a line of trees. Since traffic was nonexistent, I parked only partway off the road. While Deb and the dogs waited, I walked down the hill to photograph the lake from the optimal angle. Though I wasn't gone long, my stop coincided with the first vehicle of the day.

I had just climbed back to the edge of the shoulder when a man in a pickup truck slowed down to scream, "Get the fuck off the road!" as he passionately presented the international one-finger salute.

I waved, smiled, and jumped back into the truck.

"What was that about?" asked Deb.

"Just some jerk who thought I hadn't pulled far enough off the road."

"He had plenty of room."

We continued down the highway in silence. The smooth gravel allowed me to drive fifty miles per hour, or faster, without shimmying.

With my mind still on the one-finger salute, we were traveling somewhere in the "or faster" range as we approached a curve fringed by trees. I handled the curve effortlessly and was delighted when the view opened up to expose another blue-green lake—even more gorgeous than the first one.

The road traversed a ridge, which dropped precipitously thirty feet to the lake immediately to our right. If I didn't stop quickly, I'd overshoot the tiny lake. I stepped on the brake while simultaneously pulling to the shoulder. This time, I'd make sure I was far enough off the road to—

"The shoulder is giving away! Martyyyy!" yelled Deb.

"Shiiiiiiiiiiiiiiiiiiiiiiiiiiiiiiit!" we screamed in unison.

I could feel the earth crumbling beneath the passenger side tires as we skidded to a halt.

Huh, huh, huh, huh. We both panted aloud before I said what Deb was already thinking: "Don't . . . move . . . a muscle."

I slowly turned my head to look out the side windows. We weren't teetering, but if the road collapsed any more, we'd roll into the lake. "Okay, Deb. I'm going to stay in the truck. My weight should help keep us stable. Do you have room to get out on your side?"

"I . . . think so, . . . but it's steep."

"Get out, and take the dogs with you."

"Are you sure?"

"Yes. Do it!"

Deb eased open her door and gingerly lowered herself to the bank before opening the extended cab door to release the dogs. Once everyone was clear, I crawled out my side.

"That was *too* close!" said Deb.

"The shoulder *looked* firm," I said with a forced chuckle.

"We're gonna need to hire a tow truck."

"From where?"

"I don't know. Probably Watson Lake, seventy miles back."

I walked to the front of the truck and got down on my hands and knees for a better view. The vehicle was listing precariously, but the crumbling under the passenger side had stopped—at least temporarily. "I think I can back it out."

"Don't be stupid! It's not worth risking your life for."

I cupped my chin between my thumb and forefinger and resurveyed the situation. "I'll lean out the door. If the truck rolls I can jump to safety."

Deb put her hands on her hips. "If you roll it, we're totally screwed!"

"This should work. Stand in front, so you can direct me."

I climbed back into the cab, perched myself on the outer edge of the seat, and engaged the four-wheel-drive. "Hold onto the dogs!" I yelled before gently pressing the accelerator.

Zzzzzzzzzz. The wheels spun for a moment before taking hold.

"Don't turn so sharp! The front end is swinging out!"

I adjusted my steering and pushed harder on the accelerator.

Rrrrrrrrrrrrrr. Just a few more feet to—"Yes!"—solid ground.

Deb opened the door, and she and the dogs jumped in. "No more driving on shoulders. Okay?"

"You don't need to worry about that. I won't trust another shoulder till we reach Montana. Oh, wait! I'll be right back. I still need to photograph the lake."

The rest of our day was less stressful. Around lunchtime we entered British Columbia's temperate rainforest. The new ecosystem provided a dramatic change of scenery. Now the flora was lush and green with just a hint of fall colors. As we experienced firsthand, the reason for the lushness was rain—copious rain.

Don't get me wrong. I liked the change. The mountains were now snowcapped and a dense mass of clouds rested atop their peaks, hemming us in. Like a scene inside a toy snow globe, we were in our own little world. When someone gave us a shake, rain enveloped us, and fog wafted through the treetops to add a touch of mystery.

Three hundred miles south of Boya Lake Provincial Park, we veered onto Highway 37A and headed west. When we departed Inuvik, traveling to Alaska wasn't on our itinerary; then Deb discovered a promising side trip to the neighboring towns of Stewart, British Columbia, and Hyder, Alaska. The excursion would add a day to our journey, but since we were making good time and would have a chance to see glaciers and grizzly bears, the opportunity was irresistible.

Thirty minutes later, I parked the truck in a gravel pullout across from a spectacular sight that wasn't alive but was definitely moving. The Bear Glacier poured down between two mountains, like a bumpy six-lane highway, to the edge of Strohn Lake. We sat on the opposite side of the tiny three-hundred-foot-wide lake for a head-on view of the glacier's toe. While the glacier had a white crust, its dominant color was windshield-washer-fluid blue. The color was particularly intense along newly exposed edges where chunks of ice had calved off into the lake.

The glacier's influence on the elements was impressive. When I stepped outside for some photos, I was shocked by how much colder and windier it was than when we had stopped to exercise the dogs a few miles back. I didn't linger outside for long.

We continued westward, passing several of the beautiful high mountain waterfalls that British Columbia is known for. The slender falls dropped from the snowcaps, dividing and merging on their way to the valley floor. Since Highway 37A was only forty picturesque miles long, we soon reached Stewart, where we rented a room at the Ripley Creek Inn.

Before World War I, Stewart had ten thousand residents, but now only seven hundred call it home. The end of the mining boom was the major reason for the decline in population. Weather was another factor. According to the Stewart/Hyder International Chamber of Commerce Web site, the town gets "unbelievable amounts of snowfall."

The Ripley Creek Inn occupied a historic building constructed in 1920 for Katherine Ryan, the original Klondike Kate. Ryan was one of Canada's early heroines. Though trained as a nurse, she gained fame for accomplishments that were unusual for a woman: she staked claims during the Klondike gold rush and worked as a jail keeper, Mounted Police special constable, and gold inspector.

Our room at the inn was on the ground floor in a section that had been added on. Although the room wasn't historic, its natural wood furnishings and pine board walls made it easy to imagine we were staying in a gold-rush-era cabin.

For dinner we walked across the street to the Bitter Creek Café. The restaurant was rumored to have the best food in town, and it had an eclectic little gift shop. We placed our order, then perused the antiques and other items for sale. When I came across the guest book, I noticed a couple from Essen, Germany, had made the most recent entry.

Of all the trips for this book, this one offered me the fewest opportunities to interact with others. Although my last name has nothing to do with Germany (my great-grandfather changed his name to Essen when the factory he worked at in Sweden had too many Hendricksons), it provided a good excuse to start up a conversation.

Four other couples were seated in the intimate dining room. After our meal arrived, I listened for an accent that wasn't American or Canadian. The elegantly dressed fiftyish couple at the table next to us was the only possibility. The woman was speaking in rapid-fire sentences, and the man was holding up his end of the discussion with nods and an occasional short utterance. I waited for a lull before introducing myself.

"Good evening. When I signed the guest book, I noticed the people who signed before me were from Essen, Germany. My last name is Essen. Are you the couple from Germany?"

"No," said the woman. "We're from New Zealand."

"Oh, I'm sorry. Confusing a New Zealand accent with a German accent is embarrassing."

"No need to apologize. Now if you had confused us with Australians— *that* would be another story."

"Why? Don't you like Australians?"

"I can't stand them. They're so uncouth. I have relatives in Australia, so I *have* to go there often. I can never get home soon enough."

The man shot me a look of embarrassment.

"So, what brought you to Canada?" I asked.

"We came to see the grizzly bears," said the woman. "And wouldn't you know, on our way here we got stuck on a bus *full* of Australians!"

While I chuckled, the man stared at the floor.

"Have you seen any bears yet?" I asked.

"No, we just got here," said the woman. "We're going to the viewing platforms, near Hyder, tomorrow."

"We're doing the same thing," I said.

"Where are you two from?" asked the woman.

"We live in Montana, in the United States."

"Oh! George Bush—he's a *lunatic!* You're brave to admit you're from the States while traveling."

The man's jaw dropped.

"Well, I have considered proclaiming myself an honorary Canadian— until Bush is out of office, of course."

Once the man knew his wife's comment hadn't offended me, he joined our conversation. "Your president seems to be a very unstable person."

"I can't disagree with you," I said.

"Bush is a loose cannon!" barked the woman. "He's just itching to start a war!"

Deb, who had been quietly listening, spoke up. "I hope you understand, many Americans are as worried as you are. We don't want Bush to start a war either."

"We know that," said the man.

"Tell me about New Zealand," I said. "We hope to visit your country someday. . . ."

Miles traveled so far: 4,170

Wednesday, September 18, would be our twelfth day on the road. I could have sworn we had just left Montana. Then I remembered, right next to the physics law "Two Annies cannot occupy the same state at the same time" is another, better-known law, "Time travels twice as fast when you're on vacation."

Rain had fallen all night, and it was still pouring in the morning as I carried our gear to the curb and tossed it into the truck. The weather wouldn't delay our Alaska visit, and U.S. Customs wouldn't slow us down either. We reached Hyder, three miles to the west, within ten minutes. Because no towns were accessible by road beyond Hyder, the United States government didn't supervise the border. We would, however, have to clear Canadian Customs upon our return.

We planned to spend a good portion of our day along the Salmon Glacier Road. The twenty-three-mile-long gravel road follows the Salmon River northwest out of Hyder, kisses the Tongass National Forest, turns northeast back into Canada, and dead-ends at the summit of the Salmon Glacier.

Hyder, population one hundred, took less than two minutes to drive through, and that included a stop to photograph the main street. On the far side of town, we picked up the Salmon Glacier Road and proceeded to where it crossed Fish Creek. From July through September, the creek is filled with salmon that have swum up from the ocean (via the Portland Canal) to spawn. Since the fish attract grizzly bears, the Forest Service had erected two long viewing platforms beside the creek to attract bear enthusiasts.

Deb and I stopped at the platforms eager to see the grizzlies. Because of our recent incredible luck with animal sightings, I naturally expected they'd be waiting for us when we arrived. No streak lasts forever, though. According to the park ranger on duty, the viewing season was winding down, and bears hadn't been seen in the area for several days. We hung around for a bit, watching salmon swim in the crystal-clear creek and hoping a grizzly would show up just for us. Eventually we accepted our fate and decided to move on. Perhaps we'd find a bear somewhere beyond the platforms.

We continued up the road as we scanned the forest for wildlife. Seventeen miles from Hyder, we reached the toe of the Salmon Glacier, the fifth-largest glacier in North America. Unfortunately, we had entered a cloud of foggy drizzle, so all we could see was an undistinguishable mass of white.

Other than grizzly watching, our goal for the day was to reach the top of the glacier. Hyder was at sea level, and the summit was at 4,300 feet. Although we had already climbed some, the bulk of our ascent would take place during the next six miles, as the road paralleled the glacier.

Deb and I briefly discussed turning around, but neither of us wanted to pass up the unique opportunity to follow a major glacier from toe to summit. The road wasn't intimidating—at first. That changed, however, as the gravel surface became progressively narrower and steeper.

Unlike other mountain roads I've driven, this one made my balls suck up into my lungs. As for Deb, despite compliments people have given her for having balls, she doesn't actually have any—I've checked. So, rather than sucking body parts into her lungs, she pushed one hand against the dashboard while clutching an armrest with the other.

Between the road and the glacier was a sheer drop of several hundred feet—I think. I couldn't actually see the drop because fog obscured everything from the edge of the road out. From my window, it looked as if we were driving alongside a smoky abyss.

Now, I know what you're thinking. We've all driven fogged-in, narrow, steep gravel roads that drop directly into hell. But there's more. The road not only angled up, it also tilted down, so its outside edge was lower than its mountainside edge. The first time we hit washboards I thought the truck would vibrate off the road. Oh, one last detail—no guardrails.

During the final few miles, I found myself gripping the steering wheel so tight I worried I might rip it from its column. Once we reached the summit, the fog hovered below us, and the drizzle became mixed with snow. Suddenly I had a new worry: what if the water on the road froze?

Deb, I, and the dogs piled out of the truck for a better view of the glacier. After everything we had gone through to reach the summit, the scene was anticlimactic. We could see the upper third of the Salmon Glacier, and though it was bigger than the Bear Glacier, it wasn't as colorful or dramatic. Instead, it was mostly white with a hint of blue.

Because of the weather, we didn't linger at the top for long. Heading down was even more nerve-racking than going up. The truck felt as if it wanted to race to the toe. I rode the brakes, ready to react if we started to slide. By the time we reached bottom, my lungs ached from holding my breath too much, and my muscles burned from being held taut too long. In all, the drive had been both tense and fun—like a scary amusement park ride with real danger.

We continued past the glacier and soon discovered an unmarked two-track road angling west through the forest. We decided to check it out. During our Canadian travels, exploring unmarked roads had become a regular activity. Though often short, they usually led to secluded spots for picnics and nature watching. In this instance, we popped out on the east bank of the Salmon River, in a section where the main road had curved away from the water.

We followed the two tracks as they paralleled the riverbank and soon spotted one golden eagle and three bald eagles perched low over the river. If we couldn't find a grizzly, the eagles made an excellent consolation prize. We stopped briefly to admire and photograph the raptors, then moved away so they could contemplate their next salmon meal in peace.

We had a task to complete before returning to Stewart. Finding water too cold for Kate to lie in had become the trip's running joke. Whenever we'd stop, Kate would jump out of the truck and into the nearest body of water. Since she had already declared the waters north of the Arctic Circle "balmy," this was our last opportunity to chill her out. The Salmon River flows directly from the Salmon Glacier. A river any colder would be frozen.

When I parked the truck near a wide stone-covered beach, the dogs began their adventure dance. As soon as I opened their door, they raced to the river. Annie arrived first, walked in just far enough for a drink, and stepped back out. The water was obviously too cold for her. Kate, on the other hand, waded out to the proper depth and plopped down for a leisurely drink. Just watching her made my balls suck back up into my lungs. (I apologize to my women readers, who can't relate to how testicles react to heights and cold water. But guys, you know exactly what I'm talking about.)

The dogs had been cooped up in the truck for much of the morning, so they eagerly took advantage of their opportunity to get some exercise. I didn't want them to run for long, however, because the river was full of salmon, and the grizzlies, while out of sight, were certainly nearby. When I called them back, Annie refused to come. She had found a dead salmon downriver and decided to stay and chew on it for a while. I yelled for her several times, using my authoritative "Dad voice," but she had developed river deafness.

The facts were undeniable: the bad Annie had found us. Since we had been continually on the move, the good Annie had accompanied us this far without interruption. The bad Annie was often close behind, but choosing the correct portal from Idaho was tough work. She caught the break she needed when she learned we were heading to the top of the glacier. With a stop to play in the water on the way back virtually guaranteed, all she needed to do to pull a switch was wait inside one of the portals hidden along the Salmon River.

This was a dangerous situation. Although the bad Annie was cunning, she had no experience with grizzly bears. If one took exception to her borrowing a salmon, she wouldn't stand a chance. I'd have other opportunities to watch grizzlies, but there was only one, make that two, Annies. If the bad Annie were killed during a switch, the good Annie would be stuck in Idaho forever.

I scanned the woods for bears before jogging downriver to retrieve the Labrador from Idaho. Though she pretended not to hear me, I wasn't buying her river deafness act and scolded her anyway. As I reached down to grab her collar, something flashed in the corner of my eye! I wheeled toward the light, but it was gone in an instant. When I turned back, the good Annie dropped the salmon and ran to the truck.

The bad Annie had returned to her proper state, where she'd remain for the duration of the trip.

Since the Stewart–Hyder area had some hiking trails and other places to explore, we considered staying another night at the Ripley Creek Inn. The weather, however, showed no sign of improvement, and neither Deb nor I felt like slogging through the woods with muddy dogs. We decided instead to head east in hopes of clearer skies.

The next twenty-four hours were uneventful. The rain didn't stop, so we kept going. We spent Wednesday night at a hotel in the town of Burns Lake, halfway across British Columbia, and by Thursday afternoon were in Jasper National Park, heading southeast on Highway 93. Though we still had roughly seven hundred miles of driving ahead of us, we'd never have to take another major road, because Highway 93 would pass within five miles of our house in Montana.

When Highway 93 passes through Jasper and Banff national parks, it's called the Icefields Parkway, and Parks Canada publicizes it as "The most beautiful road in the world." While the mountainous terrain along the paved parkway was scenic, Deb and I both agreed that the Campbell, Dempster, and Cassiar highways were more beautiful.

For us, the biggest shock—and detraction from beauty—was that once again cars were a common sight. On the Campbell, Dempster, and Cassiar highways, we had seen an average of one or two vehicles per hour; now we were seeing four or five vehicles per minute. While it wasn't exactly rush hour traffic in a major city, we had become so spoiled that it seemed like a lot.

Wildlife along the Icefields Parkway was plentiful. Our sightings would include numerous bighorn sheep, several mountain goats, a few deer, a black bear, and an elk. Unlike the rest of our trip, most of our wildlife spottings here were group experiences. The first spotters would pull to the shoulder to view their find, then others would join in. Often we'd encounter lines of cars with people watching animals. While the extra eyes meant more sightings for everyone, sometimes the experience felt a bit zoolike.

Late Thursday, Deb and I had the privilege of being the first spotters of the largest elk on Earth. Okay, Deb spotted it without my help, and it probably wasn't the world's largest elk, but everything else in the previous sentence is true. We were driving fifty-five miles per hour along a section where the Icefields Parkway parallels the Athabasca River. A strip of forest was shielding the river from the highway with occasional gaps providing fleeting views of the water.

"Elk!" shouted Deb.

"Where?" I asked.

"Back there. I only caught a glimpse of him. I'm not even sure it was an elk—it could've been a deer."

"There's only one way to find out." I eased us to a stop, U-turned, and headed north.

"I doubt we can spot him again. The gap between the trees was narrow."

"There he is! Definitely an elk." I U-turned again before parking.

The dogs launched into their adventure dance!

"Sorry girls," said Deb, craning her neck to the back. "You two have to stay in the truck. Dad and I won't be gone long."

We shut the doors and started toward the river.

"Wait! Dad! Mom! You forgot the dogs!—*Again!* This isn't fair. Wait! The Labrador Retriever Union isn't gonna like this. Come back! Mommmmmmmm!"

We picked our way through the trees and soon had a clear view of the elk. He was standing at the edge of the woods, on the opposite side of the Athabasca River.

"He's huge!" I whispered. "Look at those massive antlers!"

If he wasn't the biggest elk on Earth, he was darn close—and I thought only the moose in Canada took steroids.

I ducked behind a boulder and snuck to the river for some photos. The weather had only marginally improved since we left Stewart, and the dim misty day challenged my equipment. When I extended my zoom lens, the camera's light meter blinked in protest.

What happened next made me rethink my literalist traveler assumption about the Canadian government erecting signs to warn me about possessed elk. Perhaps using a reflector for an eye actually meant the elk were psychic.

In the past, wild animals had acquiesced to my photographic efforts, but never before had one actually helped me with the process. The river was more than one hundred feet wide, and the elk was thirty feet beyond the water. When the big bull spotted me with my camera, I expected him to react like a normal elk and vanish into the forest. Instead, like a psychic, he seemed to know I wouldn't harm him and only desired a quality photo. He walked to the edge of the river and posed for a head-on shot. After I captured the image, he turned sideways for a profile view. I pushed the shutter button again, then glanced over my shoulder to exchange grins with Deb.

The image stabilizer in my lens had stopped working earlier in the trip. As helpful as the elk had been, the malfunctioning equipment combined with the poor weather conditions meant we were still too far apart for anything but an average photo. With the river between us, closing the distance seemed unlikely. Then, as if he understood my predicament, the elk stepped into the river and waded toward me.

I continued pushing the shutter button as he approached. Once he reached mid-river, water began splashing against his chest. Suddenly his confident demeanor changed, his eyes grew wide, and he refused to take another step. Had I done something to upset him? Was the river too fast or too deep?

Deb touched my elbow. "We should go."

"You're right. We should back up to give the elk more room to cross."

"No! We need to go. . . . *Look.*"

When Deb pointed toward the road, I understood her insistence. Numerous cars were lining the shoulder, and people were peering between the trees with their cameras.

Our special moment with the elk had ended, and now we needed to set an example for the others. The elk, who was neither possessed nor psychic, would stand in the frigid water, too frightened to move, until he had a clear path to safety. We hurried to the truck, shot the gawkers a look that said, "Follow us," and sped off down the road.

Deb and I decided to spend the night at Honeymoon Lake Campground, one of the few campgrounds in Jasper National Park that remained open during the off-season. Because of the reduced facilities, we were fortunate to find a secluded spot to pitch our tent.

After dinner, we walked the dogs and built a campfire. Nothing beats relaxing by a crackling fire on a cool dark—

Wrrrrrrrrrrrrrrrrrrrrrrrrr. . . . The growling RV startled me. I peered over my shoulder as the mammoth vehicle backed into the adjacent site. "Damn!" I whispered under my breath.

Soon engine noise gave way to yard lights nearly bright enough to wash out our fire. When the occupants filed out of the RV, a middle-aged woman smiled at me. I smiled back, trying not to sneer.

Though the sudden change of events displeased me, at least our new neighbors were quiet. I couldn't blame them for taking advantage of their lights while organizing their gear, and once everything was in place they'd certainly turn them off.

—Okay, maybe not.

As the evening wore on, I considered asking for a little darkness. My request became unnecessary when nature intervened with a shower that sent our neighbors scurrying for the comfort of the great indoors, flicking off their lights in the process.

Deb and I surrendered to the elements as well and crawled into our tent. Although our campfire had been cut short, nothing beats falling asleep to the pitter-patter of rain on a cool dark night.

Miles traveled so far: 4,907

The rain changed to snow overnight. Even though the two inches of crystalline fluff wouldn't last the morning, waking to a snow-covered camp was a great way to begin our last full day in Canada.

The Icefields Parkway passes within viewing distance of seven ice fields and twenty-five glaciers. To get the most out of our drive, we stopped at the Icefield Centre near the Jasper–Banff boundary (Jasper, Banff, and Kootenay national parks run in succession along the British Columbia–Alberta border). There we could get information, view exhibits, eat lunch, and—if we wanted—even take a "snocoach" onto the Columbia Icefield.

Despite being the off-season, the Icefield Centre was bustling with tourists. I stepped to the information desk, where a man with round wire-rimmed glasses and a harried expression greeted me.

"What's the difference between permanently snowcapped mountains, glaciers, and ice fields?" I asked.

"Finally, an intelligent question!" said the man.

"Oh, really? I thought it was pretty basic."

"You wouldn't *believe* the questions people ask me. No, we don't take the animals inside on cold nights. No, you can't ride a mountain goat. No . . . Forgive me. I've had a bad morning."

"Maybe you'd like to answer my second question first. Is it okay if I feed the bears?"

"You joke, but I've been asked that question many times."

"I believe you."

"To answer your serious question. Both ice fields and glaciers are large nonseasonal bodies of snow that have compressed into ice over time. Ice fields occupy flat land, and they don't move; glaciers occupy mountain slopes and valleys, and they do move. No one's ever asked me about snowcapped mountains before. But if the snowcap doesn't melt in the summer, then it would have to be a glacier, because the slope of the peak would make it move."

I said good-bye to the man and perused the Icefield Centre exhibits with Deb. We had now visited three glacial regions on our trip—Glacier National Park, Stewart–Hyder, and the Icefields Parkway. In all three areas, educational brochures and signs had one thing in common: the glaciers were receding due to global warming.

Despite overwhelming evidence, in America we still debate whether global warming is real. To those who refuse to acknowledge what is happening, I'll just say this: Increasing automobile fuel efficiency, moving away from fossil fuels, recycling, and insisting factories dramatically reduce their pollution are all good things we should be doing anyway. Even if global warming were a figment of the scientific community's imagination, taking proactive action to protect our planet would still undoubtedly benefit us all.

Marty with Annie and Kate at home in Montana. *(Photo by Deb Essen)*

Belize • American crocodile.

Belize • Brown pelican.

The Amazon • Orchid-mimic spider.

The Amazon • Dr. Devon Graham with a black caiman.

The Amazon • The *M/N Tucunare* on the Amazon River.

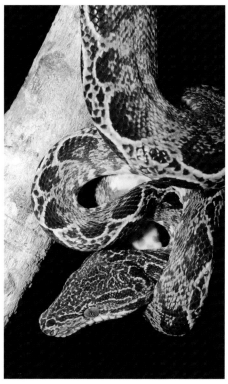

The Amazon • Amazon tree boa.

The Amazon • Fer-de-lance.

The Amazon • Poison dart frog.

The Amazon • This is the same frog!

The Amazon • Anaconda.

The Amazon • Leaf-mimic katydid.

The Amazon • Deb jumps off the *M/N Tucunare.*

The Amazon • Giant ceiba borer beetle.

Australia • Deb with Herbie the agile wallaby.

Australia • Boyd's forest dragon.

Australia • Carolyn & Gary Bondeson.

Australia • Marty with Frog the tawny frog-mouth. *(Photo by Deb Essen)*

Australia • Marty with Bonnie the silver wallaroo. *(Photo by Deb Essen)*

Australia • Burton's legless lizard.

Australia • Spectacled flying fox.

Australia • Mudskipper.

Australia • Lace-lid frog.

Australia • Chris Leach.

Australia • White-lipped tree frog.

Australia • Lace monitor.

Australia • Marty with the 7½ foot-long amethystine python. *(Photo by Chris Leach)*

Canada • The Alaska Highway.

Canada • The Campbell Highway.

Canada • Close-up shots of tundra plant life.

Canada • Porcupine.

Canada • Deb approaches the Porcupine caribou migration.

Canada • LEFT: The Bear Glacier.
ABOVE: Annie checks out the Athabasca River.

Antarctica • Gentoo penguins.

Antarctica • Adélie penguin.

Antarctica • Gentoo chicks.

Antarctica • Chinstrap penguin.

Antarctica • Olle Carlsson.

Antarctica • Southern elephant seals.

Antarctica • The Iceberg Graveyard.

Antarctica • Sara and Laurel.

Antarctica • Antarctic fur seal.

Antarctica • Marty gives Atlas a break. *(Photo by Deb Essen)*

Antarctica • Zodiac outing on Paradise Bay.

Antarctica • Humpback whale.

Antarctica • A humpback tail and the *Professor Multanovskiy*.

Antarctica • A humpback whale approaches the kayakers.

Antarctica • Leopard seal.

Borneo • Painted leech.

Borneo • Unidentified Bornean caterpillar.

Borneo •
Luang, Deb,
Jonathan,
and Blonsai.

Borneo • Orangutan on our
backpacking trip.

Borneo • Ugan.

Borneo • Nanga Sumpa longhouse.

Borneo • Leaf monkey.

Borneo • Comb-crested agamid lizard.

Borneo • Stick insect.

Borneo • Orangutan at the Sepilok Orang Utan Rehabilitation Centre.

Borneo • Charging Asiatic elephant.

Europe • Castillo de Albuquerque.

Europe • Emad at the Zermatt train station.

Europe • Angel pours a glass of sidra natural.

Europe • Deb at La Garganta Divina trailhead.

Europe • The Matterhorn.

Europe • Spanish ibex.

Zimbabwe • Greater kudu.

Zimbabwe • Our first camp on the Zambezi River.

Zimbabwe • Cape buffalo.

Zimbabwe • Marty with the 7½ foot-long African rock python. *(Photo by Skip Horner)*

Zimbabwe • African painted dogs.

Zimbabwe • Spotted bush snake.

Zimbabwe • Sunset on the Zambezi River.

Zimbabwe • A hippo approaches.

Zimbabwe • The yawn of aggression!

Zimbabwe • Deb and Marty after the hippo bites through their canoe.
(Photo by Brian Worsley)

Zimbabwe • Marty with the 10½ foot-long African rock python. (*Photo by Skip Horner*)

Zimbabwe • Lion.

Zimbabwe • African elephants.

Zimbabwe • Zebras at sunset.

Zimbabwe • Humphrey, Ashley, and Brian (with camp staff members in the truck).

Zimbabwe • Victoria Falls from the air.

From the Icefield Centre, we continued southward through the national parks. Once past Kootenay, we debated what to do for our final night. Since the tent and sleeping bags were wet again, staying at a hotel was our initial choice. We did have two other options though: we could go on a caffeine-assisted marathon drive home or pretend our gear was dry and sleep outdoors.

For me, the most unexpected part of our trip was how much I looked forward to nights in the tent. Deb and I would squeeze into the middle with Kate against the wall on Deb's side and Annie against the wall on my side. Sleeping between the dogs was snuggly, and we rarely felt cold.

When Deb found White Swan Lake Provincial Park on the map, we unanimously—dogs included—voted to spend the night there. We knew nothing about the park but reasoned that since it was located on a gravel road, twelve miles off the highway, it wouldn't be crowded.

We arrived to discover four campgrounds spaced throughout the park. The first was packed with RVs; the second was next to the road; the third resembled a parking lot; and the fourth, while sparsely treed, had only three occupied campsites. The last campground was the obvious choice, and we selected the site with the most trees.

At the beginning of the trip, Deb and I would set up and break down camp in a haphazard manner with much discussion about who was to do what. We improved with experience and now went about our tasks with drill team precision. Our increased efficiency paid off on this evening, because immediately after we set everything up a hailstorm hit.

We piled into the tent to wait out the storm. The hail soon gave way to heavy rain with gusty winds. To think only hours ago our plans were to stay in a nice, warm, dry hotel. I tried to remember what possessed us to choose camping instead—oh yeah, it was snuggly.

When the rain diminished to a drizzle, we took Kate and Annie for a walk along a nearby creek. The cold, wet weather didn't bother the dogs at all. They had a wonderful time, thoroughly enjoying all the new sniffs. Deb and I, on the other hand, found ourselves doing everything we could to stay warm.

Once we returned from our walk, we shivered through dinner and went to bed early. Though the dogs, tent, and sleeping bags were damp, we soon warmed up enough to fall asleep.

Wrrrrrrrrrrrrrrrrrrr. . . . The rumble of an approaching diesel vehicle jolted me awake. The night was so dark that when I opened my eyes I saw nothing but blackness. As the sound grew louder, headlights flashed our tent. The campground had at least fifteen unoccupied sites. Surely anyone arriving so late would pick a spot where they wouldn't disturb others. Just in case I was wrong, I sent out a telepathic message: "Don't camp next to us. Don't camp next to us. Don't camp next to us. . . ."

Wrrrrrrrrrrrrrrrrrrr. Rup-pup-pup-pup-pup-pup-pup. . . . I'm a terrible telepath.

Before we continue, I need to get you into both Deb's head and mine. That way you can experience the dramatically different reactions we'd each have to the same event.

When you're in my head, I'm tired and angry. Two rude and irresponsible people are ruining my last night in Canada, and I'll make matters worse by stewing in my anger.

When you're in Deb's head, Bob & Doug McKenzie are camping next to us, and she's trying not to laugh out loud.

If you're unfamiliar with Bob & Doug McKenzie, they were fictitious brothers played by Rick Moranis and Dave Thomas in an early 1980s parody of Canadians that became famous for its over-the-top accents and routines about "hosers," "back bacon," and "the great white north."

I'll narrate from my point of view, but if you don't mind, I'm going to hang out in Deb's head until morning. I already lived through the night once in my own head, and that was quite enough. As for you, feel free to bounce back and forth between Deb and me as often as desired. Now, let's go back to that dark, drizzly night in Canada:

Pup-pup-pup-pup-pup-pup-pup. . . . Though my eyes wouldn't confirm what I heard until morning, a diesel pickup truck, carrying a large camper and pulling a trailer with two off-road vehicles, was idling forty feet from our tent. As the engine grumbled, two doors squeaked open and slammed shut. Then footsteps approached and moved away.

"Over here, eh?" The loud voice came from a young man, who sounded as if he was in his late teens. I determined he was the son.

"No, no! Der udder site is better." The second loud voice came from a man, who sounded as if he was in his midforties. I determined he was the father.

The father and son walked the grounds, shouting to each other the various campsite possibilities. Upon their return, they milled around a bit, climbed back into the truck and slammed the doors.

I breathed a sigh of relief, thinking, "They've decided to move on."

A door squeaked opened and slammed shut. *Shhhhhhwww, shhhhhh-www, shhhhhhwww, shhhhhhwww. . . .* Footsteps dragged across the gravel, as if a monster in a horror movie were approaching.

"Okaaay! Back up!" yelled the son.

I whispered under my breath, "Damn!" and sent out another tele-pathic message: "No, no! The other site is better. Go to the other site. Go to der udder site. Go to der udder site. . . ."

Wrrrrrrrrrrrrrrrrrr. . . . The truck roared as the father pushed the accelerator.

"Turn right, eh? Noooooooo! Right!"

Wrrrrrrrrrrrrrrrrrr. . . .

"No! No! Der udder way!"

Wrrrrrrrrrrrrrrrrrr. . . .

"Stop!"

Rup-pup-pup-pup-pup-pup-pup. . . .

"Okaaay! Go left!"

Wrrrrrrrrrrrrrrrrrr. . . .

"No! Forward! Hollllld iiiiiit. Hollllld iiiiiit."

Rup-pup-pup-pup-pup-pup-pup. . . .

"Okaaay! Now back!"

Wrrrrrrrrrrrrrrrrrr. . . .

"Go left, eh? Left! No! No! Der udder left! Stop!"

Rup-pup-pup-pup-pup-pup-pup. . . .

"Okaaay! Now go straight. No! Back! Hollllld iiiiiit. Hollllld iiiiiit. Okaaaaay! . . ."

I buried my head under my pillow—fuming.

Eventually the father and son maneuvered their truck and trailer exactly where they wanted it. I sighed, ready to go back to sleep.

Pup-pup-pup-pup-pup-pup-pup-pup-pup. . . .

They were going to turn off the truck, weren't they? Loud voices, slamming doors, rattling beer cans, and other noises filled the next ten minutes. Finally, the father cut the engine. I sighed again.

The two shuffled about awhile longer, adding occasional door slams for good measure; then their camp went silent. I waited until I was sure they'd gone to sleep, took one last deep sigh, and curled alongside Annie—she sighed too.

"Maaaaaaaaaaaaaaaaax! Max! Here, dog!" screamed the son.

"Maaaaaaaax! Here, Max!" bellowed the father.

They both whistled.

I sat up, ready to explode. The father and son obviously hadn't read the sign at the campground entrance: "Dogs must be leashed or tied at all times. Strictly enforced."

The two tromped through camp, yelling and whistling, until they located their dog.

I looked at my watch. It was after midnight. Now, too wound up to sleep, I closed my eyes and imagined myself sneaking over and releasing the air from their tires. The thought didn't put me to sleep, but it made me feel better.

"Bob? Bub! Bub! Buuuuuuuuuuuub! Here, dog!"

Yes, they had two dogs. This time I had to crack a smile. As the son crisscrossed camp, calling and whistling for his dog, Bob, he sounded more like a chicken than a human.

"Bub! Bub! Buuuuuuuuuuuub! Here, dog! Bub! Bub! Buuuuuuuuuuuub! Here, dog! . . ."

I fell asleep shortly after one o'clock, contented with the belief that the father and son would sleep in. In fact, maybe *I* could wake *them* up.

Miles traveled so far: 5,219

Grrrrrrrrrrr. Grrrrrrrrrrrr. Rup-pup-pup-pup-pup-pup-pup. . . . The diesel engine dislodged me from my slumber. I glanced at my watch. It was five past six. I felt a surge of irritation before consoling myself with a pleasant thought: "They'll be leaving soon."

Pup-pup-pup-pup-pup-pup-pup-pup-pup. . . .

For the next fifteen minutes, the engine grumbled, doors slammed, and voices yelled. Then a woman, from the opposite side of the campground, began shouting in anger. I couldn't make out her words, but she'd obviously had enough of our inconsiderate neighbors.

The camp went silent. Except, of course, for the idling engine.

While I should have been pleased, I lay in my sleeping bag feeling ashamed. I should have been the one to approach the father and son.

"Maaaaaaaaaaaaaaaax! Max! Here, dog!"

That was it! I stormed from the tent and glared at the lanky teenager. "Quiet! People are sleeping!"

"My dog. He's lost, eh?"

"Your dog is *supposed* to be tied up!"

"Whaaaatever." He slipped his pinkies into his mouth and whistled.

Though the teenager was my height, I was definitely bigger than he was. His flippant attitude surprised me until I realized his father was standing by the trailer, watching me. I returned the father's glare but didn't say a word. The father and son were obviously unconcerned about the effect of their crass behavior on others, and pursuing the issue wouldn't make them change. Besides, they were both dressed in camouflage fatigues, prepared for a day of shooting whatever crossed their path. The sooner they departed, the less chance of them confusing my dogs for elk.

Ten minutes later, they slammed their doors a final time and roared out to the main road. Although a few well-placed trees blocked my view, I didn't need to be a telepath to know what condition they left their campsite in. I walked over, picked up the scattered beer cans and candy wrappers, and tossed them into the trash barrel—twenty feet away.

The saddest part of the incident was that this had been a father and son outing. The father had taught his son to be a slob camper, and later that day he'd likely teach his son to be a slob hunter. Unless the chain is broken, the son will teach the same practices to his children, and they'll pass them to their children, and so on.

Though we don't like to admit it, at one time or another we have all wished something bad would happen to someone. In my case, I hoped something would happen to the son to remove him from the gene pool. Considering my nonviolent nature, this was a difficult thought for me. I wouldn't want anything painful or life threatening to happen to the boy. Hmmm . . . what would it take for him to freeze his balls off anyway?

We arrived home late Saturday afternoon. The trip had been hard on my truck. Several flying rocks had cracked the windshield, and one of the ball joints had developed a loud squeal. Both items would need to be replaced. Still, considering what the truck had been through, it had held up quite well.

Kate and Annie's enthusiasm for getting in and out of the truck never waned. I thought for sure they'd tire of traveling by the end of the trip, but instead, they would have been thrilled if we'd kept driving all the way to Mexico. The only time they were unhappy was when we arrived home, and they had to get out of the truck for the final time. Both dogs were depressed for days.

As for Deb and me, though we looked forward to taking a break from riding in the truck, this was yet another trip we hoped to repeat. Next time, however, we'd have to come up with a more efficient travel method. If Annie would just show us the portal between Idaho and the Yukon border, we could head directly to the Campbell Highway and . . .

Total miles traveled: 5,572
Driving distance from Los Angeles to New York: 2,824

5
Antarctica the Beautiful

A ntarctica was supposed to be our final adventure for this book.
When Deb and I saw magazine advertisements listing Antarctica
trips from $8,000 to $15,000 per person, we agreed: before forking over
that kind of money we had to survive the other six continents first.

In July 2002, a year before we even expected to begin planning an
Antarctica trip, my curiosity led me to do some preliminary Internet
research. Knowledge, after all, is a good thing. Right?

First, I learned that the best way to get from the United States to
Antarctica was to fly to Ushuaia, Tierra del Fuego, Argentina, and sail
the rest of the way by ship. Because of Antarctica's extreme weather,
most commercial ships restrict their voyages to late November through
early March (essentially the Southern Hemisphere's summer).

Next, I wanted to see if we could reach Antarctica for less than the
cost of a new automobile. Within a few clicks, I found prices lower than
in the magazine ads, and from there, I narrowed my search to Polar
Cruises, a firm out of Oregon.

Although I intended to do a more thorough search later, I dialed
the number for Polar Cruises and reached the owner, Lynn Cross. I
expected Lynn to be a typical brochure-quoting travel agent and was surprised to learn she had worked for six years on Antarctica-bound ves-
sels. Not only did she have firsthand answers for all my questions, she
also had access to multiple ships ranging in capacity from 49 to 150
passengers. The smaller ships, which would provide more intimate
wildlife viewing, piqued my interest.

Near the end of our conversation, I asked, "If I decide to do this, how far should I book in advance?"

"Most people make reservations at least a year ahead," she said. "This coming season is already pretty much booked up."

"Is there anything left on the smaller ships?"

"That depends. Would you want a cabin with two or three berths?"

"I'll be traveling with my wife, so I'd need a double."

"As of two days ago the *Professor Multanovskiy,* a forty-nine passenger ship, had one double cabin left in February. But I'm not sure if it's still available."

Although she was telling the truth (she couldn't know for sure because other agencies also booked the ship), she had used the classic "limited availability" sales close.

"Can you check for me?"

"One moment, please." She put me on hold for a few minutes before returning to say, "Yes, it's still available."

"Great. I'll take it."

Just because a close is a classic doesn't mean it's no longer effective.

After giving Lynn my address and credit card number, I hung up, shocked yet excited by what had transpired. I ran upstairs to find my wife.

"Deb! Guess where we're going in February."

"Where?"

"Antarctica! I booked the only cabin left on the ship, and it was a *really* good deal."

"You did what!" Her initial reaction told me I was in trouble. Then she cracked a smile and started laughing.

You're probably wondering, so I'll tell: our voyage on the *Professor Multanovskiy* cost $4,495 per person, plus airfare. Since rooms with private baths ranged from $5,295 to $6,395 per person, we would be "slumming" it on the deck with shared bathrooms. Where we stayed on the ship wasn't a concern for us, however. As Deb pointed out, "We didn't have a problem sharing bathrooms on our Amazon trip. Why would this be any different?"

What is the attraction of visiting Antarctica? The answer will take this entire chapter, but for starters, it's the Earth's least explored continent. The first landing on the Antarctic Peninsula likely took place in 1821, and the first landing on the continent's round section happened in 1895. Although tourism has increased in recent years, according to the *Antarctic Explorer* (published in 2002 by Ocean Explorer Maps), fewer than 200,000 people have ever walked on the continent.

Antarctica is a land of extremes. While most people would expect it to be the coldest and windiest continent on Earth, few would expect it to also be the driest and highest (averaging 7,544 feet above sea level). As for size, it comprises 9 percent of the world's land (it's almost twice as big as Australia).

As part of my pre-trip research, I read Alfred Lansing's book *Endurance: Shackleton's Incredible Voyage.* From that moment on, I knew thoughts of Sir Ernest Shackleton and his ship, the *Endurance,* would follow me from Montana all the way to Antarctica:

In August 1914, Shackleton launched the Imperial Trans-Antarctic Expedition with the goal of being the first to cross the continent on foot. The *Endurance* sailed from England to Argentina and into the Weddell Sea off the coast of Antarctica. Weather conditions turned treacherous, and by late January 1915, the ship had become trapped in the pack ice. In October, the shifting ice floes crushed it.

With no way of signaling for help, the situation seemed hopeless. Undeterred, Shackleton led his twenty-seven-man crew across the frozen sea, dragging three small wooden boats behind them. Soon hazardous ice conditions made travel impossible, forcing them to spend the next five months living on the northward drifting pack ice.

Upon reaching open water, they launched their boats and sailed the stormy Southern Ocean to Elephant Island—an inhospitable place with precipitous snow-covered mountains. Shackleton knew they couldn't survive on the island for long, so he left his crew hunkered down in a makeshift shelter and took five men on an 870-mile voyage to South Georgia Island.

Rough seas almost swamped their little boat. Then high winds and a broken rudder forced them to land on the uninhabited southern side of South Georgia Island. Though he and his men were weak and exhausted, Shackleton led a trek north across the island's mountainous interior. After thirty-six hours of nonstop hiking, they reached the Stromness Whaling Station.

Three days later, Shackleton began the first of four attempts to rescue his crew on Elephant Island. Pack ice and inadequate ships doomed his first three efforts. His fourth try, using a tugboat borrowed from the Chilean government, was successful. The date was August 30, 1916. Remarkably, everyone survived.

For speed and efficiency of travel, give me Amundsen.
For scientific discovery, give me Scott. But when disaster strikes
and all hope is gone, get down on your knees and pray for Shackleton.

—SIR RAYMOND PRIESTLY, ANTARCTIC EXPLORER

Although Deb and I didn't have worries of being shipwrecked like Shackleton, we were traveling with some trepidation. As with most of our trips, we'd be out of touch with world events for an extended period. Normally I enjoy catching up with the world after a good adventure. This time, however, George W. Bush was set to order an attack on Iraq at any moment. In fact, coinciding with our departure was the largest worldwide antiwar protest in history. Would Bush listen to the protesters? If he did order an invasion, would retaliatory terrorist attacks take place in America? Would our family and friends be safe? What about our return? Our schedule included a flight from Buenos Aires to Washington, D.C. If attacks closed any airports, Dulles International would be a likely candidate.

Our outbound schedule routed us from Missoula to Denver to Miami to Buenos Aires and finally to the city of Ushuaia in Tierra del Fuego, Argentina. While we waited to pass through immigration in the Buenos Aires airport, a tall, heavyset American woman in her early thirties ducked under the ropes and cut in front of us in line. Her companion followed moments later. I was about to say something to the women regarding their rude actions, when Deb noticed they were carrying Quark Expeditions folders. Since Quark was the company in charge of our trip, we knew they were two of our shipmates. I decided to stay quiet.

As we soon found out, the heavyset woman was Mildred, and her companion was Rose. We ended up sitting across the aisle from them on the flight between Buenos Aires and Ushuaia. When Mildred discovered that several expedition participants were on the flight, she introduced herself to everyone. What began as a nice gesture rapidly turned into a brag session, as she brought out pictures and boasted in detail about her scuba diving accomplishments.

Scuba diving was an optional add-on to the expedition. Though Deb rarely passes up an opportunity to dive, she would have had to get extra training and expensive specialized gear for Antarctica's frigid water. After listening to Mildred's stories for a few minutes, Deb cupped her hand to my ear and whispered, "This woman doesn't have a clue what she's doing. I'm so glad I won't be diving with her."

While on the airplane, we also met some of our other shipmates, including members of a film crew who were along to shoot an Antarctica documentary. Although we were too tired to do much socializing, we could tell our expedition would include some intriguing people.

On Sunday evening, February 16, 2003, we arrived in Ushuaia (population 58,000), the southernmost city in the world. After visiting Inuvik, in far north Canada, I expected Ushuaia's similar harsh climate would make it equally depressing. Instead, the towns were polar opposites. Unlike Inuvik, Ushuaia was bright, friendly, and clean with small freshly painted houses in vivid reds, blues, yellows, and greens—bold colors to warm up the long winter nights.

Quark put us up at Los Ñires Hotel at the edge of the city. The hotel was well kept, and we had a stunning view of the Beagle Channel from our room. After more than thirty hours in airplanes and airports, Deb and I were grateful to have a comfortable place to sleep.

In the morning, we hired a taxi and sped off to downtown Ushuaia for some shopping and sightseeing. Spanish is Argentina's official language, and only a few of the locals we met spoke English. Deb had picked up some Spanish when we were in Peru and augmented what she had learned by browsing through a language book. In all, she knew about fifty short phrases, which was forty-seven more than I knew. My Spanish vocabulary was limited to *muchas gracias* (many thanks), *buenos días* (good morning), and *buenas noches* (good evening)—all of which I proudly used whenever the opportunity arose.

Trying to communicate with people who didn't speak English was surprisingly fun. Gestures and a few basic words were usually sufficient to get our point across. Everyone was patient with us and seemed to appreciate that we were at least attempting to use their language.

Even though communication was an enjoyable challenge, paying for things was frustrating. While Argentina's paper money was easy to figure out, I would have needed an electron microscope to read the value printed on their coins. Therefore, my purchases all went the same way: I'd pay what I could with bills before pulling out a handful of coins and staring at them as if I hadn't passed second grade math. Eventually I'd dump all the change on the counter and gesture for the clerk to take whatever I owed. Then I'd leave, muttering to myself, embarrassed that I'd just reinforced the image of a stereotypical ignorant American traveler.

I bought the English language edition of the Buenos Aires newspaper—probably paying twenty dollars in Argentine coins—and read about the worldwide protests against President Bush and his determination to invade Iraq. Some of the protests in Buenos Aires had changed from anti-Bush to anti-American. I agreed with the protesters' feelings about Bush and the war but found their chants of "Death to America" unsettling. Chanting for the demise of the United States put me and other peace-loving Americans in the same boat as a corrupt administration that obviously believed first-strike violence was an acceptable way to solve problems. Broad generalizations are part of human nature, but now more than ever I hoped people in other countries would not hold *all* Americans accountable for the impending actions of a unilateralist president elected by a minority.

Once we finished exploring Ushuaia, we headed to the marina and boarded the *Professor Multanovskiy*. A small ship (234 feet long by 42 feet wide), the *Multanovskiy* was closer in size to Shackleton's *Endurance* (144 feet long by 25 feet wide) than to modern cruise liners such as the *Carnival Conquest* (952 feet long by 116 feet wide). Built in 1982, the white ice-strengthened vessel had three decks of passenger cabins and a navigation bridge on top. Two Russian diesel engines powered the ship to a maximum speed of 14 knots (16.1 miles) per hour compared to the *Endurance's* 10.2 knots (11.7 miles) per hour and the *Carnival Conquest's* 22.5 knots (25.9 miles) per hour.

I was delighted to learn our fellow shipmates came from all over the world and was surprised to find out women outnumbered men twenty-eight to eighteen. Joining us were passengers from China, Czech Republic, Finland, Germany, Great Britain, Italy, Japan, Mexico, Switzerland, and the United States. This would truly be an international expedition.

Twenty-four crew members were also onboard, but we'd never see close to half of them because they worked nights or in off-limits areas like the engine room. Crew members we would have contact with included Captain Sergey Nesterov from Russia, Expedition Leader Olle Carlsson from Sweden, Ship Doctor Andrew Hughes from Australia, Biologist/Zodiac Driver Jackie McPhadden from Canada, Naturalist/Zodiac Driver Ty Milford from the United States, Dive Master Henrik Enckell from Sweden, and Bartender Katja Paulsson from Sweden.

We departed Ushuaia and sailed through the Beagle Channel toward the Atlantic Ocean. With seventy-five miles of calm channel water ahead, the expedition staff (crew members who worked directly with the passengers) used the opportunity to lead us through our mandatory lifeboat drill. The lifeboats looked like orange Tylenol gel capsules, only *slightly* bigger. The *Multanovskiy* had two lifeboats, and each one supposedly accommodated forty passengers. For this drill, approximately twenty-five people squeezed into each boat. Once we were seated, the doors were shut to seal us in. Had this been an actual emergency, we would have had to share the lifeboats with the entire crew— a feat that looked impossible.

We sat like peas in a pod while the staff gave us instructions and passengers asked questions. The smell of everyone's breath was overpowering—who had garlic for lunch anyway? Several passengers, including me, were getting a wee bit claustrophobic. Every time someone asked another question, I could see a half-dozen faces cringe, silently pleading, "Please, no more questions. I've got to get out of here!" Finally, after what seemed like hours of discussion, the staff released us from our tomb.

Ah, fresh air!

We reached the open ocean shortly after dark. The body of water between South America and Antarctica is called the Drake Passage. Known for unsurpassed rough seas, the passage crosses the only navigable waters on earth without a wind-breaking landmass somewhere to the east or west. Sailors call the latitudes between the two continents the "furious fifties" and the "screaming sixties" for good reason.

Crossing the Drake Passage would take two days. The staff biologist, Jackie McPhadden, told Deb and me the ocean was so rough during the *Multanovskiy's* most recent voyage that everyone was seasick by the second day. When I asked her if the acupressure wristbands we brought along actually worked as advertised to prevent seasickness, she was unsure and led us to the doctor's infirmary for an opinion.

Dr. Hughes wasn't in, so Jackie left to page him over the intercom. While we waited, a puffy-cheeked American in her mid-fifties joined us in the infirmary. The trim young Australian doctor entered moments later. Before I could utter a syllable, the woman stepped between the doctor and me and launched into a lengthy monologue about her medical history: "I take a green pill for this problem and a red pill for that problem, and I'm allergic to this, and that gives me diarrhea and . . ."

I watched the doctor's brown eyes glaze over. Most perplexing was that the woman was literally describing her pills by color rather than by name. Upon completing her list, she demanded some seasickness medicine.

The doctor asked a few qualifying questions, then began counting out tablets.

"I hope those won't react badly with the seasickness pills I've already swallowed," she said.

"I'll need to know what you've taken before I can answer that," he replied.

"They're round pink pills about this big," she said.

The doctor's face twitched. "*Perhaps* you should go to your cabin and bring me the bottle."

The woman scowled. "What kind of doctor are you anyway!"

An awkward silence hung in the air before she turned on her heels and left in a huff to get her pills.

I hesitated a second, then held my hand out to the doctor and said, "Hi. I'm Marty, and this is my wife, Deb."

"You two aren't with her?" he asked, gesturing to the space where the woman had been standing.

I chuckled. "No, believe me, we're not. I just wanted to find out if acupressure wristbands really work to prevent seasickness."

"It depends on the person. They work for about 20 percent of the people who use them."

We continued our conversation for several minutes, and when Deb and I departed, the doctor handed us each a precautionary supply of seasickness pills—the pretty blue kind.

While neither of us had a history of motion sickness, having a few pills at our disposal seemed like a good idea. As the doctor informed us, the key with seasickness pills is that you must take them before symptoms begin—once the nausea starts, it's too late. Also, like wristbands, they don't work for everyone.

Before long, almost every passenger would have a supply of the little blue pills. No one wanted to risk wasting even one precious day tethered to a toilet.

The Drake Passage wasn't living up to its rough reputation. Though the ocean swell was high enough to make some people ill, Deb and I made it through the first day without incident. I took a pill to be on the safe side but soon decided seasickness couldn't be much worse than the drugged feeling the medicine gave me.

If nothing else, the effect of the waves provided everyone with a good opening subject to use during the awkward getting-to-know-your-shipmates process. A typical conversation would start like this:

"Hi, Seijiro, I didn't see you at lunch. Are you feeling okay?"

"I wasn't feeling too good, but I took a pill and now I feel a bit better."

"You're from Japan, aren't you? . . ."

Other than seasickness, the main introductory subject for conversations was inquiring about one another's career. I was pleased to learn I was one of three writers on the ship. The others were Kitty, a journalist from Hong Kong, and Barb, an American who was writing a book on Antarctic history.

As for the other passengers, the majority had successful, high-powered careers. Surprisingly, most were humble about discussing their work, and no one was as blatant as Mildred had been on the airplane about trying to make an impression. I think we were all eager to get the obligatory small talk behind us.

Even though we were hundreds of miles away from any significant landmass, our Drake Passage voyage was never boring. I spent much of my time outside on the bow enjoying the crisp Antarctic air and photographing the wandering albatrosses. Beautiful slender white birds with black and white wings, wandering albatrosses belong to the order Procellariiformes. The descriptive name for birds in this order (which also includes petrels, prions, and shearwaters) is *tubenose*, and it comes from their ability to drink ocean water and excrete the salt through the tubular nostrils on their upper bills.

Wandering albatrosses are impressive creatures with wingspans up to eleven feet—the widest of any bird. Imagine one flying a short distance overhead. On land it might look like a pterodactyl swooping down to carry you off, but on the ocean there's nothing for size comparison, and you have to remind yourself just how big the bird really is.

As masters of riding the wind currents, wandering albatrosses seldom need to flap their wings. With just a dip of the head or a subtle tilt of tail feathers, they could adjust their flight to keep even with the ship. Sometimes they'd glide in close, and I'd gaze into their shiny black eyes and feel as if I were flying myself.

Wandering albatrosses spend the majority of their lives at sea. When young, they may go five or more years without touching land. When mature, they come ashore on a two-year breeding cycle and lay one egg each time.

Sadly, these great birds are a "vulnerable species" (as classified by the IUCN), with fewer than twenty thousand breeding pairs remaining in the world. Their population is declining because their slow reproduction rate can't compensate for the 10 percent that perish each year trying to scavenge bait from the longlines of commercial fishing boats. Although albatrosses have the entire ocean at their disposal, they seem to prefer the company of ships. Theories for their attraction include curiosity, air currents, and easy access to food churned up in wakes. Whatever the reason, I never would have suspected they were in peril, as one or more were usually gliding nearby.

While my favorite spot on the *Professor Multanovskiy* was on the bow, most of the other passengers preferred the bridge. And who could blame them? The warm and spacious glassed-in control center provided unobstructed views to the bow, port, and starboard sides. Best of all, it was high above the water, so whales and icebergs could be spotted far off in the distance.

Passengers were allowed to visit the bridge twenty-four hours a day and stand or sit anywhere they pleased, as long as they didn't interfere with the operation of the ship. Although navigating in the Antarctic is serious work, the crew kept things light by playing New Age music over the loudspeakers and placing Otto, a five-foot-tall inflatable penguin, at the wheel whenever the ship operated on "Otto-pilot."

For me, being on the bridge was a surrealistic experience. At night, when the stars were shining, I felt as if I were on the *Starship Enterprise*. Like on the *Star Trek* ship, it sported padded captain's chairs, radar screens, and various controls that did who knows what. I couldn't resist sitting in one of the chairs like Captain Jean-Luc Picard, pointing forward, and reciting his famous one-word command, "Engage!"

Also surreal was sailing on a Russian ship with a Russian bridge crew. The captain and his officers always communicated among themselves in their native language, and all the controls were labeled using the Cyrillic alphabet. Having grown up during the Cold War, when the Soviet Union was "the enemy," I wondered what I would have thought as a teenager had I been able to glimpse into the future and see my older self standing on the bridge surrounded by Russians.

My next thought was all too real. Our species had made tremendous progress when both sides in the Cold War showed restraint. If the United States could refrain from attacking a country that actually had nuclear weapons pointed at us, attacking Iraq—a country posing no threat to our borders—was certainly unnecessary. Then I smiled. Perhaps the entire Iraq situation was just a bluff. America was a peaceful country, and no American president—especially one so religious—would order an invasion that would send us back to a more primitive era.

The expedition staff used our time crossing the Drake Passage to turn the *Multanovskiy* into a floating university. Three times a day they presented lectures to educate us on the unique region we were about to visit. For instance, on Tuesday Deb and I attended Olle Carlsson's presentation on seabirds, Ty Milford's slide show on Antarctica's geography, and Jackie McPhadden's talk about the Antarctic food web.

Barb, the Antarctic history author, also gave a series of lectures. When I first met Barb, I was eager to tap into her knowledge and learn more about Sir Ernest Shackleton and his Imperial Trans-Antarctic Expedition. Unfortunately, after only a few questions, she looked at me with obvious irritation and said, "Shackleton wasn't the only explorer down here, you know."

Later, when I learned one of Barb's lecture subjects was "little-known aspects of Shackleton's life," I had to presume unflattering information was on her agenda. Normally I'm open to hearing all sides of a story, but not this time. Shackleton was my official patron saint for the expedition.

While we were visiting his domain, his name could only be spoken with reverence. Anything less would be blasphemy.

Coincidentally, I found several other shipmates who felt the same way about Sir Ernest. Instead of attending Barb's evening lectures, we watched a four-part movie on Shackleton's expedition. Most of the people playing hooky from the lectures had read at least one book about the expedition and were curious to see how it played out on film. To our disappointment, part of the movie was dedicated to an alleged extramarital affair Shackleton had before the expedition. Since none of us had read about the affair in our books, we unilaterally decided that the screenwriter made it up to add spice to the movie. The memory of some heroes should always stay pure.

On Tuesday evening, Deb went to bed early. I was still wound up and decided to walk the ship to see if anyone else was wandering about. As I headed toward the dining room, I heard the distinct sound of a chicken clucking.

"Buck, buck, buck, buck-ock! Buck, buck, buck, buck-ock!" The food served by our European chefs tasted fresh, but not *that* fresh.

I rounded the corner and found three people standing at the dining room bulletin board checking off their meal selections for the next day. The clucking sound was coming from an exotic-looking man in his late forties—apparently he wanted the poultry selection for dinner. The man's head and face were shaved bald, except for a "soul patch" on his chin. The first image that came to mind was a young version of the cleaning solution icon, Mr. Clean. As for his companions, they were an attractive, athletic-looking British couple in their mid-thirties.

We greeted each other and made small talk while I filled in my meal choices. The three of them had such an easy camaraderie, I felt out of place—like the last person to arrive at a party. Then the woman turned to me and said, "We're heading to the bar. Would you like to join us?"

So, I wasn't late for the party after all. The four of us walked upstairs to the empty bar and had a delightful visit. The woman, Sasha, was an executive for a multinational corporation, and her husband, Simon, worked as a management consultant. Emad, the clucking man, was born in Egypt—the son of a diplomat—and lived in several other countries before settling in Switzerland. He spoke five languages, had a doctorate in engineering, and developed fuel cells for a living. Most impressively, he could imitate almost any sound. Though a chicken clucking and a baby crying were his signature effects, he could quickly pick up the vocalizations of almost any animal.

We spent the evening learning about one another's countries, discussing politics, and fretting over the looming war. Two Brits, a Swiss-Egyptian, and an American listening to each other's point of view and agreeing on nearly everything—that's something you don't see every day.

People from at least fourteen different countries were on the *Multanovskiy*, and we were sailing to the only continent on earth that had never seen war. I envisioned us as a microcosm of the world. Could such an internationally diverse group live harmoniously for nine days on a small boat? I looked forward to finding out.

The ship had two side-by-side dining rooms in the lower-level bow. Early in the trip, passengers began self-segregating into their chosen eating area. Segregation wasn't based on age, sex, religion, or nationality. Instead, it was simply the rowdy side and the quiet side.

The two groups separated gradually, and the divisions didn't become firmly established until several days into the expedition. As a result, sometimes the rowdy side would fill up first, leaving Deb and me no choice but to sit on the quiet side. That didn't stop us, however, from laughing and telling humorous stories under the watchful frowns of passengers who were just too serious to appreciate our antics.

A smaller, similarly aged group of us usually dined at the same table. Along with our new international friends Simon, Sasha, and Emad, Americans Michael, Laurel, and Sara also joined us. Michael was a reconstructive eye surgeon; Laurel was an executive in the hotel business; and Sara was a doctor for NASA. With such a successful and well-educated group, one might expect a certain amount of snobbishness, but these people were the antithesis of snob. Everyone had a great sense of humor and took turns providing laughs for each meal. Everyone, that is, except Emad, who was so consistently funny he merely had to change his facial expression to make us chuckle.

Deb and I found the location of our cabin played an important role in both socializing and avoiding seasickness. I wouldn't have traded our cabin for any other room on the ship. Tucked away on the lowest passenger level, our compact living quarters consisted of two small bunks, a desk, a sink, and some storage compartments.

All of the cabins, including the expensive upper-level suite, were utilitarian. The primary differences were a private bathroom and a bit more space. Per maritime tradition, the class and price of the cabins increased with their relative height on the ship. Sailing calm seas makes this arrangement logical—the views up high are better—but when you add waves, everything changes. To demonstrate, put your elbow on a table with your hand in the air. Imagine your arm is the ship, your hand is the suite, and your elbow is a budget cabin. Now add the motion of waves by swinging your arm back and forth like a windshield wiper. Suddenly, your elbow becomes the best, most stable, room on the ship.

The other reason I wouldn't trade cabins was the camaraderie on the lower level. Using the old ocean-liner term for inferior tourist-class cabins, we collectively called ourselves "the steerage passengers." A fitting term, we decided, "Since everyone knows the people in steerage on the *Titanic* had more fun." The atmosphere was like a college dorm. While the upper-level hallways were quiet, private, and tidy, we left our cabin doors open and littered the hallway with boots, coats, and life preservers.

Laurel and Sara shared the cabin next to us and were a pleasure to have as neighbors. Sara always had a smile on her face, and Laurel had the most infectious laugh I'd ever heard. The smallest joke would make Laurel laugh longer than any other human being on Earth. Just when I'd think she was done, another round of laughter would bubble up from her diaphragm. Sometimes, when Deb and I were in our cabin, we'd hear her laugh sift through the walls and start laughing ourselves.

Once, when Laurel was laughing particularly hard, I peeked through their open doorway and found the two attractive dark-haired women busily melting squares of chocolate with a hair dryer. After neglecting to turn off the dryer when leaving their cabin, they had returned to find a gooey piece of chocolate next to the overheated appliance. Loath to waste the candy, Sara dipped an apple into it. The combination was so tasty they decided to make more. When Sara noticed the inquisitive look on my face, she smiled, licked the chocolate from the corners of her lips, and held out a piece of chocolate-covered apple. "Hair dryer fondue. Want some?"

The Drake Passage continued to behave like a sleeping giant. The ship's radar showed a large storm to the south, but along our course, the weather remained mild and the ocean swells peaked at just six to nine feet. On Wednesday morning, Olle announced that we were making great time. If the weather held, we'd stop at Aitcho Island for our first shore landing.

Penguins swimming in the ocean provided the first hint we were nearing land. The Antarctic birds flew through the water using a technique called *porpoising*. Like dolphins, they'd come out of the water to breathe and dive back under in one graceful motion. Sometimes, when many penguins porpoised together, they looked like a large solid body, and I'd have to do a double take to make sure they weren't actually a rising whale.

I was standing on the bow when I overheard two women talking about a "school of penguins" they saw swimming. Calling them a *school* didn't sound correct, but it did bring up an interesting question: what do you call a group of porpoising penguins?

I reasoned that since penguins are birds, which "fly" through the water, the correct term would be *flock*. To verify my hunch, I asked Olle at the next lecture.

Olle was a tall man with gray hair and a goatee. He was in excellent shape and looked like he had spent a good portion of his life at sea. I guessed he was in his early sixties, but it was hard to tell. His playful sense of humor combined with his authoritative demeanor made him the ideal expedition leader.

"I'm not sure," he said before pausing to think. "How 'bout a *gang* of penguins?"

"I know," said someone from the back of the lecture room. "Since they're birds, they must be a *gaggle.*"

"Reminds me too much of geese," said someone in the front. "How 'bout a *pod?*"

Both staff and passengers continued throwing out suggestions until someone near the aisle proposed, "How 'bout a *penguimonium?*"

"That's it!" said Olle.

Everyone promptly concurred—penguimonium was by far the most fitting term.

Despite our enthusiasm for the new made-up word, I consulted some reference books to get a definitive answer. Initially I found several authors who weren't sure what to call a group of porpoising penguins. Instead, they wrote around the issue and limited their terminology to *colonies* of penguins on land. When I dug deeper, I reached a consensus of authors. The correct term is *flock*. Still, as anyone who has seen penguins in action knows, *penguimonium* is a far more accurate word. Merriam-Webster, are you paying attention?

Shortly after lunch, we gathered in the lecture room to receive instructions for our first landing. Weeks before our departure, Quark Expeditions issued every passenger a packet of materials listing the various requirements for the trip. As is typical of any group, a few people still came unprepared. For instance, some didn't bring waterproof boots or pants.

To transfer from the *Professor Multanovskiy* to land, we would ride in twelve-person, nineteen-foot-long, outboard-motor-powered inflatable rafts called Zodiacs. Getting wet was an inevitable part of the experience. While in the Zodiacs, we'd often encounter rain, waves, and spray, and when we disembarked, we'd step into the frigid water near shore. Anyone failing to wear appropriate clothing would become soaked to the skin and risk hypothermia. Fortunately, the expedition staff had extra gear stashed away for forgetful passengers to use.

Also, as we'd soon find out, a few of the passengers overestimated their physical abilities. Regular activities would include climbing steep gangway stairs, getting in and out of unstable Zodiacs, and walking over snow-covered ground. To participate in the expedition, each member had to have a doctor sign a form verifying his or her fitness level. Nevertheless, some people would have difficulty performing basic physical tasks without assistance from a staff member or shipmate.

For those believing dangers only applied to people during Shackleton's era, recent events proved Antarctica is still an unforgiving and dangerous place where things can turn ugly in a hurry. The staff informed us that two weeks earlier, on a different ship, a scuba diver got separated from his partner and was found dead on the ocean floor. A month and a half before that, on the *Professor Multanovskiy*, an unexpected storm came up during a landing. When the Zodiacs couldn't handle the waves, staff and passengers had to huddle together under a makeshift Zodiac shelter until the storm abated twenty-one hours later.

After discussing the requirements and dangers, and making sure everyone was outfitted properly, Olle announced the rules for shore landings:

"First, no one may go to the bathroom on land because urine and feces can take years to decompose in the cold climate. [That's also why sled dogs were banned from the continent in 1994.] Our time on shore will usually last two and a half hours [or fifteen minutes longer than the average bladder can comfortably withstand], so plan accordingly.

"Second, no food or drink is allowed on land. In light of what happened two months ago, we've amended the rules to allow you to bring a bottle of water, but it's for emergencies only—keep it zipped in a pocket. [A sensible rule, in terms of preventing both accidental littering and exploding bladders.]

"Third, you may not approach any animal closer than fifteen feet. However, the animals may get as close to you as they wish—at which point you must resist touching them. [This rule would be the toughest to follow.]

"Anyone ignoring the rules or failing to follow instructions from the expedition staff will be banned from future landings."

The time for our first landing had arrived. Everyone was excited. Some looked forward to wildlife encounters, and others—especially those suffering from seasickness—looked forward to standing on solid ground again. Deb and I were definitely among the people eager to experience the wildlife. We walked down the gangway stairs, boarded the Zodiacs, and sped toward Aitcho Island. An eerie fog limited our view as we approached. Gradually, the island's wide rocky beach and tall rounded hills materialized.

Aitcho Island is located ninety miles west of the Antarctic Peninsula, and it's part of the South Shetland Islands. Being so close to Antarctica, I expected to see lots of snow. Instead, I stepped onto an island with only a few patches of snow and lots of gravel, moss, and guano.

The guano was from the resident penguins. Hundreds of them lined the beach, and they generated quite a racket. Robinlike chirps and donkeylike brays were two of the many noises they made.

Seven species of penguin inhabit the Antarctic region: Adélie, chinstrap, emperor, gentoo, king, macaroni, and rockhopper. Chinstrap and gentoo penguins cohabited this island. Both species were about thirty inches tall and had white chests and black backs. Beyond that, they were substantially different birds. The dramatically marked chinstrap penguins had black skullcaps, white faces, and a thin black line under their chins. They resembled little boys dressed as soldiers. The more plainly marked gentoo penguins had completely black heads except for a white patch above each eye, which gave them a perpetually surprised look.

What gentoos lacked in appearance, they made up for with a curious and playful disposition. Almost all of my close-up penguin encounters were with gentoos. The aloof chinstraps were just too handsome to be bothered with humans and went about their business as if we didn't exist.

Other than my house cat, who I swear is a minion of Satan, I love all animals. If I were to list animals in order of my affection for them, most birds would hover near the middle. But not gentoos—they were way too much fun for a middle ranking. If any species of wild animal is more receptive or friendly to humans, I'm unaware of it. Like most Antarctic animals, they didn't see us as predators. Although they'd flee rapid movement, they couldn't resist taking a closer look at anyone standing still. I was thankful the fifteen-foot-buffer rule applied only to people approaching wildlife and not vice versa.

The three-quarters-grown, down-covered gentoo chicks were especially amusing. They looked like overstuffed toys and ran—squawking with each step—with their wings extended behind their backs for balance. If I knelt down, they'd use their beaks to tug on my camera straps and zipper pulls. If I walked away, they'd follow behind like vocal little shadows.

After we spent some time with the penguins, Olle led us on a hike through the drifting fog. With the intent of reaching the opposite side of the island, we took a direct route up a moderately steep hill. To minimize our impact on the terrain, we walked single file and avoided the moss.

When we reached the top, we threaded our way through small groups of southern giant petrels, Antarctic skuas, and kelp gulls. Although the birds could fly, most stayed where they were and casually watched us. Once again, fear of humans wasn't an issue. In fact, I was able to circle two skuas (gull-like birds with brown plumage), set up the proper camera angle, and shoot their portrait without them even ruffling a feather.

We cut short our bird-watching when Olle spotted a wallow with six female southern elephant seals on a rocky outcrop near the ocean. We hiked down to investigate. Elephant seals are the world's largest seals. They grow up to twenty feet in length and rank third behind whales and elephants in overall mammal size. Interestingly, no other mammal has a greater size disparity between the sexes. Males weigh up to five times more than their mates and have a large proboscis, which they inflate when roaring. Although I would have loved to see a male, the two-thousand-pound females were quite impressive.

On a good day, elephant seals would never win a mammalian beauty contest. On this day, they looked so miserable they couldn't win a contest against a tapeworm. They were in mid-molt and had large pieces of skin sloughing off their bodies. To get a general idea of their appearance, imagine a giant furry slug with leprosy.

The odor emanating from the seals helped us maintain the fifteen-foot rule. They smelled slightly sweet, like roses, and considerably pungent, like rotting carcasses and excrement. The stench probably came more from what they were lying in than from the animals themselves, as moving from the area to urinate would have required too much energy. Large rocks bordered the wallow, and for all the seals to fit, two had to sprawl on top of the others. The thought of being at the bottom of the pile was enough to make me glad I wasn't an elephant seal. The claustrophobia alone would have driven me to suicide.

Deb sidled up to me and whispered, "Okay, I'm beginning to feel like I'm in a *National Geographic* special."

"Yeah," I answered, "and there are no boring parts to edit out. Everywhere I look there's something new."

"It's amazing this harsh environment can support so many animals."

Deb and I watched and photographed the seals for about ten minutes. We would have stayed longer, but Olle had already taken the rest of our group two hundred feet ahead to yet another remarkable animal. We hurried to catch up.

A lone Antarctic fur seal was sitting upright, supported by his front flippers, on a flat section of rock. Fur seals are truly beautiful animals. They have cute doglike faces, tiny earflaps, dense chocolate-brown fur, and long whiskers. Small when compared to elephant seals, females weigh up to 150 pounds and males up to 460 pounds.

One thing elephant seals and fur seals have in common is that they were both hunted to near extinction. Sealers killed elephant seals for their blubber and fur seals for their luxurious coats. After witnessing how close we could get to the seals, I could only imagine what it was like when they were brutally massacred: one day a pristine beach would be covered with seals and the next it would be covered with blood. Fortunately, international protection arrived before total extinction, and both species have made remarkable comebacks.

We continued along the outcrop until we reached four more fur seals. The handsome pinnipeds watched us for a few minutes before breaking into a sparring match. They chased each other with a rolling bearlike gait and wrestled with the quickness and agility of bears as well. While I observed the battle royal from my ringside seat, I wondered—were they showing off for us, or were we just an irrelevant piece of landscape?

As Olle and the others meandered away, I lagged behind to take some photos. In the midst of setting up a shot, I inadvertently invaded the personal space of a fur seal. He bared his sharp teeth and charged me with a terrifying roar!

I stood tall, raised my hands in the air, and shouted, "I'm big! I'm big!"

Ten feet short of me he stopped, turned, and retreated with a whimper. I had called his bluff.

I wasn't the first person charged by a fur seal. A few minutes earlier, the same thing had happened to Olle. Having witnessed his stand-tall technique, I copied it, trusting my seal would be as predictable as his was. Luckily, the seal stopped when he did, because another foot or two and I might have violated the rule against defecating on shore landings.

With time running out on our Aitcho Island visit, we headed toward the Zodiacs. A small group of us stopped to visit the elephant seals again and lost sight of Olle and the others in the fog. No worries, Dr. Hughes had stayed back with us. We could walk with him to the landing site.

What we didn't know was this was also the doctor's first Antarctic trip. Together, we, "the great explorers," did the impossible and got lost on a tiny island with no trees. When we finally found the Zodiacs, the beach was vacant—except for penguins. Somehow, we had passed by Olle's group without seeing them.

While Deb and I were on the island, the scuba divers were on their first dive. By the time we returned to the ship, people were already buzzing about a diving incident involving Mildred and her partner, Rose. Apparently Rose was floating on the surface, trying to figure out her gear, when Mildred abandoned her and went down on her own. Henrik, the dive master, helped Rose into the Zodiac, then anxiously scanned the waves for signs of Mildred. No one knew if Mildred was dead or alive until she surfaced twenty minutes later. Even though both women had dive cards and claimed to have extensive experience, their actions indicated otherwise. Rose didn't have the necessary mastery of her equipment, and Mildred had broken the number one rule of diving by leaving her partner. With the latest Antarctic scuba death only two weeks in the past, Henrik prudently banned both women from future dives.

Rose took her banishment gracefully. Mildred, on the other hand, refused to accept her fate and belligerently insisted she'd done nothing wrong. Later that evening she proclaimed, in her deep, gravelly voice, "They ruined my trip, so now I'm going to ruin everyone else's."

While no one who heard Mildred's threat took it lightly, ruining the trip would be a monumental task. The majority of us were having a wonderful time and were eagerly anticipating our next adventure.

We arrived at Deception Island on Thursday morning. Sealers in the early 1800s named the mountainous island for its inhospitable outer shores. They could sail around almost the entire island—looking for a suitable place to land—before spotting Neptune's Bellows, a narrow, windy inlet leading into an interior bay.

Deception Island is a dormant volcano. The interior bay is seven miles in circumference, and it's literally a flooded, collapsed caldera. From the ship, I could see a ring of steep, craggy rock surrounding us. Even so, I had a hard time believing we were actually sailing inside a volcano. Perhaps if I had witnessed the 1923 eruption, when the water in the bay boiled and stripped paint off boats, I would have been more easily convinced.

When Olle mentioned that ongoing subterranean volcanic activity sustained semihot springs at Pendulum Cove, several of us volunteered for a dip. Unfortunately, whipping winds made a Zodiac landing inadvisable.

We went ashore instead at the more sheltered Whaler's Bay. There we were able to see firsthand the devastation caused by the most recent (1967–1970) volcanic eruptions. Black ash and mud had engulfed a British research station, which was active at the time (everyone escaped), as well as the adjacent vacant Norwegian Hektor Whaling Station. Rather than rebuild, the countries left everything in place as an unattended outdoor museum. Included among the partially buried relics were whale-processing equipment, wooden fishing boats, and a rusty tractor.

Visiting Whaler's Bay was a solemn experience. Not for the ruins, but for the remnants of the butchery that happened from 1911 to 1931 when the Hektor Whaling Station was operational. Perfectly preserved whale bones protruded from the volcanic-sand beach—a testament to a coldhearted industry that, if left unchecked, would have exterminated multiple species of whale. Perhaps the eruptions were Neptune's way of saying, "Enough!"

We spotted our first live whales shortly after returning to the ship. Mother and calf fin whales were swimming directly in front of the Hektor Whaling Station. Although Deception Island is a regular stop for the *Professor Multanovskiy,* this was the first time the crew had seen whales inside the caldera.

Fin whales can reach a length of more than eighty feet and are the second-largest whales in the world after blue whales. The IUCN classifies them as an "endangered species." As with all whales we'd see on this expedition, fin whales are baleen whales—toothless whales that feed by taking in ocean water and using the horny bristle-edged plates inside their mouths to trap small sea creatures when they push the water back out.

Everyone on the ship was excited about the fin whales, and many of us laughed at the irony of seeing them in front of the old station. Our encounter, however, was brief and not as close as we would have liked. Since the mother had a calf, the captain prudently kept us at a distance and soon steered us away.

As we departed through Neptune's Bellows, the weather started getting rough (and yes, our somewhat tiny ship was sort of tossed). The temperature was a hair above freezing, the wind was blowing, and we were heading directly into a series of tall swells. When Deb, Emad, Henrik, Dr. Hughes, and I walked to the tip of the bow, Olle spotted us from the bridge and called out over the loudspeaker, "You should come in now. The waves are getting too high. You're going to get wet."

Getting wet was *exactly* what we wanted. We were on a water ride that dwarfed the largest ride at any amusement park. Each time the *Multanovskiy* labored to the top of a wave we'd lean over the chest-high gunwale for a face-first plunge into the trough. Then, if the next wave came quickly enough, the ship would cut through it, and water would gush over the bow.

"Here comes a good one!" I'd yell.

"Whooooooo!" we'd scream in unison as the spray hit us.

"Not big enough," Emad would proclaim.

Our routine continued for several minutes, but the ship wasn't hitting the second wave quite right. Then it happened.

"This is it!" screamed Deb.

"Yessssssssssssssss!" we shrieked, as water whooshed over the bow.

Sopping wet, we howled with laughter and leaned over for the next wave.

Olle's voice boomed over the PA, "Everyone, off the bow. *Now!*"

"Oh, Dad! You always ruin all our fun," I called back with a wink.

As we sloshed inside, Deb declared, "We've been baptized by Neptune!"

The waves remained rough all night. Although a few more people got seasick, Deb and I were still feeling fine. Fighting the motion was the quickest way to become ill. I attributed my good health to thoroughly enjoying each wave and allowing the boat to dictate my direction. Going to bed was especially pleasurable—the waves rocked me to sleep.

Friday morning at six-thirty, Olle's voice crackled over the cabin PA. "Oop-a-dup-a-dooooo! [He really needed to take rooster crowing lessons from Emad.] Ladies and gentlemen, breakfast will be served in the dining room in one half hour."

Wake up calls often came early—something much more painful for Deb than for me. While I would typically already be up, she would usually cover her head with a pillow and mutter something about being on vacation. No one ever forced her to get up, but she knew sleeping in would likely result in missing out on something good. Eventually she'd crawl out of bed and stagger to the dining room for her coffee fix.

In addition to scuba diving, passengers could also pay extra for a sea kayaking option. On this morning, as Deb and I donned our gear for a Zodiac outing to Cuverville Island, the kayakers were already paddling away from the ship.

We were about to descend the gangway stairs when someone yelled, "Whale!"

I looked up just in time to see a minke whale gliding in to check out the kayakers. As baleen whales go, minkes are small. Even so, imagine the size difference between a skinny sixteen-foot-long sea kayak and a mammal that could be as long as thirty-five feet and weigh as much as twenty-two thousand pounds.

Michael was one of the passengers who had selected the kayaking option. Unfortunately, an outfitter in the United States had sold him the wrong class of dry suit for Antarctica's ice-cold water. Without the proper clothing, the kayaking guides couldn't allow him to participate. To Michael's credit, he handled his misfortune gracefully and didn't complain about it ruining his trip.

Then his luck changed. After he missed the initial kayak outing at Aitcho Island, two staff members and one passenger volunteered to take turns lending him a dry suit for the rest of the expedition. Now, minutes into his maiden paddle, he was in the kayak closest to the minke whale. As I watched from the ship, I was thrilled for Michael—and a wee bit jealous. His whale-sized grin said it all.

After the whale's brief visit, we rafted over to Cuverville Island and stepped onto a long, stony beach. We had two hours to explore on our own. Since Deb and I desired a little privacy, we paused to see where the others were headed and walked off in the opposite direction.

Beyond the beach, we found a snowfield that flowed down from the low interior mountains. Hundreds of gentoo penguins had congregated on the snow, and some were climbing the slope and tobogganing down on their bellies—the penguins had their own ski resort.

Where the snow leveled off, it took on the distinct reddish tint of penguin guano. In fact, whether we were on the snow or rocks, our boots continually squished through excrement. Our walking mantra was, "Don't slip, don't slip, do not slip, don't slip, don't slip, do *not* slip!"

Nevertheless, I didn't go on this expedition to take hundreds of photographs angling down on my subjects. Creating the proper image sometimes required getting on the ground and literally rolling in guano—*squish, click, squish, click, squish, click!*

I was thankful for my waterproof pants and parka.

Our wildlife sightings on this island were limited to penguins and skuas. A greater variety of animals were certainly around, but the mountains restricted our exploration to the area near the beach.

When the time came to walk back to the Zodiacs, Deb and I found ourselves cut off by a thick wall of penguins that stretched from the mountainside to the ocean. Returning would be impossible without breaking the fifteen-foot-buffer rule. We zigzagged through the colony and paused often to let penguins waddle out of our way. Though we felt badly about infringing on their space, no one in the colony seemed to mind.

Upon reaching the Zodiacs, Deb looked at me and announced, "Honey, you're a mess!"

She was right—I was covered with penguin poo. A modified version of Black Sabbath's song "Iron Man" popped into my head. Since I could only remember one line from the original song, my lyrics were simple:

> *I am Guano Man!*
> *Na, na, na, na, naaa*
> *Na, na, naaa, naaa!*

Happily humming my new song, I waded into the ocean and washed off the guano. Once I was clean, I stepped into the bow of the Zodiac.

Entering behind me was the woman with the colorful pills, whom I'd met in the infirmary. Following Zodiac boarding protocol, I sat on the pontoon and slid toward the stern to make room for her. The woman hesitated, reached into her pocket, pulled out a tissue, and began wiping the pontoon.

Deb sat on the pontoon opposite me. When our eyes locked, she flashed a wide grin. I bit my tongue, trying not to laugh, but the combined sight of the woman cleaning her sitting spot and Deb's mischievous smile was almost too much to take. I looked away, regained my composure, and avoided making eye contact with my wife for the next few minutes.

Ty, our Zodiac driver, was a quiet man with the outdoorsy yet unblemished look of someone who could be a model for an outdoor equipment catalog. At his suggestion, rather than returning directly to the ship, we went on an iceberg tour. Since the woman with the pills was the last person to board, she ended up in the bow. Though she was dressed head to toe in rain gear, she soon began complaining about the spray from the waves. When I volunteered to switch places with her, she had to decide between putting up with the splashes and sitting on an "unclean" section of pontoon. After one more splash, she accepted my offer. I moved to the front and averted my eyes. If I caught a glimpse of either the woman wiping or Deb smiling, I would've had to bite through my tongue to keep from laughing.

Floating ice comes in all shapes and sizes. While *iceberg* is a familiar term for a massive piece of ice that has broken off from a glacier, smaller pieces of ice also have their own names. For instance, fragments of ice that look slushy are called *brash ice, growlers* are sports-car-sized hunks of low-floating ice, and *bergy bits* are larger and higher floating than growlers.

Deb loved to say *bergy bits.* She'd pronounce the term in an endearing, childlike manner, and use it as often as possible—even if it had little to do with our conversation.

Marty: "Weren't the penguins wonderful? They cracked me up."

Deb: "Yes, especially when they were swimming around the burrr-geee bits."

Ty piloted us into a bay bordered by snow-covered mountains. A foggy drizzle muted our view, and the peaks faded into low clouds. Before us was a labyrinth of bergy bits and icebergs. Most of the ice formations were smooth and ringed with horizontal depressions, almost as if whales had licked them like giant ice cream cones, and many were larger than a two-story house. We were getting only a hint of their true dimensions, however, as roughly 90 percent of an iceberg floats below the surface.

The water was so clear we could see huge formations extending far beneath our raft. In some places, turquoise-colored ice shelves jutted beneath us, giving the water a swimming pool-like appearance.

As inviting as the water looked, its temperature wasn't the only reason to stay dry—a curious leopard seal had swum over to check us out. Reaching ten feet in length and weighing up to one thousand pounds, leopard seals are second after orca whales at the top of the Antarctic food chain. The seals are called "leopards" as much for their spots as for their aggressiveness. According to Alfred Lansing's account of the Shackleton expedition, crewman Thomas Orde-Lees barely escaped when a leopard seal chased him across the pack ice. Even so, unprovoked attacks are extremely rare.

Our seal wasn't aggressive at all. She'd rise vertically out of the water, look at us, swim underneath our Zodiac, and do the same thing on the opposite side. Once she figured out we weren't prey or competition, she lost interest and swam off into the mist.

Our iceberg tour had been so rewarding I barely noticed the continuous drizzle and occasional splashes. My cameras, on the other hand, weren't as water-resistant as I was. By the time we returned to the *Professor Multanovskiy,* my Canon film camera and Sony digital were both fogged up inside and unusable. Fortunately, I had packed a spare film camera in my luggage. On previous trips, I chided myself for bringing more photo gear than needed. For once, I was glad I hadn't packed light.

Even with the extra camera, my photo taking would be limited. My two most powerful lenses had been with me on the Zodiac, and now they were also temporarily out of commission. The only dry lens I had left was a small wide-angle zoom, which was unsuitable for images of distant wildlife. I'd have to be satisfied with scenic shots when photographing from the ship.

I put my damp gear in the cabin to dry and headed out to the bow with camera number three and the little lens. Joining me were Deb, Emad, and Paul. Emad had a huge top-of-the-line Canon telephoto lens mounted on his camera, and Paul, the documentary cinematographer, had a similarly long lens mounted on his camera.

Observing their oversized equipment, I turned to Deb and said, "I feel so inferior."

Paul and Emad immediately picked up on my double entendre and showed off their lenses in a suggestive manner.

"So that's why you boys keep buying bigger lenses," said Deb, snickering with amusement.

"Emad, I've lusted after your lens from the day I first saw it," I said.

"Yes. It's very big, isn't it?" he replied.

"Is it heavy?"

"Yes, it's quite heavy."

"May I hold it?"

"Here, let's trade lenses for a while."

As soon as I attached Emad's lens to my camera, Olle announced over the PA, "There are two humpback whales at one o'clock!" (Olle often used the face of a clock to indicate direction, with the bow at twelve and the stern at six.)

When I turned to take a photo, I realized Emad's unfortunate situation. "I suppose you want your lens back already."

"Yessss!" he hissed.

We quickly exchanged lenses and leaned over the gunwale to look for the whales. They were right next to the boat! I had the perfect lens after all.

For the next twenty minutes, the humpbacks did what Captain Nesterov said he'd never seen whales do before—they literally played with the ship. The captain steered the *Multanovskiy* in a slow circle while the whales took turns surfacing on one side, diving under, and resurfacing on the other. Each time they dived, we'd all race to the opposite side of the ship and wait for them to come up again. The water was so smooth and clear, we could see them rising (we'd spot their white flippers first and then their black bodies) and have our cameras ready when they emerged. When I ran out of film, I hurried down to my cabin, grabbed my freshly dried digital camera, and still had time for more photos before the whales moved off.

Listed by the IUCN as a "vulnerable species," humpback whales reach forty-nine feet in length and weigh up to sixty-six thousand pounds. They're famous for their extra-long flippers, friendly disposition, and spectacular breaching.

To the best of my knowledge, Deb was the only expedition participant lucky enough to see a humpback breach. It happened later in the trip, while she was standing alone on the side walkway. A humpback came straight out of the water three times in a row, each time landing on its back with a thunderous splash. When she reported her sighting, we were all incredibly jealous—especially when we learned the whale was right next to the ship.

The thrill of seeing humpback whales up close leaves each person with a specific unforgettable memory. For some, it's the whales' huge size, incredible beauty, playful disposition, or earthy smell. For me, it's the sound they made releasing air from their blowholes when they surfaced. *Pssshhhhhhhhhhhhhp!*—it was much louder than I expected, like sea monsters.

Because humpbacks are inquisitive animals with little fear of boats, whalers were able to slaughter them by the tens of thousands before they became a protected species. While I can't imagine an ethically justifiable reason for killing a whale—especially in modern times—I have no problem imagining what a hunt is like:

> A whaling ship motors through the morning mist. A mother humpback hears the noise and swims over to investigate. "Hi, I'm a humpback whale, and this is my baby. Do you wanna be friends?"
>
> The soulless whaler can't see the beauty or sense the intelligence—all he sees is a commodity. He pulls the trigger.
>
> *Ka-boom!* An exploding harpoon pierces the mother humpback's flesh, shocking every nerve in her body. Her blood pours into the ocean, as she slowly dies in agony.
>
> The whaler smiles.
>
> The baby humpback frantically nuzzles his mother. "Wake up!"
>
> As blood covers the baby's eyes, his world turns red. Confused and frightened he floats by his mother's side, softly whistling a song of sorrow.
>
> *Ka-boom!* His world goes black.
>
> The whaler smiles.

Fact: One of the hunting methods used by whalers is to wound a calf and wait for its cries to lure in the mother and other nearby whales. Once the group is in range, they kill them all. Though this method of hunting is now illegal, not every whaler follows every law.

Since 1986, the International Whaling Commission has maintained a worldwide ban on commercial whale hunting. The ban isn't permanent, however. In fact, a proposal from Japan to reinstate whaling was defeated as recently as the June 2005 IWC annual meeting (the vote was twenty-three in favor to twenty-nine opposed).

Even with the ban, whalers from Norway, Japan, Iceland, and various native villages slay almost fifteen hundred whales per year. Norway justifies its actions by refusing to acknowledge the validity of the regulations; Japan and Iceland claim their hunts are for "scientific purposes"; and native people are allowed hunts for "cultural and subsistence purposes." Whatever their excuse, I don't have a problem with it, as long as each whaler agrees to tie the anchor end of the harpoon rope around his testicles before firing.

After our humpback adventure, we ate lunch and prepared for our only landing on mainland Antarctica. Setting foot on the continent was a planned but not guaranteed part of the expedition. Sudden changes in ice or weather conditions could thwart our goal without notice. Deb and I, however, were unconcerned. We had spoken Sir Ernest Shackleton's name with reverence and been baptized by Neptune. A successful landing was not in doubt.

We dropped anchor in Neko Harbour. Gigantic cliffs of glacial ice bordered the narrow bay to the north, and a glacier rose from the water like a ski slope to the south. Our Zodiac glided across the calm water to the southern shore, and we stepped onto Antarctica.

As I looked out over the snow-covered mountains, a shiver of appreciation worked its way up my spine. Early explorers had reached Antarctica at great risk and with enormous sacrifice. The continent didn't become readily accessible until modern ice-hardened ships with advanced navigation systems replaced antiquated wooden ships that navigated with a sextant. Although our journey couldn't compare to the adventure of the early expeditions, it didn't lessen the thrill I felt of standing on the last continent on earth to be discovered.

We had the option of mingling near shore with the gentoo penguins or following Ty on a hike to the top of the glacier. Since reaching the summit would require a moderately steep climb through calf-high snow, I figured about half our group would be physically unable to make the ascent. Therefore, I was surprised when we started walking and only a few people remained behind.

Soon nickel-sized snowflakes began parachuting from the clouds. We paused to stick out our tongues and catch a few of the magical flakes. By the time we reached the halfway point, the air was so thick with fluffy snowflakes that the *Multanovskiy* below looked like a ghost ship fading into the underworld.

Though the snow muffled the sound of our voices, Antarctica wasn't a quiet place. Every few minutes we'd hear the rumble of an avalanche or a glacier giving way. We'd look across the bay, expecting to see an ice cliff plunging into the water, but each time the source of the noise was out of sight.

"Wouldn't it be great if one of those glaciers calved off?" said Deb as she pointed north.

As if on cue, a cliff started to crumble. What sounded like distant thunder soon intensified into a roar, as an ice chunk the size of the *Endurance* crashed into the water! Shackleton was saying, "Hello."

Upon reaching the summit, we all plopped into the snow to catch our breath and revel in the beauty of Antarctica. Looking toward the toe of the glacier, we could just make out the black specks of the penguin colony and the clusters of white brash ice floating in the blue-green water.

While I mounted my camera onto my monopod/trekking pole and took some photos, Deb got into a playful snowball fight with some of the others.

The purity of Antarctica made us feel like kids again.

Not wanting to miss out on the fun, I turned to Ty and asked, "Is it okay if I slide down the glacier?"

"No, you better not. A sprained ankle would ruin your trip."

"Aw, come on, Dad," I whined in my best little boy voice. "I promise to be careful."

"You'll break your camera," he said sternly.

"I'll hold it in my lap. It'll be fine."

Ty was about ten years younger than me. My little-boy act caught him off guard. "Okay, but slide over there where you won't hit anyone."

"Thanks, Dad!"

I moved to where Ty had pointed and secured my camera. The powdery snow blanketing the glacier's icy crust was more than a foot deep. Even though the incline here was steeper than where we had hiked up, I didn't expect to be able to slide very fast on my rear end.

I was wrong. Speed wouldn't be a *problemmmmm!* Snowflakes plastered my face as I shot down the hill.

Simon and Sasha were halfway down the glacier, unaware I was directly above them. When they too started to slide, I plunged my feet into the snow to avoid colliding with them and then followed in their track. I reached bottom, gleefully grinning, gliding on my back with my knees against my chest.

While the fetal position was great for speed, it had funneled snow underneath my shirt. Normally snow against my bare back would feel cold, but on this day I was ten years old again, playing in the northern Minnesota winter. Feathers wouldn't have felt any warmer. I fanned out my shirt and watched the flakes float to the ground.

I had a debt to pay for our successful Antarctica landing. Besides Shackleton and Neptune, another larger-than-life being had been guiding our expedition. Now, on Antarctica, I could finally follow through with the favor I had promised to Atlas.

Before taking on such a Herculean task, however, I wanted to give Deb my camera so she could snap a photo for posterity. I waited until she had walked most of the way down the glacier before calling out, "Deb, I need you!"

When she arrived, I glanced down at the guano-stained snow. The penguins on the lower section of the glacier added an unexpected element. Had I been thinking, I would have made use of the clean snow near the summit. Oh well, a promise is a promise. I leaned over, pushed the top of my head against the glacier, propped my hands out on either side for balance, and lifted my legs straight into the air. Anywhere else I would have been doing a headstand, but here on Antarctica I was holding up the world!

Perhaps you remember a brief unexplained sensation of falling on February 21, 2003. I could only hold the world for a few seconds—just long enough to provide a short break—and Atlas wasn't ready to get it back so soon. We almost fumbled the exchange.

The euphoria of walking on the Continent of Peace came crashing down as Deb and I approached the Zodiacs. Mildred, furious with Olle for refusing to overrule Henrik's decision to keep her from diving, was in the midst of a tirade. "You're a male chauvinist pig!" she screamed.

Her diatribe continued with words I won't repeat here. What I will say is that each time she paused, Olle calmly tried to explain his position. No matter what he said, she just grew more belligerent. When Olle's face reddened, I thought he might explode in anger, but to his credit, he kept his cool and walked away. Mildred followed, bellowing at his back.

Deb and I boarded one of the three Zodiacs, hoping we'd made a correct choice. No such luck—Mildred plopped down on the pontoon directly across from me. Since Olle was piloting one of the other Zodiacs, she continued her argument with anyone in earshot. "They won't let me dive because I made one mistake. This entire trip is disorganized. Quark Expeditions has been totally unprofessional. . . ."

I ignored her for a while, but unlike Olle, I had paid a lot of money to come down here, and tolerating ill-mannered shipmates wasn't in my job description. Speaking in my most authoritative voice I said, "First, Mildred, this trip has been well organized from day one. If *you* weren't prepared, that's *your* problem! Second, Antarctica is an unforgiving place. I'm not a diver, and even I know the number one rule of diving is that you *never* leave your partner!"

"You don't know what you're talking about!" she screamed, launching into another rant. Again, I won't repeat all her words. What I will say is that according to her, everyone on the ship was conspiring to make her miserable.

I shook my head in disgust. Arguing was futile. Thank Neptune; the ship was only a short distance away.

We remained on the *Professor Multanovskiy* only long enough to eat a snack and sail a short distance south to Paradise Bay. The aptly named bay was dotted with blue-streaked icebergs and surrounded by beautiful glacier-covered mountains. Everything sparkled in heavenly shafts of sunlight, which pierced through gaps in puffy white clouds.

We boarded the Zodiacs and headed across the bay for a late-afternoon cruise. As we passed a cluster of small odd-shaped icebergs, Deb couldn't resist announcing, "Burrr-geee bits!"

When I turned to smile at my wife, Ty shouted, "Humpback!"

I snapped my head toward the bow just in time to see the whale surface beside the Zodiac in front of us. "Wowwwwwwwwwwwww!" I said, drawing out the word until the whale disappeared.

Humpbacks are so huge that their surfacing and diving routine often seems to take place in slow motion. Not every dive was the same, but the best ones—like the one I had just watched—concluded with a tail hanging in the air for just a moment before it disappeared underwater.

The only flaw with a sight so grand was that it was at least a quarter mile away—we were in the wrong raft again. Ty gunned the engine to bring us closer, but by the time we arrived, the whale had moved off. Because this one had a young calf at her side, she was more cautious than the humpbacks from earlier in the day. Once she satisfied her curiosity, she led her baby to the far side of the bay. Rather than pursue, we gave them space.

A half hour later, on our way back to the *Multanovskiy*, Ty spotted a leopard seal lounging on a low benchlike section of iceberg. The rotund two-toned-gray seal was unconcerned with our presence and allowed us to move in close for as many photos as we desired. While we were busy with our cameras, another leopard seal swam in and spy-hopped—popping out of the water like a periscope—multiple times. Though the new arrival obviously aimed to acquire the occupied prime section of ice, the reclining seal had no desire to move and closed his eyes for a snooze.

On any other day, our leopard seal experience would have been the talk of the ship, but on this day, humpbacks ruled!

Before the expedition, Deb considered signing up for the scuba diving option, and I considered the kayaking option. Once the trip started, we never regretted passing on the options, as we would have missed too many wonderful Zodiac and shore-landing experiences. Deb was especially pleased with her decision, because the divers were reporting that the sea life was sparse, small, and dull colored.

The divers did have one notable exception to the mundane, however. They got to swim with the humpback whales!

As one of the divers told us, "The most amazing thing about the whales was the control they had over their huge bodies. They gracefully swam between us without ever touching us—we felt like such klutzes."

Shipmate discussions about whales often revolved around the aura of intelligence they projected. In contrast to our observations, I found a statement on the Japan Whaling Association Web site equating whale brainpower with that of cows or deer. Though the JWA obviously wants people to think they're only proposing to kill "dumb" animals, it does bring up the question: how do you measure whale intelligence?

Humans still have much to learn on the subject. The first studies of whale songs as a form of communication didn't even begin until the early 1970s. In addition, conflicting physical characteristics complicate intelligence estimates. Although whale brains are physically larger than human brains, they're smaller in proportion to their bodies. Conversely, the folds in the cerebral cortex (which scientists consider a trait of intelligence) are more numerous in whales than in humans.

One thing we do know is that humpback whales work cooperatively, blowing bubbles to herd small prey together for efficient consumption. The use of tools, in this case bubbles, points to a high level of intellect. Where whales rank on the intelligence scale in relation to other animals may not be known for many years, but putting them in a class with cows is insulting. As much as I like cows, a "moo" just doesn't compare to a complex whale song, which may contain information about food, location, migration, and mating.

As soon as we returned from our Zodiac cruise, wind and snow moved in to whip up a blizzard. I walked downstairs to my cabin and hung up my parka. Though I had rinsed off the parka at Cuverville Island, the pungent smell of penguin guano wafted through the room. I decided to move it to a hook in the hallway. When I stepped out the door, Sara and Laurel were there removing their boots.

Laurel looked at me and scrunched up her nose. "You're not gonna hang *that* out here, are you?"

"Me? No. I was just gonna throw on some shoes and head up to the deck to hose it off," I lied.

Now committed, I carried the parka outside to the boot washing station and started scrubbing. Soon the ricocheting high-pressure spray had me soaked to the skin. I returned to the cabin, hung up my clean parka and wet clothes, and lay down for a nap.

I had barely closed my eyes when Olle clicked on the PA: "Minke whale at eleven o'clock!"

Whale sighting announcements were becoming increasingly common. In fact, many passengers were now either ignoring them or watching from the bridge. For me, each sighting was still cause for excitement. I slipped into some lightweight pants and a windbreaker and ran up to the bow.

By the time I reached the gunwale, the minke was gone. Since no one else was outside, I started back in. Halfway to the door a thought turned me around: "When will I ever have a chance to experience an Antarctic blizzard again?"

I returned to the tip of the bow. Simon soon joined me, and together we faced into the wind and looked out for whales.

The temperature was near freezing, and the speed of the ship pushed the windchill even colder. Since the blizzard contained more wind than snow, we could still see several hundred feet in front of the ship—if we squinted.

When another minke whale surfaced, Simon and I turned and looked up to the bridge to see if anyone there saw it as well. To our surprise, more than a dozen passengers were watching us through the glass—we had an audience.

Though we were both outwardly too mature to admit to it, an unspoken contest of who could withstand the blizzard longer had begun.

In my regular Antarctic gear, I could have stayed outside indefinitely. But now, dressed in clothing only suitable for a brief whale sighting, I felt chilled for the first time on the trip. As for Simon, I don't know what he had on underneath his nylon parka, but he certainly wasn't wearing the usual layers. Every few minutes he'd jump up and down to speed up his circulation.

I'm proud of living in Montana, but in frigid weather I revert to my northern Minnesota roots. Part of being a Minnesotan is believing that the state is actually located a few miles west of the North Pole. In fact, any Minnesotan caught losing to a Brit in a cold-weather tolerance contest would be promptly excommunicated and set adrift on the ice of Lake Superior.

We stood in the wind and talked for what seemed like hours. Simon kept me laughing with his dry humor, and I did my best to reciprocate. The laughter was good for both of us—it helped pass the time and made us look as if we were unaffected by the cold. I wish I could quote for you parts of our conversation, but all of the blood that normally occupies the memory section of my brain was busy trying to keep me warm. I honestly can't recall a word we said.

Eventually, at least for me, cold-weather tolerance became secondary to bladder capacity. Perhaps Simon was getting outside help. Shackleton would never allow a fellow Brit to lose to an American in Antarctica. On the other hand, I definitely had Atlas on my side.

Olle ultimately saved our egos with an announcement over the PA: "Dinner is now being served in the dining room."

Our contest had ended in a draw. Simon and I walked together to the side door.

"After you."

"No, that's okay, you first."

The blizzard concluded shortly after dinner, and by evening the weather was calm. We anchored for the night in a sheltered bay near Vernadsky Station. The Ukrainian-run research facility was located on a tiny island off Antarctica's western shore. We were now approximately

250 miles down the Antarctic Peninsula and had reached the southernmost point of our trip. In the morning, we'd raft over to the station for a visit and then head north.

Other than when we had anchored for Zodiac landings, this was the first time the *Professor Multanovskiy* wasn't moving. Now that I had my sea legs, walking about the stationary ship required extra concentration. I kept feeling as if I should grab a railing or shift my weight to compensate for the roll of the waves.

Falling asleep was even more difficult than walking. After four nights of the ship rocking me to sleep, my body craved the motion. Now I understood why sailors become addicted to the ocean. Months on the water would make a stationary bed feel stifling—like being strapped to a gurney.

At the same time, the night without movement was great therapy for our seasick shipmates. By morning, everyone was back to normal.

Emad and I were pleased our fellow passengers felt better, but it was now Saturday—the expedition was more than half over—and we had yet to experience the massive waves of a true ocean storm.

Each morning I'd check the weather forecast on the ship's bulletin board—"Damn! Another beautiful day."

As for Emad, whenever the subject of storms came up, he'd break into a chant of "Rock and roll! Rock and roll! Rock and roll!"

Frequently, we'd check with Olle to see if the extended forecast showed any hint of oncoming bad weather. Each time he'd look at us as if we were crazy and say, "You *really* don't want a big storm. Trust me. But I'll see if I can order up a one-hour demonstration storm for you."

Olle gave us a nickname, which we proudly accepted. We were the Storm Boys.

We cruised over to Vernadsky Station after breakfast. The facility was called Faraday Station until 1996, when Ukraine acquired it from the United Kingdom and renamed it after scientist Vladimir Vernadsky. The historically significant station is the oldest post on the Antarctic Peninsula, and it's where scientists made the discovery of the hole in the ozone layer.

The building itself wasn't as interesting as its history. The main floor was a simple, long hallway connecting living quarters and offices. The highlight of our tour was the attic, because it contained the atmospheric and meteorological equipment. The base commander gathered everyone around and pointed to a large piece of equipment. "This is very important," he said solemnly. "The name of the machine used to discover the hole in the ozone layer is Daphne."

The base commander doubled as postmaster, giving us the opportunity to mail home postcards with a Ukraine-Antarctica postmark. Although delivery was supposed to take six weeks, the cards Deb and I mailed would take ten months to reach their destinations.

Our ability to freely visit a Ukrainian research station is an example of what makes Antarctica such an exemplary model for international cooperation. In the early 1900s, seven nations claimed large portions of territory on the continent, and three of the claims overlapped. In 1959, twelve nations originated and signed the Antarctic Treaty. Although the treaty didn't invalidate the seven historical claims, it did make them irrelevant. Key issues in the treaty include limiting the use of Antarctica to peaceful activities, keeping the continent free of nuclear explosions and waste, cooperative sharing of all scientific discoveries, and unrestricted inspections of boats and stations. The Madrid Protocol, an important treaty amendment, was added in 1991 to ban mining until 2041. As of 2005, forty-five countries had signed the Antarctic Treaty, and twenty-six maintained scientific research stations on or near the continent.

Our day was just getting started. After our Vernadsky Station visit, our schedule included a late-morning landing at Petermann Island followed by an afternoon Zodiac cruise through the Iceberg Graveyard.

Petermann Island provided us with our first opportunity to see Adélie penguins. Adélies are classic "dinner-suit" penguins with a white front, black back, and black head. What made them memorable were their exotic eyes, which had large black pupils and light-blue irises framed with a thin band of white. The splash of blue jumped out from the otherwise black-and-white setting.

Overall, Adélies were every bit as handsome as chinstrap penguins, and they seemed to share their aloof disposition as well. They had no desire to approach us and waddled about as if we were part of the landscape.

In addition to penguins, an accommodating fur seal also occupied the island. The seal could have had a successful career as a supermodel.

She'd strike a pose, hold it for a moment, change positions, and pose again. After everyone had enough photos of her on all four flippers, she rolled onto her back to provide a more intimate perspective. Similarly, like a supermodel, she roared when we stopped paying attention to her.

The Iceberg Graveyard is the unofficial name for Pléneau Bay. Ocean currents carry icebergs into the bay, where they run aground to form a sculpture garden of awesome beauty. Perhaps a more fitting name for the bay would be Neptune's Cathedral, as it looked as if a supernatural being had carved all the icebergs. For instance, one iceberg resembled the Great Sphinx of Giza, and another resembled the face of the Statue of Liberty.

One of the most impressive formations was a huge iceberg shaped like a band shell. I imagined the animals using the shell for concerts when humans weren't around. A typical show would begin with a tuxedoed Adélie penguin swimming to center stage and introducing the entertainment for the evening: "Ladies and gentlemen, please put your flippers together and welcome the new Antarctic sensation—Minke and the Whales!"

The colors were spectacular. Injected into pure-white icebergs were nature's most beautiful shades of blue. Some veins of ice were windshield-washer-fluid blue, like the glaciers I'd seen in Canada, and others were greenish blue, with a little more green than blue. Each iceberg glistened under the cool Antarctic sun.

The combination of vivid colors and chiseled shapes created a dreamlike atmosphere. Even the inquisitive leopard seal that swam up to greet us seemed more like a mermaid than a thousand-pound carnivore. I felt as if I were in a living Maxfield Parrish painting.

Bringing us back to reality, Deb and I were once again stuck on a raft with Mildred—and her mood wasn't improving with time. We were under strict orders not to stand in the Zodiacs, and with six people sitting on each pontoon, one or more passengers would invariably end up in the way of someone else's photo. In such instances, whoever was blocking the shot would simply lean over or kneel down. No one ever took a request to move personally—except Mildred.

Near the end of our cruise, she misinterpreted a move request intended for someone else and threw herself on the Zodiac floor like a two-hundred-pound child. "Fine, I'll just stay down here where I won't be in anybody's way," she whined.

Zodiac drivers stand when they steer, so they can more easily see obstacles ahead. When Mildred launched into her tantrum, she landed at Olle's feet. A little more momentum and she would have knocked him into the water. Somehow, Olle managed to control his temper and ignore her. As for the rest of us, we likely shared the same thought: "Let's throw her overboard. She's wearing a life jacket. We can always pick her up later."

We returned to the *Professor Multanovskiy* and gathered in the dining room for tea. By now, Mildred was infamous throughout the ship, and many people had stories of encounters with her. While some laughed when hearing about her tirades, others were concerned that she might progress beyond words and become physically violent.

If, as I had envisioned earlier, our internationally diverse group was indeed a microcosm of the world, then Mildred was a nation of one, trying to start a war when others desired peace.

The captain anchored the ship for the evening in a bay near Port Lockroy "Base A." The two-person staff from the British station rafted over to join us for a barbecue on the bow. The temperature was thirty-five degrees, and an invigorating breeze swept down from the surrounding ice cliffs. To counteract the chill, Katja the bartender brewed up a tasty batch of hot rum punch.

Food for the barbecue included steak, chicken, corn on the cob, and beans. Even though the cooks served us directly from the grill, our food was cold by the time we carried it to the table. No one seemed to mind, however—we were having a picnic off the coast of Antarctica!

Our usual group shared a long table on the port side of the bow. I sat across from Sara and watched as she attempted to cut her steak with the plastic tableware. Before long, her fork splintered into little white pieces. Being a gentleman, I walked over to the grill area and acquired her another one.

When she started back in, her knife snapped in two.

Once again, I retrieved a replacement. Handing it to her, I said, "Are you sure you're really a doctor?"

This time Sara wore the determined look of a surgeon performing a delicate operation. She poised her utensils over her meat and made an incision.

Crrrrack!

She froze with her head down, shards of plastic cupped in her petite hands.

"Thank God you're not my doctor!" I said. "If you were, I'd never make it through airport security. All the broken needles under my skin would set off metal detectors everywhere!"

Soon everyone was laughing and watching to see if the esteemed doctor from NASA would break another utensil. Sara laughed with us, making her task all the more difficult.

She finished her meal using the broken handles of two forks.

On Sunday morning, we rafted over to Port Lockroy "Base A." During World War II, British intelligence thought Germany might use Antarctica as a hiding place for ships and weapons. "Base A" was one of several stations built to monitor such activities. Following the war, Britain used the station for ionospheric research. They closed it in 1962, and it remained vacant until 1996, when the British Antarctic Survey renovated and reopened it. The station is now used for an environmental monitoring program studying gentoo penguins and the effects of human contact.

The Spartanly furnished base was the size of a typical single-story house. A small kitchen and sleeping area accommodated researchers, while other rooms contained a museum about the station's history. The most noteworthy piece of equipment was the Beastie, a renovated ionosande, which researchers once used to gather atmospheric data. The Beastie was bigger than a refrigerator, and it had primitive circuit boards with components the size of my index finger. It looked more like a prop for a mad scientist in an old horror movie than a legitimate piece of scientific equipment.

As we were preparing to leave Port Lockroy, a dozen or so juvenile gentoo penguins in a small cove distracted us. We delayed our departure to watch a live nature show worthy of an Oscar.

I was surprised to discover that penguins have to learn to swim. Beginner chicks would stand in shallow water, lean forward to submerge their heads, hold their pose for several seconds, then joyfully race around the rocks announcing their accomplishment to the rest of the rookery.

Intermediate chicks would flap their wings continuously and thrash their way across the water for short distances. After each demonstration, they'd celebrate their triumph with a loud proclamation of achievement or a vigorous game of chase—running, falling face-first into the water, getting up, and running again.

As we delighted in the slapstick antics of the young penguins, another observer was taking a keen interest in the proceedings: a leopard seal was lurking a short distance off shore. Should a penguin graduate from intermediate to advanced and venture out too far, its accomplishment would be short-lived.

I filmed the penguins using the movie setting on my digital camera. Knowing the leopard seal was within striking range, I was torn as to what I wanted to happen. On one hand, seals have to eat, and filming a successful hunt would be a dramatic event. On the other hand, I was already attached to our flock of little gentoos, and seeing any of them harmed would have been devastating.

As things turned out, the conclusion to the drama would forever be a mystery. Before the leopard seal could make its move, we boarded the Zodiacs and returned to the ship.

Most of us were hungry after our entertaining morning. We were assembling in the dining room for brunch when a shipmate burst through the doorway and blurted out, "Mildred is on the deck stabbing the Zodiacs with her dive knife!"

"They've got to do something about her now!" someone shouted.

"Yes!" everyone agreed.

The PA clicked on. A tense hush engulfed the room as Olle announced, "The rear deck has been closed for repairs and is off-limits to all passengers."

We all knew what Olle really meant—Mildred had finally snapped. She'd have to be disarmed, sedated, and locked up for the remainder of the expedition. We ate our brunch in silence—concerned for the safety of whoever had to disarm her and relieved that our encounters with the woman would finally be over.

Mildred's previous behavior had us primed to believe anything, but this time the story had been blown out of proportion. Eventually I learned, from a reliable source, that Mildred hadn't attacked anything with a knife. Instead, she dressed in her scuba gear and attempted to board the dive team's Zodiac. After Henrik turned her away, she sat on the rear deck and waited. Later, when a crew member walked by, she muttered something about damaging the equipment, so no one else could dive either. Despite the lack of a direct threat, her dive knife became a concern, and the story escalated from there. Once the staff assessed the situation, they decided Mildred wasn't dangerous and reopened the rear deck. As far as I know, she didn't have to be disarmed.

The next time I saw Mildred was on the bow deck, an hour later. While Deb, I, and others enjoyed the sunny afternoon, she sulked on a mooring cleat, refusing to budge.

I moved up to the bridge and watched as we sailed through the Neumayer Channel and entered the Gerlache Strait. Steep mountains towered over the water's edge—some were frosty white with snow, and others were windswept down to slate-gray rock splashed with volcanic-red deposits. Midway through the strait, we passed three leopard seals lying on densely packed brash ice. Moments later Olle announced, "Minke whale at twelve o'clock!"

I hurried back outside. Though the sky had clouded up and a misty rain was falling, the crisp clean air and Antarctic sights made the bow irresistible.

Soon the captain ordered a full stop. He had spotted humpback whales on the far side of a wide but calm bay. It was the perfect opportunity for a final Zodiac cruise.

Giddy for another close encounter, we donned our life jackets and gathered on the bow deck. I was surprised to see Mildred. I thought for sure her sulk would last the rest of the day. She stood in line by the gangway as the staff lowered four kayaks and four Zodiacs into the water. Several people discreetly counted heads and positioned themselves to avoid being trapped on a raft with Mildred—Deb and I did the same thing.

Unbeknownst to us, Mildred intended to board the scuba divers' Zodiac. When Henrik turned her away, she had to choose between staying on the *Multanovskiy* and getting on the last Zodiac for the whales. Her dilemma led to another tantrum. She stomped down the gangway, slipped over several stairs, and leaped into the raft. A nasty argument between Mildred and another passenger ensued, but fortunately Deb and I didn't have to hear it. We were already on our way!

Though once again we were in Ty's Zodiac, this time we reached the humpbacks first. Ty cut the engine as we peered through the rain at the whales. Two were together, several hundred feet ahead of us, and one was a half mile away. When the nearest whales dived, my heart sank. One thing I had noticed about Antarctic wildlife was that animals of the same species could be shy, indifferent, or bold when reacting to people. While I found their varying dispositions fascinating, the last thing I wanted on this day was shy whales.

Psssshhhhhhhhhhhhhp! The humpbacks surfaced eighty feet away and headed toward us!

Everyone gasped as the lead whale drew near. If she stayed on top of the water, she'd swamp our raft!

Instead, when she was almost close enough to touch, she ducked underneath us and resurfaced on the opposite side. We all gasped again, and many of us broke into smiles.

The curious humpbacks were roughly two and a half times the length of our raft. Alfred Lansing had mentioned in his book that Shackleton's crew worried about whales surfacing beneath their dinghies and capsizing them. Some people in our Zodiac had similar fears. While I could see how such an accident could happen, our previous encounters had proven that whales are well in tune with their surroundings—I had complete confidence in them.

As the humpbacks swam around us, sometimes they'd gradually sink underwater, and other times they'd do full-blown dives. I wanted to photograph a tail high in the air during a dive, but doing so wasn't as easy as it looked. On several occasions, the whales came through for me with wonderful displays. It wasn't their fault that each time they flashed a tail I was either changing film or cleaning raindrops off my lens.

Observing the whales was a breathtakingly delightful experience. Every so often, we'd see the water churn as they played with each other—or, as some speculated, mated.

I think the whales enjoyed observing us as well. Since their eyes normally remain underwater when they surface, they'd occasionally tilt their bodies sideways to raise an eye in the air. While the distant whale never approached, the two that were together took their time checking us out. They also investigated the kayaks and the other Zodiacs, so everyone shared in the thrill.

I can't remember an hour and a half ever going by so quickly. Even though the temperature was near freezing and I was wet from the rain, I could have been out there in a swimsuit and never felt cold.

What a privilege to be able to watch humpbacks up close and at water level. In my book, humpbacks are the coolest of the cool!

We awoke on Monday morning to the high rolling swells of the Drake Passage. Although not nearly rough enough to satisfy the Storm Boys, the waves did create an opportunity for fun.

At breakfast, I noticed my shipmates were having a hard time carrying their meals in from the buffet in the opposite dining room. They'd enter with a plateful of food in one hand and a drink in the other. Inevitably, as soon as they made it through the doorway, the ship would rock hard to one side and they'd have to lean the other way to avoid falling against a wall or a table. Then, once they regained their balance, the ship would roll in the other direction and force an opposite reaction.

When someone made a particularly clumsy entrance, I barked out an Olympic-style score, "Two point five!" Soon another person lurched through the doorway, and I announced, "Five point eight!"

Michael recognized the entertainment potential and joined me in rating the entrances. We set up our scoring system on a scale of one to ten with mandatory two-point deductions for spillage and wall or table touches. Entrance speed and grace in handling difficult waves were the primary factors for earning a higher score.

Our game rapidly caught on, and we soon had a panel of international judges representing the United States, Switzerland, Germany, China, and the American Indian Nations. We discussed whether Emad would be the judge from Switzerland or Egypt. In our capacity as the game's founders, Michael and I decided he had to represent Switzerland, since that was where he currently lived. Naturally, since Switzerland was a neutral country, all his scores had to be fives.

The best part of our game was judging people entering for the first time. Barely awake shipmates would stagger into the room and find everyone staring at them. Each steadying touch or drip of coffee on the floor would lead to an audible gasp. After the "contestants" slid into their seats, we'd announce our scores and howl with laughter.

Judging people who got up for seconds was almost as much fun. Knowing we were watching them, some got into the spirit of things and put on a show. While almost everyone enjoyed the game, a few gave us disdainful "humphs" as they toddled by.

When Olle arrived, he nonchalantly put his hand on a wall—the judges gasped in horror. He then sat at the table behind us—the recipient of the morning's lowest score—chuckling whenever we announced another tally. Once he finished his breakfast, he walked toward the door, launched into a perfect midair pirouette, and landed with his plate balanced on one hand and his cup in the other. The judges roared in approval and awarded him perfect tens! Everyone, that is, except Emad, who had to give him a five.

With our return voyage under way, the day's activities consisted mostly of attending lectures and of Emad and me lobbying for a big storm.

Late in the afternoon, Olle invited everyone to the bar for an expedition recap. Surprisingly Sara didn't attend. When Deb and I found her later and asked where she had been, she told us a story that could have been right out of *The Twilight Zone:*

Having been asleep when Olle announced the gathering, she awoke to a ship that appeared abandoned. She checked the halls and dining rooms and saw no one. She looked out on the decks, and they were deserted. She hurried up to the bridge and found only Otto the inflatable penguin at the wheel. In a panic, she ran down to the lecture room and peered around the corner. There she was, sitting on a bench, the lone sign of life on the ship—Mildred!

Okay, sing it with me now: *"Do do do do, do do do do, do do do do."*

Tuesday, February 25, was our last day on the ship. The waves were bigger than at any other time during our voyage. Rougher seas meant most passengers had developed at least some level of seasickness. Deb and Emad were the only ones I knew for sure didn't have any symptoms. I was doing okay. My slightly queasy stomach wasn't enough to keep me from hoping the Drake Passage would stir up more action.

Though I presumed veteran sailors grew accustomed to the waves, I checked with Olle to be sure. "No," he said, "I've worked at sea for eighteen years and still occasionally become ill. Seasickness isn't something you grow out of."

The waves intensified as the day progressed. Emad and I never experienced the big storm we hoped for—but we came close. We stood on the bridge photographing the waves as they crashed over the bow, sprayed high into the air, and splashed against the glass in front of us.

"How high are they now?" I asked.

Olle checked with the captain and repeated the information to me. "Nine meters."

Twenty-nine and a half feet is high enough to wash over a typical two-story house. Nevertheless, since the waves came in rolling swells instead of choppy whitecaps, they didn't look as impressive as their measurements sounded. The *Professor Multanovskiy* handled them with ease.

In 1616, Willem Cornelis Schouten became the first person to sail around Cape Horn (the southern tip of South America). From Schouten's time to the present, treacherous seas have wrecked or disabled hundreds of ships as they've attempted to circumnavigate the horn. Strong winds, heavy currents, and icebergs have all contributed to making the journey a sailor's nightmare.

We were an hour away from Cape Horn when a distress call came over the radio—the Cape had another victim. The *Hexagon* was competing in a solo around-the-world sailboat race when it rolled and broke its boom. A support boat was supposed to be nearby, but it wasn't responding to hails. The *Multanovskiy's* first mate relayed calls on behalf of the *Hexagon* until the support boat answered, forty minutes later. With assistance on the way, we passed a short distance from the crippled sailboat but didn't stop.

As I hurried out the side door of the bridge to photograph the *Hexagon*, Mildred blocked my way with her big body. "Excuse me, I need to get by," I said, but she feigned deafness and refused to move. I pushed past her and stepped onto the narrow walkway just in time to capture an image of the tiny sailboat silhouetted by the jagged mountainside of Cape Horn.

Rumor had it that Mildred planned to catch the next boat to Antarctica and vowed not to return home until she got to scuba dive. While I felt sorry for both her and the passengers of whatever ship she booked, I had to admire her determination.

As for Deb, me, and the vast majority of our shipmates, the voyage had been a spectacular success worth every penny we paid. Our contingent of Swiss, Swedish, Russian, Mexican, Japanese, Italian, German, Finnish, Czech, Chinese, Canadian, British, Australian, and American passengers and crew had delighted in the wonders of the Continent of Peace and learned that nationalities could be irrelevant.

When a group of us discussed the possibility of stepping off the *Professor Multanovskiy* and finding America at war, Deb commented,

"If the leaders of opposing nations were required to sail together to Antarctica before firing a shot, we'd have a lot fewer wars."

Setting aside thoughts of what our president might have done, I concentrated on enjoying the remaining hours at sea. As Cape Horn faded into the distance, the waves died down and I returned to my favorite spot at the tip of the bow. I leaned over the gunwale and inhaled the salty air.

This had truly been an unforgettable journey. Fond memories of curious wildlife, gorgeous scenery, and interesting new friends would follow me north and remain with me for the rest of my life.

I said good-bye to Shackleton and braced myself for civilization.

6
Borneo We're Going to Die

Our guide had abandoned us deep in the jungle. Deb and I were unarmed and didn't have a compass or a map. Our lives were now in the hands of four rough-looking, knife-toting men from the Iban tribe. We trudged single file up a faint trail. Three Iban led the way, followed by me, Deb, and another Iban.

My first concern was my wife's safety. Although the tribe had supposedly given up headhunting for good in the 1970s, what would they do with an attractive blond-haired woman? I tried to form a defense plan, but the results never came out in my favor. I was outnumbered and out of my element. I glanced along the line to size the men up. I looked behind Deb. The Iban in the rear had his gun pointed at her back!

We were on Borneo, the third-largest island in the world. At that particular moment, either of the two larger islands, Greenland or New Guinea, would have seemed like paradise. We had chosen Borneo for our Asia trip because of its exotic reputation. I was looking forward to an adventure that included encounters with interesting people and bizarre animals. The travel gods—who are known for their selective listening—only heard that I desired "an adventure" and nothing about what kind of adventure I sought. To them, being dropped off in the middle of nowhere with four armed men was exactly what I was looking for.

Even before we left the United States, our Borneo trip seemed questionable. Both the war with Iraq and the SARS (severe acute respiratory syndrome) scare were in full swing. Although I figured we had a better chance of winning the lottery than catching SARS, I couldn't help wondering if terrorists would shoot down a commercial airplane in revenge for the war or if we would be poorly received in a predominantly Muslim region. Despite the uncertainties, we never seriously considered canceling our trip. Fear of the unknown wasn't going to dictate our actions.

Borneo is located on the equator south of Vietnam. Sharing the island politically are the Sultanate of Brunei, the Malaysian states of Sabah and Sarawak, and the Indonesian provinces of East, West, Central, and South Kalimantan. Borneo has a population of approximately thirteen million people, 75 percent of whom live in the Indonesian provinces. Of the more than thirty ethnic groups comprising the population, the largest are the Dayaks (which include the Iban and other aboriginal people), Malays, Chinese, and Indonesians. Collectively, the various groups speak nearly one hundred languages and dialects.

The island extends roughly 800 miles from north to south and 650 miles from east to west. Deb and I would remain in Malaysian Borneo throughout our stay, exploring Sarawak in the west and Sabah in the north. Though the Indonesian provinces take up more than half of the landmass, we'd still have a six-hundred-mile-long intra-island flight between Kuching, Sarawak, and Sandakan, Sabah.

Our adventure began on Friday, April 11, 2003, when we landed at Kuching Airport. Our guide, Bayang, picked us up with the Borneo Adventure van. He was a muscular, round-faced man in his early thirties. Although Bayang was a member of the Iban (pronounced *ē-bon*) tribe, he no longer lived with his people in the rainforest. Like many other English-speaking people we'd meet in Borneo, he spoke a dialect that sounded like a hybrid of English and Iban or Malay. Deb and I had a hard time understanding him but could usually recognize enough words to figure out what he was trying to say.

"How's the war?" he asked.

The question, spoken in perfect English, caught me by surprise. I wasn't sure how to answer it. Can war ever be good? Back home, when George W. Bush ordered the attack on Iraq, I was angry. Here, I felt something I never thought I'd feel about my country—I was ashamed.

Attacking another nation without provocation just seemed un-American to me.

"We wish there wasn't a war," I said.

"Peace is always a better answer," added Deb.

"Yes, peace is better," agreed Bayang.

Since we wouldn't depart for our backpacking trip until the following morning, Bayang dropped us off at the Kuching Hilton. After our long overseas flight (the airline's route actually took us more than halfway around the world), we had to resist the temptation to indulge in a midday snooze. If we didn't force ourselves to stay awake until evening, we'd be up again in the middle of the night and off schedule for days. We showered, dressed, and decided to go for a walk.

Hand in hand, we strolled across the street to the waterfront. Leafy trees, circular gardens, and manicured grass buffered us from city traffic, while schoolchildren scurried by on the brick walkway paralleling the Sarawak River. We intended to follow the walkway, but a surprise downpour forced us to find shelter under the eaves of a food stand.

As a steamy mist from ricocheting raindrops enveloped us, we watched small fishing boats putter up and down the quarter-mile-wide river and tried to wait out the storm. When the rain outlasted our patience, we dashed back to the hotel, laughing as our freshly changed clothes became shapeless pieces of waterlogged fabric.

Once the storm passed, we walked down the street to Borneo Adventure's headquarters. Carsten, the senior sales manager, greeted us at the door and introduced us to everyone in the office.

Months earlier, I had contacted several local outfitters to request a custom backpacking trip into the rainforest. The people at Borneo Adventure were the only ones who responded without trying to push me into something prepackaged. Judging an organization based solely on e-mail correspondence is difficult, but now that we were face-to-face, I felt comfortable that I'd chosen the right guide service. Carsten and the rest of the fourteen-person staff treated Deb and me like dignitaries.

Just as important as their courtesy was their declared commitment to ethical and sustainable tourism. By working to minimize their impact on tribal peoples and the environment, they increase the chances of having a worthwhile product for their clients in the future. A less forward-thinking organization would have attempted to cash in quick with a jungle-theme-park mentality.

After our visit with Borneo Adventure, Deb and I wandered the streets. Kuching is the capital of Sarawak, and it has a population of 460,000. Even though we didn't have time to acquaint ourselves with the entire city, the parts we did see were friendly, clean, and safe. The rarity of multinational corporations was a particularly refreshing sight. Other than automobiles, hotels, and a few fast-food chains, all the commerce appeared to be locally owned. International businesses, such as the Hilton, looked out of place among the traditional storefronts.

Bayang picked us up early Saturday morning, and we set off on a six-hour drive into Borneo's interior. We followed a road south, almost to Indonesia, then turned east and skirted along the border. At the time of our trip, Indonesian Borneo was under a travel warning from the U.S. Department of State, Bureau of Consular Affairs, because of violent ethnic clashes and possible terrorist activity. When we came upon an armed checkpoint for illegal immigrants, I became concerned. "We left our passports in Kuching!" I said.

"No worry," said Bayang. "They see Borneo Adventure sign on van and not stop us."

The road ended an hour later at the Batang Ai Reservoir. Sky-blue water stretched on for miles, and a wall of lush green rainforest bounded the shores. We had gone as far into the interior as we could go by van. From this point on, we'd have to travel by foot or boat.

Blonsai and Juing were waiting for us at the dock. Borneo Adventure had hired the two Iban men to work as porters for the expedition. Although Deb and I were responsible for our personal gear, they would carry food and supplies. Both men lived in the rainforest on the opposite side of the reservoir. Blonsai was tall, thin, and muscular. Juing (Bayang's father-in-law) was medium height, physically fit, and had geometric tattoos covering his upper torso. Neither man spoke English.

The five of us embarked on a ninety-minute voyage aboard a skinny, flat-bottomed canoe called a *longboat*. The appropriately named craft was thirty feet long and three feet wide. It felt unstable until Juing cranked the outboard motor up to full speed. Then, as if a giant gyroscope took over, all the tipsiness disappeared.

The distant clouds, which looked benign when we started across the reservoir, soon drifted over us and opened into a downpour. Although the cooling storm provided relief from the hot day, the fast-moving longboat made the raindrops sting like tiny balls of hail. I shielded my face with my arm as we skimmed over the water.

Once we reached the Ai River, the storm dissipated. With the sun peeking through the clouds, we sped upstream to the Nanga Jelia longhouse.

The Iban live in simple stilted rectangular buildings called *longhouses*. While one might assume the tribe is just into long things, the purpose for the shape of their houses is to accommodate their close communal lifestyle. Some longhouses exceed six hundred feet in length and hold forty or more families. Each family has a living compartment within their house, and when a male child marries, he moves out of his parents' unit and builds a new section on an end.

Our stop at Nanga Jelia was brief. Just long enough to pick up some extra fuel and meet a young schoolteacher who was eager to practice his English.

"Where are you from?" he asked.

"The United States," I said.

"How's the war?"

I stared at the teacher in disbelief. Here we were, miles away from phones, roads, and electricity, yet still unable to escape the war's reach. As with Bayang, I explained my preference for peace, and the teacher expressed his agreement.

Two solidly built women in their mid-twenties joined us in the longboat, and we continued upriver. After several miles, we encountered a mass of floating logs caught in a bend. The river was about thirty feet wide at this point, and though the water was clear, it was too deep to see bottom.

I assumed the river was impassable—we'd either have to get out and walk or turn around and go back. The Iban, however, had another option in mind—we'd go through the logs. Blonsai and the women stood in our tippy craft, balancing on one foot while using the other to push logs out of the way. As soon as they'd clear a small opening, Juing would gun the engine and lift the propeller out of the water a split second before ricocheting logs could crush it. In places where going between logs was impractical, Juing made use of the longboat's flat bottom and powered us over the top. Logjams were obviously a routine hazard for the Iban.

Five minutes past the logs, we reached the foot of a waterfall and the end of navigable water. Our trail, which we planned to follow for a four-day backpacking trip, was in the mass of greenery above the falls. I had assumed we were hiking an out-and-back route and that the two women were coming with us. Instead, they pushed off from the riverbank and floated downstream with our longboat.

I felt a twinge of trepidation. We were now committed to a point-to-point route, and the only way out of the rainforest was to hike the trail to its end—wherever that was.

Deb and I stood with Bayang, Juing, and Blonsai on a narrow rock shelf at the bottom of the falls. I wanted to adjust my backpack but couldn't do so without knocking everyone into the water. At Bayang's suggestion, I led the way to the top, so I'd have extra time to tweak my gear. Feeling as if I had a twenty-pound weight on one shoulder and a forty-pound weight on the other, I cautiously climbed the slippery rocks beside the fifteen-foot-high waterfall, then crossed over the river on a one-log bridge. The treacherous course provided advanced warning that my backpack was overloaded for the terrain and needed more than just a simple adjustment.

I had done a foolish job of packing. I should have left my binoculars, a blanket, one of my cameras, and several other items in Kuching. I had also packed the wrong footwear for walking in water. Since I anticipated only a few river crossings, I brought paddle shoes along to supplement my hiking boots. Paddle shoes are designed for kayaking, not hiking. They have slippery rubber soles and are difficult to pull on and off. As I was about to find out, we'd be spending much more time in the water than expected. Changing back into hiking boots made sense only if we had a long stretch of land ahead of us. In fact, on this day I wouldn't have a single opportunity to remove my paddle shoes. Teva sandals, like Deb had, were better suited for the conditions. They were wide, stable, and simple to remove.

When we were riding in the van, Bayang told us our first day would consist of an easy hike to a primitive shelter. Based on my definition of *easy*, I had assumed we would be hiking gentle hills with solid footing, similar to what we had encountered during our dry season trips to the rainforests in Peru and Australia. Now that we were here, I could tell our hike would be the antithesis of easy. The terrain was mountainous, the rainy season was just ending, and a blanket of wet leaves camouflaged slick tree roots, rocks, and mud. As we slipped and tripped along, each step was an invitation to a broken arm, leg, or ankle.

Twenty minutes into our hike, we reached an S in the river. The trail was supposed to follow high along the outside riverbank, but a recent mudslide had obliterated it. The only way to proceed was to cross the river at the bottom of the bend, scramble up a muddy ten-foot-high wall, cross to the middle of the S, slide down into a waist-high section of rapids, and wade to the other side.

The first part of our crossing went okay, but when I stared down at the rapids, I couldn't resist asking, "Should I just take my cameras out of my pack now and toss them into the river to get it over with?"

"It be okay," said Bayang. "I used to walking in river. Switch packs with me, so I carry your cameras across."

Since Blonsai and Juing had gone off on their own, I slid into the water first, followed by Deb and Bayang. Deb and I made it across okay, but Bayang, who was shorter than either of us, slipped. As he fought to stay upright, I tossed him my trekking pole. He jammed it between the rocks, regained his balance, and crossed to our side.

> —Jungle lesson #1: Educate yourself about the trail before hiking it. Your guide could be washed away at any moment.

We were hiking the Red Ape Trail. Named for its route through one of Borneo's last remaining wild orangutan territories, it follows an old tribal hunting path, which Bayang and two other men had restored. The trail had opened with international fanfare just seven months before our expedition. Borneo Adventure and Orangutan Foundation UK had jointly promoted a high-profile inaugural hike to publicize the need for orangutan conservation and raise money for local orangutan projects.

According to Bayang, we were only the third outsiders to attempt the trail since the inaugural hike. Calling the route a "trail" stretched the meaning of the word to its limit. Without a knowledgeable guide, staying on course would have been nearly impossible. A typical section of trail would go up the river, cut through the rainforest, disappear, and then reappear on the opposite side of the river. Bayang told us that when he led the first hike, one of the backpackers broke down and cried several times. While neither Deb nor I are the crying type, I could understand how the physical and mental demands of the trek would cause such a reaction.

We reached the shelter just in time to avoid another rainstorm. The stilted three-room hut had been constructed out of nearby trees, and its windows were open frames with one-inch wire fencing substituting for screen. The wet rainforest climate had aged the hut rapidly, making it look more like a remnant of the Japanese invasion of World War II than a one-year-old structure.

Although we hadn't traveled far, I was already wondering what possessed me to schedule a backpacking expedition into the Bornean jungle. This wasn't a day hike, where we could get help quickly if something unforeseen happened—we were on our own. No wonder other outfitters had been so hesitant about deviating from their controlled prepackage menu. As I listened to the rain, I feared this day had been only a mild foretaste of things to come.

> —Jungle lesson #2: Know your limitations before it's too late.

The rain stopped after we settled in and had a bite to eat. Rather than sit inside the lantern-lit hut, we decided to go for a night walk. I was eager to do some exploring and prove to myself that my worries were unnecessary. Finding some interesting creatures would remind me why I wanted to visit Borneo in the first place.

With flashlights in hand, Deb, Bayang, and I walked to a nearby stream. The mass of vegetation overgrowing the trickle of water restricted our exploration to a small, relatively open area. There we found several colorful medium-sized frogs, but none that were unusual or rare. After a bit, we departed the stream and meandered up the trail.

Since Deb and I were both wearing hiking boots, and wanted to stay dry, the river limited how far we could walk. While going off trail was an option, neither of us was enthusiastic about working that hard. We returned to the shelter with our only finds being frogs and the most bizarre-looking stick insect I'd ever seen.

The four-inch-long walkingstick was thicker than a pencil and looked like a broken branch covered with thorns. Though his camouflage was nearly perfect, the sharp spikes covering his body guaranteed that only the most determined foe would mess with this bad boy.

The hike had raised my spirits. Walking wasn't nearly as difficult as it had been when I was carrying my backpack. Now at least I knew I could walk through the jungle without feeling as if I were wearing roller skates.

I figured that if I got my pack in perfect balance, and wore my paddle shoes only when absolutely necessary, I'd be okay. But for now, all that mattered was sleep. I hadn't slept on the airplane on the way over, and the eight hours I got in Kuching wasn't enough to get me caught up. I joined Deb under the mosquito netting in our room and closed my eyes.

Tsssssssssshhhhhhhh—the rain returned before I could fall asleep. It came down so hard it washed away my newfound optimism. Except for rapid-filled narrows, the river's depth hadn't been an issue. But what if the water rose so high overnight that we couldn't make our crossings in the morning?

I never think as rationally at night as I do during the day. With three days of difficult hiking ahead, all I could think about were worst-case scenarios: Deb and I could have such a hard time walking that weeks later we'd end up crawling out of the jungle; one of us might break an ankle or a leg and develop gangrene while crawling out of the jungle; maybe the SARS virus infected us on the airplane flight and we would become too sick to crawl out of the jungle; or our guide might suffer a fatal fall and we'd be forced to live the rest of our lives aimlessly crawling through the jungle.

The last possibility worried me the most. Bayang guided without a compass or a map. If something happened to him, I wasn't sure if Blonsai and Juing would help us or if they even knew where we were headed. Without someone to point the way, we could walk for hundreds of miles in several directions without ever seeing another human. If we got lost or hurt, a rescue party might have an easier time finding weapons of mass destruction in Iraq than finding us in the jungle. Unable to turn off my brain, I lay awake all night thinking of ways to die in Borneo.

In the morning, I tried to force rational thoughts into my head, but my mind games continued when Blonsai and Juing engaged in a spirited argument. Even though I couldn't understand their words, they were obviously quarreling about who was carrying the heaviest load. "Great," I thought, "just what we need is for the porters to quit over their disagreement."

Once all five of us were back on the trail, my confidence began to return. The rain had stopped, and we had a nice long stretch where I could wear my hiking boots. What a difference from my paddle shoes! I still had an occasional slip or trip, but nothing like the previous day.

When I had to revert to paddle shoes for an extended river hike, I was surprised to find the water clear and only slightly higher than the day before. Only rarely did we have to wade in depths above our knees.

To my relief, I soon got the hang of river trekking. In fact, I enjoyed it. The key to staying on my feet was avoiding rocks in the shallows near the banks. The fully submerged rocks near the center had less algae on them and provided better traction.

Footing wasn't the only thing that took getting used to. The extreme heat and humidity made me feel as if I were hiking in a sauna. My T-shirt couldn't have gotten any wetter if I'd dunked it in the river. I knew from experience that my body would adapt to the tropical conditions within a few days—I'd just have to endure until then.

As the morning progressed, the unpleasant heat became secondary to a change in the trail. We had climbed to higher ground and now had to contend with several elevated portages around deep water, rapids, and waterfalls. All the portages were precarious, the most memorable being a shoe-width path along the edge of a steep wall of mud. Though I was moving cautiously, my feet slipped out from under me, and only a reflexive grab of a small tree saved me from sliding seventy-five feet down to the river.

I was so relieved to be unharmed that the incident seemed humorous. I turned to Deb and said, "Remember in the movie *Romancing the Stone,* when Kathleen Turner and Michael Douglas were caught in the jungle rainstorm? I thought for sure I was going to reenact their mudslide scene—minus the face-first landing between Kathleen Turner's legs, of course."

Deb and I were amazed at the terrain we could conquer when hiking forward was our only option. The situation reminded me of the time I learned to skydive (my attempt at height-aversion self-therapy). My instructor told me, "You can abort your jump anytime up to the point you put your feet outside the airplane door. Once your feet are out, it becomes too dangerous to let you back in, and you *have* to jump." Sitting on the edge of the airplane floor and placing my feet out on the step was the easy part. Grabbing onto the wing strut, sliding out, and letting go was much more difficult. Knowing I had to continue after my feet were outside helped me do something I might not have been able to do otherwise.

Here in the rainforest my feet were firmly outside the airplane. Giving in to my fear of heights wasn't an option. Sometimes, on high ravine walls, all I wanted to do was freeze and refuse to move another inch. Other times I couldn't even allow my legs the luxury of shaking, as I'd quiver right off my foothold.

The confident Iban provided a stark contrast to Deb's and my cautious trekking style. They walked with effortless precision—as if the ground were perfectly level—and though they must have grown tired, they never showed it.

When we took a break for lunch, Blonsai and Juing immediately went to work preparing our food. Despite a passing rain shower, they soon started a campfire using kindling cut with their knives and resin accelerant gathered from trees. Our meal included rice, rainforest plants, and chicken chunks (complete with all the bones) cooked inside a thick section of bamboo. When the concoction was hot, they poured it onto our plates. It looked like canned dog food, but it tasted fine—at least for one meal.

Nothing, however, was ever wasted. Once we finished eating, Blonsai turned the bamboo into "jungle-Tupperware" by stuffing it with the leftovers, plugging the ends with leaves, and carrying it along for dinner.

We pushed on after lunch, heading away from the river and into the mountains. While the terrain provided better footing than the moist river basin, and had no dangerous drop-offs, its steepness made the hiking more strenuous. Unlike mountain trails in America, which usually climb gradually with numerous switchbacks, Iban trails go straight up the mountainside. To conquer each ascent, we'd hike for as long as we could, stop to catch our breath, and repeat the process.

Because we had been spending most of our time watching where we stepped, we hadn't seen much wildlife. Animals on my wish list included the orangutan and the reticulated python. Since snakes were something the Iban would traditionally eat or avoid, I offered a reward to the first person who found a python—unharmed, of course. When Bayang relayed my offer, Blonsai and Juing smiled and shifted their concentration to likely snake hiding spots.

By late afternoon, we reached the high point of our climb. The mountains in this part of Borneo reminded me of the mountains in Belize—low compared to the Rocky Mountains, but definitely not hills. The particular mountain we were on had a gently rolling, rainforest-covered top that stretched out for as far as I could see.

We followed the ridgeline and soon came upon a small break in the trees. "We camp here, tonight," said Bayang.

With sighs of relief, Deb and I removed our backpacks and melted to the ground.

Though resting felt fabulous, the rainforest floor may be the least relaxing place in all of Borneo—a convoy of leeches crawled toward us.

Every tropical ecosystem has its signature annoying creature, be it ants, bees, flies, or mosquitoes. Borneo's primary irritants are brown and painted leeches. Both species would inch across the ground and vegetation, frequently stopping to wave their heads in the air and home in on something bloody good to eat. Leeches are common throughout Borneo and nearly impossible to avoid (some tourists buy gaiterlike leech socks, but they looked too hot to consider). Our goal was simply to pluck them off before they started sucking. Painted leeches have earned the nickname "tiger leech" because their bite is supposed to sting. I seldom noticed bites from either kind of leech—at worst, they felt like a prick from an acupuncture needle.

The main problem with leeches is the anticoagulant they inject. Not only does it keep the blood flowing while they're feeding, but it also makes the bleeding continue long after they're gone. Consequently, my socks always sported several fresh bloodstains. Still, when compared to other skin-piercing creatures in the tropics, leeches aren't too bad.

While Deb and I dodged leeches, Blonsai and Juing went to work constructing our camp. First, they cut down some small trees, then they bound them together with vines to make supports for hammocks and a rain tarp.

Since we still had a few hours of daylight remaining, Bayang suggested that instead of watching the porters, we go on a slow walk to look for wildlife. Though our bodies were saying, "Hell no, we want to stay here and feed the leeches," our brains overruled. We coaxed ourselves to our feet and followed our guide.

We were about a quarter mile from camp when Juing's yell pierced the forest. Had he found an orangutan or a python? I grinned in anticipation. We hurried back to find out.

Two strange Iban men were standing in our camp, and another was sitting, rummaging through our food. All three men looked rough—like stereotypical terrorists or guerrillas. An animated Iban language conversation took place between Bayang and the men. When they finished, Bayang turned to Deb and me and said, "My father just died. Juing and I must go."

"You must *what?*" I asked. My muscles tensed and my throat grew dry.

"I need to leave immediately. This is Jonathan, Luang, and Ugan. They will be replacing me."

"Are any of these people guides?"

"Jonathan is my associate. He is very capable guide. Luang and Ugan help carry gear."

"Does anyone speak English?"

"Only Jonathan. He speak good English."

I pointed at the rifle propped up beside Ugan. "What about the gun? Guns aren't supposed to be part of this trip."

"Gun only for protection from sun bear," replied Jonathan. "Very dangerous."

"You can't shoot any animals while you're with us," I said.

"No shoot," said Jonathan.

Deb and I stepped away from the men and whispered to each other.

"We do have options," said Deb. "We could go with Bayang."

"He's gonna cut straight through the jungle. We'd never keep up."

"Yeah, you're right. It's just hard because we bonded with him. Maybe things will be okay."

"They're gonna *have* to be okay. We can't exactly tell Bayang not to go to his father's funeral."

We rejoined the men.

"We're sorry for your loss," said Deb.

"Yes, we're very sorry," I agreed.

"Thank you. I must go now," said Bayang.

We watched in shock as Bayang and Juing disappeared into the forest. Of all the things I had thought could possibly go wrong, having our guide hand us off to strangers in the middle of nowhere wasn't one of them. In five minutes' time, all the confidence I had built up during the day had been sucked right out of me.

An awkward silence engulfed the camp as Deb and I turned our eyes toward Jonathan. He was a stocky man in his early forties who spoke in a high-pitched voice that didn't match his build.

Jonathan took three quick steps toward me, grabbed my hand, and shook it vigorously. As his sweaty palm sloshed against mine, he said, "Congratulations on the war! Way to go, America! We Iban glad you got rid of Saddam Hussein!"

His overly enthusiastic attempt at being friendly came off as nervous and shifty—I didn't trust him. I also didn't know what to say. Responding pro or con to his offer of congratulations seemed inappropriate.

Jonathan continued, "You must put on your packs. We have better place to stay tonight."

"We're exhausted. Can't we stay here?" I asked.

"We have camp already set up one hour from here. You be more comfortable there."

Mental alarms clanged in my head. Deb and I were unarmed and had no idea where we were. The Iban had knives and a gun and knew the jungle well. My first concern was my wife's safety. At least for now, cooperating seemed to be the best thing to do. Deb and I looked at each other and reluctantly heaved our packs onto our backs.

We walked single file up a faint trail with Luang in the lead, followed by Blonsai, Jonathan, me, Deb, and Ugan. The Iban were once a fierce headhunting tribe, but I was more worried about what they'd do with a good-looking woman deep in the jungle than losing my head. No defense plan I could think of came out in my favor. I was outnumbered and out of my element. I glanced along the line to size everyone up. I looked behind Deb. Ugan had his gun pointed at her back!

I stopped dead in my tracks.

The rifle was slung under his arm with the barrel facing forward. I wasn't about to risk a shooting—accidental or otherwise.

"The man in the rear can't carry his gun pointed like that!" I yelled.

"It's okay. Not loaded," said Jonathan.

"It's *not* okay!" I said. "He must move to the front. We can't walk with a gun pointed at us."

I stood firm until Jonathan reluctantly waved Ugan into the lead.

We trudged forward.

I felt better for a moment. Then I realized Ugan was no longer on the trail with us—he had vanished like a ghost.

I wasn't thinking rationally to begin with, and now my train of thought careened out of control: "Maybe Ugan is hiding in the trees with his gun aimed at us. Maybe all the Iban will disappear, one by one, leaving us hopelessly lost in the jungle. Maybe once we reach the camp they'll rape Deb and take my head as their secret trophy. Maybe—"

I reined in my imagination and focused on the positive: "I'm just tired. Everything will be okay once I get some sleep. Our lives now depend on Jonathan and the others. We have to trust them and make the best of the situation. We have to—"

"Orangutans!" whispered Jonathan. "Come here! Come here!"

He grabbed my wrist and pulled me through the vegetation to the best viewing position. I looked up and saw two females and a half-grown youngster—my mood changed from apprehension to exhilaration.

As the orangutans bounded from tree to tree, Jonathan continued pulling me to the optimal sight lines. When we got too close, the orangutans snapped off branches and hurled them at us. I knew primates sometimes tossed feces at people but never expected a barrage of large tree limbs. It sounded as if the forest were coming down around us.

I tried to shoot some photos, but unobstructed views were so brief that I couldn't get my camera focused in time. Soon the orangutans disappeared into the canopy. Though I didn't have an image to document the event, the disappointment was minor. I had witnessed something few people ever get to see—orangutans in the wild!

Orangutans are the world's largest tree-dwelling animals. In the Malay language, orangutan means "man of the forest." Considering they share 96.4 percent of their genes with humans, the term is uncannily accurate.

The red apes live only in Borneo and on the Indonesian island of Sumatra. At the time of our expedition, researchers were estimating that the total population of wild orangutans had declined by 50 percent since the 1980s. With a current population of just fifteen thousand, they could become extinct within the next ten to thirty years (the IUCN classifies them as an "endangered species"). The primary factors contributing to their demise are poaching, illegal pet trade, and habitat destruction. Malaysia has taken steps to protect orangutans and, to a lesser extent, so has Indonesia, but neither country is doing enough.

The orangutan sighting was good for more than just the obvious reason. I now realized I had misjudged Jonathan. He was so excited when he pulled me through the forest that he was like a child with a new puppy. If he had planned to harm or abandon us, showing us the orangutans wouldn't have delighted him so much.

Deb whispered to me, "This is a good omen. We would've missed the orangutans if we were still with Bayang."

—Another jungle lesson learned.

An hour later, we arrived at our destination for the evening. The camp was a crude hunting shelter the Iban had built a few months earlier. Although it didn't have walls, the thatched roof supported by wooden poles would provide a dry place to sleep.

The mystery of what happened to Ugan was solved. While I was imagining him sinisterly hiding in the trees with his finger on the trigger, he was actually hurrying ahead to get an early start on dinner. Tonight's meal was chicken chunks and rice.

The Iban cook their chicken with a pungent curry. At lunchtime, I had been able to handle the seasoning okay, but this time it made me feel nauseated after a few bites. I had to force myself to eat enough to keep up my energy. Deb, on the other hand, thought the chicken tasted just fine.

Despite my lack of appetite, the meal provided an opportunity to have a relaxed conversation with our new guide. When Jonathan filled my cup with hot tea, I asked him, "How did you ever find us so deep in the jungle?"

"We knew when you started hiking and how far you should have traveled. Cut through jungle to where we thought you'd be."

"Did it take you long to find us?"

"No. Found you right away."

"Amazing!"

Then Jonathan had a question for me: "What is itinerary?"

"What do you mean?" I asked.

"Where we supposed to take you?"

I was taken aback by his question. How could our guide not know where we were going? I relayed what Bayang had told me earlier: "We're supposed to hike all day tomorrow and camp by a river. After that we have a half-day hike to a longhouse."

"That is Nanga Sumpa—my longhouse," he said. "I guess your itinerary work, but there is festival at Nanga Sumpa in two days you would enjoy very much. Miss most of festival with your schedule. If we hike longer tomorrow, we reach longhouse by dark."

Although I suspected Jonathan was more interested in the festival for himself than for either Deb or me, reaching the longhouse early did have an appeal. I conferred with my wife before saying, "We're willing to try to make it to your longhouse tomorrow, as long as we have the option of staying one more night in the jungle if we get too tired."

"No problem," he said.

After dinner, Jonathan and the others went to work constructing hammocks. When I learned we were going to sleep in hammocks, I expected the kind that swing on ropes between trees. Instead, these were like stretchers. The Iban assembled them by stringing pre-sewn fabric between two delimbed tree trunks and then resting each trunk end horizontally on a large perpendicular log. To complete the project, they placed Deb's and my hammocks side by side and hung a mosquito net over the top. The white netting reminded me of a wedding veil. "Look honey," I said, "they've prepared the bridal suite for us!"

When Deb and I turned in for the night, the Iban slept next to us in similar hammocks—minus the mosquito netting. Every hour or so one of them would wake up and break into spontaneous conversation with the others. Laughter followed each exchange. Generations of communal living had made the Iban extraordinarily social people.

I wished for an understanding of their language. Were they talking about us? Then again, perhaps the language barrier was a good thing.

Deb and I awoke feeling mentally refreshed but physically beat from our various nicks, cuts, and sore muscles. As a consequence of being wet for much of the previous two days, blisters encased my toes, and a rash inflamed my inner thighs. I wrapped my injuries with medical tape to prevent further injury. Since the tape would rub off too easily if I placed gauze underneath it, I had to stick it directly to my wounds—I'd deal with the pain of removing the tape later. At least today, the sun was shining. Perhaps I'd have a chance to dry out a little.

Jonathan hadn't told us that switching to his itinerary meant leaving the Red Ape Trail, but figuring it out didn't take too long. After hiking up the steepest mountain yet and surviving a controlled fall down the other side, I asked the obvious question: "We're not on the original trail, are we?"

"This is shortcut," he said sheepishly, "old hunters' trail."

Even though the route was more demanding than the Red Ape Trail—something I wouldn't have thought possible—I did get a certain perverse pleasure from witnessing that even the Iban were having trouble hiking it. When the sure-footed Jonathan took a nasty fall and hit his head on a rock, my pleasure turned to concern—we couldn't lose another guide.

Deb's travel theory, "the worse the road, the better the surprises along the way," also applies to trails. In this case, we could hear an orangutan in the distance moving through the trees.

Rustle, snap, crash! Rustle, snap, crash!

Ugan cupped his hands around his mouth and let loose a series of whoops. I figured he'd never fool such an intelligent animal, but within minutes, the male orangutan was in sight. He was much larger than the females from the previous day and likely weighed 175 pounds. Once he spotted us, and realized we'd tricked him, he started lobbing treetop missiles at us. I wasn't sure if he was angry, frightened, or a little of both, but his fury made him appear Bigfoot size—the Sasquatch of Borneo was raining weapons of mass destruction upon us!

Fortunately, the trees were close enough together to block any branches thrown horizontally. As long as he didn't climb directly above us, we were safe.

Eventually the orangutan realized we weren't going to harm him, and curiosity took over. He moved to a big tree, thirty-five feet away from us, and peered down from a low branch. With his hairless forehead, rusty beard, and intelligent eyes, he looked so . . . human.

Many scientists believe orangutans and humans evolved from a common ancestor, and many Iban believe their dead live again as orangutans. As I stood there admiring and photographing the orangutan, I couldn't disagree with either belief.

As the orangutan grew more at ease with us, a strange feeling came over me. I felt as if I were looking back in time and into the eyes of one of my own ancestors. Great-great-great-great-great-great-great-great-great-grandfather, is that you?

If Deb and I had our way, we would have spent the entire day with the orangutan. Jonathan, however, was determined to reach the longhouse by nightfall. After fifteen minutes, he insisted we move on and started walking off without us. Although we were upset about being pulled away from a once-in-a-lifetime event, we were in no position to argue and hurried to catch up.

The heat and humidity had drained off all my energy. I drank water and tea to keep myself hydrated but quickly sweated off whatever liquid I consumed. After lumbering to the top of a steep climb, I physically couldn't go any farther and had to remove my pack and rest. My stomach was in knots and my head felt as if it were going to burst into flames—I had heat exhaustion.

Though I knew heatstroke was a possibility if I continued, I also knew we were a half hour from a river. If I could make it that far, there'd be plenty of water to cool me down. After a ten-minute break, I told Jonathan I was ready to go.

We began another controlled fall down a mountainside. As we progressed, we grabbed trees, roots, and vines to slow our descent. Just as I was about to grasp the trunk of an ordinary-looking tree, Jonathan yelled, "Don't touch! Tree poisonous! Your hand burn for weeks!"

I pulled back with an inch to spare.

—If you're counting, that was jungle lesson #27: What you don't know *can* hurt you.

Before long, I was overheating again—even worse than before. When the ground leveled off, I could hear the faint gurgle of water in the distance. We were almost there. As I plodded forward, I dipped into the river with my mind. It was so cool, so refreshing.

I froze in midstep—a break in the trees revealed my goal. The river was in a deep gorge bordered by walls of slick mud and rock. The descent was steep enough to warrant a rope. Did anyone bring a rope? Ha! What would the Iban need a rope for?

I flashed back to a cartoon I'd seen depicting the skeleton of a man who had died in the desert a few feet before reaching an oasis. Although I couldn't remember what made the cartoon funny, I felt a certain kinship with the skeleton. I could practically smell the river, yet if I attempted to reach it, I would almost certainly fall onto the rocks below and die just a few feet from the water.

By the time I finished my thought, Luang and Blonsai were already halfway down the wall. God, I hated the Iban!

Like an obedient servant, I followed. Whether I died on top of the gorge or on the way down really wouldn't matter in the end. My brain went numb, and my legs tensed with anxiety. As I slid down the wall, my hands and feet, and even my butt cheeks, grabbed whatever they could along the way. Somehow, we all made it to the river.

I stripped off my backpack, eased into a shallow pool, and leaned back until my head was underwater. Soon I began to feel better.

"From here, we walk in river," said Jonathan.

"That'll be great," I replied. "It should help keep me cool."

The river averaged twenty feet in width and varied in depth from six inches near the banks to more than six feet in pools and narrow passages. As we proceeded, we encountered some sections where the water squeezed between gorge walls and others where the gorge was wide enough that we could walk on spits of dry rock and pebble. Like the previous day, we had numerous precarious portages around deep water, rapids, and waterfalls.

The relief I felt from lying in the river was temporary. Soon my stomach cramps and burning headache returned. When Jonathan mentioned an old hunting shelter, forty minutes downriver, reaching it became my short-term goal. I slogged along, thinking of nothing but the next step.

By the time we arrived at the shelter, I was feeling as miserable as I'd ever felt in my life. Then the aroma of Ugan's curried chicken chunks wafted in my direction.

I thought my stomach would turn inside out.

Moving away from the cooking area helped—until Jonathan handed me a plateful of the pungent dish. Out of both politeness and the need for energy, I choked down a few bites. Afterward, I excused myself to lie down on a bed of narrow tree trunks stretched between two logs.

Jonathan let me rest for a while before announcing we had to make a decision. If we wanted to reach the longhouse before dark, we needed to leave immediately. Otherwise, we could spend the night where we were and hike out in the morning.

"What's the rest of the hike like?" I asked.

"All downhill," he replied. "The worst is behind us."

From a medical standpoint, I should have elected to stay at the shelter, but I was too stubborn to hold us up. "Let's go for it," I said.

"Are you sure?" asked Deb. "Don't feel pressured. Staying here tonight isn't a problem."

"I'll be okay. Besides, the rash on my thighs is getting worse. I'm gonna have a hard time walking tomorrow."

Twenty minutes later, we were in the midst of our most dangerous portage yet. I was forty feet above a roaring waterfall, clinging to a muddy gorge wall, while trying to find just one solid root to hold on to. When I discovered every exposed root within my reach was rotten, I barked at Jonathan, "Damn it! You said the 'worst was behind us'!"

"I forgot to mention this spot."

"Is this the *last* portage?"

"Easy past here," he said as he jammed his walking stick into the mud to make a handhold. "Don't look down."

I looked down. God, I hate heights!

I shimmied past the waterfall and cautiously descended to the river. I waited until Deb caught up and whispered to her, "This feels more like a rescue operation than a guided backpacking trip."

"You're right," she whispered back. "And to think we paid good money to do this."

"Honey, you can't buy moments like this."

The sky rumbled! Soon we could hear rain hitting the trees, getting louder by the second. We had been concentrating so hard on not falling that we had failed to notice the clouds. Moments later we were drenched in sheets of rain. As the drops pummeled the river, they hissed like a radio tuned to static and turned all the way up.

"Great," I yelled to Deb, "just when I thought we'd get out of here alive, Mother Nature throws a thunder-and-lightning storm at us!"

My pessimism was premature. I hadn't considered the effect the wonderfully cool rain would have on my body. My temperature started to drop, and I immediately regained my energy. After several minutes, I felt better than I had since the beginning of the trip. The rain had saved me.

Of course, it only saved me so I could put up a good fight before it drowned me. Before long, the river resembled a giant centipede—each leg a newly formed tributary pouring into its body.

"We need to move quickly!" screamed Jonathan. "River get very deep."

Though I hadn't thought it possible, our hike had taken on more urgency.

Now that I was feeling better, it was Deb's turn to suffer. She was so exhausted she was shaking. Because Jonathan's new rapid pace made it difficult for her to keep up, I yo-yoed between the two—reminding Jonathan to slow down and making sure Deb was okay.

"Do you want to rest?" I asked. "I can tell him to stop."

"No, no, let's get this over with!" she shouted. "I just need to get myself pissed off, and I'll be okay."

The rising water frequently forced us out of the river to avoid rapids, pools, and other hazards, and the perilous gorge walls repeatedly forced us back in. Deb slipped and fell several times on the slick rocks near the water's edge but each time returned to her feet and marched on.

I had just scrambled over some boulders when out of the corner of my eye I saw her go down again. This time she tripped on a submerged rock and fell face-first into the river. I raced back to her, but she was already pushing herself up, cursing in pain. Although for the most part her Teva sandals worked great, they provided little protection for the tops of her feet.

"Are you okay?" I yelled.

"I caught my toe on a rock, and it hurts like hell! I think it's broken."

"This is stupid! I'm gonna tell Jonathan we need to stop. If we keep up this pace, someone's going to get seriously hurt—or worse."

"No, let's just go! If we stop now, my foot will balloon up. The cool water will help keep the swelling down."

I knew arguing would be fruitless. She was as stubborn as I was. We were either going to reach the longhouse by nightfall or die trying.

A bit farther downstream, the gorge narrowed and forced us to wade waist deep in rapids. Each step had to be deliberate because we could no longer see our feet. This was one place where the Ibans' open-weave basket-packs had a distinct advantage over Deb's and my nylon backpacks. If we tripped, our backpacks could fill with water and hold us under.

The river rushed around a corner and dropped into an impressive waterfall. We had been wading as far to the right as possible. When we peered over the falls to find a way down, the "safest" route was on the opposite bank. Since the water at mid-river was deep, we'd have to cross at the crest of the falls, where the river had deposited a line of rocks.

We started across, leaning against the current and hoping our feet wouldn't slip out from under us. I glanced back at Deb. She wore a look of grim determination as the water pounded her hipbone and threatened to wash her over the edge.

The rocks grew larger as we approached the bank; the last one stuck out of the water. Concentrating on keeping my weight upriver, I tried to step onto the boulder in one smooth motion. My momentum sent my feet sliding in opposite directions, and I landed in the splits on top of it. "Luckily," men have evolved with two natural pillows between our legs to break our falls on such occasions. I caught my breath and clambered to my feet.

Once everyone made it across the waterfall, we started down a near-vertical wall of hard, slick mud. Jonathan led the way, followed by me, Deb, Blonsai, Luang, and Ugan. This time we didn't even have a rotten root to grab. Although the wall wasn't as high as some of the others, a fall would have been just as deadly. As we descended, visions of all our narrow escapes flooded my brain—the slips where footing suddenly took hold, the last-second grabs of trees or roots—we could only be lucky for so long. I knew I'd make it down. Deb was the one who worried me. I had gotten her into this mess and was afraid of losing her. She was exhausted and walking on a badly injured toe. If she slipped now, nothing could stop her from crashing onto the rocks below. I couldn't look up because I had to watch my feet. Instead, I listened for the tumble I knew was coming.

"Take your time, Deb."

"I'm okay."

"Don't take any chances. When I get down, Jonathan can climb back up and help you."

"No, really. I'm okay."

And she was okay. When I reached bottom she was right behind me. I breathed a sigh of relief. We had survived another portage from hell.

My relief turned into anger. I was tired of risking my life. Jonathan was leading us on an insane route—there had to be an alternative. As we hurried downriver, I shouted to him, "I don't care if we have to slide down every waterfall or swim rapids over our heads, I'm *not* doing another portage like that!"

"No more. Easy past here."

I wanted to snap back that I'd heard that line before, but antagonizing the man responsible for getting our butts to the longhouse didn't seem like a wise idea.

We were running out of time. The river was still rising, and evening was approaching. "How much farther to the longhouse?" I yelled.

"One hour, thirty minutes," he shouted. We puffed along for a few moments before he continued. "I have idea. I send Ugan for longboat. He pick us up at end of river. Save forty minutes."

As rain poured over the brim of my baseball cap and thunder crashed above me, my anger turned into anticipation. We were beyond exhaustion, and although forty minutes was a small amount of time to save, all we needed was a little good news to raise our spirits. Deb was so pale she looked like a drowning victim. Once she knew we were near our goal, some color returned to her face.

Yes, we had to tackle more portages, but at least the steepest ones were behind us. We maintained a brisk pace and reached the mouth of the river a few minutes shy of Jonathan's predicted time.

We'd made it!

The old hunters' trail river we had been following flowed into the wider, slower-moving Delok River. We expected to find Ugan at the confluence, but neither he nor the longboat was in sight. The rain, which had felt wonderfully cool when we were moving, was now just plain cold. We sat on the riverbank and shivered while we waited.

After twenty minutes with no sign of Ugan, Jonathan hinted we might have to give up on the boat and start walking again. The thought of another hike was almost too much to bear. Our adrenaline had worn off, and all the injuries we'd been able to ignore were now at the forefront of our minds. My blisters and jungle rash ached, and my triceps were black and blue from the continuous pounding of my backpack frame. Deb, who had hiked several miles on a lame toe, was in even worse shape than I was.

We didn't fret for long, because we soon heard the glorious growl of the longboat motor in the distance. We would be warm and dry in fifteen minutes. I expected to see Ugan, but instead two boys pulled up beside the riverbank. Both looked about ten years old—one worked the engine and the other watched for obstacles. We boarded the long-boat and sped downriver.

Along the way, we encountered numerous rapids, logs, and rocks. The boys handled all the hazards with veteran precision. I leaned back and shouted to Deb, "These kids are amazing! I don't remember white-water rafting being part of our itinerary, but this is fun."

She laughed in agreement.

When we arrived at Nanga Sumpa, no one showed us where to go. Jonathan, who had told us earlier we'd be staying in his room, left us standing on the dock and went to bail out a nearby longboat.

The dock sat in a narrow inlet, and on each side of the water were stilted buildings. On the near side was a new, uniformly constructed, wooden building. On the far side was an older, larger building—obviously the longhouse—that appeared to have been haphazardly constructed over time with randomly acquired building materials. When Ugan noticed Deb and me abandoned on the dock, he walked over and escorted us into the new building. We would be spending the next two nights in the guest lodge.

Although we were still in the rainforest and far away from electricity, the lodge felt almost luxurious. Our room had an uncovered open-frame window, a curtain door, and a mosquito-net-covered mattress on the floor. The dining room had elaborately carved wooden tables, and the bathrooms had cold-water showers and flush toilets.

I was curious about how the Iban accomplished running water and learned they piped it down from a mountain spring. The elevation drop created the water pressure.

After settling in, Deb and I discussed our adventure. We both agreed we had never pushed ourselves so hard before.

"It's amazing what you can do when your only alternative is death," I said. "Still, I wouldn't trade the past three days for anything."

"You're right," said Deb. "I'm glad we did it. I really learned something about myself."

"Of course, we only say that now that we've made it safely to the longhouse," I added.

We both laughed.

Jonathan knocked on our doorframe and peeked around the curtain. "Village headman is here. Please join us for drinks."

We hobbled into the dining room and sat at a large table with the headman, Jonathan, Blonsai, Luang, and Ugan. The headman appeared to be about seventy years old, and he had a shapeless blue tattoo covering his throat. Since Jonathan was still our only English-speaking contact, our greetings were limited to handshakes and smiles.

"Thank you for getting us here, Jonathan," I said. "Although I must say, I wasn't thankful on the trail when you kept telling us the section ahead would be easy. Every time you said the terrain would get better, it got worse."

"I said that so it not seem so hard. Didn't want you to get discouraged."

I considered telling him that being straight with us would have saved a lot of frustration, but I let his comment pass.

"I was impressed with how gracefully all of you moved through the jungle," said Deb. "You carried yourselves so effortlessly."

"We felt so inferior," I added.

"No need to feel inferior," replied Jonathan. "Very few of my people have hiked the trail you did. Too difficult. Less than 5 percent of longhouse could do it."

I had a hard time believing Jonathan. The Iban were at home in the rainforest, and many of them had sculpted oversized calf muscles as proof of their frequent strenuous climbs. Even so, his compliment was a nice ego boost.

An hour later Deb and I excused ourselves to go to bed. As much as we would have enjoyed spending the entire evening drinking tuak (a strong rice wine) with our hosts, we had to get some rest.

"You can sleep in tomorrow," said Jonathan. "Festival postponed. Man who runs it delayed at another longhouse."

Although the festival would have been interesting, we weren't disappointed. A solid eight hours of sleep followed by a day of relaxation would feel wonderful.

Unfortunately, an undisturbed night of slumber was not to be. One of the resident cats was in heat, and she and her suitors yowled throughout the night. When the cats took a break, crowing roosters, squealing pigs, and the ever-talking Iban filled the silence. At least now I knew what had driven the tribe to headhunting—they never got any REM sleep.

In the morning, we found Blonsai sitting at the breakfast table. Since he lived at a different longhouse, he had slept in the room next to ours. When Deb mimed to him all the places she was sore, he surprised her by miming back all the places he was sore.

The Iban had appeared to be such superhuman jungle trekkers that we never imagined they too felt the effects our adventure. Perhaps Jonathan's compliment from the night before wasn't just flattery after all.

Deb and I relaxed until Jonathan came by to offer us a longhouse tour. Though we weren't moving well, we were eager to see how the Iban lived when they weren't leading Americans up mountains and down rivers. We limped over the wooden bridge spanning the inlet and climbed the ramp to the building.

In the United States, we often strive to make our homes neutral or pleasant smelling. That wasn't possible here. The combination of a tropical climate and 209 people living under the same roof gave the longhouse a, shall we say, "distinctive" odor. Physically, the Iban divided their home the long way down the middle, with one side containing private living quarters and the other side left open for its entire length. Woven mats covered the floor on the open side to create a commons area for weaving, net making, and other crafts.

Deb is an accomplished weaver. When she learned the Iban were also weavers, she asked to observe their techniques. Jonathan granted the request by leading us to the living quarters of one of the master weavers.

When he opened the door without knocking, we surprised the topless old woman inside and had to quickly back out so she could put on a blouse. When we reentered, she was sitting at her loom, working on a stunning creation. The living quarters were significantly hotter than the open side. No wonder the woman was working topless. Jonathan explained that despite the stifling heat, many of the best weavers worked in privacy to prevent other weavers from stealing their patterns.

With Jonathan serving as an interpreter, Deb asked the old woman questions about her work. I tried to follow the interview, but two languages discussing the technicalities of weaving exceeded my attention span. When Deb noticed I was lost, she brought me back into focus. "Weaving is basically the same all over the world," she said. "Everyone just has their own variations."

The old woman's living quarters were spacious, if for no other reason than she had few possessions (a mattress, washbasin, propane stove, and shelves stocked with necessities). The walls were made out of debarked tree trunks, and linoleum remnants covered the wooden plank floor. I had to be careful where I stepped, as the floor bowed under my weight and threatened to give way at any moment.

Three little girls (most likely the woman's grandchildren) watched me from across the room as I photographed the weaving session. The girls, with their big brown eyes, wide smiles, and straight black hair, were melt-your-heart cute. When I noticed they were fascinated by my digital camera, I took their photograph and showed them the result on the screen. They giggled with delight. I took several more and giggled along with them.

Unlike traditional film cameras, which don't produce immediate results, digital cameras are great tools for breaking down language and cultural barriers. People usually relax after viewing their first digital photo. When I show them I can erase undesirable images, they loosen up even more.

We proceeded into Jonathan's living quarters to watch his mother weave. In contrast to the starkness of the master weaver's space, Jonathan's quarters had amenities such as framed pictures, varnished furniture, and a television.

"How are you able to watch TV?" I asked. "I didn't think you had electricity."

"I have generator."

"How many channels do you get?"

"Very few. None come in too good."

I suspected Jonathan was the only person in the longhouse who owned a TV. He was in charge of Nanga Sumpa's relations with Borneo Adventure, a position that undoubtedly paid him enough to buy some extra possessions.

The three of us walked back into the commons area, paused to watch Ugan work on a fishnet, then stepped outside to tour the community gardens. Continuing on the arts and crafts theme, Jonathan pointed out various plants his people used for dying yarn, making baskets, and weaving mats. He then insisted I take a picture of him with two small *Calophyllum blancoi* trees. "These trees illegal to remove," he said. "May have cure for AIDS."

I've often wondered how many of the tropical plants I've walked by contain unknown but important medical remedies. Key ingredients for an estimated 40 percent of all prescription drugs originate from tropical rainforests. Add to that the large percentage of plants that have never been studied for medical use, and you have a compelling reason to protect the rainforest. Who knows how many lifesaving cures have already been lost because of irresponsible human activities? At least in the case of the *Calophyllum blancoi* trees, the Malaysian government was taking proactive action to protect a medically promising plant.

We returned to the guest lodge for the remainder of the afternoon. As we sat in the dining room, Dirk and Sabine, two medical doctors from Germany, joined us for tea. They had arrived earlier in the day—the easy way—via longboat from the Batang Ai Reservoir.

Dirk and Sabine were a delightful couple in their late thirties. Like other Europeans we had met during our travels, they were on a multi-month trip. Since Americans traditionally take short one- or two-week-long vacations, I asked Sabine, "How do German businesses manage to remain productive with important employees gone for extended periods?"

"We come back refreshed," she said, "and we're much more productive than we would have been without the extra time off."

I pondered her point. Even if the productivity of German workers didn't increase in proportion to their time away from work, at least they were having more fun than the average American worker.

After a bit, our conversation morphed into politics. "I'm surprised how well we've been received during our travels," I said. "With everything our president has been doing, I expected to encounter people who hated Americans."

"I wouldn't worry too much about that," said Dirk. "Most people can separate George Bush from the American public. We all know what happened in Florida."

"But what happens if we reelect him?"

"You don't seriously think *that* would happen—do you?"

"It's too early to tell."

"You know, I heard a rumor that Angola has offered to send representatives to the United States to monitor your next election. . . ."

We also discussed the events of the past few days, including Deb's fall in the river. Since she was still wincing in pain with every step, the doctors volunteered to examine her toe.

"It's definitely broken," said Dirk. "Unfortunately there's not much we can do for it, except show you how to tape it."

"*Anything* would help," said Deb.

Dirk carefully wrapped her broken toe and taped it to an adjacent healthy toe. When he finished, Deb stood, gingerly took a few steps, and smiled. "Much better!"

We went back to the longhouse in the evening to socialize, drink tuak, and purchase crafts from the various artisans. Deb and I presented the headman with gifts we had brought from the United States (mostly school supplies for the children) and made a special point of buying a basket from Ugan and weavings from the two weavers we had met. The tribe did exceptional work. Unfortunately, we had to pass on many beautiful pieces, because they would have been too cumbersome to carry along for the remainder of our trip.

Staying with the Iban was a great learning experience. One thing I wouldn't learn until the following day in Kuching was that Ugan was the village shaman, and he supposedly had the power to heal by touch. Had I known our porter was also a shaman, I would have asked him to examine Deb's toe and my jungle rash.

I'd love to revisit the longhouse someday and get to know Ugan better. The knowledge he could share about medicinal plants alone would be well worth the cost of the trip. In our brief time together, we had already developed a connection. Whenever he saw me, a big smile would light up his face, and he'd reach out to shake my hand.

Then again, perhaps Ugan had used his powers and I hadn't known it. Upon completing the backpacking segment of our trip, my rash was so raw and infected that I thought for sure I'd be in pain for weeks. Instead, the symptoms would disappear within a few days after departing Nanga Sumpa. Ugan had undoubtedly noticed my limping. Had he healed me by repeatedly shaking my hand? I'm generally skeptical about such things, but who knows? I do know that he had many talents. If the Iban had use for résumés, his would be impressive: shaman, porter, cook, orangutan caller, net maker, basket weaver, and gun-safety instructor. Okay, maybe not the last one, but at least if he had accidentally shot Deb on the trail, he might have been able to nurse her back to health.

In the morning, we waved good-bye to the longhouse, boarded a longboat, and returned to Kuching—the easy way. Jonathan accompanied us,

as Borneo Adventure requires all guides to personally deliver their clients back to the city.

Our first stop was the Borneo Adventure office to pick up some gear I had stored there. Sporting a five-day beard and looking as if I'd been to hell and back, I limped across the room to the desk where Carsten was sitting.

"You won't believe what happened!" I said. A shocked expression flowed over the senior sales manager's slender face. "But before discussing it, I'd like take my gear to the hotel and clean up."

"How much time do you need?" he asked.

"Forty-five minutes will be fine."

"I'll call you then, and we'll set up a meeting."

An hour later, Deb and I met Jonathan, Carsten, and Emong (the operations manager) for drinks at an outdoor pub. I could see the concern on their faces and got straight to the point.

"Deb and I want to thank you for the most memorable backpacking trip of our lives. But needless to say, things didn't go quite as planned. . . ."

I filled everyone in on the events of the trip, then said, "Since the trail is new, I'd like to offer a few suggestions for future treks. First, you need to make sure your clients have a more accurate description of the expedition. The e-mail Charlie [another sales manager] sent me stated, 'The hike will be slow and quiet for better wildlife spotting,' with an average pace of 'one kilometer [six-tenths of a mile] for an hour.' If we'd known what we were really getting into, we still would have gone—we just would have been better prepared. I had packed for four leisurely days of rainforest photography, not racing down rivers and clinging to gorge walls. Second, the mental part of a trip can be just as difficult as the physical part. When the unexpected happens in the jungle, imaginations can run wild. I know switching guides in midtrip is unusual, but it would have made a *huge* difference if Jonathan had shown us something to prove he actually worked for Borneo Adventure."

I turned and looked at Jonathan. "Don't get me wrong. Now that we know you, we love you. But being handed over to strangers, armed with knives and a gun, was a frightening experience."

When I finished my lecture, I braced for a defensive response. Instead, all three men were apologetic and appreciative of my comments—a sign of a good organization. As for the e-mail I had received, Carsten sheepishly explained that Charlie had never actually been on the trail himself.

With business talk out of the way, we enjoyed a few drinks and shared several laughs. As we said good-bye, I reiterated, "Please understand, we're not upset. You gave us an adventure we wouldn't trade for anything, and I'd personally recommend your organization to anyone. We just want to make sure people who hike the trail in the future know exactly what to expect."

After everyone nodded in agreement, we shook hands and went our separate ways. The first part of our trip was complete.

The next morning, Thursday, April 17, we flew to the city of Sandakan in the state of Sabah. The flight was notable only because Malaysia Airlines attendants walked the aisle handing out a choice of three newspapers printed in both English and Malay. I've been on other flights where newspapers were handed out, but never have I seen almost every passenger take and actually read at least one paper. Since I wanted to learn as much as I could about what was happening in Iraq, I read all three.

The balanced war coverage by the Malaysian press both surprised and impressed me. While most U.S. papers were slanting their reporting to accommodate the Bush administration, Malaysian papers were printing both sides of the story—often running pro-war articles from U.S. newspapers alongside antiwar stories from other sources.

A newspaper I saved from April 11, the day we arrived in Borneo, provided a good example of the balanced coverage. Inside was a two-page full-color photo spread. The heading on the left page stated, "Suffering of young innocent," and below it was a heartrending photo of an Iraqi man carrying a young girl whose legs had been blown off in a U.S. led air strike. The heading on the right page proclaimed, "Statue of Liberty!" and under it was a photo of a U.S. soldier in Baghdad draping the American flag over the statue of Saddam Hussein.

The effect of the war photos, however, was unbalanced. Even though the papers printed "happy" photos, such as Saddam Hussein's statue coming down and a group of Iraqis celebrating in the streets, I couldn't clear my mind of the graphic photos of the maimed and the dead. If mainstream newspapers throughout the United States had printed the same disturbing photos, they would have put a human face on what for many Americans was an abstract concept and dramatically reduced support for the war.

Our new guide, Rudy, met us at the Sandakan Airport. He would be escorting us on a forty-minute shuttle-van ride to the Sepilok Nature Resort. Rudy was a polite, neatly dressed young man with round-framed glasses. He looked more like a preppy than a jungle guide. After introductions and small talk, I thought he might ask "the" question, but instead we rode in silence.

I looked out the window as the busy city of Sandakan gave way to tranquil tropical forest. So far, other than orangutans, we hadn't seen much wildlife. Now, with the survival portion of our trip—hopefully—behind us, I planned to focus my efforts on finding more of Borneo's cool creatures. My mind wandered to some of the possibilities: Sumatran rhinos, mouse deer, spitting cobras, proboscis monkeys, clouded leopards, slow lorises, western tarsiers, pangolins—

"How's the war?" asked Rudy, interrupting my train of thought.

This time I couldn't help smiling. While I had anticipated the question, I hadn't expected him to use the exact same words as Bayang and the schoolteacher.

My response was the same as well: "We wish there wasn't a war."

Deb and I had scheduled our trip in three parts. For most of the middle section we'd have separate adventures. I would spend all three days at the Sepilok Nature Resort, and she would spend one day with me before departing for the Lankayan Island Dive Resort.

I had considered accompanying Deb to the dive resort, but Lankayan Island was tiny, and I wanted plenty of time to photograph orangutans at the nearby Sepilok Orang Utan Rehabilitation Centre.

While I looked forward to some leisurely days with my camera, I was also concerned about a warning the U.S. Department of State, Bureau of Consular Affairs had posted on its Web site: "The Abu Sayyaf Group (ASG), a terrorist group based in the southern Philippines, has kidnapped tourists from resort islands off the eastern coast of Sabah. U.S. citizens are urged to use extreme caution when traveling in the coastal region and islands of eastern Sabah." Even though the warning didn't mention that three years had passed since the most recent kidnappings, no one could predict if the war would incite new terrorist activities.

Once we arrived at Sepilok Nature Resort, I found myself half hoping that Deb would talk me into changing my plans and hesitantly said to her, "I'm a little worried about you going to the dive resort alone."

"Oh, will you stop it!" she said.

Then I remembered what a tough and nasty woman she is when she's pissed off—and interrupting her scuba diving would definitely piss her off. If terrorists did abduct her, they'd quickly drop their ransom demands just to get rid of her.

The Sepilok Nature Resort had small lakeside cabins on well-kept grounds. The accommodations were basic, but after our time with the Iban, just having hot water and air-conditioning seemed like a decadent luxury.

After settling into our cabin, Deb and I walked over to the Orang Utan Rehabilitation Centre to watch the semi-wild orangutans. Although the experience wasn't as exciting as the encounters we had had with the wild orangutans, it did provide an opportunity for easy observation and photography.

Both the resort and the rehabilitation centre sit on the edge of the Kabili-Sepilok Forest Reserve's eleven thousand acres of protected rainforest. Since 1964, the centre has been taking in orangutans that have been orphaned or confiscated from the pet trade and returning them to the wild. The rehabilitation process often requires more than just food or medicine. The babies, for instance, must be taught everything they would have learned from their natural mothers. They start in quarantine and advance in developmental stages until they can fend for themselves. The centre isn't fenced in, and rehabilitated orangutans and other rainforest animals are free to come and go.

The staff fed the orangutans at ten and three o'clock each day. During my stay, I caught several feedings. What impressed me most was each primate's uncanny sense of time (or ability to pick up some signal I was unaware of). No orangutans would be in sight until ten minutes before the hour. Then I'd spot them, slowly climbing out of the treetops, pacing themselves to reach the feeding platform moments before food arrived.

That evening, Rudy took Deb and me on a walk to search for wildlife. Although our outing wasn't productive in terms of numbers, we did find a Wagler's pit viper and a giant flying squirrel. Each animal was high in a tree. The height was unsatisfactory for viewing the snake but perfect for viewing the squirrel. When it launched itself into an amazingly long flight, we could see it silhouetted in the darkening sky.

One of the ways rainforests in Borneo differ from rainforests in most other areas is that here the upper canopy doesn't grow to a uniform height. Since the varying layers create the need for extended jumps between trees, a variety of animals have developed gliding ability. In addition to flying squirrels, we also had the possibility of seeing lemurs, snakes, frogs, and lizards take to the air. Observing all five kinds of unusual flyers was a goal I hoped to achieve.

Deb departed in the morning for her diving adventure. With a gorgeous sunny day all to myself, I leisurely explored the rehabilitation centre, photographed the orangutans, and entered trip notes into my laptop computer. By evening, I was eager for some action and set out on another night walk with Rudy.

Normally when I think of wilderness, I think of places far away from civilization, such as where Deb and I had backpacked with the Iban. At Kabili-Sepilok Forest Reserve, the virgin rainforest was only a few minutes outside Sandakan. Even so, I had no problem forgetting the city of 325,000 even existed.

I was looking forward to a productive night. The lush flora hid innumerable creatures—we just had to find them. Rudy and I walked for about twenty minutes without seeing anything unusual. Then an eerie sound, unlike anything I had heard before, weaved its way through the trees.

"What kind of animal is making *that* noise?" I asked.

"That is Muslim call to prayer," said Rudy.

I could feel my face flush with embarrassment. "I'm sorry. That was the *last* thing I expected to hear in the rainforest. . . . The trees muffled the sound. . . . I couldn't hear it clearly."

Once I finished my awkward apology, I looked for the nearest hole to crawl into. The Muslims I had met in Borneo had treated me with respect, and I certainly intended to treat them the same way. I wasn't sure of Rudy's religious persuasion, but he ignored my faux pas and continued looking for wildlife.

Our luck improved. During the next hour we found several unusual caterpillars, a burnt-orange tree crab, a whiplike bronzeback snake, and a huge moth with big red eyes that were so reflective they appeared to glow in the dark. Later we detoured to where we had seen the Wagler's pit viper the previous night. The bright-green snake was still there, posed in the same position. This time, however, I came prepared with a more powerful camera lens and was able to capture several good images.

The rainforest was hot, and I frequently needed to replace the fluids I had sweat off. Near the end of our walk, I took a big drink from my water bottle. As I gulped, I felt something smooth and slimy—dangling toward my throat. A tiger leech was attached to my lower lip!

Pthhh! I spit it out, but it still hung from my lip. *Pthhh! Pthhh!* I tried to spit it off, but it wouldn't let go. I gave it a tug, and it grabbed onto my finger. I tried flinging it to the ground, without success. I pulled it off with one hand, and it stuck to the other. Finally, I rolled it into a ball and flicked it into the forest—victory at last!

Earlier, when I mentioned my preference for leeches over ants, bees, flies, and mosquitoes, I wasn't considering taste. The earthy flavor of the leech and the odd sensation of its sucker on my lip remained for hours. Even after the bleeding stopped, I occasionally found myself wiping my mouth with the back of my hand to make sure the leech was actually gone.

I returned to the resort for a late dinner. Other than the leech, the food during my stay was delightful. Almost every meal included jumbo prawns, fresh fruit, and various tropical delicacies. After all the gut-challenging food the Iban had served me, this was just what I needed. And my mom would have been so proud of me: I belonged to the Clean Plate Club for every meal.

Okay, I confess—I cheated. The dining area was on a deck, which overlooked the same small lake my cabin was on. Whenever I'd eat, a large school of ravenous fish would watch me with their snouts sticking out of the water. Whenever I'd grow full, I'd fling the scraps over the railing and watch the water boil from their feeding frenzy. Under normal circumstances, I'd never feed fish in such a manner, but guests had obviously been tossing them leftovers for years.

On the afternoon of my final solo day, I hiked across the Kabili-Sepilok Forest Reserve with Rudy and two other staff members. The terrain wasn't as rough as it had been in Sarawak. The hills climbed gradually, and though the flora was luxuriant and green, the ground was relatively dry.

This was a beautiful rainforest with mosses and ferns blanketing the ground and huge two-hundred-foot-tall dipterocarp trees reaching for the sun. Even so, after walking for more than an hour without seeing any fauna, I decided to spice things up by reinstating my reward for finding a python.

Upon hearing my offer, one of the staff commented, "Since you like snakes so much, you might be interested in knowing that a large black spitting cobra has been around here lately."

"Okay, I'm tripling my offer for the cobra!" I said. "My only stipulation is that I have to be able to get close enough to photograph it."

Despite our efforts, the wildlife spotting didn't improve. Hikes during the midday heat are seldom productive—even a tasty rodent couldn't have coaxed the cobra out from its cool hiding spot.

Our trek concluded at a research station at the edge of the Sulu Sea. Rather than returning by foot, Rudy arranged for us to take the easy way back: we traveled by speedboat to Sandakan and from there took a shuttle van to the resort.

Deb returned from Lankayan Island on Sunday morning. She was beaming with pleasure and talking faster than an auctioneer. "That was the *best* diving experience of my life! The reef was in pristine shape, the water was warm, and the fish were incredible. Oh, and it was so cool—all the dives were macrodives! I spent much of my time exploring crevices—looking for camouflaged creatures."

"What kinds of sea life did you see?" I asked.

"I saw batfish and scorpionfish and stonefish and clownfish and blue starfish and a hawksbill turtle and thousands of tiny glass fish and giant clams and even a seven-foot-long zebra shark!"

"That's great! You had your heart set on seeing a whale shark. Did you have any luck?"

"Yes, I did! But I wasn't diving at the time. I was on the boat, heading for Lankayan, when I spotted one feeding along the surface. He was huuuuge!"

"I'm so pleased you had a good time."

"It was wonderful. I just wish you had been there. I missed you. Oh! Remember your concern about the kidnappings? I was well protected. At least five heavily armed guards patrolled the island at all times."

Deb and I continued sharing stories of our two days apart while traveling south by shuttle van toward Danum Valley. We would be spending the next four nights at the Borneo Rainforest Lodge, the sole accommodations in the Danum Valley Conservation Area. Comprised of

108,000 acres of virgin lowland tropical rainforest, the conservation area protects one of the most biologically diverse ecosystems in the world. Information provided by the lodge stated that the area's ever-growing species list included 275 birds, 124 mammals, 72 reptiles, and 56 amphibians. Researchers have also found as many as 200 tree species within a single hectare (2.47 acres).

The ride to Danum Valley would take five hours. Three hours into our journey, we stopped in downtown Lahad Datu (population 81,000) to switch shuttles. Our driver, whom we had known only since the beginning of the ride, removed our luggage and set it on the sidewalk. "If you want lunch, restaurant two blocks away," he said as he pointed. "While you eat, new driver transfer belongings to his van."

Trusting strangers was becoming routine. Despite the possibility that all our travel possessions could disappear in an instant, Deb and I just looked at each other and shrugged, both thinking, "What the hell, we've been lucky so far."

As we strolled down the busy street, I realized we were the only foreigners in town. Our light skin made us stand out like a cat at a dog show. Being the object of numerous smiles and stares made me feel a bit self-conscious. I flashed back to a similar occurrence in Iquitos, Peru, and concluded that every white American should experience being a minority at least once. A glimpse from the other side can make anyone a better person.

We ate at a crowded open-air Chinese restaurant. The portions were generous, and the price was a steal. When I converted the ten Malaysian ringgits I paid into U.S. dollars, the total bill for our meal came to $2.63. No wonder so many people were in the restaurant.

We met Stephen, our fourth and final guide, shortly after lunch. Since he lived near Lahad Datu, he joined us in the shuttle van for the ride to the Borneo Rainforest Lodge. He was a quiet man who limited his speaking to answering questions and providing interesting tidbits of information. His gentle voice and liberal use of native terms forced me to concentrate whenever he spoke. He didn't ask about the war but obviously knew about it from the newspaper he read during lulls in our conversation.

Stephen had a husky build and appeared to be about fifty years old. We couldn't have asked for anyone more knowledgeable about the area where we were headed. As a member of the Dusun Segama tribe, he grew up in the Danum Valley rainforest. In fact, he told us that he hadn't seen a town until the age of nine, when he followed his schoolteacher on a three-day hike to Lahad Datu.

As we proceeded west on a gravel road, into the heart of Borneo, Stephen pointed out landmarks and told us about his tribe's history. Because I was still getting used to his hybrid dialect, this is what I heard: "That is rntwaysp, which my people grow for food. When I was young, we walk along the slstrepatgs. My father helped build dyweplk and he ayesdg until—Elephants! There are elephants up ahead!"

A mother elephant and her calf had crossed in front of us and were slowly walking into the rainforest. We pulled to the edge of the road so I could take some photos through the open window on the right-hand side. I squeezed off several shots. Then, like a scene from the movie *Jurassic Park,* a low rumble rattled our van. The sound was so low and powerful I could feel it in my chest. I twisted to the left and looked into the eyes of a three-quarters-grown male elephant! He wanted to cross the road, but we were in his way. Our driver cranked the ignition and accelerated forward before stopping again.

I craned my neck to the rear. "Is it okay if we get out and walk back to the elephants?"

Stephen hesitated a moment before answering, "Yes, okay."

The elephant hadn't crossed the road yet, and when he saw us get out of the van, he grew nervous and backed off. Stephen waved Deb and me to the far side of the vehicle. Once we were out of sight, the young bull hurried across to join his family.

I crept down the road to where the elephants had entered the forest. Their path cut straight through the thick foliage. I held my breath and peeked around the corner. Five elephants—two mothers, two babies, and the young bull—were ninety feet away. The larger mother was standing sideways, partially blocking my view of the other members of the herd. I decided to walk down the path. Not too far—just enough to get a good picture of one of the babies peeking out from between her mother's legs. Deb and Stephen followed behind me.

Five steps, stop; four steps, stop; three steps, stop; two steps—the mother turned and charged!

While Deb and Stephen ran, I held my ground, waiting for the perfect shot. Everything seemed to happen in slow motion. In the short time it took the elephant to halve its distance to me, several thoughts whisked through my brain: "Don't move. You survived backpacking with the Iban—this is nothing. Hold the camera steady. You'll never have a photo opportunity like this again. Steadyyyyy. Now! That was really stupid! Run!"

The elephant was roughly thirty feet away when I pushed the shutter button. She aborted her charge as soon as I dashed off in the opposite direction.

When I think of elephants, the first thought that comes to mind is African elephants on the open plains. Observing Borneo's elephants in the thick rainforest was a curious experience. They looked out of place—and some would say they were.

At the time of our visit, the prevailing opinion was that the Sultan of Sulu had introduced Asiatic elephants to Borneo in 1750. Lack of fossil evidence and accepted local tradition supported the introduction theory. Stephen, however, disagreed and said, "My people's history goes back much further than that. Elephant always part of our history."

Unknown to us was that the *Public Library of Science Biology* would soon be publishing a scientific study on Borneo's elephants. Researchers, led by Prithiviraj Fernando of Columbia University, had conducted DNA tests and determined that the estimated two thousand elephants on Borneo were genetically distinct from other Asiatic elephants.

While the debate over the elephants' status as a Borneo native will likely continue, the DNA tests corroborated the accuracy of Stephen's tribal history. Furthermore, now that evidence suggests that the elephants have been isolated on Borneo since land bridges last linked the island to the mainland (eighteen thousand years ago), the conservation of these unique mammals takes on additional importance.

We returned to the van and continued our drive. When Stephen spotted a snake near the middle of the road, our driver pulled to the shoulder so we could check it out. As we walked toward the bright-green, three-feet-long grey-tailed racer, he cocked his head and contorted his body in a way I'd never seen a snake do before. He looked as if he could easily spread his ribs out enough to catch the wind like Borneo's flying snakes (which actually glide, not fly).

"Is he venomous?" I asked.

"Mild-venomous," said Stephen.

Later, I'd consult several wildlife books and find that none of them mentioned the grey-tailed racer as being either a flying or a venomous species. One thing I learned was that much of the wildlife on the island was either unstudied or understudied. Often books would list aspects of a Bornean animal's natural history as "unknown," and occasionally, such as with the elephants and something else I'll share with you later, they'd restate common beliefs that were likely untrue. Therefore, while I trust sufficient research has been done to verify that grey-tailed racers are nonvenomous, I'm still not convinced they can't fly.

The roar of a logging truck cut short my admiration session. I had to get the grey-tailed racer off the road before the truck ran him over. Since at the time I believed the snake to be venomous, I couldn't just pick him up. I tried herding him, but herding a cat would have been easier—he reared up and defended his position.

Stephen, Deb, and I hurriedly searched the roadside for a stick. When I found one, I slid it under the snake and carried him to the shoulder—an instant before the truck thundered by.

I was disturbed to see numerous logging trucks on the road. I had presumed the Malaysian government was protecting the entire Danum Valley but, apparently, only the Danum Valley Conservation Area was safe from chain saws. Signs posted in the area claimed that "selective logging" was being done, but based on the size of the logs on the trucks, the only things being selected were the biggest and best trees.

Although I've loosely used *jungle* and *rainforest* as equivalent terms in this book, technically *jungle* best describes what virgin/primary rainforest becomes when it regrows after logging. Natural plant growth in the rainforest depends on large trees forming a canopy to block out direct sunlight. When trees are removed, sunlight readily reaches the forest floor, allowing faster-growing plants to choke off slower-growing trees. In a primary rainforest, the undergrowth is limited. In a secondary rainforest, the undergrowth forms a *jungle* of near impenetrable tangles. Recovery from deforestation takes much longer than you might expect. As Marco Lambertini notes in his book, *A Naturalist's Guide to the Tropics,* it can take five hundred to a thousand years after wide-scale deforestation for a rainforest to totally recover.

We escaped the rumble of logging trucks and entered the serene Danum Valley Conservation Area. A permit is required for public access to the area, and overnight stays are limited to the Borneo Rainforest Lodge's thirty-one double-capacity chalets.

At the time I made our reservation, the reasonable price for chalet rental combined with the exclusivity of the accommodations caused me assume the lodge would be continuously filled to capacity. Once we checked in, I was delighted to learn that we shared the entire lodge with only six other guests. When I asked one of the staff why they had so many vacancies, he told me that an already slow week had been compounded with SARS and war-related cancellations. In fact, four guests would be checking out the next day, leaving just us and a couple from the Netherlands.

After settling into our chalet, Deb and I walked over to the open-air dining room (located on the second floor of the main building) for dinner. The Sepilok Nature Resort had spoiled me with a wide variety of delicious meals, and I had high hopes the Borneo Rainforest Lodge would do the same. To my dismay, the food placed on our table was virtually identical to the repetitive meals the Iban had cooked for us. The lodge did add a fish course, but that was even less appetizing than the chicken chunks. A three-day break from heavily curried food wasn't nearly long enough for me.

We met Stephen after dinner for a night drive. I had never been on a night drive before and looked forward to covering a lot of territory quickly. Our transportation was an old, smelly, barely running flatbed truck. We sat on a bench in the rear while a lodge employee perched on the cab roof and shined a high-powered spotlight on the trees. As we puttered down the road, Deb whispered to me, "I feel like a Montana poacher."

I had to agree. Montana certainly has its share of poachers who hunt at night using similar spotlighting techniques.

Our drive wasn't as productive as I had hoped it would be. We did see some unusual frogs, a flying squirrel, a whip snake, and a buffy fish-owl, but they were scarcely worth the headache I got from breathing the diesel fumes. I went to bed looking forward to a day of exploring the rainforest on foot.

Stephen met us after breakfast for a short hike along one of the trails leading from the lodge and immediately put his keen eyes to work finding hidden wildlife. Unguided travel may save money and appeal to one's pioneering spirit, but as Deb and I had learned on previous trips, nothing beats a local guide for successful wildlife spotting. Because guides are usually familiar with the territory they work, they're more likely to notice something new in a scene and less likely to be fooled by an animal's camouflage.

On this morning, Deb and I would have walked right past several comb-crested agamid lizards and a blue-necked keelback if Stephen hadn't pointed them out.

The two-foot-long blue-necked keelback was the most exotic-looking snake I'd ever seen. She was two-tone reddish-orange, with white speckles along her spine and a dark red chevron on the back of her neck. Her skin looked velvety.

"Is the snake venomous?" I asked.

"Harmless," said Stephen, "but many of my people believe it to be venomous."

When I reached down and touched the snake, she raised her head high and flattened her neck to mimic a cobra. "Are you *sure* she's not venomous?"

"Yes—harmless."

I considered catching the snake for closer examination but decided instead to take a few photos and let her disappear under the leaf litter.

A subsequent check of my wildlife books revealed that the blue-necked keelback was another understudied species. In general, authors either didn't address the issue of venom or stated that the snake *might* be venomous. Lacking a definitive answer, I decided the most fitting description for this exotic cobra-mimic would be "probable-nonvenomous with delusions of grandeur."

When Stephen pointed out the morning's first comb-crested agamid lizard, I immediately thought of the Boyd's forest dragon I had seen in Australia. While both species belong to the same family, comb-crested agamid lizards are a little smaller (about a foot long) than Boyd's forest dragons and not quite as outlandish looking.

We saw four comb-crested agamid lizards during our hike. Each one had an expressive face, a frill down its back (males have longer frills than females), and a green or brown body flecked with scales of gold, black, and red. They all clung to tree trunks, and like the Boyd's forest dragon, I could get very close to them, because they were convinced their camouflage was infallible. A female allowed me to get my camera lens within a few inches of her nose before she tilted her head inquisitively for a perfect photo. In retrospect, she likely saw her reflection in my lens and was trying to figure out who the beautiful lizard was staring at her from inside the black cylinder.

After lunch and another short hike, I suggested to Deb and Stephen that we stroll a half mile down the road to the canopy walkway.

"I'm surprised you'd want to go there," said Deb. "You know how much you hate heights."

"After all the gorge walls we traversed with the Iban, I don't think heights will ever be a problem again," I said confidently.

"Oh, I didn't think of that. I suppose you're right."

I was wrong.

The canopy walkway stretched in two sections between three giant dipterocarp trees. A small wooden platform wrapped around each tree, and upper and lower sets of parallel support cables ran between the trees. A series of vertical cables connected the support cables to the actual walkway, which consisted of wooden crossbeams covered lengthwise with wooden planks. Strung between the upper and the lower support cables were four-foot-high sides of netting, and the top was left open. In all, the hanging footbridge was 350 feet long with an average height of 89 feet.

I climbed the stairs to the first platform and stepped onto the walkway. Intellectually I knew I was safe, but four things made me nervous. First, the ironwood floor planks were only one inch thick. While ironwood is known for its strength, many of the boards were cracked, and some of the nails attaching them to the crossbeams had worked loose. Second, the walkway swayed with each step, creating the illusion that it could roll upside down at any moment. Third, the walkway was more exposed than I had expected it to be. I had visualized it as being closely surrounded by trees with nearby branches to grab in an emergency. Fourth, similar structures have been featured in countless action-adventure movies, and in each one a cable or plank breaks just about the time the hero reaches the middle. The hero, of course, miraculously swings to safety, but someone always suffers a fatal fall.

As I gingerly proceeded, my balls sucked up into my body, my legs begged to buckle, and my instincts urged me to drop to my hands and knees and crawl. I had a lively conversation with myself. "Don't stop! If you keep walking, you eventually have to reach the other side. How can you tell stories of adventure and bravery in Borneo if you chicken out on something Deb will do without a second thought?"

And so I went, slowly and deliberately. The first section was shorter and more stable than the second section, which swung vigorously. Deb and Stephen followed but stayed a section behind to minimize the motion.

I continued talking to myself. "Come on. . . . You can do it. . . . Just a few more steps. . . . I made it!"

The far side of the walkway dead-ended at a platform with no way down. At that moment, all I wanted to do was become a tree hugger—literally—and wrap my arms around the trunk until a helicopter arrived to rescue me. The tree, by the way, was so massive that three of me would have been necessary to reach all the way around it for a proper hug.

Now I had to reverse my course. I eased back onto the walkway, jabbering to myself as the wooden planks creaked beneath my feet. "Wimp! Come on! You can do it. Walk like a man!"

My return trip was easier, if for no other reason than the element of choice had been eliminated. Opting for a helicopter rescue would have shattered my travel budget—and my ego—for the next decade or so.

I tried to figure out why heights bothered me so much. I couldn't recall any bad falls from my past. Then I remembered what I had learned about the Iban believing their dead live again as orangutans. That was it! If humans can become orangutans, then the process should also work in reverse. I must have been an orangutan in a previous life. One day, while I was happily jumping from tree to tree, a branch broke and I crashed to my death. That would also explain my love for banana bread, banana cream pie, banana liqueur, and just about everything else banana. Now, if I could just grow more than a half-dozen chest hairs my theory would be confirmed.

Upon reaching the first platform, I was eager to return to solid ground. I looked back for my companions. Deb and Stephen—who had practically skipped across the walkway—had decided to hang out on the middle platform to wait for a flying squirrel that regularly emerged from its nest at dusk. "Damn!" I muttered to myself. Back I schlepped to the middle platform, where I pretended to have a good time, waiting for a squirrel that refused to follow a human schedule.

One creature that did follow a schedule was an insect called a "six o'clock cicada." I was familiar with a variety of cicadas but had no idea an individual species could accurately tell time. According to Stephen, within five minutes of either side of six, the cicadas would begin their song.

The word *song* may not be the most accurate word to describe the noise they made—think electric buzz saw instead.

As we listened to what sounded like a construction crew busy in the rainforest, Stephen said, "When I was little boy, my mother always have me come home when six o'clock cicada start."

The cicadas, incidentally, would be on time every evening for the rest of our visit.

Our wait for the flying squirrel was rewarded, but not by the elusive rodent. Instead, we saw two wrinkled hornbills (classified as "near threatened" by the IUCN) and several white hornbills. Although the birds chose perches well out of my camera's effective range, just being able to observe them through binoculars was a thrill.

A hornbill is a large bird with an oversized beak topped with a bony protrusion called a *casque*. Eight species of hornbill live in Borneo, and each one has a different-sized casque. For instance, the wreathed hornbill has a modest casque, and the rhinoceros hornbill has a substantial casque worthy of its name.

Aside from their distinctive appearance, hornbills are unique in the way they protect their eggs and chicks from predators. With the exception of ground hornbills, when the female is ready to lay her egg(s), the male will lure her to a hollow in a tree and wall her in with mud. While the female is incarcerated, she'll receive food from her mate through a small slit in the mud. Then, after about three months, she'll break out and the chicks will seal themselves back in until they're ready to fly.

Just when I thought we were finally going to descend from the canopy walkway, Stephen put a finger to his lips and pointed to a tree, two hundred feet away. "*Shhhhh.* See movement in treetop? Orangutan making nest." I stared at the treetop but saw only a mass of stationary greenery. Stephen concentrated on the spot for a moment, then added, "We must come back here early tomorrow before orangutan wake up."

By morning, I'd be excited about the possibility of seeing another orangutan. But at that moment, the last thing I wanted to do was return to the canopy walkway. "Great," I whispered to myself, "as soon as my balls return to their normal position they'll be yanked back up into my lungs again."

As we walked toward the lodge, Stephen continued educating us about the local wildlife. "You've probably read in books that orangutan make new nest out of branches each night. Books wrong. I see orangutan reuse nest many times. First it step into old nest to test, then it adds reinforcements if necessary."

Once again, Stephen's knowledge was at odds with prevailing opinion. Even though making a new treetop nest each night is a rather insignificant piece of information, both books and experts commonly repeat it as "an interesting fact about orangutans." Is this another case of "if you repeat it enough it must be true"? Without spending years in the rainforest watching orangutans, I can't say for sure. But then that makes my point. Who would know more about orangutans than someone who has lived in the rainforest for most of his life? I side with Stephen on this one.

We returned to the lodge for dinner. Other than a few minor variations, the chef had prepared the same entrée for every meal except breakfast. I had lost almost ten pounds during the first part of our trip, and now keeping the weight off was just a little too easy. After a few bites, my stomach would feign being full. Even Deb, who liked the food, was tired of the monotony.

We both craved something sweet. The only dessert served to us anywhere in Borneo was a melon plate. Although technically the melon was sweet, eating it day after day was unsatisfying.

As we stared with contempt at yet another plate of neatly sliced orange, pink, and green triangles, Deb exclaimed, "Chocolate! We need some chocolate."

"A chocolate ice cream bar," I suggested.

"*Any* kind of chocolate would be good. . . . Wait a minute. I still have some Hershey's Bites in my bag."

"Sorry, I ate them while you were scuba diving."

"How could you!"

"There were only a few left, and they were calling to me."

"Damn!"

"They must have chocolate here somewhere. I'll go ask at the front desk."

I ran downstairs and found the manager. "Do you have any chocolate for sale? Perhaps some ice cream or a candy bar."

"I'm sorry," said the petite young woman. "We don't have any chocolate on the premises."

"Do you know where I can get some?"

"You'd have to go back to Lahad Datu."

I returned to the dining room, trying not to look as dejected as I felt. Before I could even sit down, Deb asked, "Did they have any *choc-o-lat?*"

"Noooo, the nearest chocolate is two hours away in Lahad Datu."

"Bummer!"

"Wait a minute! There's a helicopter pad behind our chalet. . . ."

After sunset we headed out on a night drive. The thought of spending another evening breathing diesel fumes was almost enough to warrant skipping the drive, but I really wanted to see some of the unusual nocturnal mammals in the area. For instance, we had a chance of spotting slow lorises and western tarsiers—two adorable primitive primates with oversized eyes and expressive faces. On the other end of the spectrum, I hoped to see a pangolin. Relatives of anteaters and armadillos, pangolins have scales instead of hair and resemble little tanks with legs. If I were directing a science fiction movie and needed an animal to walk through the ruins of a nuclear war or represent a species from a far distant planet, a pangolin would be my first choice.

As with our previous night drive, once it started, I was eager for it to end. The smell of exhaust was overpowering, and the few animals we did see were too far away to enjoy. Our sightings on this night included a binturong (a large civet known locally as a bear-cat, and classified by the IUCN as "vulnerable") and a Malayan civet.

A typical night drive spotting went like this:

"See those two shiny eyes near the top of that tall tree?"

"No."

"Look way up, close to the trunk. Now do you see them?"

"No."

"Okay, look just above that large branch on the left. Now do you see them?"

"Yes . . . I think so."

"That's a bear-cat."

I'd take the spotlight operator's word for it, but in reality, the actual animal providing the eyeshine was irrelevant. Two fireflies sitting the proper distance from each other on a tree would have looked virtually the same. Deb and I vowed to do night walks instead of night drives for the remainder of our stay.

Tuesday morning we were up at six to meet Stephen for another hike to the canopy walkway. I was surprised Deb willingly got up so early. She was definitely setting a new personal travel wake-up-time record. But then, how often does one get the opportunity to see an orangutan emerge from its nest?

The three of us climbed the stairs to the walkway and crossed to the middle platform. Although I wasn't ready to dance on the walkway yet, the going was much easier than the day before, and the white and rhinoceros hornbills flying among the trees kept me distracted.

When Stephen noticed movement in the nest, he whispered, "Orangutan waking up."

We stared at the foliage for several minutes, waiting for the red ape to appear. Eventually Stephen announced, "Orangutan went out other side. We go find him."

We descended from the walkway and tried to locate the best route to the orangutan. The treetop we had been watching was in dense forest, about a third of a mile from the road. With no direct way in, we'd have to find our own route. Deb, still nursing her broken toe, elected to wait for us by the road.

I faithfully followed my guide as he zigzagged through small openings between trees, vines, rocks, and spider webs. A third of a mile isn't far on open land, but our natural obstacle course made the distance seem five times longer. Finally, we came upon a trickling spring, and just beyond it was the orangutan's tree. Stephen put a finger to his lips as we slunk below and gazed up.

"Orangutan slept there and went out that way," he said as he pointed. "You can see where he climbed through branches."

I couldn't see anything but the tall trunk and leafy crown of a normal-looking dipterocarp tree. Nevertheless, I pointed in the same direction and said, "Yes, he went just like that."

We searched the immediate area for the orangutan before starting back toward the road. Stephen picked a different route through the trees than the way we came in. After a few minutes, he stopped and scanned the terrain. He looked confused. My sense of direction told me we were going to miss our mark, but how could I ask a man who was born in the jungle if we were headed the right way? He continued walking, stopping, looking, walking, stopping, looking—I felt a twinge of anxiety. Eventually, after what seemed like a roundabout route, we stepped onto the gravel road—two hundred feet away from where we had entered. I never asked him what happened.

As soon as we met up with Deb, Stephen said, "I am very sorry we miss orangutan. Really wanted to show him to you."

"That's okay," I said. "We saw four wild orangutans in Sarawak and at least ten semi-wild orangutans at the Sepilok Rehabilitation Centre. Seeing more would've been nice, but I'd much rather find some other primates."

"Yes," agreed Deb, "any of the monkeys would be great."

Stephen's face lit up. "I hear Bornean gibbons across river."

Deb and I shot each other looks of astonishment before following our guide down a short path to the water's edge.

"I can hear them, but I can't see them," I said.

Stephen pointed to the trees along the opposite bank of the Danum River. "Remember what I told you about orangutan reusing nest? I show you something else you won't read in books. Hear 'wooooooing' sound? That's the female. Hear 'bubbling' sound? That's the male. The female starts the call and the male finishes it. Now watch. As soon as the male stops bubbling they will all move to different branches."

"Oh, now I see them!"

Knowing when the gibbons would move made spotting them easy. We counted six gibbons in all (a pair with their offspring), and though we were roughly sixty feet away, the distance was beneficial, as we could observe all their choreographed movements at once.

Like orangutans, Bornean gibbons are apes. The major differences between apes and monkeys are that apes stand more upright, are tail-less, and are more intelligent. The major differences between Bornean gibbons and orangutans are that the gibbons are smaller (10–18 pounds versus 80–200 pounds), less intelligent, and more social (orangutans tend to be solitary).

The Bornean Gibbon Ballet continued for about fifteen minutes, and during that time their routine never deviated. Every few minutes, the sequence of calls would start again, and the entire family would change positions.

The three of us took a break for brunch at the lodge before heading out on another hike. Rainforests have poor soil because heavy rains have leached away the nutrients. Since trees must get their food on or near the surface, they have adapted by growing buttress roots that reach out rather than down.

When we came upon a dipterocarp tree with massive buttress roots, Stephen took the opportunity to show us how trees could save our lives if we became lost or injured. In our jungle survival lesson, he taught us to clear a sleeping space between the roots, gather resin for starting a fire, and call for help by pounding on a buttress with a rock. To demonstrate, he hit a root several times. Like a giant megaphone, the tree broadcast the thumping sound, which would-be rescuers could hear for miles. Finally, he pointed out that we could use vines for navigating, as they always wrap around trees with the lower portion of the loop pointing downriver.

Secure that we could now survive almost anything, we spent a good portion of the afternoon looking for animals and enjoying the rainforest. I was still unsuccessful in my trip-long quest to find a reticulated python, and now, with only two days left, my search for the world's longest snake was taking on more urgency.

Although once again the snake would elude me, my consolation prize for the afternoon was being able to add to my list of unusual flying animals. This time we spotted two gliding lizards, each clinging to its own small tree. Both reptiles were about eight inches long and blended in perfectly with the bark. When Stephen wiggled one of the trees, the lizard flung itself into the air and sailed to safety. Aided by large skin flaps (which are supported by extralong ribs), gliding lizards can fly quite far and even make midflight steering adjustments to land on their chosen spot.

After our hike and survival lesson, Deb and I returned to the lodge for another déjà vu meal. We didn't plan to meet up with Stephen again until after dark. When we finished eating and realized we had several hours of daylight left, we decided to take advantage of the opportunity to do absolutely nothing.

The Borneo Rainforest Lodge has a network of raised walkways and ground-level boardwalks made out of evenly spaced wooden slats supported by four-inch-high boards on each side. The walkways lead from the dining room to the chalets, and the boardwalks connect to the walkways via stairs and lead to the gardens and the Danum River.

With thoughts of relaxing on our balcony with a cool drink, we strolled along the walkway toward our chalet. Something gold flashed in the corner of my eye! I spun to my left just in time to see the back half of a large snake slip between the slats of the nearest boardwalk. "Snake! I think it's a cobra!" I shouted.

I sprinted down the stairs to where the snake had vanished and peered between the slats. A tail zipped by! The snake appeared to heading toward the thick bushes beside the stairs.

As I stepped toward the bushes, I put on my sunglasses—in case it was a spitting cobra. Then . . . slowly . . . carefully . . . I parted the branches. Nothing!

Deb joined me in the search. While I continued sifting through the bushes, she stood on the boardwalk, looking between the slats. "There he is! He's right under my feet!"

The sight of my wife standing with a suspected cobra inches below her feet brought two simultaneous thoughts to my head. One was a flashback to our wedding day. Would she still have married me if the minister had asked, "Do you promise to love, honor, and assist your husband in the search for deadly serpents?"

I put my other thought into words: "Get *off* the boardwalk!"

"It's okay. He took off as soon as I saw him."

I took a deep breath and knelt on the boardwalk for a closer look beneath where Deb had been standing. "Which way did he go?" I asked, knowing her answer no longer mattered.

The two of us searched the bushes and every inch of the boardwalk, but the snake was gone.

We returned to our chalet and flipped through my wildlife identification books. Although neither Deb nor I had seen the snake's head, based on its speed, size, and elegant gold and brown skin pattern, we were able to conclude with certainty that it was a cobra—a king cobra.

Having experienced enough adventure for the day, we sat on our balcony, put our feet up, popped open some beers, and watched the river go by.

After a bit, Deb looked at me with a smile of contentment. "*Mmmm,* it feels so nice to be able to just sit and relax for a while."

"Yes . . . it does feel nice . . . but . . ."

"You can't take it, can you?"

"No, this is great. . . . I'm really enjoying watching the stork-billed kingfishers fly back and forth over the river. They're stunning—the turquoise on their wings is just about my favorite color. I was thinking about photographing them, but they're moving so fast. . . . And with that tree right there, I'd have a difficult time getting a clear shot."

"Go on. I can relax without you."

"Are you sure you don't mind?"

"Go."

I picked up my camera and hurried out the door. The rest of the afternoon whizzed by as I enjoyed my kind of relaxation: walking the grounds, photographing birds and dragonflies, and doing a little light cobra hunting.

When Deb and I met up with Stephen for a night walk, we told him about our king cobra sighting, and he told us about a spitting cobra he saw just before sunset. With at least two cobras in the area, the prospects seemed great for a productive night of creeping through the jungle with flashlights.

Tonight our plans were to concentrate on finding snakes. In the past, when Deb accompanied me on searches of this type, she was a relatively passive participant. This time, Stephen offered her a stick, and she took it and put it to proper use.

As we headed down a trail, I couldn't stop grinning. Deb loves to joke about how she trained me after we got married. It's true—I've been domesticated. I now wipe off the bathroom sink, put down the toilet seat, and even throw my dirty clothes in the hamper. I hadn't considered that spousal training could work in reverse, but there she was, diligently using her stick to lift any foliage that could hide a snake. I recalled my imaginary wedding vow from earlier in the day. Perhaps the reason our marriage has lasted so long is because we've both changed a little for each other.

Searching for snakes can be a tedious process that leaves plenty of time for thinking. While we slowly worked the edges of the trail, I continued my sentimental thoughts about our marriage. The faces of all the eligible women I knew before Deb flashed through my brain. I couldn't imagine any of them traveling with me to Borneo, much less willingly hunting for pythons and cobras in the dark. I was fortunate to have married the right woman on the first try.

Deb interrupted my thoughts with an announcement: "I like scuba diving better than snake hunting. There's more immediate gratification."

Okay, so she's not perfect.

On this night, however, even I was beginning to feel a little antsy. After more than an hour, our only sightings were a walkingstick and a giant frog. The walkingstick was close to a foot long—by far the biggest I'd ever seen. As for the frog, it was about the size of a large grapefruit. "Giant frog," said Stephen admiringly. "Very edible."

As appalling as eating rainforest animals seemed to me, I didn't say anything. Stephen grew up in the forest, and expecting him not to see the indigenous animals as a source of food was unrealistic. He always showed respect for the wildlife we encountered and never attempted to catch a meal while working as our guide. As long as his diet didn't include protected or endangered species, what he ate on his own time was none of my business.

A short distance past the frog, Deb informed us that her toe hurt too much to walk any farther. Ever since she broke her toe, various inanimate objects—luggage, doors, beds, and backpacks—had been leaping out of nowhere to stub it. One such object pounced earlier in the evening, and now her toe had swollen up in her hiking boot. We altered our route to cross near the lodge, and Deb hobbled back to the chalet for the night.

Stephen and I continued, but our luck didn't improve. The next hour and a half produced only a flying frog and another giant frog. Finding the flying frog was fun because it was another airborne animal to add to my list. The giant frog, on the other hand, must have been a real delicacy, as Stephen couldn't resist another comment: "Giant frog. Very edible. My people eat these frogs. Two enough for good meal."

Fortunately for the frogs, no human predators would be eating them on this night. As for Stephen and me, we were tired, sweaty, and dirty. We abandoned our search and hiked back to the lodge for some sleep.

Deb and I awoke on Wednesday with plans for another hike. Mother Nature, however, had a better idea and brought the action to us. While we were eating breakfast in the open-air dining room, Deb's eyes suddenly grew wide. "Monkeys! There are monkeys in the trees behind you!"

I turned and was delighted to see seven leaf monkeys (also known as maroon langurs) enjoying a breakfast of tender leaves. Since they were engrossed in their meal, I took a chance they'd stick around and ran back to the chalet to grab my camera.

When I returned, they were still in the trees, forty feet away from the dining area. A day earlier, I had caught a glimpse of some leaf monkeys fleeing into the canopy. Now, knowing they were shy, I approached gradually. I figured they'd eventually spook, no matter how stealthy I was, but instead they only shot me occasional glances as I maneuvered underneath them.

Prior to my first tropical rainforest visit, this was how I had imagined it would be: monkeys lounging in the trees, unafraid of the humans below. The reality of multiple rainforest visits made me fully appreciate the rare treat before my eyes.

Leaf monkeys have long tails and handsome black faces. They're roughly the size of a two-year-old child, and they look like little people in furry suits. I found them most amusing when they jumped from tree to tree. Their routine was reminiscent of the famous cliff-jumping scene from the movie *Butch Cassidy and the Sundance Kid.* They'd race along a sturdy treetop branch, launch themselves into the air, and crash-land on a neighboring tree. Though each one must have done the same routine thousands of times, none appeared to enjoy it. Every jump matched the desperation of Butch and Sundance, complete with a similar midair scream: "Aaaaaahhhhhhhhhhhhhh!"

When the monkeys proceeded upriver, I followed. As we moved away from the lodge, the forest canopy began to close. I wanted to get a photo of a monkey in flight while I could still see open sky between the trees. I moved ahead, found a somewhat bug-free area under the last tree of opportunity, and lay on the ground with my camera ready. Although each monkey gave a verbal warning before jumping, the shot was difficult because each leap came from a different branch. I missed the first few shots, got lucky on one, and then became distracted when a Malayan flying lemur glided by in the opposite direction. The shock of seeing the lemur caused me to pause just long enough for the remaining monkeys to make their jumps.

The flying lemur was an exciting sight because it completed the quinquepartite list of unusual flying animals I wanted to see. Presuming the grey-tailed racer was capable of flight, I had now seen a flying snake, flying squirrel, flying frog, flying lemur, and gliding lizard.

Flying lemurs are neither true lemurs nor members of the primate family. Instead, they're in an order all their own, called Dermoptera. Based on their appearance, I've formed my own origination theory:

Millions of years ago, when Borneo's tree squirrels were evolving into flying squirrels, one industrious—and very horny—squirrel decided to take an evolutionary shortcut and mate with a bat. Its offspring were awkward creatures, resembling flying foxes with big puffy tails, who instantly became the laughingstock of the rainforest. In the first ever case of evolution due to embarrassment, descendants plucked the hair from their tails each morning until eventually the hairless appendage became part of their kite-shaped flight membrane and the modern flying lemur was born.

My attention returned to the monkeys. Although the chances for more in-flight photos were gone, I observed the band for nearly two hours, as they slowly worked their way through the trees by the river. I would have stayed with them longer, but Deb—who had been splitting time between the lodge and the monkeys—was eager for me to see a surprise Stephen had in the reception area.

As I headed for the lodge, I almost walked straight through a knee-high spider web, strung horizontally between three plants. A horned spider guarded the center of the web. The bizarre-looking arachnid had a bright-red abdomen—the size of a quarter—and two long horns protruding from its rear.

Deb hadn't noticed I was distracted and was far ahead of me when I yelled, "I'll be there in a moment! Right after I photograph this really cool spider."

The only problem with photographing the spider was that it was clinging to the underside of its web—facing belly-up. To get an image of the spider from the proper side without disturbing it, I'd have to shimmy on my back underneath the web. I should have thought to check the ground first, but I didn't want to keep Deb and Stephen waiting.

As soon as I clicked the first shot, I felt the unmistakable sensation of a leech crawling up my inner thigh. I could see on the digital camera screen that my first image was out of focus. I desperately wanted to reach up the leg of my shorts to remove the leech, but I was committed to producing a crisp photo and couldn't risk spooking the spider into dropping from its web. I'd have to hope the leech settled before inching too far north.

I squeezed off three more shots. They looked okay on the screen, but I couldn't be sure. As I aimed the camera once more, numerous creatures began crawling up my legs. They were too small and too fast to be leeches.

"Oh, shit, ants!" I shouted.

If I injured an ant, they'd all start stinging. If I stood, I'd be tangled in the web. If the spider bit me, I could have a reaction to its venom. As for the leech—it was *definitely* nearing a major blood-flow area!

I limboed out from under the web and leaped to my feet. I had an instant to decide whether to first remove the ants or the leech. The decision was easy—the ants had to go. I gingerly flicked them off my skin before reaching up the leg of my shorts. The leech had already attached its suction cup, but fortunately I was able to grasp the wormlike creature between my fingers and yank it off before it filled with blood.

Now, suitably creeped out, I brushed the dirt off my legs—and anything else that felt buglike—and hurried to join Deb and Stephen.

When I arrived at the reception area, Stephen was sitting on a bench with a rhinoceros beetle clutching his pant leg. The three-inch-long beetle had two large spikes near the top of its head and a smaller spike centered above its eyes—it looked like a triceratops dinosaur.

The rhinoceros beetle is considered by some to be the world's strongest animal. Tests have shown it can carry an enormous load in proportion to its weight. How much the beetle can actually carry is subject to debate. Although the prevailing opinion is 850 times its weight, a study published in *Discover Magazine* (April 1996) contends that one hundred times its weight is a more realistic figure. Either way, we should all be thankful the beetles don't grow to the size of elephants. Imagine the damage they'd do.

I placed the rhinoceros beetle on the ground for a photo. Although it had been calm on Stephen's leg, it now refused to stay still. I took several shots, but none looked good on the camera screen.

"How am I supposed to take your photo if you won't stand still?" I asked.

The beetle didn't answer.

I pushed the shutter button again.

"That picture turned out good," said Deb impatiently.

I didn't answer.

Deb looked over my shoulder as I squeezed off another shot. "Come on, you have several good pictures. Stephen and I have been waiting for you all morning. We wanna go on a hike."

Close-up photography of a moving subject is harder than it looks—finally an acceptable image showed on the screen. Both Deb and the beetle were thrilled I was done.

After I released the beetle, we decided to take the riverside trail. A few minutes into our hike, Stephen paused and sniffed. "I smell leaf monkey. Very strong."

We scanned the forest and soon spotted two leaf monkeys sleeping on a large branch midway up a tree. Although this was the only time Deb and I witnessed our guide using his nose to find animals, he told us he could detect and identify most of the resident mammals by smell alone. I sniffed the air and picked up the faint musky scent of the monkeys. Yes, they had a detectable odor. But could I smell the difference between a leaf monkey and a Bornean gibbon? I doubt it.

Other than leaf monkeys, our animal experiences on the outward portion of our hike were limited to our sense of hearing. For instance, we could hear but not locate a barking deer and a great argus pheasant. Once we reached our turnaround point, we sat on the wide stony bank of the Danum River and reveled in the stunning day.

As we enjoyed the sunshine and the river's cooling breeze, Stephen pointed to a small clearing on the opposite bank. "My grandfather once settled over there to protect area from development. No one lives in Danum Valley anymore. Government convince my people to move to Lahad Datu so children could go to school."

Stephen's grandfather had obviously been successful in preserving the area, and I was happy for that. On the other hand, I felt badly for Stephen. Even though he didn't say it directly, I could see the pain on his face when he spoke of his people leaving the valley. This was his home, and working as a guide was his way to return and make sure it remained protected.

Next to us was a patch of *Mimosa pudica*. Commonly known as sensitive plants, the small fernlike shrubs would wilt when touched and recover minutes later. Playing with the plants was therapeutic. The aggressive side of my personality enjoyed watching them wilt under my touch, and the nurturing side enjoyed observing their recovery. Admittedly, I had more fun making them wilt.

Eventually we rose to our feet and started toward the lodge. Stephen led the way, followed by me, then Deb. We had walked only a short distance when Deb called out, "Marty, Stephen, look at the snake you two almost stepped on!"

We turned around and saw a small black and orange snake, partially covered by a large leaf. "Worm snake," said Stephen. "Harmless."

I reached down and removed the leaf. I expected the snake to lie motionless, but instead he slithered off the trail. His diminutive size kept him from going very far, and I quickly found him again. Deciding he would be easier to photograph if he was in my hand, I gently grasped his midsection between my thumb and forefinger. As I picked him up, he lashed out with several sharp bites!

"Ouch! He's a feisty little guy," I said.

"Are you bleeding?" asked Deb.

"No, he's too small to break my skin."

I snapped a few photos, and let the snake go.

Once we completed our hike, I turned on my digital camera and matched the images I'd taken of the snake with a photo in *A Field Guide to the Snakes of Borneo.* Stephen's jungle knowledge was amazing but not perfect. I wasn't holding a worm snake—I was holding a highly venomous banded coral snake!

Banded coral snakes do not have the distinctive alternating bands of color that coral snakes in the United States have. Instead, they have subtle bands of black, which come partway up from their orange bellies to merge with their orange-tinted black backs. According to the field guide, the Iban call the snakes "pig cobras," as they occasionally bite and kill the wild bearded pigs that nuzzle them by mistake. Since a snake's poison is most concentrated when it's young, I was indeed fortunate the pig cobra I picked up was too small to pierce my skin.

Our last evening at the Borneo Rainforest Lodge had arrived. If I could think of a bright side to leaving such a captivating place, it was that we had only one more dinner to endure. The meals had been repetitious, to say the least. Not eating almost seemed like a better option than choking down the same fare again.

When we sat at our table, I noticed several additional guests had arrived. And what was that in the corner? Yes!—a buffet with numerous new food options. I bounded from my chair to check it out. No chocolate, but by now *anything* different would taste heavenly.

Obviously, the chef served a greater variety of food when the lodge had more than just four guests. I suppose I could have gotten upset about this, but the chef was simply being efficient and using up ingredients he had already opened. The monotonous meals were a small price to pay for having the place virtually to ourselves.

At the beginning of our stay, Stephen mentioned he had a broken foot that had healed well enough to walk on. While at first he seemed fine, the more we hiked, the more noticeable his limping became. By the time we rendezvoused for our final night walk, he was in so much pain he had to use his walking stick as a crutch. Deb and I offered to cancel our outing, but Stephen was determined to help me find a python and even turned away another guide who offered to take his place.

Our hike began with an appearance by a bearded pig and several unusual insects. After that, we didn't see much. One interesting discovery was that the comb-crested agamid lizards, which we always found on tree trunks during the day, were now at the far end of branches. Deb suggested a plausible explanation for their new position: "It helps keep them safe from predators. If anything crawled out after them, they could feel the movement and escape."

I had hopes of replicating the Australia trip's last-minute python find, but that kind of magic only happens once in a lifetime. On this night, we cut our hike short. After forty minutes of watching Stephen struggle on his injured foot, Deb insisted we turn around, and I concurred. Although Stephen was suffering too much to object, when we said good night at the lodge, he couldn't resist giving us instructions for one last animal find. "Get up after midnight and look behind chalet for sambar deer," he said.

As things turned out, we didn't have to wait to see the deer. Deb shined her flashlight out back as soon as we reached our chalet and spotted two of them grazing in the tall grass. While the sambars likely weighed over 350 pounds, their size was difficult to judge at night.

"They don't look very big," said Deb, "but they were right where Stephen said they'd be."

"He's an amazing guide, isn't he?" I added. "We'll have to tell him his recommendation paid off."

On Thursday, April 24, I awoke at sunrise and let Deb sleep in. Our return shuttle to Sandakan would be leaving shortly after lunch, and I wanted to squeeze in some solo exploration before then.

As I strolled past the lodge, I was surprised to find Stephen lying on a bench.

"Are you okay?" I asked.

"I couldn't walk. Slept here last night," he said.

"Can I help you to your chalet?"

"No, I'm fine. Car with medicine and crutches on way from Lahad Datu."

"Is there anything I can do for you?"

"No. Enjoy your hike."

I reluctantly said good-bye and continued toward the river.

My morning hike would be the final test of an informal experiment. I had walked the riverside trail four times during the previous three days. Even though I had had little success finding animals on my own, I had become quite familiar with the terrain. Would following the trail a fifth time improve my wildlife spotting?

The initial results were encouraging—well-camouflaged lizards and geckos materialized before my eyes. I passed by them for the time being, however, because I had a specific animal in mind.

Up to this point, I had taken 100 percent of my Borneo photos with digital cameras. I had used film exclusively on the Belize and Amazon trips and split shots between film and digital on the Australia, Canada, and Antarctica trips. When I noticed the majority of my best images were digital, I decided to forgo film and bought a second digital camera to complement the one I already had. The new combination worked fine, except for medium- to long-range shots where trees muted the sunlight. Upon realizing that most of my leaf monkey photos had turned out mushy, I dug deep into my luggage and pulled out my emergency film camera. If I could find the monkeys again, I'd give film the opportunity to regain my favor.

An hour into my hike, I heard the faint sound of rustling leaves. I froze in my tracks and scanned the forest for monkeys. A day or two earlier and I wouldn't have been able to find them, but now that I had jungle eyes, locating them was easy. Perched on a branch, partway up a huge tree, were two beautiful leaf monkeys—one in the ever-popular red coat and the other in the less popular, but equally stunning, blond coat.

I focused my camera. The light meter screamed, "More light! Give me more light!" My film camera wasn't going to solve the mushy photo problem.

To make matters worse, I blew my chance for even a mushy image by assuming the monkeys were part of the same band I'd seen the day before. These two were much more skittish. When I approached them like old friends, they leaped spectacularly from tree to tree to escape.

I followed the red-coated monkey until she settled on a branch high above the river. Even though this time I approached more cautiously, as soon as I got within camera range, she exploded into another series of jumps. The noise from her acrobatics made me think of Tarzan swinging through the jungle after a few too many drinks: "Aaaaaahhhhhhhhhhhhh!" *Crash!* "Aaaaaahhhhhhhhhhhhh!" *Crash!*

Following each crash was the crack of breaking branches. When a particularly large branch splashed into the river, I thought for sure the monkey would follow. I immediately withdrew my pursuit. As much as I wanted a good leaf monkey photo, I hadn't traveled to Borneo to terrorize the wildlife. I turned and headed toward the lodge.

Along the way, I found a comb-crested agamid lizard on a tree trunk, twenty paces off the trail. Since I had plenty of time, I decided to wade through the knee-high ferns to get close enough for some photos. My approach didn't startle the lizard, but it did wake up a swarm of mosquitoes. Bugs aren't supposed to be intelligent, but how do they always know when I can't swat them? I swear, they never even attempted to bite me until I was ready to push the shutter button. In a way, I was thankful. The malaria pills I had purchased for the trip cost a fortune, and this was the first time any mosquitoes had shown interest in me. Now, at least, I felt as if I'd spent my money wisely.

I finished with the lizard and continued down the trail. Soon I spotted four leaf monkeys—two of each color—draped over a large branch, sound asleep. When they heard the click from my camera, they lazily opened their eyes to look at me, yawned, and went back to sleep. These four were obviously from the same band I'd seen the day before. The sight of them sleeping together was quite humorous. Even though they had an entire forest of trees to choose from, they all crammed against each other with their arms and legs hanging limply. They looked like fuzzy rugs hanging on a clothesline.

I blew the monkeys a kiss and said farewell to the rainforest.

My experiment had been a success. Now that my eyes had grown accustomed to the surroundings, wildlife spotting was substantially easier. A few more days and I certainly would have found the thirty-foot-long reticulated python I kept walking past. Okay, maybe not, but it's my fantasy, and I'm sticking with it.

Deb and I checked out of our chalet and met Stephen by the shuttle van to say good-bye. I snapped a photo of my injured companions: Stephen with his crutch and swollen foot and Deb with her swollen and heavily taped toe. Other than the sorry appearance of their feet, they looked ready for another day of jungle trekking.

Our shuttle driver had a bright smile and was about twenty-five years old. He wasn't the same person who had delivered us to the lodge. I tried to engage him in a conversation, but the language difference between us was too great, and we soon ended up riding in silence.

So far, our shuttle rides had been relatively tame. Though we had had a few tense moments here and there, we'd grown to trust that somehow our drivers would avoid a fatal accident. After all, it's not good to kill the client.

On this day, maintenance crews were laying new gravel on the road between the lodge and Lahad Datu. If our driver hadn't learned to drive by watching James Bond movies, I'm certain he would have exercised proper caution, but instead he zipped along as if we were in a sports car. On several turns, I was sure we were going to slide off the road.

To make matters worse, the workers had dumped piles of gravel in visually obstructed sections of the road. We'd zoom around curves and nearly collide head-on with four-foot-high walls of gravel. Casually, with no loss of speed, our driver would swerve around the piles—practically grazing them in the process.

Upon reaching Lahad Datu, the road surface changed back to pavement. Since we'd no longer have to worry about sliding off the road or crashing into piles of gravel, I relaxed and looked forward to enjoying the scenery for the rest of the way.

Our driver surprised us when he pulled up behind an unmarked pickup truck and transferred our gear into its box. No one had told us we were going to switch shuttles, but we probably should have expected it, considering our earlier trip. We climbed into the truck and continued on our way.

Our new driver was in his late teens and didn't speak English. He seemed to be a calm person however, as he contentedly followed two feet behind a gasoline tanker truck and turned down opportunities to pass where gaps in the traffic were large enough for even the most timid driver. No worries. We weren't in a hurry. As long as the tanker didn't stop unexpectedly, we'd reach Sandakan alive.

When traffic on the narrow two-lane road thickened, the near-continuous streams of approaching vehicles transformed our driver into Joe Suicide of Borneo. He pressed his foot to the floor, whooshed past the tanker, narrowly avoided a head-on collision, and swerved back into the driving lane! He then accelerated until his front bumper nearly touched the rear of the next vehicle and repeated the process.

The worst part of his passing technique was that after he steered into the oncoming lane, his eyes would glaze over, and he'd forget about returning to his own lane. Several times I had to yell and frantically point at approaching vehicles before he'd veer out of the way.

The Sandakan city limits saved us from becoming someone's hood ornament. As soon as we reached the residential streets, our driver transformed back into a meek teenager and leisurely followed the traffic.

Once we departed the shuttle, Deb and I laughed about surviving yet another brush with death. We loved Borneo, and as with all the trips in this book, we'd suffer a bout of post-trip depression, wishing we had stayed longer. This time, however, at least a small part of us was ready to go home.

For our final night, we splurged and rented a suite at the Sanbay Hotel. Our spacious room had a large, comfortable bed and all the modern conveniences. A bigger contrast from the Iban hunting shelter would have been hard to find.

I undressed and stepped into the bathroom to take a shower. Just as I was about to turn on the water, Deb swayed in wearing a big amorous grin. Naturally, I smiled back.

"Guess what's in the refrigerator," she said.

"Beer," I replied.

"No. Something even better—chocolate!"

7

Surprisingly Europe

July 13, 2003, Pamplona, Spain—I'm with Mike Holmes, a former teammate from my adult men's baseball team. We're standing in a mass of humanity at the Festival of San Fermin, preparing to race for our lives. We had hatched our plan to run with the bulls (the *encierro*) a year earlier, while drinking a few beers at a Minnesota Twins baseball game. Now I'm thinking, "I must have had one beer too many."

A rocket blasts off, signaling the bulls have left the corral. As the crowd roars, my heart begins to pound. Soon I hear the thunder of hooves on cobblestone!

Mike grins and yells to me over the commotion, "Are you ready?"

"This is a really stupid idea!" I scream back.

"Don't worry, we'll be okay. Just stay to the side!"

"I can't do this!"

"You have no choice! All the exits are blocked!"

"I'm serious. I *can't* do this! I thought I could run without feeling responsible for the fate of the bulls, but I was wrong."

"Here they come! You better move your ass!"

"What right do I have to use the abuse of animals for my own entertainment?"

"If you don't move to the side, you're gonna be entertainment for the bulls! Watch out!"

A wall of flesh and horns converges upon me! I try to leap out of the way, but my feet refuse to move! A huge bull lowers his head and—

Crrrrack! Baroommm!

I open my eyes. Everything is pitch-black. Something heavy has me pinned down, and for a moment I can't breathe. When I finally inhale, I taste hot, moist breath. I work an arm free, reach over my head, and flick on a light.

"Annie, get off me! It's only a thunderstorm!"

My eighty-five-pound Labrador retriever is sprawled across my chest, and her tongue is inches from my mouth—she's panting as if she'd just run to Idaho and back. When Annie is outdoors, she's fearless. But indoors, during stormy weather, she's a bundle of nerves. I comfort my dog as we fret together—she about the storm and I about the bulls.

Participating in the encierro was something I had fantasized about since the eighth grade, when I read Ernest Hemingway's *The Sun Also Rises*. I fully intended my run to be more than just a dream. In fact, I had already booked airline tickets and reserved a hotel room in Pamplona (Deb was coming along, but as a spectator only).

My fantasy ended when I read Gary Gray's *Running with the Bulls* as part of my pretrip research. Although I enjoyed Gray's book, his detailed portrayal of bullfighting festivals made me realize I couldn't separate the encierro from the actual killing. While I would have never gone to a bullfight—cheering for the bulls probably would have gotten me in trouble anyway—my plan to make my run and enjoy the people watching was still unacceptable. Attending Pamplona's Festival of San Fermin would have been condoning the slow, brutal slaying of a noble animal.

When I informed Mike of my decision to cancel the trip, he seemed relieved (and Deb was thrilled). Instead of going to Spain in July, he went to Africa, and I stayed in Montana. The matadors still slaughtered the bulls, but at least we weren't accomplices.

With the festival out of the picture, Deb and I had to come up with a new plan for our European trip. For many people, visiting Europe is a lifetime dream; for me it was something hard to get enthusiastic about. I had no desire to explore major cities or partake in traditional touristy activities. I purchased some travel guides for ideas, but they all concentrated on the things that interested me the least.

I wanted to see Europe's wildlife. Since the travel guides practically ignored the subject, I logged onto the Internet and searched "Europe+wildlife." To my dismay, the theme for the majority of hits was "extinct or endangered animals." Surely the Europeans hadn't decimated all their wildlife!

Eventually I found two books, *Wild France: A Traveller's Guide* and *Wild Spain: A Traveller's Guide,* which provided useful suggestions on where we could go to enjoy nature. Using the books to point us in the right direction, we decided to fly to Madrid, explore wild areas in Spain, then work our way northeast into France and Switzerland. We wouldn't have a set schedule or firm plans, except to rendezvous with Emad (our friend from the Antarctica expedition) for a few days in Switzerland. Although I still wasn't as excited about Europe as I had been about the other continents, good things sometimes happen when expectations are low. Perhaps Europe would surprise me.

Deb and I arrived in Europe on Wednesday, September 10, 2003. The trip's first surprise occurred when we didn't have to go through customs. Immigration looked at our passports when we changed airplanes in Amsterdam, but that was it. Upon landing in Madrid, we retrieved our luggage and walked directly to the automobile rental counter.

Since our recent travels hadn't changed my inability to sleep on airplanes, once again I was faced with adjusting to a foreign land after being awake for more than twenty-four hours straight. I was barely functioning by the time I signed the rental car contract and crossed the parking lot to the attendant's booth.

"Your car is in stall number twenty-two," said the attendant in English.

"Gracias," I said.

Deb and I lugged our belongings to the stall and gazed down at a tiny two-door compact. "This isn't what I ordered," I said. "I reserved a station wagon, so we'd have a place to sleep if we ever got stuck without a hotel room."

I walked back to the booth. "Excuse me, sir. You gave us the wrong car."

"Your car is in stall number twenty-eight," he replied.

I ambled down the row and spotted a silver Opel wagon. I inserted the key into the rear hatch lock and turned it—nothing. I pulled the key out, reinserted it, twisted it, and jiggled it, but it still refused to open.

"Let me try," said Deb.

After Deb's try failed, I trudged back to the booth. "Excuse me, sir. I think you gave me the wrong key. The hatch won't open."

The young, gangly, bald, and oh-so-cool attendant gave me a "you are a stupid American" look, sashayed over to the car, inserted the key into the rear hatch lock and turned it—nothing. He pulled the key out, reinserted it, twisted it, and jiggled it, but it still refused to open.

"*So,* I'm not such a dumb American after all," I whispered under my breath.

The attendant removed the key and inserted it in the driver's side door. "You need to open the hatch by turning the front door lock, like this," he said.

While I loaded our luggage into the back, the attendant returned to his booth. When I finished, I shut the hatch with a typical amount of force. Instead of locking tight, the hatch door protruded out of line, as if it hadn't fully latched. I raised the hatch again and slammed it shut—same result. I tried one more time, with brute force, but it wouldn't latch.

"Let me try," said Deb.

After Deb's try failed, I trudged back to the booth. "Excuse me, sir. The rear hatch won't shut tight. I think it's broken."

The attendant gave me a "you are an *incredibly* stupid American" look, sashayed over to the car, and with two fingers gently closed the hatch.

"See, just like this," he demonstrated again, pushing down the hatch as if it were made of fine china.

Satisfied the car was quirky, not defective, I thanked the attendant and started the engine.

"Don't forget to put diesel, not gasoline, in the car," he said before I shut the door.

Although I could have been offended by the insinuation that I was incapable of fueling the vehicle, I appreciated his comment. The Opel had a quiet engine, nothing like the monster-sized diesel pickup trucks that rumble through the streets in Montana. My inclination would have been to fill the tank with gasoline. I'd need to be careful each time I added fuel, or we'd end up stranded with a very sick automobile.

Since the day was only half over, we decided to travel one hundred miles west to the town of Arenas de San Pedro. Deb, who had slept some on our flights, was the logical candidate to drive. My name, however, was the only one listed on the rental car insurance policy.

The excitement of driving in a new country kept me alert, for a while. But once we got out of the hectic city of Madrid, the traffic dissipated and the excitement wore off. Vehicles in Spain travel on the right side of the road. Other than roundabouts, the driving and scenery were similar to what you might encounter in flat sections of Utah or Nevada—lots of rock, scrub, and wide-open spaces.

"I'm having trouble staying awake, and my eyes keep going out of focus," I said to Deb between yawns.

"Will it help if I talk to you?"

"I think so."

I've had conversations with Deb where she's talked for an hour or more with little or no input from me. In fact, when it comes to talking, she has no peer. I know some of my readers will disagree and say, "You haven't met so and so," but trust me on this: in a talking contest my wife would smoke all contenders.

Except on this day.

When Deb ran out of things to say, I tried to tune in a radio station but found only static. With nothing but the soothing hum of tires to occupy my brain, the car's comfortable seat and gentle sway felt *soooo* relaxing. If I could just close my eyes for a second—I jerked the wheel!

"What was that!" screamed Deb.

"I think I fell asleep."

"Did you know that in Spain . . ." she said, launching into a monologue that would last all the way to our destination.

When we reached Arenas de San Pedro (population 6,350), the town appeared deserted. Unencumbered by traffic, we drove down cobblestone streets looking for a hotel. The main road was barely wide enough for two lanes of traffic, and the side streets were seldom much wider than our station wagon. A few streets had narrow sidewalks, but elsewhere stucco-walled buildings abutted the cobblestone. This was a typical rural Spanish town, built long before the advent of automobiles.

After turning onto one of the side streets, we found ourselves lost in a maze of old two- and three-story buildings. The direction of traffic within the maze was determined by who got there first, and despite sharing the entire town with only two other moving vehicles, we soon encountered each of them. Both times, I had to back blindly out of the way.

We escaped to the main road before frustration set in. "Pull into that parking lot," said Deb. "I think we'll have better luck finding a hotel on foot."

I squeezed the car into the only open space, and we stepped out onto the hot pavement. Directly to our right was a well-preserved castle.

Normally such a sight would have excited me, but what Deb said next made me—at least temporarily—forget about the ancient structure: "There's a hotel right there!"

The Gran Hotel La Hosteria de Bracamonte stood in front of us, a little to our right. It was easy to miss because it was at the end of a row of interconnected buildings. Its exterior reminded me of a seedy old boardinghouse in a western movie. Not exactly what I had in mind for our first night in Spain, but I was too tired to be picky.

The front section of the hotel had a bar and restaurant, and the entrance to the lobby was on the side, ten feet from the castle wall. I opened the door and peered inside. The interior, while somewhat stark, was nicer than I expected.

We stepped to the counter and rang the bell. A thin man in his fifties sauntered in from the kitchen and greeted us in Spanish. Deb, anticipating the need to speak Spanish, had spent a few evenings before the trip adding a few key phrases to her limited vocabulary. Now, using one of those phases, she hesitantly inquired about a room, and then stared blankly as the clerk responded in rapid-fire sentences. She asked the clerk to repeat himself but still couldn't understand him. (Reading Spanish was obviously much easier than understanding a native speaker.) Finally, she asked in desperation, "Do you speak English?"

His response (which Deb translated later) was, "Madam, this is Spain. And in Spain we speak Spanish."

Once the clerk assigned us a room, we hauled our gear to the lobby and squeezed into the world's smallest elevator. Feeling like gelatin in a mold, we popped out on the third floor and waddled to the end of the hall. Our cozy room was only slightly larger than the elevator, and it didn't have any windows except for a small skylight peeping out through the ceiling.

I looked at my watch; it was ten minutes till four. On past trips we had stayed awake until dark to get our bodies synchronized for the following day. This time we were too tired and decided to take a nap.

The bed felt *soooo* good. We closed our eyes and snuggled in. Soon we slipped into slumber—*Bong! Bong! Bong!* . . .

I opened my eyes. Though my mind was in a fog, I tried to find the source of the noise. When I noticed an old radio mounted in the wall above my pillow, I figured it had to be the culprit and fiddled with the knobs until the sound stopped.

I closed my eyes again. Sleep didn't come as fast this time, but eventually I drifted to the paradisiacal edge between consciousness and unconsciousness—*Bong! Bong!* . . .

I squinted through one eye. Directly above the radio was a wall lamp with frayed electrical wires hanging from it. I languorously reached up and pulled on the wires until the clanging ceased.

Satisfied that I'd solved the problem, I took a few deep breaths and concentrated on blocking all thoughts from my brain. Within five minutes, I was totally relaxed; within ten minutes, I was no longer cognizant of where I was; within fourteen minutes, I started to dream; at fifteen minutes—*Bong! Bong! . . .*

I jerked up from my pillow.

"What is it?" asked Deb.

"That noise. I think it's church bells."

"That's definitely what it is. Don't worry, I'm sure they won't ring all night."

I got out of bed and put on some clothes. I couldn't sleep knowing that as soon as I dozed off the bells would ring again. If I was going to be awake, I wanted Deb to get up with me, so we could walk the streets together. The bells, however, didn't bother her the way they bothered me, and she had already resumed her nap.

If I blatantly woke her up, she'd snap at me. Instead, I had to be subtle. With a sigh, I plopped onto the bedside chair and stared at her. As the moments passed, I began to wonder if she'd fallen asleep too deeply for my wife-watching trick to work. Finally, she opened her eyes.

"I suppose you want me to get up."

"I was thinking about exploring the town. If you'd like to come with me, I'd enjoy the company."

Deb moaned softly before answering, "Okay. Just give me a few minutes to get ready."

Looking like zombies with beanbags under our eyes, we rode the world's smallest elevator to the main floor and stepped outside into the bright sunlight.

Our first mission was to locate the source of the bells—*Bong! Bong! Bong! Bong! Bong!* That was easy. The church belfry stood directly behind the hotel, practically towering over the skylight in our room.

"No wonder the bells were so loud," I said.

"And look how many people are wandering about," added Deb. "I guess siesta is over."

I knew Spaniards took an afternoon siesta but never imagined it would have such a dramatic impact on the population. In Arenas de San Pedro, siesta lasted from one-thirty to five. During that time, most of the stores were closed, and a blanket of quiet covered the town—except, of course, for the church bells. Now that it was after five, automobile traffic had returned, and the town buzzed with activity.

Other than the bells, the main reason I wanted go exploring was to check out the castle. Although at the time all I could do was admire its physical attributes, later I'd learn more through various sources, which I'd have translated from Spanish. For instance, the castle's name, Castillo de la Triste Condesa, means "Castle of the Sad Countess."

Deb and I walked around the castle's exterior, hoping to find a way inside, but all the doors were locked. The medieval complex took up the equivalent of a typical city block, and the keep (the main section) stood as high as a six-story building. While not as architecturally spectacular as some of the castles we'd see later, it did have simple, yet impressive, stonework around its windows.

As with all medieval castles, this one had been built to protect its inhabitants from attack. The lowest windows were more than thirty feet off the ground, and at the edge of the roof, above each window, were balconies with gaps in the floors for dropping objects on anyone attempting to climb the walls. The one thing missing was the moat, which had been filled in long ago.

Since the castle was dark inside, and many of the window openings were partially shrouded by vines, it had a haunted appearance. And who knows? Perhaps it was haunted. Its history includes multiple sackings, and its grounds were once used as a graveyard (the corpses have been relocated).

The mysterious Castle of the Sad Countess isn't famous, but perhaps it should be, as it was once owned by a woman who was gutsy enough to stand up to the Crown, and a man whose matchmaking efforts would ultimately affect both your life and mine:

Constable Ruy López Dávalos commenced building the castle in 1393, finished it in 1423, and was kicked out one year later when King Juan II stripped him of his rank and possessions. The castle then became property of the Count of Benavente, who gave it to Don Álvaro de Luna in 1430 as a dowry for marriage to his daughter, Doña Juana de Pimentel.

Don Álvaro de Luna was King Juan II's closest friend and second in command. During their long relationship, de Luna ran the government for the king (who was more interested in books and the arts than ruling) and on multiple occasions boldly risked his life to save the king.

After Juan II's first wife died, de Luna arranged for the king to marry Princess Isabella of Portugal. The new queen soon became jealous of de Luna's power and conspired against him. In 1453, three years after the royal wedding, Isabella successfully convinced the king to order the public beheading of de Luna.

Distraught over her husband's execution, Doña Juana de Pimentel began calling herself "the Sad Countess" and signed all documents as such. One year later, King Juan II died of remorse for what he had done to his loyal friend.

Following de Luna's death, the Sad Countess fought to prevent the Crown from repossessing her late husband's assets. In 1461, Juan II's son, King Enrique IV, grew tired of her resistance and sentenced her to death. Fortunately for the Countess, influential citizens interceded on her behalf and convinced Enrique to rescind his order. Although the Sad Countess lost much of her wealth, she retained her castle and lived there until shortly before her death in 1488.

How did de Luna's matchmaking affect you and me? When King Enrique IV died, Queen Isabella I, the daughter of Isabella and Juan II, ascended to the throne. Queen Isabella I and her husband/cousin, King Ferdinand V, were the initiators of the Spanish Inquisition and the sponsors of Christopher Columbus's historical voyage to America.

The Castle of the Sad Countess is now an Artistic Historical Monument owned by the town of Arenas de San Pedro, and at the time of our visit, workers were restoring the interior with plans to turn it into a museum.

I enjoy old architecture, and the Castle of the Sad Countess had whetted my appetite for what was to come. Even though nature would be the focus of our trip, I knew now we'd have to set aside some time to explore Europe's man-made wonders as well.

Deb and I returned from walking the streets, hungry for dinner. As we'd soon learn, meals in rural Spain were going to be among the trip's most memorable experiences. At home, we eat dinner around six o'clock, and because it was already a half hour past that time, we hoped to grab a quick bite to eat and head to bed early.

Our first lesson in rural Spanish dining was that we couldn't eat on American time. Since siesta had pushed the entire town's schedule back, no restaurant would even take our order until after eight.

Evening meals would always be major productions (Madrid was the only place in Spain where we'd see a fast-food restaurant). Our initial dinner was typical of what we'd experience during the coming days. We arrived at eight-fifteen; the waiter brought us menus and wine at eight-thirty, took our order at nine, served our first course at nine-thirty, and continued bringing us unexceptional food for the next hour.

Our other lessons would revolve around language difficulties and the actual food served to us. At home, I'm a vegetarian wannabe. In other words, I have aspirations of someday becoming a true vegetarian, but for now I eat poultry and fish and abstain from mammal. Eating a vegetarian-wannabe diet would have been easy in one of Spain's big cities or tourist towns, but in rural areas virtually every dish would come with some sort of sausage made out of who-knows-what. After a few frustrating meals of trying to stick to my diet, I'd eventually give up and eat the traditional foods.

For some reason, I had presumed restaurants would have English language menus available. Again, restaurants in big cities or tourist towns could have accommodated me, but in rural areas, no such luck.

Confronted with menus in Spanish, Deb and I used a book and an electronic translator to help us figure out foods we didn't recognize. Our translation tools, however, were never comprehensive enough to decipher every item. Occasionally even familiar words would turn out to mean something unexpected. For instance, at one point in our trip I ordered a tortilla, expecting folded unleavened Mexican bread filled with meat, beans, and cheese but received a dry omelet between two slices of hard bread instead. Likewise, when I ordered a tostada, I expected crisp Mexican flatbread topped with meat, beans, and cheese but—yippee!—received toast instead.

Rural Spanish food will never make my top-ten list. Worse than the mystery meats and misinterpreted ingredients was that restaurants served everything dry, without condiments or sauces. For instance, sandwiches would consist of a naked slice of meat tossed between two pieces of hard dry bread. If I asked for something to liven up my meal, such as butter, mayonnaise, or ketchup, I would usually be turned down or glared at—as if I'd just requested horseradish sauce to slather on chocolate ice cream.

I hate to stop complaining while I'm on a roll, but I have to tell you about the wonderful wine we had in Spain. I'm not a wine snob. Neither the price nor the vintage of a bottle impresses me—either I like it or I don't. I've always disliked red wines because they make me pucker up, as if I'd consumed something sour. I was skeptical when Deb ordered a Spanish red to accompany our first meal, but it turned out to be smooth and flavorful.

As our trip progressed, we'd enjoy several more bottles of Spanish red wine. Although each one was unique, all were excellent. Later we'd try French and Swiss wine. They were also good, but to my palate, Spanish wine was the best.

I'll have more nice things to say later, but I'm not done complaining yet. Once Deb and I finished our introductory marathon meal, we were both so tired we could barely keep our eyes open. I don't even remember riding the tiny elevator to our teeny room. I do remember, however, the blissful feeling of collapsing in bed and closing my eyes. I fell asleep at precisely 10:59 PM.

One minute later—*Bong! Bong! Bong! Bong! Bong! Bong! Bong! Bong! Bong! Bong! Bong!*

The motto on the Arenas de San Pedro coat of arms states: "*Siempre Incendiada Y Siempre Fiel,*" which translates to: "Always Set Afire and Always Faithful." Before our visit, I would have assumed the motto summarized the city's history of being plundered and burned by marauding armies. Now I knew the truth: "Always Faithful" refers to the belief that the church bells will ring precisely every fifteen minutes for eternity, and "Always Set Afire" is what happens to your temper when they ring one too many times.

The ringing continued all night. Hopefully the Catholic Church will forgive me for the string of obscenities I muttered in their honor the first few times the bells woke me up. Was there a reason I needed to know it was two-fifteen in the morning? Eventually even the bells' toll couldn't keep me awake. I fell asleep and had a bizarre dream about a hunchbacked Ernest Hemingway.

On Thursday morning, we stuffed our gear back into the car and attempted to leave town. *Attempted* is the key word here. All the street signs pointed the wrong way, and the lone road leading in the correct direction quickly petered out.

"I don't think we're ever going to get out of here," said Deb.

"I know," I agreed. "I feel like we're in the 'Hotel California' of towns. We can check in, but we can never leave."

We pulled into a gas station so Deb could look at a map and I could fill the tank. Remembering the car took diesel, I stared at the pumps and tried to locate the correct hose. Since nothing looked even close to the word *diesel,* I was relieved when an attendant noticed my dilemma and walked over to offer assistance. Though he didn't speak English, he understood my problem. "Gasolina A," he said.

When I returned to the car after paying the bill, Deb announced that she had successfully plotted our escape from Arenas de San Pedro. We departed on the east side of town, traveled north for several miles, and then turned west toward the mountains of Parque Regional de la Sierra de Gredos (a 213,099-acre regional park).

Twenty minutes into our drive, we rounded a corner and came upon a classic crusader-era castle. Perched alone on a hill, it had a circular tower at each corner and appeared to be in pristine shape. I didn't see any signs identifying the castle, but later, when I purchased John Gibson's book *Anatomy of the Castle,* I opened right up to a full-page photo of it. Called the Castillo de Albuquerque, it was built between 1461 and 1476 by the first Duke of Albuquerque, and it is still owned by his descendants.

Aside from the all-night church bells and adventuresome food, I was warming up to Spain. Without even trying, I had already seen two ancient castles. Of course, now I expected to see one around every corner (since approximately 2,500 castles exist within the country, my expectation wasn't too far-fetched). Even better than the castles was the stunning scenery. The farther we got away from Madrid, the more picturesque it became.

Spain is geographically special because it supports a variety of distinct ecological regions condensed on a landmass smaller than the state of Texas. Within a day's drive, we could go from the rainy coast to the arid interior or from the flat plains to the steep mountains. In our current location of west-central Spain, the mountains were always nearby. Sometimes we'd zigzag over high passes, and other times we'd head straight across rolling valleys with mountains on either side. Between the massifs were endless fields of golden-brown grass, islands of ground-hugging shrubs, clusters of charcoal-gray boulders, and groves of cork oak and olive trees. The intense golds, grays, and greens contrasted beautifully with each other—especially when viewed from up high. Occasionally we'd get out of the car, look far into the distance, and become overwhelmed with the urge to exclaim "Wow!"

By late afternoon, we reached Plataforma, the trailhead at the center of Parque Regional de la Sierra de Gredos. Although I was looking forward to our first outdoor adventure, I was shocked to see almost fifty cars in the parking lot. When Deb and I hike in Montana, we pass up any trailhead with more than three cars nearby, as it's "just too crowded." If we hadn't been desperate to do something—*anything*—outdoors, we would have kept on driving.

Despite all the cars, once we started hiking we rarely saw other humans. Several trails went off in different directions, and since we didn't have a detailed map, we picked the one that looked most promising.

Our trail led us into an oblong bowl-shaped valley, where climbable mountains encircled us and a small stream trickled down the middle. Even though the valley was devoid of people, we weren't alone. A small herd of range cows lounged in our path, chewing their cud. The cows kept a watchful eye on us as we walked among them, but they didn't seem to mind our presence. Each one had a large bell hanging from its neck that gently tinkled with every movement.

We wound around clusters of rock and patches of broom (small shrubs). Sometimes we'd lose the trail, but if we looked ahead, we could always find a cairn on top of an outcrop to mark our route. Interspersed with the rock and broom were wide carpets of grass, perfectly manicured by the cows.

Cows and wilderness don't mix. Similar ranching methods in the United States and other countries have caused tremendous environmental damage. Here, however, they seemed to belong. Perhaps it was the breed of cow or the small size of the herd, but other than the trimmed grass, their visible impact was minimal.

Deb and I weren't hiking in Parque Regional de la Sierra de Gredos to see cows. We wanted to see Spanish ibex, the top animal on our European wish list. A Spanish ibex is a type of mountain goat with ribbed, curved horns. Once a plentiful species, they are now IUCN classified as "near threatened." As with so many other animals, human activities are responsible for their peril. In this instance, overhunting has reduced ibex numbers to fewer than thirty thousand.

Even though ibex were supposed to be in the area, I wasn't sure where to look for them. Trying to sound as if I knew what I was talking about, I suggested to Deb, "Watch for ibex mingling with the cows."

After an hour of hiking, we neared the spot where the valley floor ascended to the lip of the bowl. Between the lip and us was a wide outcrop with another small herd of cows.

"Ibex! I see ibex!" said Deb in a hushed shout.

"I don't see anything but cows," I said.

"Look next to the cows."

"Oh, there! I think you're right."

We inched closer before Deb declared, "Yes, they're definitely ibex."

At that moment, ibex were my favorite animal in the world. How could I not love an animal that made me look so smart?

We crept along the valley wall to get a better view of the small herd, which contained three adult females and two half-grown kids. The largest of the females stood two and a half feet high at the withers and her horns were roughly eight inches long. While these weren't the glorious four-foot-high males with four-and-a-half-foot-long horns commonly featured in nature books, we weren't disappointed. Just seeing an ibex was a thrill.

Although ibex are now a protected species, their long history of being hunted irresponsibly has made them extra wary of humans. One hundred fifty feet was as close as we could get before they spooked. Once we learned their comfort zone, we shadowed them until they climbed up the mountainside and disappeared.

Where Deb and I were hiking, the valley floor was at approximately six thousand feet and the surrounding mountain peaks varied between seven and eight thousand feet. The floor's height made the peaks seem deceptively low.

At the end of the valley, we had a choice of turning around or climbing to the lip. As we were experiencing firsthand, Parque Regional de la Sierra de Gredos stretches across one of the coldest regions in Spain. When we left the car, we were comfortable in our shorts, but as the day grew late, the wind picked up and the temperature dropped. Having accomplished my goal of seeing an ibex, I was content to head back.

"Oh, let's hike to the top," said Deb.

Who was I to deny my lovely wife's wishes?

We serpentined around the last few cows and ascended the moderately steep slope. Although the climb wasn't strenuous, it increased our body heat enough to make us forget about the weather.

Upon reaching the crest, we stood on the ridge, staring in awe. I had expected to see a continuation of the mountain range, but to my surprise, the mountains angled dramatically down to a wide, flat valley. The drop was at least five thousand feet and the valley spread out past the horizon. I could see a large lake and a small town in the distance. Closer in I watched eagles circle and swoop into crevices to catch small rodents. The eagles weren't above me—they were hundreds of feet *below* me.

I couldn't imagine a more stunning view anywhere on earth. As I said to Deb, "If I were a king during medieval times and I wanted to look down over Spain, this is where I'd stand."

Eventually I turned around and gazed over the valley we had just crossed. The opposite view was almost as breathtaking. At eye level, Egyptian vultures and other birds of prey rode the wind currents, and below me, the gently curving stream meandered down the valley.

Listen: *dwint doont, dwint doont, dwint doont, dwint doont . . .*

It sounded like a calypso band playing steel drums. The valley bowl made an ideal amphitheater for the cowbells. In fact, now that we were high on the ridge, we could hear more bells than we heard when we were among the cows. All the bells were perfectly tuned, and the harder the breeze blew, the louder the song became.

Deb spread her arms and turned in circles, singing, *"The hills are alive with the sound of music!"* Then she added, "I'll have to remember to sing that again when we reach the Alps."

After our musical interlude, we decided to reverse course. As we started down the slope, we were delighted to see the five ibex again. This time they were grazing in the middle of the valley, and since the breeze was blowing toward us, our scent wouldn't give us away. Using boulders and shrubs as cover, we slunk to within eighty feet of the herd. We probably could have approached closer, but a line of natural obstructions near the stream allowed us to parallel them.

The three females were handsome animals with brown coats, white chests, and a streak of black down the front of each leg. The two kids had the same markings, but their shorter muzzles and rounded features give them a puppylike cuteness. All five blended in seamlessly with their surroundings.

We hung with the herd as they leisurely munched their way down the valley. Once the sun dipped below the peaks, we pried ourselves away, and hurried to the car.

Exhilarated by our surprisingly wonderful hike, I started the engine and turned the wheel to exit the parking lot. "We might as well go home now," I said with a smile. "Nothing's going to top today."

"Ibex! More ibex—right there!" exclaimed Deb.

I switched off the engine and hopped out the door. Fourteen ibex fixed their eyes upon me before resuming their activities. Some drank in the stream next to the lot, and others mingled among the rocks on the far bank. This herd was obviously habituated to humans. I didn't know whether to be excited or disappointed. After stealthily stalking the ibex in the valley, seeing these up close and unafraid was anticlimactic. Unlike the previous herd, this one had several medium-sized males with foot-long horns. Now at least I had a feel for what the big bucks must look like. I took some photos in the remaining light and returned to the car.

With Plataforma being a popular destination, and only the little town of Hoyos del Espino nearby, I worried we'd have a difficult time finding accommodations without a reservation. Fortunately, a small two-story restaurant-hotel combination on the outskirts of town had a vacancy. I looked around—no churches in sight. Finally, I could catch up on my sleep.

Deb and I finished our dinner at ten-thirty and with big yawns crawled into bed. I closed my eyes and immediately opened them. A roar that sounded like a party of drunken auctioneers was reverberating through our room. The hotel had ceramic tile floors, and there was scarcely a soft surface anywhere to absorb the noise. While I could have sworn people were standing right outside our door, all I was hearing was the usual hubbub flowing up the stairs from the restaurant below. If we were in a similar rural establishment in the United States on a Thursday night, the kitchen would already be closed, and the patrons would be drinking their nightcaps. But here in Spain, the evening was just getting started.

Soon Deb, who can sleep through almost anything, began to snore. Resigned to being awake for a while, I got dressed, carried my laptop computer to the hotel sitting room, and worked on my writing. Three and a half hours later, I went to bed with the rest of Spain.

Deb and I slept late and had a leisurely breakfast before continuing our journey. Our goal for the day was to reach Parque Natural de Monfragüe (a 44,113-acre park), eighty miles to the southwest. Since I also wanted to buy a compass, we stopped in some of the tiny one- and two-store towns along the way. I didn't think finding a compass would be difficult, but then, so far our trip had been full of surprises.

Eventually we reached Plasencia, the largest city in the region. Even though the city's population was only 43,300, automobiles and pedestrians packed its narrow streets. We tried to find an outdoor equipment store, but when we realized how easily we could get lost, I squeezed the car into the last remaining parking space in town.

We were in a tangle of streets bordered by solid walls of four- and five-story buildings. As we set off on foot in search of a compass, we memorized every turn to make sure we could find our way back.

Somehow, we stumbled across a mountaineering store. Since the store was barely big enough for a dozen shelves and a cash register stand, we were able to quickly conclude that today wasn't going to be my day to buy a compass. As we headed for the door, a clerk approached and offered his assistance.

Deb, unsure of the Spanish word for compass, pointed to the palm of her hand and said, *"Norte, sur–"*

"Ah, compass!" said the clerk.

He ducked behind the cash register and retrieved two boxes stuffed with compasses. I looked through the selection and chose the unit with a handy-dandy bonus thermometer.

Mission accomplished, we strolled to the town square and had lunch at a sidewalk café. This time our communication didn't go as smoothly, and we were both served food completely different from what we had expected.

Plasencia was where I learned that Spanish tortillas are nothing like Mexican tortillas. As for Deb, she thought she had ordered a sandwich piled high with numerous ingredients and received a thin slice of dry ham between two pieces of rock-hard bread instead. Since no condiments were available, we both needed multiple soft drinks to wash everything down.

After lunch, we walked a few blocks out of our way to check out a massive thirteenth-century Catholic church. The Cathedral Viejo was as large as the castles we had seen earlier, only much more elaborately designed. An aerial view would have been necessary to see everything, but from my vantage point, every inch of the roof seemed to be taken up by a spire, statue, or tower. Equally impressive were the outside walls, which were covered with hundreds of intricately carved stone gargoyles, cherubs, skeletons, angels, and faces. The detail was so lavishly overdone I couldn't absorb it all in one viewing. The church looked like it had been a project for architects who were given an unlimited budget and forced to add adornments until all the money was gone.

The extraordinary exterior made me wonder what the interior was like. I pulled on the front doors; they were locked. I checked the sign; the posted hours coincided with siesta. We had missed getting inside by only a few minutes.

As we walked back to the car, I noticed the hustling and bustling city of twenty minutes ago was now a virtual ghost town. The dramatic effect of siesta would take awhile for me to get used to.

I turned to Deb and said, "It feels like aliens swooped down and abducted the entire population."

"You're right," she said. "And it's a perfect time to get out of town. We won't have to fight the traffic."

Our short eighty-mile drive turned into a five-hour-long event. Winding roads, gorgeous landscapes, and interesting distractions slowed our progress. Birds of prey in particular caught our attention. Almost every time we looked up, we spotted another hawk, eagle, or vulture.

We decided to stay in Torrejón el Rubio, which is just south of Parque Natural de Monfragüe. The town had a population of 750, and its main street stretched six blocks long. We found the Hotel Carvajal on the corner of the last block.

The restaurant-hotel combination had small clean rooms for the U.S. equivalent of forty-five dollars. Like on our first day in Spain, registering for a room proved challenging. This time communication difficulties between Deb and the proprietor turned a simple check-in into a twenty-minute ordeal.

As you may recall from the Antarctica chapter, when discussing our brief time in Argentina, I wrote, "Trying to communicate with people who didn't speak English was surprisingly fun." I don't know what I was drinking in Argentina, but I take it all back. Communicating with people who didn't speak English was extremely frustrating. During our previous trips, language problems came in small doses. Here in rural Spain, very few people understood English. I was thankful Deb had taken some time to study Spanish. Although she often became discouraged in her efforts, without her I might have given up on human contact and lived in the back of the station wagon, eating hard bread for every meal.

Okay, even with Deb I couldn't escape the bread thing, but at least it wasn't the *only* thing I had to eat.

After transferring our gear to the hotel room, we stopped by the tourist information office for a hiking trail map and headed out for an adventure. The map, unfortunately, was easy to misinterpret, and what we thought was our trail dead-ended after several hundred feet.

Glancing up from the dead end, we spotted a castle on a hilltop. I checked the thermometer on my new handy-dandy compass: it read one hundred degrees Fahrenheit. Under normal circumstances nature would have taken precedence, but on this day, the stifling heat made us distractible. Rather than search for the real trail, we returned to the car and followed a gravel road up to the castle.

If medieval real estate agents existed, they would have listed the Castillo de Monfragüe as a "starter castle." Built in the fifteenth century, it was much smaller than the previous two castles we had seen. The unusually shaped building had six flat sides and a flat top. Each side was about twenty-five feet wide, and its total height was about the same as a three-story house. Although the castle didn't have elaborate architecture or towers, it did have one exciting feature: an open door.

We stepped inside and were surprised to see only a single large square room with stone walls and a high ceiling. Medieval real estate agents would have had to avoid using the word *cozy* when describing the castle's interior. An enclosed staircase led up from an opening in the far wall. We climbed the stairs to a midlevel embrasure window, which was big enough to support a cannon but not tall enough to for us to stand in. We hunched over and gazed down on the Rio Tajo (the major river in the area) valley, then continued to the top of the stairs and popped out on the roof. Surrounding us were walls six feet thick and seven feet high. Defensive crenellations (openings) allowed for weapon launching in all directions, and steps made it easy for us to get on top of the walls. In its heyday the castle was a strategic lookout. With views extending for miles, it would have been difficult for an enemy to cross the river without being spotted.

A medieval real estate agent might have advertised the castle like this:

> Starter Castle. One large room for easy cleaning. Six-foot-thick walls provide all the protection you and your family will ever need. Roof doubles as a patio—great for entertaining friends, boiling caldrons of oil, or tossing heretics. Outstanding views allow for easy surveillance of neighbors. Built to last—six hundred years from now, it will still look as good as new.

After Deb and I finished exploring the castle, we decided to head down to the Rio Tajo. A two-lane highway paralleled the river, with a buffer of forest shielding the water from the highway. We followed the pavement until Deb spotted a dirt side road, which led us to a riverside picnic area. I switched off the ignition and stepped out to look around.

Striking me first was not the beauty of the river but the trash and feces-stained toilet paper littering the ground. I hoped the garbage would be restricted to the picnic area, but when I walked along the river, it too was lined with clumps of toilet paper. This wasn't a picnic area—this was a giant outhouse! Carefully watching where I placed my feet—the deep-treaded soles of hiking boots are great until you step in the wrong thing—I walked back to the car.

Spain has a dreadful trash problem. The picnic area on the Rio Tajo was typical of what I saw at every automobile pullout we stopped at. When it comes to garbage thrown out automobile windows, Spaniards are almost as bad as Americans. When it comes to defecating wherever they please, Spaniards are the worst I've seen. The one good thing I can say is that they kept their litter close to the roads. All of the wilderness areas we explored were clean.

On the way back to the hotel, we crossed a bridge over a dried-up riverbed. I glanced down just in time to see a small pool of water—something was moving in it. I U-turned, drove down a two-track road next to the bridge, and parked in a clearing near the riverbed. A sign might have warned "No Trespassing," but for once, ignorance of the language worked to our advantage. I bounded from the car and hurried across the rocks.

The river, which at high water would have been more than thirty feet wide and three feet deep, had dried up and left two ponds that were roughly fifteen feet wide and two feet deep. When I reached the first pond, it came alive with dozens of *plop, plop, plops.*

I stood still and gazed over the murky water. Although I didn't see anything at first, eventually the rounded snouts and bulbous eyes of dark-green frogs began to break the surface. I wasn't sure what species they were, but they looked similar to North American bullfrogs.

I crept over to the second pool. *Plop! Plop! Plop!* More frogs! Then a snake! Then a turtle!

When the river dried up, it concentrated all the water-loving reptiles and amphibians into the ponds. Even reptiles that didn't spend much time in the water, such as lizards and skinks, stayed close and crawled about on the rocks. Never before had I seen so many different kinds of herpetofauna together in one place.

I didn't attempt to catch any of the herps, as they were already stressed from lack of water. Instead, I sat on the rocks with Deb and watched them.

When we realized the sun would soon be setting, we decided to walk up the riverbed to see what else we could find. Five minutes past the ponds, I noticed numerous rodent-sized holes in the side of the riverbank. I gently stuck the end of my monopod/walking stick into one of the holes. When I pulled it out, hundreds of daddy longleg spiders oozed toward my feet. Even though daddy longlegs are common arachnids (technically they're not true spiders), seeing so many of them at once was shocking. Masses of them crawled on top of each other, and they moved like a living ball. All that was missing was the screech of a B-grade horror movie soundtrack.

I called out to Deb, who was dawdling behind me, "Come here. You've got to see this!" When she caught up, I thrust my stick into an untapped burrow. "Watch what happens when I pull this out."

"Ooh!" she said as the writhing ball rolled onto the riverbed.

Daddy longlegs normally don't bother me, but these were creepy—I quickly found another hole and woke up another batch.

Deb and I walked until we came across another pool of water. Like the other ponds, this one was full of reptiles and amphibians. We sat on a large rock and observed the herps until twilight. We would have stayed longer, but since we had left our flashlights in the car, we had to hurry back before it got too dark.

Our hasty departure left me with a desire to experience more of this special place. I vowed to return the following evening for further exploration.

By the time we reached the Hotel Carvajal, it was already after nine o'clock. The residents of Torrejón el Rubio were out for walks and milling about in the streets—the town was buzzing as much as a tiny town could buzz. Deb and I took advantage of the beautiful evening and strolled to a restaurant a few blocks away. When we stepped inside, the bartender informed us that they didn't serve food on Friday nights. In fact, the only place in town serving dinner was the restaurant at our hotel.

We ambled back to the Hotel Carvajal. Unlike our austere room, the hotel's restaurant was elegant and probably the best in the area. We were early, by Spanish standards, and people were just beginning to trickle in. Within the hour, all the tables would be full.

Once the proprietor seated us, a young woman waited on us. Most of the time, Deb and I found communicating with younger people to be easier than communicating with older people. This time the opposite was true—our waitress soon grew frustrated with us.

After watching Deb place her order with considerable pointing and repeating, I decided to make things easy for our waitress by ordering the five-course dinner special. I had no idea what the meal included but figured Saint Ambrose's wisdom about Rome would adapt quite well to our current situation: "When in Spain, eat as the Spaniards do."

Placed first on our table was the traditional loaf of hard, crusty bread. I hadn't seen any butter since arriving in Spain but couldn't see any harm in requesting some. I looked up *butter* in our Spanish book and showed the word to Deb.

The next time our waitress walked by, Deb asked, *"Mantequilla por favor?"*

The woman stopped dead in her tracks, shot us an icy glare, and repeated in a shrill voice, *"Mantequilla!"*

A man sitting with his family at the table next to us halted his conversation and craned his neck to stare at us.

Apparently, we had just insulted the entire country of Spain. Although the waitress acquiesced to our wishes, she defiantly deposited the butter on our table as if it were a forty-pound sack of flour.

Minutes later, she returned with a bowl of soup and a tray full of sausages. She tilted the tray to show me its contents. Although I was trying to eat like a Spaniard, a news story I had seen in the United States about environmentally destructive hog farms flashed through my brain. I mimed a polite "No, thank you."

The waitress scowled at me for a moment, then thrust the bowl of soup in front of my face.

"I think the soup is mine," said Deb.

I knew the waitress couldn't understand, so I took the bowl and handed it to my wife.

The young woman's eyes grew wide. She clenched her teeth and stormed off to the kitchen! A muffled but lively conversation drifted through the doors. The next time she entered the dining room, I noticed her deliberately avoiding eye contact with me.

"I think our waitress fired us," I said.

"No, she just got confused," said Deb.

When the next course arrived, the proprietor served us, and the waitress stayed as far away as possible.

"Oh, my god, you're right!" said Deb with a wry smile. "She *did* fire us!"

Our meal progressed smoothly until the proprietor served me a plate of fried potatoes. I took a bite. Not bad, but they needed something—ketchup.

I knew I should have eaten the potatoes plain, but as the person paying for the meal, I felt it was my prerogative to season my food how I pleased. When I asked Deb for language assistance, she shot me frosty glare that even the waitress couldn't beat. This was something I'd have to do myself.

The next time the proprietor checked on us, I requested in English, "Ketchup, please?"

A moment passed before the man figured out what I wanted. Then a look of revulsion flowed over his face. Roughly interpreting his Spanish words, he said, "I'm sorry sir, but we do not serve *caaatch-up* in this restaurant!"

What is it about ketchup that is offensive? Even in the United States, people get upset if you put ketchup on their dishes. It's just an innocent concoction of tomato sauce and spices! No one ever feels insulted if you season with salt or pepper. Ketchup manufacturers need a better public relations firm.

In fairness to the proprietor, cultural differences could have caused me to misinterpret the tone of his voice. Perhaps he wasn't upset with me for insulting his chef and was just disappointed that he didn't have a generous supply of the red delicacy on hand. Yeah, that must have been it.

Our dinner concluded a little before midnight. Although we were both stuffed, the meal had been draining. Deb's words echoed my thoughts: "Next time I wanna find a place where we can just eat and get out. I'm tired of every meal being an event."

Shortly after we went to bed, my body began to ache. I felt as if I were a punching bag for a heavyweight fighter. My first thought was, "Oh, great, food poisoning," but then I began to cough. Considering how many people I had come in contact with during my travels for this book—especially on airplanes—I had been amazingly healthy. I was due to get sick. The chills came next. I wrapped myself in an extra blanket, cranked up the heat, and shivered. Poor Deb could hardly stand it: trying to sleep in a sweltering room while listening to me cough and shiver made her as miserable as I was.

My condition had improved only marginally by morning. A tranquil restaurant-free day seemed like a grand idea, but first we'd have to buy some groceries. The hotel proprietor gave us directions to a grocery store—which promptly got us lost. Even though Torrejón el Rubio was small, its labyrinth of car-width side streets made finding anything a difficult task. In frustration, we looped over to the tourist information office for a fresh set of directions.

We often made use of tourist offices because they were the most likely places to find someone who spoke English. In this instance, the helpful college-aged woman behind the counter knew just enough English to get us where we needed to go.

She was also the perfect person answer a question I had been thinking about for the past day: "How many American visitors do you get here each year?"

The woman paused to carefully count in her head, then answered, "Thirteen."

When Deb and I travel, we dress inconspicuously and avoid clothes with writing or brand names on them. Even so, I'd been noticing people staring at us, as if we each had a sign on our back proclaiming, "We are Americans."

Since Spain is a major U.S. tourist destination, I was initially surprised that we weren't blending in. The woman's response confirmed what my observations were telling me: only a small percentage of Americans venture beyond Spain's large cities and coasts.

We returned to the hotel with a bag of groceries and spent most of the day in our room. For me, nothing is more frustrating than wasting time in bed when there are adventures to be had. By late afternoon, I convinced myself that I was no longer sick and suggested to Deb we head out for the evening.

Our first goal was to find a place along the Rio Tajo to have a picnic dinner. We drove for almost an hour, but every pullout had a generous supply of litter and that oh-so-appetizing feces-stained toilet paper. As we continued, our expectations decreased. Eventually we found a spot on the riverbank that looked clean—as long as we didn't turn our heads too far to the left or right.

We couldn't have asked for a more glorious evening. The sky was clear, the temperature was in the mid-eighties, and all the trash in Spain couldn't ruin the beauty of the wide, slowly drifting river.

After our picnic, we enjoyed a leisurely drive through the countryside looking for red deer (a subspecies of elk). The deer were common in the area. In less than an hour, we found at least ten, including several bucks with impressive antlers.

As we crossed over a branch of the Rio Tajo, Deb spotted a fox (called a *zorro* in Spanish) on the far riverbank. I pulled the car to the side of the road and trotted to the middle of the bridge. When I looked down, I saw a large fox intently watching an old woman, who was fishing. Although the fox stayed a safe distance from the woman, the two seemed to know each other.

When the woman noticed me taking pictures, she grabbed a large fish out of her bucket and called to the fox. The fox moved closer before having second thoughts and backing off. The woman continued tempting the fox until he couldn't resist any longer. In one quick dash, he grabbed the fish and darted into the woods.

Training a fox to take food from humans isn't a good thing, but I enjoyed the moment nonetheless. Before returning to the car, I made eye contact with the old woman and smiled a thank-you.

With less than an hour of daylight left, Deb and I decided to revisit the ponds in the dried-up riverbed. This time we carried flashlights, so darkness wouldn't force us to hurry back.

First we checked the ponds near the bridge. Our friends the frogs, turtles, snakes, and lizards were all waiting for us. Then we walked up the riverbed to the far pond. A shelf of flat rock at the edge of the water provided a perfect spot for us to sit and watch nature put on a show.

The snakes immediately disappeared and never visibly resurfaced. The turtles were just as shy, but their body shape made it harder for them to hide. Occasionally we'd see them surface, take a quick gulp of air, and sink back under the murky water. I wanted to get an identification photo, but doing so meant selecting a section of water and hoping I had picked the right spot.

I never got my turtle photo, because several medium-sized bats distracted me. Even though the sun had dropped below the mountains, the sky still provided enough light to watch the bats as they swooped down and skimmed the water for insects. Sometimes they flew so close, I could feel the wind from their wings.

The bats presented me with the irresistible challenge of a close-up photograph. Since the only time I could track them was when they were silhouetted in the sky, to get one in frame, I'd have to prefocus my camera over the water and time the push of the shutter button from the start of its dive. If you've ever watched bats in flight, you know they never fly in a straight or predictable manner. I took nearly twenty shots that produced only flat water before finally achieving one lucky bat shot. The bat was barely recognizable in the photo—it looked like a B-2 stealth bomber—but hey, I got it.

On Sunday morning, I awoke feeling much better. After three memorable days in west-central Spain, we decided to head north. As we said good-bye to Parque Natural de Monfragüe, nature presented us with two parting gifts:

First, we spotted an impressive flock of Eurasian griffon vultures atop a towering crag. The birds would take flight, circle for several minutes, and land again. With wingspans up to nine feet wide, they were bigger than the eagles we had seen at Plataforma. While I took photos, Deb counted forty-eight vultures—or to put it another way, up to 432 feet of total wingspan.

Our second gift happened quickly. We were driving along a narrow section of mountain road, with rock face on one side and a steep drop to a river on the other. As we approached a blind turn, a huge male red deer with three-foot-tall antlers galloped around the corner and headed toward us down the middle of the road. I slammed on the brakes—the deer did the same. Had we arrived a second or two earlier, he would have crashed through our windshield. The big buck sized us up for a moment before turning and majestically trotting back around the corner. My instinct was to grab my camera and follow, but if a car was coming in the opposite direction, I'd immediately regret it. Instead, I held back so the big buck could safely get off the road.

Our goal for the day was to reach the town of Cangas de Onis near the Atlantic Ocean's Bay of Biscay. Although we had to cover nearly three hundred miles, we took time for some stops along the way.

One of our stops included the twelfth-century walled city of La Villa de Castrotorafe. I had spotted the city from the highway and turned onto a dirt road that led us right to it. Deb and I had the city (which consisted of mostly rubble and deteriorating rock walls) to ourselves. As we walked among the ruins, everything was ghostly quiet. For a moment, I felt as if we were the last people alive on earth.

Because of its strategic location between Castile, Galicia, León, and Portugal, La Villa de Castrotorafe was once an important military post. The city, however, had been poorly constructed and began deteriorating by the fourteenth century—that's what happens when you fail to build using union slaves. Several rebuilding projects were attempted, but when the bridge spanning the Esla River collapsed during the sixteenth century, the commanders finally said, "Screw it," and abandoned the site.

Another stop helped us answer a question that had been puzzling us since the day we arrived. We had noticed large nests on the peaks of many churches, but they were all either temporarily empty or too high for us to see inside. When we passed through a small town, Deb yelled for me to stop. I zipped around the corner and pulled into the church parking lot. There she was, bright and beautiful, standing contentedly in her steeple-top nest—our mystery bird was a white stork.

Traveling north meant a dramatic change in environment. In west-central Spain, the weather was dry and much of the flora was golden brown. In northern Spain, the weather was humid and everything was lush and green. The change between the two ecosystems occurred suddenly. We literally crossed a high mountain pass and drove into a world of green.

Also notable was that the closer we got to the ocean, the more tourist oriented the towns became. We had picked Cangas de Onis for our evening destination because the dot on the map led us to believe it would be a tranquil little town with lots of Old World charm—I know that's a lot to infer from a dot, but it was the cutest dot I'd ever seen.

When we arrived, the streets were swarming with tour buses and automobiles, and almost every block had a hotel and souvenir shop. Despite the hordes of people (the town's population, not including tourists, was 6,200), the dot wasn't completely wrong—Cangas de Onis did have some Old World charm.

With so many hotels to choose from, deciding where to stay was almost overwhelming. Rather than investigate all the possibilities, we let the town decide for us and selected the hotel next to the first parking space we found.

The Hotel Los Lagos turned out to be a good choice. Everything we needed was within walking distance, and our third-floor room was spacious and reasonably priced. I was a bit concerned, however, when I stepped out onto our shallow balcony and the first sight to greet my eyes was a church belfry. Directly below me was a large courtyard with artists, vendors, and people wandering about. As I watched the activity, I felt like a Spanish king looking down on his subjects. I gave everyone a royal wave.

I had chosen a particularly suitable location to practice my royal wave (which was identical to the Miss America wave), as Cangas de Onis was the original capital of the Kingdom of Asturias. Now one of seventeen autonomous regions in Spain, Asturias has a population of 1.1 million people and a rich history going back to 718 and the reign of King Pelayo. A key figure in Spanish history, Pelayo became the first king of Asturias after his rebel forces defeated the Muslims. Although modern historians contend that stories of Pelayo's victory are exaggerated, many local people consider his triumph to have been the turning point in the Christian reconquest of Spain.

After two days of subsisting on the few items we bought at the grocery store in Torrejón el Rubio, Deb and I were famished and ready to eat like kings. When I asked the hotel clerk what time restaurants started serving dinner, her response was, "This is a tourist town. You can eat anytime you want."

Relieved we wouldn't have to wait until late, we changed clothes and headed out for dinner at five-thirty. The clerk lied—we checked restaurant after restaurant and no one would serve us before eight o'clock. Hungry and frustrated, we returned to our room to plan our next day.

We knew we were going hiking in Parque Nacional de los Picos de Europa (Spain's second-largest national park). The only question was where to go within its 159,778 acres.

Deb looked in our *Wild Spain* book and found a possible destination. "La Garganta Divina sounds interesting. It says here that we'd hike 'along a narrow mule track that has been carved into the wall of the gorge, high above the spray of the thundering river.' Oh, I suppose the heights would bother you. Let me see what else I can find."

Smugly confident that our Borneo trip had cured my fear of heights, I couldn't let my wife's comment pass. "No, let's do La Garganta Divina. If I can hike with the Iban, I seriously doubt Spain can dish out anything that will bother me."

"Oh, I forgot about Borneo."

I stepped out on the balcony to wave at my subjects again—for some reason, they never waved back. When Deb joined me, she pointed to the people mingling a short distance beyond the courtyard. "I think that's a restaurant across the way. Let's eat there. I have a good feeling about it."

I checked my watch; it was two minutes before eight o'clock. "Okay, let's go for it."

Three minutes later, we were at the doorstep of El Molin Restaurant. After the waitress seated us, we watched townsfolk drift in and out and exchange pleasantries with the man behind the bar. This was obviously where the locals dined.

Our waitress had given us Spanish language menus, but when she noticed us laboring to translate them, she came to our rescue with menus in English. Now, for the first time in Spain, we could order with confidence. Waltzing before my eyes were shellfish and other choices that hadn't been options for our previous meals. My taste buds tap-danced for joy.

Once we finished our excellent meal, the man from behind the bar walked over and introduced himself as Angel, one of the restaurant's owners. He looked about thirty-five years old and had a round face that complemented his receding hairline. Having noticed the invisible "We are Americans" signs on our backs, he wanted to welcome us to Spain and find out what part of the United States we came from.

After several days of conversing only between ourselves, Deb and I relished the opportunity to speak with someone different. Angel spoke excellent English, a skill he had learned while visiting England and traveling as a professional kayaker.

Deb commented to Angel, "Once we got out of Madrid, we fell in love with Spain. It's much different from what we expected."

"We're not like the big cities," he said. "Everyone expects us to be all about 'toro, toro,' but that's not us."

Throughout the evening, Angel had been serving special drinks to his patrons. He'd hold an unlabeled three-quarter-liter bottle far above his head and pour the golden liquid so it just caught the edge of a tilted glass held below his waist. Each pour was enough for one drink, and each drink was swallowed in a single gulp. After serving a round, he'd leave the bottle on the table or the bar until summoned back for a refill.

"What are you pouring for everyone?" I asked.

"Sidra natural, a traditional Asturias drink made from fermented apples."

Although the two of us had already consumed a bottle of Spanish wine and an after-dinner drink, we couldn't resist a taste. "A glass for each of us, please," I said.

Angel opened a bottle and performed a showy pour. After Deb and I each downed a glass, he ducked behind the bar, brought out an English translation of the book *Asturias*, flipped to the proper page, and handed it to me. "To pour the *culines* (cider glasses) requires great expertise, but all Asturians claim they are experts," it said.

"Is there a reason for the tall pour?" I asked.

"Sidra natural is not a high-quality drink. The pour adds effervescence."

I liked sidra natural. It had a refreshing semi-sweet sour-apple taste with a bite. Even so, one pour was plenty. We had drunk more than enough alcohol for the night.

As our mostly full bottle sat in front of us, I looked around and noticed that all the other customers had finished their bottles. If we didn't do the same, would it be offensive, like butter or ketchup? We couldn't take the chance. When in Spain . . .

Next came the biggest surprise of the evening. Since I had already paid for our meal, the bill for the sidra natural came separately. How much do you think a bottle of the local special, complete with ten show pours, would be worth? In some countries you might expect to pay twenty-five, perhaps even fifty euros. But here in Spain, the entire drink and show package cost only two euros ($2.36 U.S.).

I never get sloppy drunk, but on rare occasions, I do get happily intoxicated. When Deb and I left El Molin, we were both feeling *very* happy. Since it was almost eleven o'clock, we planned to head directly to bed. Then we noticed that most of the stores were still open for business. What could be more fun than inebriated late-night shopping with a nearly empty charge card?

We strolled down the main street and ended up in one of the town's less-tacky gift stores. Shopping primarily for relatives, we picked up various items and soon found ourselves by the stuffed animal shelves.

"What about this for Fiona?" I asked, holding up a large stuffed bull.

"Great idea! She'll love that," said Deb.

"Wait! This one's softer," I said as I rubbed my cheek against the animal's plush fabric.

The bulls were perfectly huggable—understuffed, as if a child had carried them around for years. I decided testing just two bulls wouldn't be enough. With Deb laughing and the store clerk straining her neck to keep an eye on us, I applied the cheek test to every bull on the shelf. "This one's very nice. Oh, this one's even better. I wanna buy one for myself, too. Can I? Can I?"

"They're fifty euros apiece! But I suppose if you *really* want one, you can have one."

Regrettably, I had a flash of maturity. I put down the bull I had selected for myself and carried the gift bull—the softest one in the store—to the counter.

Before long we had a healthy pile of gifts. When the clerk realized we weren't going to break or steal anything, she warmed up to us and began laughing. As she rang us up, I added more items to the pile.

"Wait! I didn't buy anything for myself. How 'bout a CD, so we have something to listen to in the car? Better yet, how 'bout two?"

We carried our gifts back to the hotel, laughing all the way. Despite the inauspicious start, our evening in Cangas de Onis had turned out to be great fun—*Bong! Bong! Bong! Bong! Bong! Bong! Bong! Bong! Bong! Bong! Bong! Bong!*

On this night, not even church bells could bother me. Instead, they serenaded me to sleep.

I awoke the next morning, September 15, leaned over—though not too far—and kissed the tip of my wife's nose. "Happy nineteenth anniversary, Honey!" I said.

Wow! I couldn't believe we had been married nineteen years. An amazing feat, considering our relationship began with me lying about my age (I didn't want her to know I was three-and-a-half years younger than she was) and forgetting her name on our first date. She must have thought I was *really* cute.

Deb and I have had many special anniversaries, but waking up in Spain was hard to beat. In celebration of the occasion, we went grocery shopping.

I mention groceries only because everything was so inexpensive. We found a small store on the main street and bought two-liter bottles of name-brand drinking water for the U.S. equivalent of 20¢ a bottle and three-quarter-liter bottles of tasty Spanish wine for $1.20 a bottle. In fact, other than diesel (which ran about $4 a gallon), all the consumable goods we purchased in Spain cost substantially less than comparable items in the United States.

From Cangas de Onis we headed east to Parque Nacional de los Picos de Europa. Along the way, we listened to one of the Celtic music CDs I had purchased the night before. Although Celtic music is most often associated with Ireland, the Celts once had a strong influence in Spain, and remnants of their culture remain. The CD's flowing rhythm provided an ideal soundtrack for the view out our windows. One moment we'd be in a tiny old village, then we'd climb a mountain, swing around a corner, and look down on a bright-green valley surrounded by flint-gray cliffs. The scenery was lyrical.

Deb and I had decided to hike La Garganta Divina in part because it was deep inside the park, where we assumed we wouldn't see many people. When we arrived to find more than a dozen cars parked on the roadside near the trailhead, we thought we had made a mistake. Then we noticed everyone was hiking the trail up to the overlook instead of the route we planned to take into the gorge. With a little luck, we'd have some solitude.

I could tell as soon as we began our hike that it would be a feast for our eyes. The aquamarine Rio Cares sliced through the gorge with high gray cliffs soaring upward from its banks. The sky was cloudless, yet the gorge was so sheer and narrow that rays from the slightly askew sun couldn't reach its bottom. All the contrasting light and shadow accentuated the colors and textures, and the sun-splashed walls had a radiant glow.

Our trail followed a shelf on the right side of the river, midway up the rock face. The first section was wide enough for Deb and me to walk side by side. Even though the drop to the river was more than one hundred feet, it didn't bother me.

As we moved deeper into the gorge, the trail began to narrow, and I could feel my body tense up. No matter what I had survived in Borneo, I still didn't like heights. In fact, my experience with the Iban had made my fears worse—I was now more aware than ever of how easily I could slip.

"If the trail gets any skinnier I'll want to turn around," I said.

"I feel the same way," said Deb.

The trail expanded and contracted depending on the terrain. At one point it shrank to only a foot in width, yet despite our vows to the contrary, we kept going. Sometimes width wasn't the primary concern. In a few sections, I had to crouch to avoid hitting my head on overhanging cliffs while at the same time keeping an eye on the outer edge of the trail. Eventually the rock face angled away to give us some shoulder room.

Then I saw it: the remains of a landslide blocked our way. As I walked closer, I could see where it had rumbled down the mountainside, obliterated the trail, and poured over the cliff. Continuing would require crossing a knee-high mound of loose rock and gravel. Although the maneuver would take only a few seconds, the steep incline provided nothing to grab on to. If the gravel gave way, or I slipped, the last thing I'd hear would be the thud of my body striking the rocks below.

Hiking for our lives in Borneo was different than a leisurely afternoon stroll on our anniversary. Here I had no flow of adrenaline to help me ignore the heights and no compelling reason to risk my life unnecessarily.

"Okay, it's time to turn around," I said.

Deb looked ahead and noticed the gorge turned sharply to the right a short distance past the landslide. Unable to restrain her curiosity, she announced, "I'm gonna see what's around the corner. I'll be right back." Before I could protest, she passed by me, crossed over the slide, and disappeared around the corner.

I stood there for a moment, staring at the pile of loose gravel before me and the boulders along the river below me. If I hiked forward, I'd soon be with my wife. If I slipped, I'd soon bounce off the gorge floor. If I stood where I was, my male ego would kick me all the way back to the car.

With a bob of my head and a curse on my breath, I started over the slide. "Fuuuuuuuuuuuuuuuuuck!" I drew out the word until I reached the other side. Then I proceeded around the corner and nearly collided with Deb.

"Oh! I didn't expect to see you," she said. "I'm glad you made it. The gorge is just stunning past here."

"So I take it you wanna continue."

"Yeah. Do you wanna take the lead?"

"Sure."

The gorge grew more picturesque with every step, but I was beyond the point of being able to enjoy the view. Soon we encountered another landslide. I stopped, glanced back at my grinning wife, shook my head, and dutifully crossed over—cursing under my breath.

After a bit, we reached what appeared to be the end of the trail. I breathed a sigh of relief. Now we could finally turn around.

"Oh look!" said Deb. "The trail cuts over the side and goes down to the river. What a great place for a picnic!"

I glanced down. Even though the cliff was no longer vertical, it was still very steep. "Why don't we eat right here?" I suggested.

"Come on, it'll be fine. We'll be much more comfortable by the river."

At that moment, the least comfortable thing I could think of was to descend a hundred or so feet for a picnic by the river. Nevertheless, after nineteen years of marriage, I would still do almost anything to please my wife. If she wanted to eat lunch by the river, I'd find a way to get down.

I began my shaky descent, unsure of which way to face, but once I got going—sliding on my rear end—I did okay and made it to the river.

We found a large flat rock near a small waterfall and removed our daypacks. The view of the gorge from the bottom looking up was quite lovely, and while I was a bit too wound up to relax, I had to admit—it was a wonderful spot for a picnic.

After we finished eating, we explored the riverbed, snapped some photos, and climbed back up to the trail.

The rest of our hike was uneventful. Knowing I had to retrace my tracks helped take my mind off the heights. I even managed to cross both landslides without cursing—okay, maybe one little word slipped out.

As we neared our car, I noticed the line of vehicles parked on the shoulder now stretched down the road and around the corner. Several groups of people were walking toward the gorge. We had timed our three-hour hike perfectly to avoid the crowds.

"Look at all those cars," I said. "It's hard to believe we're here on a Monday in September."

"I know," said Deb. "Imagine what it would be like on a weekend in July."

"I can see why so many people come here, though. It's a beautiful area."

"Oh! It's gorgeous!"

"Do you wanna hike another trail while we're still in the park, or do you wanna move on?"

"I wanna go to the ocean now."

"Anything to please you, dear."

We drove northeast out of Picos de Europa. Two detours led us through several quaint mountain villages. For the first time ever I was delighted to be detoured, as the back roads showed us a part of Spain untouched by tourists. Particularly memorable was a mountaintop village where we had to snake between clusters of old houses barely a car width apart. Had we stopped at the proper spot, someone could have climbed out the window of one house, crawled through our car, and entered the window of the neighboring house without touching the ground.

Our original plan was to spend our anniversary night in southern France. Deb's request to go the ocean changed that. Now we looked forward to a romantic evening on Spain's Bay of Biscay—if we could find a place to stay.

When we reached the ocean, we were shocked to see nothing but megaresorts lining the coast. Since we didn't want to stay at a megaresort, and it was too late to drive to France, we backtracked to a little community on the outskirts of Isla. There we found an oceanfront hotel built years before the tourist boom. It wasn't luxurious, but at forty dollars for a room overlooking the Bay of Biscay, it was a steal.

Next to our hotel was an upscale restaurant with large windows facing the water. Deb and I decided it would be a splendid place for our anniversary dinner. We arrived before the nine o'clock crowd and got the best table in the house. Reveling in our good fortune, we gazed across the bay as the sun dipped below the horizon. Soon we were staring at a sea of blackness. We hadn't anticipated our view would disappear and laughed at our miscalculation. No worries, both of us were dressed up for the occasion and had better things to look at anyway.

The subject of our conversation for the evening became, "What was best." For starters, the meal we were eating was definitely the best so far on the trip. We had ordered *paella de mariscos* for two. The popular Spanish dish consisted of prawns, clams, crab, lobster, and seasoned rice served in a large shallow pan. Based on the delightful meals we enjoyed on this night and the previous night, Spanish food varies by region. The culinary differences between west-central and northern Spain were countries apart.

As we reminisced about our best times, decisions, and events, we turned to a question we would be discussing for the rest of our lives: what was the best trip and trip moment of our seven-continent journey? The answer didn't come easily for either of us, and we still had the remainder of our Europe trip and Africa to go.

"I'd have to say Antarctica was my favorite trip," said Deb. "There was something special about it that goes beyond words—it was a feeling. The whales, the scenery, the people . . . ooh, I get goose bumps just thinking about it."

"I've enjoyed every trip," I said. "But if I had to pick just one, it would be the Amazon trip, because it fulfilled a lifetime dream. On the other hand, I share your feelings about Antarctica, I had a blast holding all the animals in Australia, and I couldn't have asked for a better adventure than we had in Borneo."

"It's hard, isn't it?"

"It's *very* hard, because I liked each trip for a different reason."

"Okay, how 'bout the best trip moment?" asked Deb.

"That's a little easier," I said. "Nothing beats the humpback whales swimming up to our Zodiac in Antarctica. I don't think the English language has a word to properly describe the experience, but the closest is *spiritual*."

"I agree. Nothing beats the humpbacks."

"Second best has to be hiking on the tundra with the caribou in Canada."

"That was wonderful, wasn't it? I can still see the Three Kings watching us from the top of the hill. But for me, scuba diving at Lankayan in Borneo comes in second—the reef was *incredible*."

"Another moment that sticks with me was in Canada on the night before our eighteenth anniversary—the stunning sunset, snuggling into the tent with our dogs, and the wolves howling around us. I don't know, maybe that was my favorite moment. . . ."

And so our conversation went. We had been very lucky. Although events didn't always go as planned, every trip had exceeded our expectations.

After dinner, we strolled back to our hotel room and drank wine on the balcony. As the waves gently lapped the shore and the full moon slowly rose above us, we held hands and looked into each other's eyes. Everything was perfect for a night of passion—except for one thing. Rather than staying in the bridal suite, we had the "we've-been-married-too-long-get-away-from-me-suite" with two tiny squeaky beds separated by a table.

I assumed the desk clerk assigned us the room after misunderstanding Deb's Spanish. It was her Spanish, right? We hadn't been married *that* long.

On Tuesday morning, our thoughts turned to France. With all the hullabaloo about the country taking a stand against the Iraq war, and the childishness of certain Americans who took French fries and French toast and renamed them "freedom fries" and "freedom toast," I had to make sure a visit to France was on our itinerary. I wanted know: who were these rebels that *dared* use their vote to oppose an unprovoked attack on another country?

Outside Isla, we experienced our first congested European freeway. Navigating the freeways required a tremendous amount of concentration on both Deb's and my part. I kept us from colliding with zigzagging traffic and she kept us on course—or at least tried to keep us on course. When we hit a traffic jam, she promptly pointed to the wrong cloverleaf and sent us back toward Cangas de Onis. We were both glad we didn't have each other's job.

Beginning with the last ninety miles in Spain and continuing into France, individual drivers rigorously policed the three lanes of traffic in each direction (I never saw an actual highway patrol). Truckers and other slow-moving vehicles ruled the right lane, normal speed drivers maintained the middle lane, and the fastest driver set the pace for the left lane.

If the friendliness of a country were a reflection of its drivers, the world would be an inhospitable place. In Europe I learned that no matter how fast I drove in the left lane, someone else would always want to go faster. Every time I dared enter the lane, a lead-footed driver in a speedy vehicle would fly in from nowhere, hover inches off my back bumper, and flash his or her headlights to demand I move over. If for some reason I didn't get out of the way fast enough—because cars in the middle lane blocked my way or some other feeble excuse—the driver would respond with the European version of the one-finger salute.

The posted speed limit on freeways was 130 kilometers per hour (81 miles per hour), but in reality, that was merely a suggested starting point. Once, I floored our little Opel wagon, and it roared up to 180 kilometers per hour (112 miles per hour). As we passed the scenery in a blur, for one cocky moment I felt like a true European. Then I noticed a car—with its headlights flashing—rapidly growing larger in my rearview mirror. I humbly returned to the middle lane.

Our goal for the day was to drive a few hours east of the border and find a hotel near the Pyrenees Mountains. Since we never had trouble finding a hotel with available rooms in Spain, we anticipated similar luck in France. When the first place we checked didn't have a vacancy, we stopped at the tourist information office in the town of Bagnères-de-Bigorre.

Once again, I had to depend on Deb for our communications with local people. She had taken three years of French in junior high school and was confident she could remember enough to muddle through. Since Spanish and French are related, but different enough to be confusing, switching between the two languages was more difficult than she expected. Although Deb disagrees with me, her Spanish was better than her French.

Fortunately for us, the woman at the tourist office understood English and went out of her way to be helpful. Once Deb told her what we wanted, she got on the phone and did the talking for us. The first few places she checked were full. Then she had success.

"I found a room for you in the village of Lesponne," she said with a smile. "It's at a hotel called Chez Gabrielle. Go down the road twenty kilometers and take a right. You can't miss it. It's directly across from the church."

Deb and I looked at each other and grinned.

"Do the church bells in France ring all night?" I asked.

The woman tilted her head in confusion.

"It's an inside joke," said Deb. "We've just arrived from Spain, where some of our hotels were next to churches with bells that rang all night."

"Oh! They ring all night here too. Would you like me to find another place for you?"

"No, no, we'll be fine," I said. "Thank you."

Our drive to Lesponne gave us the opportunity to take in the sights at a leisurely pace. This was a rural area speckled with little villages. All around us was intensely green landscape, and just to the south of us were rounded tree-covered foothills backed by the majestic Pyrenees Mountains.

I was surprised to see a big difference between Spanish and French houses. Based on the appearance of the communities we drove through, I would have never guessed that Spain's per capita income was one-third less than France's. In rural Spain, most houses had brightly painted stucco walls and terra cotta tiled roofs; in southern France, most houses had flat white or unpainted gray stucco walls and dark-gray shingled roofs. On a larger scale, Spanish villages looked regularly maintained while French villages looked as if they hadn't been touched in fifty years. This is not to say that communities in southern France were unattractive, only that their beauty was subjective. The key was to forget about the lack of color and enjoy the authenticity.

Lesponne was three blocks long and likely had a population under fifty. Even so, we almost drove past our hotel. Other than its green shutters, Chez Gabrielle appeared to be a typical two-story French house. I looked for a place to park. Since the hotel and nearby buildings abutted the narrow street, the church's tiny four-space parking lot was our only option.

After pulling into one of the spaces, Deb and I each grabbed a bag and walked across the street to the hotel. Directly inside the door was a small dining room with three long wooden tables and matching benches. Meals would obviously be a social occasion.

The proprietor, Isabella, walked in from the kitchen and greeted us with a smile. She was a petite, attractive woman with beautiful long brown hair and an Old World warmth that made us feel like family.

Isabella knew virtually no English, and Deb's attempt to communicate with her in French didn't go well. Somehow, mostly through the use of hand gestures, the two women quickly got the basics out of the way: the price for a night was ridiculously inexpensive, the church parking lot was the correct place to leave our car, and dinner would be served at the reasonable hour of seven o'clock. I liked France already.

The hotel had only two guest rooms; both were Spartanly decorated and spotlessly clean. Because Deb and I were the first to check in, we could pick the one we wanted. Although we wouldn't be spending much time there, we chose the room with the view of the mountains and the valley floor. More important than the view, however, was that the window faced away from the church belfry.

Since dinnertime was still several hours away, we took the opportunity to drive up the road to a trailhead at the base of the Pyrenees. Sharing the road with us were numerous bicyclists from their teens to their seventies. Most wore colorful tight-fitting racing-style outfits, and all looked as if they had dreams of winning the next Tour de France.

Similar sights would be common over the next few days. Each time I saw another bicyclist over the age of sixty-five tackling a steep mountain road I'd smile with admiration. France was obviously a nation of all-aged outdoor enthusiasts.

A parking lot full of cars greeted us at the trailhead. While on our previous outings we had been able to hike away from the crowds, we couldn't do that this time. Several trails departed from the lot, but each one led us to more people. Even when we couldn't see anybody, we could usually hear voices in the distance. I was beginning to realize that, by necessity, European hikers had goals that were more social than mine were. For me, a perfect day of hiking is when I see lots of wildlife and no humans other than my companion(s). Here I saw lots of humans and no wildlife.

On the positive side, the forest was trash free and well worth the admiration of the throngs of nature lovers. We hiked to where a stream cascaded down the mountain in a series of small falls. The mist from the plummeting water rose and dissipated into the already moist air. Although the sun was shining, tall trees formed a rainforest-like canopy, which muted the light and kept the undergrowth at bay. Plants that thrived in dim light, such as mosses and ferns, were all flawlessly green and looked as if no insect or disease had ever disturbed them. Had we grown tired, luxurious pillows of moss-covered rocks were scattered across the ground. Any of them would have made an excellent headrest for a snooze.

Once we finished exploring, we returned to the car and followed the winding mountain road back to Chez Gabrielle. Deb and I were looking forward to our first taste of Isabella's authentic French cooking and changed into clean clothes for the occasion. Since the door to our room was on the side of the building, we had to walk around to the front to enter the dining room.

As we stepped inside, a deep voice boomed out, "Welcome!"

We stood by the door while our eyes adjusted to the dim interior. Soon we could see the greeting had come from an old man sitting at the far table. Something about him was familiar. He was slightly stocky and had a weathered face with a bushy beard—Ernest Hemingway! He looked exactly like Ernest Hemingway would have looked had he lived to be seventy-five years old.

The man rose to his feet, spread his arms wide, and repeated, "Welcome!"

This time, Deb took the man's cue and hurried across the room to give him a big hug and exchange kisses on the cheek.

"Come, join us for dinner," he said, gesturing to the spot across the table from him.

We soon learned that the old man's name was Michel, and the young man sitting with him was his traveling partner. The young man didn't speak English, and Deb's attempted French only confused the situation. With English as the only practical option, Michel did his best to serve as interpreter, and Deb used the opportunity to learn some French words at the same time.

"Please forgive me if I'm difficult to understand," said Michel. "I haven't spoken English in twenty years."

"You're doing great!" replied Deb. "I'm the one who should be apologizing for speaking bad French in France."

In the process of our conversation, we learned that Michel currently lived in the city of Marseille, but his father used to have a farm in Lesponne. Whenever he came back to visit, he always stayed at Chez Gabrielle, "because Isabella and her family are such nice people."

He was right. They were nice. In fact, so was everyone else we met in France. Before our trip, I heard a plethora of stories from Americans who claimed the French were rude and arrogant. I'm not sure how or why the French acquired their reputation, but based on my experiences, the accusations were unwarranted. Though I hate to admit it, if I counted all the rude or arrogant people Deb and I met during our travels, Americans would significantly outnumber people from all the other countries combined.

Our evening at Chez Gabrielle passed swiftly, with good company, good wine, and Isabella's house special—a rich black sausage with fried apple slices. I can't say that her black sausage was my favorite meal in Europe, but as far as black sausages go, it was the best I'd ever tasted. In retrospect, it would have been great with a dab of ketchup.

Either the church bells didn't ring that night or the black sausages contained some very special ingredients, because Deb and I both fell asleep as soon as we hit the bed and didn't wake until morning.

Another warm, sunny day beckoned, and we were eager to see more of the country. After a traditional breakfast of café au lait with French bread and jam, we hugged Isabella good-bye and continued on our route to the east.

Southern France resembled Spain in that most of the villages we drove through were compact and never fully redesigned to accommodate the invention of the automobile. Two questions arose as we wound through a village on a two-lane road barely wide enough for one lane of traffic. First, why didn't any of the buildings have marks on them from being hit? Surely someone, at some time, must have misjudged the clearance between their vehicle and a building and scraped a wall or chipped a corner. Second, why did every car have its mirrors intact? Each time a car zipped by in the opposite direction I blinked, half expecting the outside mirror on our Opel to collide with the mirror on the oncoming vehicle. The mirrors probably missed by a foot or more, but that didn't leave much room for error. Although the answers to my questions would remain a mystery, I was now convinced that the people living in the villages didn't drink and drive.

Before departing the Pyrenees, we followed a road leading to the top of a mountain. Along the way, we passed scores of bicyclists laboring up the steep incline. Some looked as if they would succeed, while others grimaced as if wondering, "How the hell did I get talked into this?"

The view from the summit gave me mixed feelings. Next to a sign indicating our altitude of 2,115 meters (6,939 feet) was a life-size statue of a man on a bicycle. While I presumed the statue marked a route taken by the Tour de France (the route changes each year), and I had fun imagining riders whizzing by, I was depressed to see such a majestic mountain carved up by commercial activities. A ski resort, hotel, and various shops all combined to strip the mountain of its natural beauty. With little reason to linger, we moved on.

Our next destination was Parc Naturel Régional de Camargue, a 210,040-acre park on the Mediterranean coast, 270 miles east of Lesponne. We took the tollway for most of the distance. Although expensive, it provided the quickest route across France. By following automobiles in the left lane, we maintained an average speed of just over Mach 1 and reached the park by midafternoon.

In contrast to parks we had visited in Spain, Parc Naturel Régional de Camargue was flat, with a maximum altitude of fifteen feet above sea level. Our *Wild France* book warned that the park was a popular tourist destination but indicated we could avoid the crowds by leaving the main road. After driving for several miles in a stream of cars headed south for the Mediterranean Sea, we took the author's advice and turned off on an unmarked two-track road. All signs of tourists disappeared.

We parked the car and set out on foot. On our left was a rice field, and to our right was an expanse of five-foot-tall native grass, punctuated with clumps of gnarly trees. A half mile from the car, the road turned and followed alongside a deep water-filled ditch coated with a blanket of bright-green algae. The ditch was home to a family of ducks and hundreds of frogs. Tall grass and reeds arched over the ditch, making it impossible to view the wildlife without disturbing it. Each time I parted the vegetation, I was greeted by the *plop, plop, quack, quack,* of frogs and ducks taking cover.

Before long, a small but fierce contingent of mosquitoes convinced us to reverse our course. I was lagging behind Deb when she called out, "Marty! Come here. I found more frogs."

She had found a ditch with only a few inches of slimy water in it. Like the other ditch, a tall wall of vegetation rose from its banks. I pushed my way through and peered over the edge just in time to see three kinds of frogs dart out of sight: one was green with black spots, one was brown with black spots, and one was brown with a neon-green stripe down its back.

Hoping to photograph them for identification, I stepped into the ditch. "Oh! I didn't expect to sink so deep. Well, you know you're having a good day when both your boots *and* your socks get muddy."

Soon I spied the frogs again. When I slopped toward them, they retreated for cover. I continued my pursuit, but all I was doing was driving them into better hiding spots and stirring up more mosquitoes. I climbed back out to solid ground.

Once the frogs had sufficient time to settle, I said to Deb, "Grab onto my hand while I lean over the ditch to take some pictures."

"I don't think I can hold you."

"Sure you can."

Though I outweighed my wife by seventy-five pounds, she dug in and held on as I leaned out to get my shots. A slip almost flung us into the mud, but our teamwork was successful.

When we returned to the car, I checked the photos on my camera screen against those in my reference books. Two of the frogs were different color variations of the lake frog, Europe's largest frog. The third frog, the one with the neon stripe, didn't appear in any of my books. So until proven differently, I'm calling it a "Deborah French hopper."

We briefly rejoined the southbound traffic, then veered east on a gravel road, and finally turned right onto a bumpy two-track road that dead-ended at a trail.

The trail didn't show on our map, but it looked inviting. We followed it south as it paralleled a lazy river and passed through sandy terrain interspersed with grasses, scrub, and small leafy trees. Since we didn't have a distance goal in mind, we took our time and stopped often to explore the riverbank.

Eh-oo-oo! Aa-a-ack! Eh-oo-oo! Aa-a-ack! Eh-oo-oo! Aa-a-ack!

I looked over my shoulder at Deb. "Do you hear that?"

"Yes. What is it?"

"I have no idea."

We picked up our pace. With each step the vegetation thickened and the high-pitched screeches grew louder. "This is gonna be good!" I said.

When I saw a break in the trees, my heart pounded with excitement. I rushed up to the edge. Past the trees was a field of calf-high scrub; beyond the scrub was a muddy beach; beyond the beach was a vast body of water; standing in the water was a flock of at least sixty greater flamingos.

As the world's largest species of flamingo, they stood five feet tall and were a slightly lighter hue of pink than the subspecies of greater flamingo found in the Western Hemisphere. Though they were still three hundred feet away, we approached slowly, being careful not to spook them.

The field of scrub was soft and waterlogged, but it adequately supported my weight. Once I halved the distance to the flamingos, the scrub gave way to semidry mud. I took a few steps, sinking a little each time. I took one step too many and sank past my ankles.

As the smell of rotting vegetation wafted to my nostrils, I glanced over at Deb. She was having no problem walking on the surface. Yes, it's good to be the girl.

I flashed back to my first day on the Amazon River. Experience had made me wiser. Before taking another step, I plunged my walking stick into the mud—its entire length disappeared with little resistance. Although I wanted to get closer to the flamingos, Deb was the only one around to pull me out if I got stuck, and she could end up just as stuck as me. I shot some photos from where I stood and gingerly stepped back to firmer ground.

Deb noticed an elevated peninsula a short distance west of the flamingos. We walked to its point and looked out over the water. I wasn't sure if we were at the edge of a large freshwater lake or at the edge of a protected bay on the Mediterranean Sea. The quickest way to find out if it was seawater or lake water was to taste it.

I climbed down from the peninsula, dipped my finger into the water, and licked it off. Mmmm—a repulsive concoction of dirt, fish slime, and decomposed weeds mixed with a hint of salt. I offered a sample to Deb; she refused it.

While puzzling at the time, the mild salty flavor had a logical explanation. In the mid-1800s, the French built a sea dike to control the tides and open land for farming. The lake before us was where the river once flowed into the Mediterranean, and the salty taste was diluted seawater that had found its way past the dike.

Deb and I stood on the peninsula and watched the flamingos until they flew away. With darkness approaching, we hiked back to the car and continued east across the park. A beautiful orange sunset filled my rearview mirror, necessitating a photo stop. Then a more important mission took precedence—Deb needed to be fed.

Rather than return to the tollway, we decided to take the alternate route. We thought the old two-lane highway would provide quick access to restaurants but soon regretted our decision. The dark and lonely road led us through miles of nothingness.

This was a dangerous, possibly lethal, situation. When Deb is hungry she's like a female black widow spider, and that would um . . . make me her mate.

"On the left!" she screamed. "There's a restaurant!"

When I glanced to where Deb was pointing, my eyes were drawn to the multiple rows of semitrailer trucks in the parking lot. I was looking forward to a meal of traditional French food, not truck stop food.

"Are you sure you want to eat *there?* Let's drive a little farther."

"I need to eat *now!*"

I dutifully swerved into the lot and parked the car.

We entered the restaurant dressed in our mud-smeared shorts, casual shirts, and invisible "We are Americans" signs. I scanned the crowded main room. About fifty men were inside. Some were standing at the bar, and the rest were sitting at tables.

"You're the only woman in here," I said.

"You're right," said Deb. "Oh, wait. The bartender is a woman."

"She doesn't count."

Imagine stepping into a restaurant filled with burly truckers. Members of the ruling party in your home country have recently insulted the truckers' nation, heritage, and even their manhood with degrading comments and jokes. Now you feel their eyes upon you, as if you were the one to blame for the insults. You look for an open table and catch your breath when you realize the closest one is on the far side of the room. You cross to it, as if walking a gauntlet. Intimidation floats in the air. Then you notice a small detail that changes everything. The truckers, many with tattoos covering their muscular arms, aren't drinking hefty mugs of beer—they're sipping dainty glasses of wine.

I know I'm playing with stereotypes here. Certainly every trucker isn't a beefy redneck looking to start a fight. But picture Arnold Schwarzenegger playing the Terminator with a glass of red wine in his hand. It just wouldn't work.

As things turned out, the restaurant's customers and employees were friendly. Our waiter even went out of his way to speak English to me while patiently encouraging Deb to practice her French.

Deb ordered from the menu, and I opted for the buffet. Midway through our meal, Deb subtly pointed to the large snails the truckers next to us were eating and said, "I'm surprised you didn't try the escargot."

"Oh, I overlooked them. I'll be back."

When I returned to the table, I smiled, pulled an escargot from its shell, popped it into my mouth, and washed it down with a splash of wine. "Mmmm—truck stop food!"

After spending the night at a large chain hotel, Deb and I traveled southeast with tortoises on our mind. Our plan for the day was to infiltrate the Massif des Maures area and search for one of France's most endangered reptiles—the western Hermann's tortoise.

The first stop in our quest was Le Village des Tortues (the Tortoise Village), a tortoise rehabilitation center near the town of Gonfaron. Our mission was to befriend a staff member, learn as much as we could, and get detailed information on tracking down the wily Hermann's tortoise in the wild.

When we couldn't find an English-speaking staff member, our mission was nearly thwarted. Only through quick thinking and improvisation were we able to acquire the vital background information we needed.

—Okay, we utilized the signs posted for British visitors.

For many people the word *tortoise* invokes thoughts of giant four-foot-long Galapagos tortoises. Western Hermann's tortoises, on the other hand, are small, reaching a maximum length of eight inches. While both reptiles make the *IUCN Red List of Threatened Species,* the Galapagos tortoise is listed as "vulnerable" and the western Hermann's is listed as "endangered." In France, habitat destruction, egg pilfering, and fire are the primary factors for the tortoises' decline.

The Tortoise Village had twenty-six stations with either open-air pens or glassed-in enclosures. Even though the village focused primarily on the native western Hermann's tortoise, the facility also housed turtles and tortoises from other parts of the world. Deb and I investigated all the species and stopped by the clinic, quarantine, reproduction, hatchery, and nursery areas.

Up to fifteen hundred tortoises may live on site at any one time. The permanent residents included foreign tortoises, which were on display for educational purposes, and native tortoises, which were too severely injured to be released.

The temporary residents, however, were the most important. Each year approximately three hundred injured or diseased Hermann's tortoises are brought to the village to be nursed back to health and returned to the wild.

Without a doubt, the most adorable residents were the baby Hermann's tortoises. Like their parents, they had lumpy, highly domed, olive-brown shells with black multi-shaped markings. Not exactly beauty queen contenders, but their miniature features made them so cute we instantly fell in love with them.

We stopped by the reproduction pen to be voyeurs in the making of little ones. Boy, am I glad I'm not a tortoise! Neither the male nor the female appeared to be enjoying the mating process. The female crawled nonstop and attempted to escape the mounted male by sliding under obstacles to clothesline him and brushing against objects to knock him off balance. The male, on the other hand, was a testament to perseverance. Staying mounted over the domed shell of a stationary female would have been difficult enough, but doing so with a continually moving mate must have been exhausting. To voice his frustration, he occasionally bellowed out a pained, throaty yowl.

We didn't stick around long enough to find out if the lovebirds successfully copulated, but chases like the one we watched must end in victory sometime, or tortoises would never lay fertile eggs.

Having completed the fact-finding portion of our mission, we were now ready to head into the nearby forest to pursue a wild western Hermann's tortoise. Although our hunt would begin with high expectations, we had no idea what we were up against.

Hermann's tortoises are elusive and cunning creatures who aren't above using stealth movements and decoys to avoid detection. Their alliance with the pine trees was especially diabolical. With all the pinecones strewn across the forest floor, I often found myself doing double takes to make sure they weren't my quarry.

Deb and I combed the forest for several hours, but the beautiful ninety-degree day made us easily distractible. While we followed wild boar trails, sampled a grape from a vineyard, and photographed a praying mantis, the western Hermann's tortoises confidently hid out in their undisclosed location.

Outsmarted and discouraged, we returned to the car, regrouped, and drove to within a few miles of the Mediterranean Sea. An intelligence leak had led us to believe that surfer Hermann's tortoises (a little-known rebel subspecies) maintained a lair in the vicinity. If they had eaten too much weed, we might be able to catch them unaware.

We followed a trail up and around a squat mountain. Unusual flora—including huge gnarly cork oaks and plants that looked like they belonged in a dry climate growing alongside plants that looked like they belonged in a tropical climate—gave the mountain a mystical, timeless feel. At any moment I expected to see a dragon emerge from the bushes or an armored knight on horseback come clip-clopping down the trail.

A scan of the terrain revealed that the surfer Hermann's tortoises were even craftier than their western cousins. The weed they consumed obviously hadn't dulled their minds, as their masterful use of decoys kept us confused and slowed us down. Not only did the pinecones look like tortoise shells, even the rocks were strategically placed so their shadows—wait what's that?

"Shhhhhhh. Deb, come over here. I think I found one. Look, inside that hollow log. All I have to do is reach in and . . . Aarrgh! Another rock!"

The tortoises were just too slippery for us. They knew the territory; they knew the hiding spots; and we were out of time. Four o'clock had already arrived and we had to meet up with Emad in Switzerland in twenty-one hours. We wished the tortoises well—wherever they were—and plotted our route to the northeast.

Future tortoise hunters please note: western Hermann's tortoises are protected by law. Picking them up in the wild or selling them is strictly prohibited.

Driving to Switzerland wouldn't be as quick and easy as it looked on the map. Much of our three-hundred-mile-long drive across France would follow winding two-lane roads over high mountain passes, and sometimes even flat straightaways would be slow going.

Deb and I learned the hard way not to take secondary highways during rush hour. As we headed north, tiny villages temporarily gave way to medium-sized towns. We'd crawl through traffic in one town, pick up speed for a few miles, hit traffic in the next town, and so on. Eventually we grew tired of rush-hour déjà vu and bolted for the tollway.

We had planned to drive for one hundred miles and to stay overnight in Gap. When we reached the city of 40,000 people and couldn't find a hotel with a vacancy, we reluctantly continued toward Switzerland. Checking every lodging possibility along the way slowed our progress. By the time we reached the village of Saint-Bonnet, we felt like we were forty miles past Gap instead of just ten. Upon spying an advertisement for La Crémaillère Hotel, we followed signs through town to what we hoped would be our home for the night.

Feeling weary and looking dirty, we entered the hotel. Although it was only a two-star property (the European star rating system is highly subjective), the establishment was elegant and well maintained. To our right was a formal dining room with several well-dressed guests eating dinner. Directly ahead of us, at the front desk, was the hotel manager. The contrast between the curly-haired manager in his dress shirt and slacks and us in our T-shirts and shorts had me worried that even if he had a vacancy he'd turn us away.

Speaking in French, Deb requested a room for the night. The manager responded in a deliberate manner, but that didn't keep Deb's brain from freezing up. In frustration, she asked, "Do you speak English?"

"Yes, madam, a little."

"Do you have a room available for tonight?"

"Yes, I would be happy to accommodate you."

"I may have to kiss you!"

A sly smile came over the manager's face. Whether he was flattered or amused by Deb's proposition was unclear. We were just pleased to have a place to stay.

Deb and I lugged our gear up the stairs to our second-floor room, showered, changed clothes, and walked back down for dinner. I must say—we cleaned up pretty good. When the manager saw our new look, he raised his eyebrows in surprise.

While a young woman served all the other guests in the dining room, the manager waited on us personally. Tonight we'd have no worries of being fired.

As dinner arrived, I said to him, "You keep busy around here. First you checked us in and now you're serving us our food. Can I assume you're also the owner?"

"I am just the husband of the boss," he said.

Deb and I chuckled and tasted our French wine and orange duck.

"Mmmm, delicious!" said Deb.

An hour and a half earlier, we had been preparing ourselves for the possibility of sleeping in the back of the station wagon. Now we were in a nice hotel, enjoying friendly service and a gourmet meal. Despite occasional periods of frustration, this had been another great day in France.

Deb and I hit the road early in anticipation of our rendezvous with Emad. One of the most pleasurable and unexpected benefits of our seven continent journey has been the friends we've made along the way. Almost every trip in this book has introduced us to people we will stay in touch with for the rest of our lives. As for Emad, we'd be seeing him just seven months after the three of us became friends on the Antarctica expedition.

Emad would be taking a train south from Winterthur, Switzerland, and meeting us between one and two o'clock at the train station in the city of Sierre. The last time we communicated with Emad was by e-mail, a week before we departed from the United States. We had planned to contact him again once we reached Europe, but we were unable to locate an Internet café or reach him via telephone. We had to trust that he didn't have an unexpected change of plans or think our silence meant we weren't coming.

We hoped to cross into Switzerland ahead of schedule, but mountain passes slowed our progress. As exhilarating as it would have been, I just couldn't drive 112 miles per hour along the skinny edge-of-the-mountain roads. In fact, in some places, fifteen miles per hour was a challenge.

When we reached Sierre, it was already after one o'clock. Based on the cute little dot on the map, we expected to find a couple-of-blocks-long town, not a several-mile-long city. What's the world coming to when you can't even trust a dot anymore?

Since Switzerland didn't provide handy graphic Canadian-style signs to point our way, we spent a half hour searching for the train station and got lost several times. Hmmm, is it possible to get lost when you're looking for something and you don't know where it's supposed to be? Eventually we stopped at a hotel, and Deb ran in to ask for directions. She returned with a smile. The station was in an alley, one block away. We could have driven all day and never found it.

The train station had a long outside wall made of glass. Deb and I walked along it, looking for the door. We hadn't gone far when I spotted the unmistakable shaven head, soul patch, and smiling face that could only belong to Emad.

He spotted me at the same time, and we both pounded our open hands against the glass wall as if we were in separate universes divided by a force field. We continued pounding along the wall until reaching the door, where the three of us exchanged hugs.

As Emad loaded his gear into our car, he announced he had a special itinerary for us. Deb and I knew we'd be exploring the Alps but had left the details up to him. His plan was this: We would drive to the town of Tasch (which was the last town on the road permitting combustion-engine vehicles), park our car, and take an electric taxi to the town of Zermatt. From there, we'd take a gondola (cable car) up the mountain to the base of the Matterhorn and stay two nights at the Hotel Schwarzsee.

The plan sounded great—except for the heights. By the time Emad finished reciting the details, the muscles in the back of my neck were in a knot. Even though I didn't say anything, I thought, "Must our activities revolve around heights? Couldn't we do something more relaxing, like explore a cave full of venomous snakes?"

On the drive to Tasch, we caught up with each other on what had happened in our lives since Antarctica. Emad had been traveling even more than Deb and I had.

When the subject of food came up, he told us a sickening story about a meal he had eaten while on a business trip in China. "I was sitting at a table, with my prospective Chinese business partners, when the chef came out of the kitchen holding a live python. I had no idea what was going on until he picked up a knife and slit the snake up its belly!"

"Oh my god!" Deb and I exclaimed in unison.

"It gets worse. Next the chef removed the gallbladder, squeezed the bile into a glass, and mixed it with rice wine!"

"Ahhhhhh!" I groaned. "You didn't drink it, did you?"

"It would have been culturally offensive *not* to drink it. They believed the concoction had medicinal properties, and that drinking it was a special privilege. It tasted absolutely *vile!*"

"Okay, I've now lost all desire to visit China," I said.

"There's more," he said. "The main course was a lobster."

"What's wrong with lobster?" asked Deb.

"It was still alive! The chef pulled off its tail-scales and set it on the table. We had to chase it around with our chopsticks to pick pieces of meat off its body!"

"That's barbaric!" I said. "I would have *never* been able to drink the snake wine or eat the live lobster. Cultural sensitivity only goes so far."

"I know. I felt terrible. If I ever go back to China on business I'm going to tell them I'm a vegetarian."

Upon reaching Zermatt, we boarded the gondola and began our climb up the mountain. Our four-person-capacity "cabin of death" hung from a flimsy cable. As we ascended to the heavens, I looked out the window and watched Zermatt shrink before my eyes.

"Does the gondola bother you?" asked Deb.

"No, not at all," I lied.

"You don't need to worry, Marty," said Emad. "The Swiss make the safest cable cars in the world."

The first gondola didn't reach all the way to the hotel, necessitating a change of cars at the midway point. Our entire ride lasted a little more than a half hour.

Having survived the ascent, we stepped out onto a treeless mountain, where a bracing wind threatened to fling our hats back to Zermatt. Though we were at a high altitude, the Matterhorn still towered above us. We took a moment to admire the precipitous snow-flecked peak before schlepping our gear to the hotel, a short distance away.

The Hotel Schwarzsee was surprisingly small. The main floor had a dining room, kitchen, and sitting room, and the upper two floors had various-sized rooms with fourteen beds total. In all, the accommodations were utilitarian but pleasant.

Shortly after we arrived, dozens of people emptied out of the hotel. The last gondolas were heading down the mountain, and all the day-trippers had to leave. Soon we were alone at the top, except for three other guests, the hotel manager, and the cook.

The wind followed the day-trippers down the mountain, and when the gondolas were turned off for the night, everything grew eerily silent. With a few hours of daylight left, Deb, Emad, and I took a short hike to get a feel for the area.

Upon our return, Emad laid a trail map out on a table so we could plan the next day. "We can take any trail you want," he said, "but I think you'd enjoy hiking up to the Hörnlihütte."

"What's the Hörnlihütte?" I asked.

"It's the base camp, where mountaineers stay before climbing the Matterhorn," said Emad.

"Will we have to follow any edge-of-the-cliff trails?" I asked.

"I don't know," said Emad. "This is my first time here as well."

"I think we should go for it," said Deb.

"Okay, I'm game," I agreed. "But both of you have to understand, ever since Borneo, heights have been freaking me out more than usual. We're up here to have fun. If it stops being fun, I wanna be able to turn around."

"No problem," said Emad.

"We'll only hike as far as you want to go," added Deb.

That being said, here are some important elevations to know: the Hotel Schwarzsee, 8,474 feet; the Hörnlihütte, 10,696 feet; the top of the Matterhorn, 14,692 feet.

The three of us spent the evening in the dining room, talking, eating, and drinking. Although Emad was born in Egypt, he had lived in Switzerland for the past twenty years and was very much a Swiss. Consequently, he made sure national food and drink were included with our meal.

We started with a bottle of Swiss wine. As I filled my glass, Emad commented that the Swiss were good at many things, but making wine wasn't one of them. I took a sip. It was light and slightly sweet—I liked it. Not being a wine snob has its advantages.

Our dinner came with *rösti,* a traditional Swiss fried potato dish similar to hash browns. I took a bite. Not bad, but it needed something. Traveling with Emad eliminated all our communications problems. If either Deb or I needed anything from anyone, he gladly served as our translator.

"Would you please ask the manager to bring me some ketchup?" I asked.

Emad looked at me with disgust. "I will *not* ask her for ketchup!"

"Why?"

"You do not put ketchup on rösti. It would be offensive."

"What's the point of the food on my plate? Is it to please me or to please the manager? I'm the one paying for it. Shouldn't I be able to put whatever I want on it?"

Emad's look softened. "You are right. I will get you some ketchup."

(Ketchup manufacturers wishing to make a generous donation toward my future travels may contact me through my Web site: www.CoolCreaturesHotPlanet.com.)

I enjoyed my rösti with ketchup, but Emad wouldn't let me forget it. His offers to get me more of the red delicacy would become the running joke for the rest of our visit.

Incidentally, the manager did find my request for ketchup offensive. When she brought the bottle to our table, the resentment on her already stern face was unmistakable. I can see it now: World War III won't be fought over oil or religion. Instead, the wrong government leader will pour ketchup over the wrong food. I'll say it again—ketchup manufacturers need a better public relations firm.

Saturday morning at six, I knocked on Emad's door. We had decided to get up before sunrise to photograph the Matterhorn—Deb, of course, wanted no part of our early rising. Emad tossed on his coat and followed me downstairs. When we reached the main-floor landing, the door to the dining room was locked. Since the hotel's entrance was on the far side of the room, we couldn't get out.

"We're prisoners!" I whispered. "If the hotel started on fire, we'd burn to a crisp."

The only main floor room we could get into was the sitting room. While Emad looked for another exit, I stepped inside and began checking the line of windows facing the Matterhorn. The first few were sealed shut. Then I located one I could open. I called to Emad, and the two of us—feeling like mischievous high-school kids—crawled through the window and escaped to the patio.

The Matterhorn at sunrise wasn't as picturesque as Emad and I had hoped it would be, yet we were still glad to be up early. The mountain stretches for the sky as if giving nature a "thumbs up," and if we watched carefully, we could see the flash of headlamps worn by climbers who were already partway up its face. Despite the Matterhorn's imposing steepness and height, the climb from the Hörnlihütte to the summit and back is a one-day event.

We were immersed in our photography when a shrill voice cried out from behind! We spun toward the sound and froze at a sight more terrifying than a high school principal. The hotel manager was leaning halfway out the open window, screaming in rapid-fire sentences. I couldn't understand her Schwyzertutsch (a Swiss-German dialect), but the tone of her voice made it clear—we had been very bad boys.

Apparently, the hotel did have another exit. We just hadn't found it. Emad spoke with the manager to smooth things over. I'm not sure what he said, but the woman's anger soon dissipated, and she ducked back into the sitting room.

Emad and I stayed outside and captured some more images of the Matterhorn. Once we had our shots, we slipped through the window and returned to our rooms. We'd meet up again once Deb was awake and ready go.

After breakfast, Deb, Emad, and I began our hike to the Hörnlihütte. The day was clear, and the temperature was in the mid-thirties. Even though the Matterhorn appeared to look straight down on us, our destination was more than two hours away. With the exception of the Matterhorn and the snow-capped peaks in the distance, our trail wasn't particularly scenic. We were above the tree line, but not high enough for permanent snow. If anything in the Alps could be considered a band of nothingness, this was it. Mostly we hiked over a near moonscape of craggy rocks and brown dirt.

The first hour of our trek didn't bother me much. We had some steep climbs, but in most cases, the mountainside sloped down gradually from the edge of the trail. As long as slipping off the edge wouldn't result in a fatal fall, I was okay.

I walked in the lead position, because I was determined to put heights out of my mind and felt it would be easier if no one blocked my way. As we entered our second hour, the trail changed and ascended sections of mountain with perilous drops over the edge.

"I'm not having a good time," I said. "This is *exactly* what I wanted to avoid."

"Do you wanna turn around?" asked Deb.

"No, we've come this far, I wanna finish it. Emad, would you mind moving to the front? That way when drop-offs bother me I can stare at your feet."

Following Emad helped me relax. Whenever I felt the need, I focused on his boots and continued forward.

The section before our final climb was a long, level ridgeline, which cut straight toward the Matterhorn. I felt as if I were walking on top of the world. Fortunately, the slope on either side of the ridgeline was gentle enough that a fall wouldn't result in anything worse than permanent disfigurement.

"Chamois! Chamois!" shouted Emad.

A lone chamois raced across the slope below us and disappeared from sight. Chamois are a type of goat with small horns and flexible hoofs (which aid in climbing). They're uncommon animals, but only certain subspecies make the *IUCN Red List*.

"I thought we were too high to see wildlife," I said.

"I'm as surprised as you are," replied Emad. "I didn't think we'd see anything up here either."

We decided to remove our packs and take some landscape photos. To the east, our hotel was out of sight; to the north, the mountainside sloped down into a rocky valley before rising into a line of mountains; to the south another rocky valley rose into a line of mountains; and to the west loomed the Matterhorn.

From our position, we could see the Matterhorn head-on. The view looked quite different from what I had seen in photographs. The bottom third of the mountain rose at a sharp angle before leveling out just enough for the Hörnlihütte. From there, the mountain made its precipitous ascent to the summit. Unlike the top section, which required ropes to climb, the bottom section was climbable via a steep trail with multiple switchbacks.

"If we make it to the Hörnlihütte, we'll be able to say we climbed one-third of the way up the Matterhorn," I said.

"Wouldn't that be great!" exclaimed Emad.

"Yes, but let's go before I have too much time to think about it," I said.

We donned our packs, walked the rest of the way along the ridgeline, and started up the Matterhorn!

The climbing soon became challenging. Past the second switchback, we came upon a spot where the trail had crumbled off the mountain, leaving only a swath of open air. In lieu of the trail, someone had bolted a cable to the mountainside. We grabbed onto the cable and pulled ourselves up to the next level.

So far, so good. I wasn't enjoying myself, but at least I was doing a fair job of blocking out everything except Emad's feet.

The next switchback took us into the shadows and something I hadn't anticipated—ice!

I looked around. With nothing to grab onto, a slip would mean sliding right over the edge. I leaned in against the mountainside, craned my neck out, and looked down. The only thing blocking my view was the ridgeline—three hundred feet below.

Before I go on, a word of warning. If you read outdoor books to travel vicariously with macho authors who, despite broken legs, loss of sight, malaria, and concussions, ultimately overcome all predicaments, please skip the next section and go directly to the paragraph beginning with the three stars ★★★. What happens next isn't pretty, and believe me, we'll both feel better if you just skip to the stars.

How did I handle the ice? I sat on my rear end. "This is it! I can't go any farther."

"Just relax a minute," said Deb.

I took a deep breath and reconsidered. The ice was somewhat dirty. Perhaps it wasn't as slippery as I thought. I slowly rose to my feet, walked a few steps, and eased back down to my rear end.

I looked at Deb and Emad, "If I knew this was the only section of ice, I could do it. I'm just worried things are gonna get worse as we climb higher."

"Let me see what's up ahead," said Emad. He disappeared around the corner and returned a moment later. "The next section doesn't look any better, but it won't be long before we're back in the sun."

Determined to try again, I stood, took several steps, and froze. "Damn! I can't do it! Listen, we're almost to the Hörnlihütte. You two go on without me. I'll climb down to the ridge and wait for you there."

"It's okay. We don't *have* to go to the top," said Deb.

"The ice bothers me, too," said Emad. "And coming down will be worse."

"We're *not* going on without you," said Deb.

At that moment, I felt like a complete failure. I wanted to continue the ascent, but I had too much to live for and wasn't willing to risk my life just to spare my ego. Had the situation been similar to Borneo, where my life depended on going forward, I truly could have done it. But here in Switzerland, reaching the Hörnlihütte was an option, not a requirement.

"Don't worry about it," said Emad. "Let's turn around."

"If it wasn't for the ice . . . Damn! I really thought I could do it."

As we descended the mountain, a myriad of thoughts raced through my mind: "Go back and try again—you know you can do it. Even if you make it past the ice, there are probably worse spots up higher—you'll have to turn around anyway. I can't wait for the Africa trip—I'll be on flat ground and will only have to worry about lions eating me. If Deb and Emad had also wanted to turn around I'd feel okay—but being the only one is humiliating. *What am I going to tell my readers!* I don't write about every second of every day. I could skip this part of the trip—they'd never know the difference. No—I'd know."

When we reached the ridge, Emad, who had been wonderful about cutting short our climb, couldn't resist a final comment: "We were *sooo* close!"

Just for a moment, I hated him.

★★★Okay, lovers of he-man outdoor writing, you can now safely start reading again. You were wise to skip down to here. No one wants to read that wimpy emotional stuff anyway. In fact, I just read it myself and had to break three computer keyboards just to get my testosterone level back up to normal. Now that I feel sufficiently manly again, I wish to present to you the properly spun facts about what *really* happened. The following section—of absolute truth—picks up right after I laughed at the ice and sprinted up the trail:

I reached the Hörnlihütte a good ten minutes before Deb and Emad. I would have made it up sooner, but the sheets of glare ice were too much for my fainthearted companions. To make their climb easier, I ran down to the ridge several times and brought up packs full of dirt for the slippery spots. Even then, I still had to carry both of them across the most dangerous sections.

Once we were all together at the Hörnlihütte, I looked out over the Alps. I could see heavenly white snow-covered peaks in every direction except behind me, where the ominous sheer face of the Matterhorn continued skyward.

"I'm glad we made the climb," I said, "but I had hoped for a better view."

"The view is fantastic!" said Emad. "I can see for miles. How could it possibly get any better?"

"We're not high enough," I said. "Imagine how stunning the Alps would look from the summit. Nothing would be in the way to block our view. I know we didn't bring any climbing equipment, but we're already a third of the way up the Matterhorn. What do you say we finish the job?"

"The way you conquered the ice to guide Emad and me up this far was an amazing and manly feat," said Deb. "But how could you possibly get us to the top of the Matterhorn without ropes? After all, you're only human."

"No problem, my little woman. You and Emad can just hold onto the back of my three-hundred-pound pack, and I'll pull us the rest of the way up. We'll be at the top in less than an hour."

"Oh, Marty! You're such a hunk!" cooed Deb.

"You da man!" exclaimed Emad.

"Just give me a second to smash these casts off my broken hands and we'll get started."

The three of us returned to the hotel for a quick lunch. Before the day was over, we aimed to reach the top of another Matterhorn. This time, the 12,740 foot-high Klein Matterhorn was in our sights, and we planned to climb it the civilized way. To reach the summit, we would take the gondola halfway down the mountain, transfer to a larger gondola, ride up to 9,642 feet, transfer to another large gondola, and ascend the rest of the way.

The gondola to the summit was the highest in Europe, and it had to be specially constructed to make the unusually steep climb. Advanced Swiss engineering doesn't come cheaply: round-trip tickets between our hotel and the Klein Matterhorn cost the U.S. equivalent of sixty-six dollars per person.

Unlike the four-person multicar gondolas, which ran at a fixed speed between our hotel and Zermatt, the large single-car gondolas had pilots and a capacity of approximately forty people. From the side, the large gondolas looked like chubby wheelless railroad cars hanging from hefty midroof hooks.

At first I thought pilot-controlled gondolas were an inefficient use of labor. When we climbed higher, and the wind picked up, I understood the reasoning behind them. As our car swung back and forth, the only way to control the motion was to slow our ascent. The most challenging part of the ride was at the top, where the cable led us into a garage-like hole in the peak. To prevent us from smashing against a wall, the pilot had to stop the car, wait for our swinging to abate, and ease us in.

After exiting the gondola, we followed a tunnel through a glacier to an elevator. We rode the elevator up to an outside staircase, then climbed the stairs to a platform straddling the summit.

Damage to the mountain aside, imagine the engineering necessary to pull the cables, erect the support towers, cut a huge hole into the peak, clear a tunnel through the glacier, install the elevator, and build a platform atop the summit. Not impressed? Keep in mind the Swiss accomplished the task at 12,740 feet, on a precipitous mountain, subject to extreme and rapidly changing weather. If the Swiss can do that, why can't Americans build a reasonably priced sport-utility vehicle that gets eighty miles to the gallon?

From the platform, I looked out over the Alps. The elevation was so high that I could see into Italy, a few mountains to the south. Surprisingly the height didn't bother me. The platform was secure, and nothing was slippery. I had mixed feelings when I noticed a tourist quaking with fear as she attempted to climb up to where I was standing. I felt her pain but at the same time was relieved to know that other people in Switzerland disliked heights more than I did.

Deb, Emad, and I stood on the platform for several minutes taking in sights, which included glistening snowcapped mountains, the wedge-shaped Matterhorn, and the town of Zermatt tucked deep inside a snowless valley. For me, the most memorable view was of a massive snow-covered glacier on the south side of the mountain. Puffy and white, it sat between the Klein Matterhorn and other nearby peaks as if it were a cloud that had become trapped. Far out on the glacier, barely visible, were four people hiking. A similar trek across the glacier would have been a stunning way to end our day.

The gondola schedule, however, left us little time to linger. We had only a half hour of leeway to reverse our course before the gondola to our hotel was shut down for the night. If an unexpected delay caused us to miss a connection, we'd have a long, miserable walk ahead of us.

Fortunately, the gondolas ran with perfect Swiss timing and delivered us to the hotel without incident. Having had our fill of Matterhorns, we spent the evening in the dining room socializing and trying more of Emad's Swiss food recommendations—this time without ketchup.

In the morning, we packed our bags and rode the gondola down to Zermatt. Our visit with Emad had come to an end. As we walked to the train depot, we spoke not of farewells but of when we would see each other again—perhaps in Montana or the Galapagos Islands. After final hugs and good wishes, Emad boarded the train to Winterthur, and Deb and I boarded the train to Tasch.

Our stay in Switzerland had been brief, and since we spent the majority of our time high in the Alps, I didn't get a feel for the country as I had with France and Spain. Switzerland, however, had a lot going for it. In addition to its stunning scenery, it had a peaceful culture and a direct democracy political system where anyone gathering enough signatures could introduce a nationwide referendum. Emad had lived in many countries before settling in Switzerland; it was easy to see why he had made it his country of choice.

We retrieved our car, drove back into France, and spent the rest of Sunday and much of Monday heading south. While our European trip wasn't providing us with as many wildlife-viewing opportunities as we had hoped for, interesting historical places were filling the void. On Monday afternoon, just when we were getting road weary, we happened upon the walled city of Villefranche de Conflent.

Located thirty-five miles west of the Mediterranean Sea and twelve miles north of the Spanish border, Villefranche de Conflent dates back to the year 1092. Despite being so old, much of the city's original architecture remains intact because the pink marble the Count of Cerdagne used to build it has resisted deterioration.

We walked through the city's main gate. Unlike the ancient structures we had visited previously, people still occupied this one. The majority of the buildings featured craft shops on the ground floor and living quarters on the upper floors. Admittance to the courtyard and shops was free, but if we wanted to get inside the ramparts and towers it would cost us a few euros.

Deb and I couldn't resist the opportunity to explore such a well-preserved site and gladly paid the fee. Once inside, we roamed the passages within the walls surrounding the three-block-long city. While the courtyard was busy with shoppers, we saw only one other person inside the walls.

Having unsupervised access gave us time to find a hidden staircase to a tower and an entrance to a cellar that looked like it hadn't been opened in years. As we inspected the battlements, walked the tunnels, and peered through the loops, I felt like an archaeologist in a recently discovered city. Where did they hide the torture chamber anyway?

A still-active Catholic church was also part of the city. We stepped into the sanctuary and looked around. You don't have to be religious to appreciate old European churches. With antique paintings and sculptures at every turn, they're often more interesting than traditional art galleries. Artwork highlights in this church included a reredos by renowned Catalan sculptor Joseph Sunyer and a fourteenth-century life-size wooden effigy of Christ.

We wrapped up our visit with some shopping. Deb's forty-fifth birthday was one day away, and she wanted her presents early. As has become our tradition, she made my shopping easy by picking out what she wanted and letting me pay for it. I mention this because the store proprietor, who didn't speak English, immediately understood the *Happy Birthday Song* when I sang it to Deb after she selected an elegant Provence tablecloth. When Deb picked up the matching cloth napkins, he flashed a big smile in my direction and asked, "Happy birthday to you?" By the time Deb finished adding to her presents, the proprietor was at least as happy as she was.

After our enjoyable afternoon in Villefranche de Conflent, we headed west toward the fourth and final country of our trip. Although we often made spontaneous changes to our itinerary, Spain, France, and Switzerland were the only countries we intended to visit. The night before, however, I had looked at a map and noticed our route would take us near the tiny Principality of Andorra.

Since I knew nothing about Andorra, other than it was sandwiched between France and Spain, I booted up my laptop computer and opened the *Microsoft Encarta Reference Library*. Soon I learned that the country was a member of the United Nations and had population of 68,403 people and a physical size of 181 square miles.

Still, I saw no point in visiting the country unless it had something of ecological interest. For that information, I checked the Andorra section in *Wild France*. Each area discussed in the book is rated from zero to three eagles, with three being the highest rating for "wildness quality." For Andorra, the author awarded three eagles—perfect.

The country had two major roads: one cutting across from the French border in the east to the Spanish border in the southwest and another leading north out of the capital city of Andorra la Vella (which according to the dot on the map wasn't quite in the center of the somewhat circular country). To reach the wild areas, the author advised taking the northbound road.

Combining what I learned from my reference sources, I envisioned the Principality of Andorra to be a sleepy rural country with rugged scenery and lots of ethnic character. With only three days left before our flight home, it seemed like a perfect location for our final outdoor adventure.

Even though the eastern border of Andorra was only thirty miles from Villefranche de Conflent, we decided to loop down through Spain and enter the country at the southwest border. We were ultimately heading west to Madrid anyway, and circling around to the far entrance allowed us to avoid a high mountain pass.

The first thing I noticed at the border were long lines of cars waiting to leave Andorra. Up till now, customs agents at borders had been nonexistent. Here they were carefully searching vehicles before allowing them to proceed into Spain.

Entering Andorra wasn't a problem. They wanted us inside. A short distance past the border, we hit heavy traffic and came to a stop below a huge billboard proclaiming, in English, "Andorra—Total Shopping!" We considered immediately returning to Spain, but they had us. Even if a break in traffic allowed us to turn around, we'd just end up at the rear of a long, slow-moving customs line.

I've been in crowded cities before, but nothing as densely packed as this. Cars were jammed in so tight, police officers had to stand at each intersection to direct traffic. I looked around. Every driver appeared to be having his or her own personal claustrophobia attack.

A small space opened in front of us—two cars collided attempting to claim it. Neither party had room to inspect the fender bender, so they continued forward as if it hadn't happened. The traffic seemed to go on forever. No matter which way we turned, tall buildings acted like a vise to squeeze us in tighter.

"Andorra's entire population is supposed to be only sixty-eight thousand!" I said. "It would take more people than that just to control the traffic and staff the businesses."

"I know," said Deb. "This is awful!"

"Tell me when to turn."

"We are so lost! Our map doesn't show any of these streets. I'm literally navigating by the sun."

Somehow, I managed to keep our car out of an accident, and somehow, Deb managed to keep us headed east. Unfortunately, once the traffic dissipated enough for us to relax, we were already halfway across the country and had missed the road we were supposed to take.

Perhaps the Andorrans had left some nature worthy of three eagles in the northern region, but nothing could make us turn back into the human beehive to find out. Instead, we decided to drive straight through to France.

Clearly, Andorra was all about tourism. To attract tourists in the winter, they carved up their most beautiful mountains and turned them into ski resorts. To attract tourists in the off-season, they opened hundreds of stores and offered duty-free shopping (which explains why Spanish officials were so interested in what people were bringing over the border). "Total Shopping" was more than just a catchy slogan; it was essentially the national motto.

I could tell Andorra was once a picturesque nation and felt sorry for any Andorrans who longed for the way it used to be. Whether they wanted the change or not, everyone had to live with the consequences of unabated greed.

We didn't quite make it out of the country. The closer we got to France, the more rural the landscape became. Since Deb and I would never visit Andorra again, we decided to spend one night there and rented a room at the Hotel del Clos. The four-story hotel was less than a year old, and it was part of the new growth sprouting up on the eastern side—heaven forbid any land remain undeveloped.

Earlier, when we were caught in the traffic jam, I wondered how the country's small population managed to staff all the businesses. If our hotel was any indication, the employees came from other countries. For instance, the desk clerk and the young man who would wait on us that evening both spoke perfect English, but neither spoke Catalan, the official language of Andorra.

The balcony of our top-floor room overlooked the scarred mountainside of a ski resort. Even so, it was a fine place to enjoy a gorgeous evening on the last day of summer. We put up our feet, drank some Spanish wine, and relaxed until dinnertime.

A large tour group of retirees from France preceded us into the hotel restaurant. We were the youngest diners in the room by at least twenty years. On the other end of the spectrum, all the waiters and waitresses were in their early twenties. Dressed in formal attire, they walked with rigidly straight postures, spoke in elegant voices, and put on a show worthy of the finest European restaurants.

From our table, Deb had an unobstructed view of the swinging kitchen doors. When she started laughing, I turned to see what was so funny. Although obviously well-schooled in restaurant etiquette, the waitstaff discontinued their show the second they entered the kitchen. In fact, before the doors could even swing shut, their postures had already collapsed into a comfortable slouch. Watching them return to the dining room was even more amusing because we could see their faces through the door window. They'd be laughing and having a good time in the kitchen until the exact moment the doors opened; then they'd square their shoulders and adopt a serious expression.

The entire restaurant crew had the fresh good looks that movie casting directors dream about—young versions of Leonardo DiCaprio, Keanu Reeves, and someone else famous we couldn't place. The waiter who looked like Keanu Reeves had his hair artificially spiked into the bed-hair look. As someone who wakes up with natural bed hair—worthy of the Sex Pistols—I couldn't resist commenting to Deb, "If I knew he'd be here in the morning, I'd come down to breakfast before showering and put him to shame."

When our waiter stopped by to check on us, Deb asked him, "Do you know who Leonardo DiCaprio is?"

"Oh, yes," he said. "Everyone thinks I look like either him or Sting."

As our chat continued, we found out that our waiter had lived in Spain and England before moving to Andorra to work at the hotel.

"Are the roads in Andorra always so busy?" I asked.

"This is the slow season," he said. "The traffic isn't so bad now. In the winter, when the ski resorts open, it *really* gets busy."

On Tuesday morning, September 23—Deb's birthday—we said good-bye to Andorra for good. Escaping the country on the French side was easy, and we were surprised not to see any customs agents.

As soon as we entered France, we cut south and returned to Spain. (Cool! At dinner parties I can now say I've been to France and Spain three times.) We had a hotel reservation in Madrid for the following evening and planned to spend one last night at a hotel en route.

Our drive across eastern Spain provided us with additional opportunities to explore castles and other ancient dwellings. Almost everything we saw had deteriorated to the point of crumbling. The castles, with their fallen or missing walls, were actually more dramatic to photograph than the intact structures we had seen earlier in the trip. I couldn't help wondering: what was the story behind their demise? Had they succumbed to a siege? Or, like La Villa de Castrotorafe, were they tragic examples of failures to build using union slaves?

Despite several interesting stops, we made better time than expected and decided to gamble that the hotel in Madrid would let us check in a day early. The reason for our reservation was because our Thursday morning flight left at six, and we wanted to be as close to the airport as possible. I had even printed up a handy-dandy map from the Internet so we'd have precise locations for both the airport and hotel.

We hit a major traffic jam ten miles outside Madrid and crawled into the city. Locating our exit was easy, but the hotel wasn't where it was supposed to be. We drove around lost for a half hour, stopped to ask for directions, and drove around lost for another half hour. When we finally located the hotel, it was booked up for the night.

At that point, we were so frustrated that no price would be too high if it kept us from getting lost again. We walked down the street to the Hotel Barajas. There, they not only had a room for us, but they also offered us a free breakfast if we stayed two nights instead of just one. Although expensive at two hundred dollars per night, we couldn't pass up a free breakfast and cancelled our reservation at the other hotel.

After staying almost exclusively in one- and two-star hotels, moving up to the luxurious four-star Hotel Barajas was a dramatic change. The bed alone was larger than some of our previous rooms.

For our final day in Europe, we decided to explore downtown Madrid. One convenience of being in the big city was that we could always find someone who spoke English. In this case, after Deb and I debated at breakfast whether to take a car, train, or bus into downtown, we decided to defer to a desk clerk's recommendation.

Since only one English-speaking clerk was on duty, and she was busy helping a middle-aged American man, we stood in line and waited. When the clerk gave the man his bill, he bellowed out to everyone within earshot, "I've been in Europe for three weeks, and this was by far the least expensive hotel I've stayed in!"

When the clerk turned away to run the man's credit card, I couldn't resist asking, "Where have you been staying? My wife and I have been in Europe almost as long as you have, and our room costs have averaged less than fifty dollars per night."

The man's jaw dropped into his double chin. "Will you book my next trip for me?"

I laughed.

He continued. "Have you been doing much golfing?"

"No, I can't say that I have."

"Well, that's the difference then. I always stay at hotels near golf courses."

"How was the golfing?"

"Excellent!"

"Well, it was nice meeting you. Have a safe trip home."

"You, too."

Once the man departed, Deb looked at me inquisitively and commented, "He came all the way to Europe to go *golfing?*"

"I know. I can't imagine traveling halfway around the world for golfing either, but everyone has different interests. I'm sure he would have thought our idea of a good time in Europe was absolutely insane."

"Yeah, you're probably right."

Following the desk clerk's advice, Deb and I took our little Opel on a final drive. Despite timing our outing to avoid traffic jams, we hit one anyway. When we finally reached downtown, we parked in one of the many underground garages. While Madrid has a well-earned reputation for its congested roads, at least it seemed to have ample parking.

Madrid is a grand old city with gigantic churches, enormous palaces, and magnificent sculptures. The churches in particular were noteworthy.

Roman Catholicism became Spain's established religion in the sixth century, and it remained that way (except for a brief period) until 1978, when the country's new constitution declared an end to state religion. The Catholic Church's long history of wealth and power was on display wherever I looked. Whether it was a store selling silver scepters, golden chalices, and precious metal accessories for the well-dressed priest or the extreme opulence in the cathedrals, all the gold and silver I'd seen in my life up to that point would be a mere speck compared to what I saw in a single afternoon in Madrid.

I felt uneasy walking through churches as if they were art galleries, but no one seemed to mind, and plenty of other people were doing the same thing. I just had to concentrate on keeping my mouth shut. Several times I repressed the urge to shout out, "Wow! Deb, come over here. You've got to see this!"

Many of the churches had massive pillars, soaring arches, beautiful gold-framed antique paintings, colorful stained-glass domes inlaid with gold, huge gold and silver pipe organs, and elaborate stations where you could drop in coins to light electric candles. Even the doors, most with intricate three-dimensional artwork, were remarkable sights. Imagine the good the churches could of done if they had invested their money into helping the poor instead of decorating their buildings.

Although we spent much of our time in churches, we also had an enjoyable walk through the streets and stopped whenever something caught our attention. Plaza Mayor was one of the places we visited. Comprised of a large courtyard surrounded by stately buildings, the plaza had a multiple-use history, which included bullfights, fiestas, and Inquisition-era public executions.

A few blocks west of Plaza Mayor was the Palacio Real (Royal Palace). We hoped to tour the palace, but when we saw the long admissions line, we changed our plans and strolled through the Sabatini Gardens instead. The formal gardens featured shrubbery manicured in the shape of a maze, statues of past royal family members, and a rectangular pond with several small fountains.

We saw no visible signs of siesta. In fact, as the day grew late the city became more crowded. After several hours, we had had enough of downtown Madrid and walked back to the car.

Instead of heading directly to the hotel, we decided to return our Opel wagon a day early. Without having to allow for a delay at the rental car booth, we could sleep in an extra hour and take a shuttle to the airport in the morning.

We followed the signs to the Terminal One rental car return lot but couldn't find the booth we were looking for.

"We must be at the wrong terminal," I said.

"Okay, let's try Terminal Two," said Deb as she pointed toward the freeway.

Upon reaching Terminal Two, we spotted a sign with our rental company's logo on it and an arrow pointing back to Terminal One.

"It *has* to be there," I said. "We must have just missed it."

"Take a left and go back along the frontage road."

We returned to Terminal One and circled the lot twice. The rental company's booth definitely wasn't there.

"Do you wanna try Terminal Three?" I asked.

"We might as well."

I steered back onto the freeway. Like rushing water in a gutter, heavy traffic engulfed us and pushed us along. Up ahead the lanes split—two going left, two going right.

"Should I take the left or right fork?" I asked.

"I don't know! Just pick one!"

I swerved left. "This doesn't look right. I should have gone the other way."

"Take the next exit. We'll turn around and try again."

We drove for what seemed like miles before spotting an off-ramp to a frontage road. From there, we looked for a way to get back onto the freeway but didn't see one. The frontage road led us toward the airport for a short distance, then curved away from the freeway. I turned onto a series of side streets to correct our course—bad idea!

We were lost again.

I pulled to the curb so we could get our bearings.

Bong! Bong! Bong! . . . As Deb looked at a map, every church bell in Spain began to ring—it was five o'clock.

8

Hippo Canoe and Zimbabwe Too

I had just started my African continent research when I met Skip Horner in the Hamilton, Montana, bookstore. If there's such a thing as "America's most famous guide," he holds the title. His specialty is leading extreme and exotic trips all over the world, and several of his exploits have received national media attention. His most notable accomplishment is being the first person to successfully guide clients to the top of the highest peak on each of the seven continents.

Like me, Skip lives on the outskirts of Victor. Though we hadn't spoken before, I was familiar with him from his Seven Summits slide show and knew he guided a variety of trips that didn't involve gasping for air at the top of Mount Everest. After introducing myself and inquiring about his latest adventure, I decided to explore the possibility of us working together on my next adventure:

"My wife and I are traveling to all seven continents for a book I'm writing. Our final trip will be to Africa, and I want it to be extra special. Do you guide many trips in Africa?"

"I guide a lot of trips in Africa," he said. "Are you interested in climbing Mount Kilimanjaro?"

"No," I laughed, "I get enough of the mountains here in Montana."

A wave of relief flowed over Skip's chiseled face, "Oh, good. Not that I mind doing Kilimanjaro, but it's one of my most requested trips. I'd love to do something different."

"I'm interested in an expedition where we can observe Africa's wildlife on foot—preferably camping along the way. I don't want a typical tourist trip, where everyone has to watch the animals from the safety of a vehicle."

"Where do you want to go?"

"I was thinking about Zambia or Uganda, but the country isn't important. I want to go where the wildlife is the best."

"I used to live in Zambia, and I still have a good contact in the area. Let me see what I can put together."

During the weeks that followed, Skip bounced destination ideas off Deb and me. Eventually we decided on Zimbabwe, a country where we could accomplish everything we wanted. Our expedition would begin with a five-day-long hike across Mana Pools National Park and a return via a three-day canoe trip on the Zambezi River; then we'd fly to Matusadona National Park, where we'd spend three days at a bush camp; and finally, we'd fly to Victoria Falls for two days of relaxation.

I thought doing an expedition with Skip would make my job easier, but it actually made it harder. Since this wasn't a stock trip we could simply join, Deb and I were saddled with the responsibility of finding at least three additional participants. With such an outstanding itinerary, the trip should have filled quickly. Working against us, however, were the high cost of the expedition ($5,500 per person, plus tips and international airfare) and numerous unfavorable news stories about Zimbabwe.

Although Zimbabwe didn't have the clout to make George W. Bush's "Axis of Evil," in November 2003 the president announced a new list of countries, which he called "Outposts of Oppression." Included on his list were Cuba, Burma, North Korea, and Zimbabwe. I chuckled upon learning that North Korea was now both an Axis of Evil and an Outpost of Oppression but worried the new catchphrase would negatively affect our recruiting.

Aside from Bush's list, Zimbabwe also made the *Forbes.com* list of the "World's 10 Most Dangerous Destinations 2004," and Zimbabwe's president, Robert Mugabe, was ranked fourth on *Parade's* (the Sunday newspaper magazine) 2004 list of "The World's 10 Worst Dictators."

Deb and I contacted everyone we knew who would be physically and mentally capable of participating in the expedition but rapidly depleted our list. Then one morning Deb announced that Jill and Sam from Spokane, Washington, had agreed to join us. Though I had met the couple only once, I remembered enjoying their company and was confident they'd be an asset to our expedition. Now all we needed was one more person.

Time was running out. If we didn't fill the trip soon, I'd either have to pay a "ghost fare" out of my own pocket or cancel the trip. As a last resort, I contacted the local newspapers, and they all ran blurbs about the expedition. Before long, several people were interested in joining us.

Of the interested people, Joe and Susan from Missoula were the obvious best fit. The three of us had an extended telephone conversation and found we had much in common. Unfortunately, they couldn't commit to the trip until clearing up some difficulties with their airline frequent flyer program. A day earlier, I would have been happy with any warm body; now I wanted Joe and Susan and hoped no one else would put down a deposit before they did.

Two days later, the couple called with good news. Deb and I were ecstatic. We had filled our expedition and were going to Zimbabwe with a great group of people!

Was visiting an "Outpost of Oppression" a foolish idea? Before we departed, I checked the Web site of the U.S. Department of State, Bureau of Consular Affairs and printed up seven pages of warnings. Had this been my first international trip, I might have changed my plans. With experience, however, comes the realization that U.S. government reports on foreign nations can be misleading—especially when the country in question isn't a close political ally.

Here's a quote from the first page: "The Department of State warns U.S. citizens of the risks of travel to Zimbabwe. . . . All U.S. citizens in Zimbabwe are urged to take those measures they deem appropriate to ensure their well being, including consideration of departure from the country."

Just what were the risks? To fill seven pages, the Department of State had to work hard. Some of the warnings I found to be petty included:

- Inter-city commuter bus travel, except 'luxury coaches,' is dangerous due to overcrowding, inadequate maintenance, and drivers who fail to adhere to local speed limits and obey traffic rules or regulations. [Couldn't the same warning apply to bus travel in many U.S. cities?]

- It is against the law to make any gesture or statements that might be construed as offensive to the president of Zimbabwe, a member of his government, or the Zimbabwean government itself. [Let's not forget that in our own country people have been arrested for wearing anti-Bush T-shirts to presidential appearances.]

• The behavior of police or military personnel is not always predictable or rational. [Can any country claim their police and military personnel are always predictable and rational?]

• U.S. citizens participating in nature and rafting excursions in Zimbabwe should be aware that even with an organized tour group, tourists are often allowed to participate in activities that may pose great risks to personal safety. Tragic attacks involving wildlife have occurred at Mana Pools. [A country where people aren't allowed to participate in risky activities would be very boring. In fact, I'd call such a country an "Outpost of Oppression."]

Sarcasm aside, Zimbabwe does have its problems. To understand the situation, a little background information is necessary:

In 1965, the ruling white minority government of Southern Rhodesia declared independence from Britain and changed the country's name to Rhodesia. Then, in 1980, a successful revolution by the black majority put Robert Mugabe in power, and the country was renamed Zimbabwe.

At the time Mugabe took over, whites made up less than 5 percent of the country's population but owned more than 40 percent of the land, including most of the best farmland. The white population soon dropped to 1 percent, in part due to a buyback program Mugabe instituted that gave the government the first right to purchase land (at market prices) from whites wishing to sell.

On the surface, the buyback program looked admirable, as it would redistribute property to black peasants and reverse the injustice of lands taken by whites in the past. Beneath the surface, the program was awash with corruption. When Britain, the primary financial sponsor for the buybacks, learned that much of the land was going to Mugabe's political supporters instead of poor blacks, it discontinued its support. Without money to fund the program, Mugabe responded by taking land from the whites without compensation.

Complicating the situation was that when black peasants were given land, they often didn't know how to farm or have the necessary seeds, fertilizer, or equipment. In fact, since the departing white farmers were major employers, life became worse for many blacks. As a result, farmland lies vacant, and Zimbabwe can no longer feed itself.

Land reform is just one of Zimbabwe's many difficulties. Others include Mugabe keeping himself in power through physical intimidation and rigged elections, severe fuel shortages, and out-of-control inflation. (In 2001, 1 U.S. dollar equaled 50 Zimbabwe dollars. In 2004, 1 U.S. dollar equaled 5,300 Zimbabwe dollars.)

From a selfish point of view, the timing of our trip would be perfect. Since news of the country's internal turmoil had frightened away most of the tourists, the chances of us running into people outside our group were slim.

From an unselfish point of view, the timing of our trip would also be perfect. Zimbabwe doesn't have the resources to maintain its national parks the way the United States does. The two parks we were going to spend most of our time in, Mana Pools and Matusadona, were essentially large unfenced sections of undeveloped land set aside for wildlife. The government fees included in the cost of our expedition would help sustain the dwindling staff of rangers who were protecting the park's wildlife from poachers. What we paid, however, would do little good unless combined with fees collected from other visitors. If tourism doesn't return to Zimbabwe's parks, the animals will ultimately pay the price.

Of all our trips, Deb and I had the most difficult time packing for this one. Even though our international flights had generous weight allowances, once we arrived in Zimbabwe we'd have three "bush flights," which would limit us to twenty-six pounds of luggage each—including carryons.

Despite needing to pack for eighteen days (the total time we were away from home), the weight limit would have been manageable for me if I wasn't a photographer. I culled my gear down to my new Canon Digital Rebel camera, three lenses, a teleconverter (a special lens that increases the power of other lenses), a small backup digital camera, and a lightweight tripod. Then I added enough batteries and memory cards to last the trip. In all, my photo gear took up more than half my allotted weight.

I joked before packing that I'd go without underwear before leaving essential camera gear at home. When I put my luggage on a scale and learned I was fifteen pounds overweight, going without underwear was no longer a joke. Next went my electric razor, binoculars, identification books, and more than half my clothes—I even cut the handle off my toothbrush. Deb also had to remove items from her luggage. After several more weigh-ins, we were each within a few pounds of our goal.

Although Skip had warned us that the weight limit was strict, neither Deb nor I could bear removing anything else from our bags and decided we'd deal with the extra pounds upon reaching Zimbabwe. If necessary, we'd dress in multiple layers of clothes or donate items to the airport staff.

Our flight landed at the Harare International Airport on Friday morning, May 14, 2004. Zimbabwe's capital city had a population of 1.5 million, yet its airport was small and eerily quiet. Since we didn't have to wade through crowds of people, meeting up with the others in our group was easier than expected.

Skip was waiting for us at the door on the far side of customs. "Hi, Marty. Hi, Deb. Welcome to Zimbabwe!"

"Hey, Skip! Great to see you," I said.

"Skip, you shaved off your mustache! I almost didn't recognize you," said Deb.

"I shaved it off yesterday. My wife has never seen me without it. I hope *she* recognizes me when I return home."

"Without your mustache, you look like Neil Diamond," I said.

Skip scowled. "Neil Diamond! I don't look as old as Neil Diamond!"

"I wasn't referring to how he currently looks. I meant it as a compliment. Women drool over Neil Diamond."

My clarification didn't appease Skip, but that was okay—now I had something to kid him about. Admittedly, others seldom agree with my opinion of whom someone looks like, as I base it on select features rather than the person's entire appearance. In Skip's case, it was his salt-and-pepper hair, squarish jaw, and the crease between his cheeks and nose when he smiled.

Once our entire group was together, we met our pilot and prepared for our bush flight to Mana Pools National Park (which is located on Zimbabwe's northern border). After I quietly warned Skip about Deb's and my overweight bags, the two of us went out of our way to be friendly to the pilot. Consequently, when the time came to cart everyone's luggage to the runway, the young aviator bypassed the scale and lifted each bag by hand instead. "Nothing feels too heavy to me," he said.

The reason for the weight limit became apparent when Skip, Joe, Susan, Jill, Sam, Deb, and I followed the pilot onto the tarmac. Waiting for us was an old six-passenger Cessna airplane that looked as if it had seen better days. Outnumbering the passenger seats wouldn't be a problem, as one of us would sit in the co-pilot seat. Since both Sam and Joe were private pilots, we all agreed that Sam would sit up front for the first flight, and Joe would take the next one.

As I fastened my seat belt, I recalled a warning I read on the U.S. Department of State Web site: "The U.S. Federal Aviation Administration (FAA) has assessed the government of Zimbabwe's civil aviation authority as category 2—not in compliance with international aviation safety standards for oversight of Zimbabwe's air carrier operations." I took a deep breath and tried to look relaxed.

The pilot gunned the engine—the airplane vibrated like an electric sander. When he released the brake, we lunged forward and raced down the runway with no feeling of lift. As we neared the end of the pavement, I thought, "Perhaps I could have left my tripod and one of my zoom lenses at home." Finally, we labored into the air.

Upon reaching cruising altitude, I whispered to Joe what I had read on the Department of State Web site.

"We were a little heavy for takeoff," he said, "but I wouldn't worry about the airplane. It may look rough, but I can tell it's well maintained."

Forty-five minutes later, we could see the Zambezi River (Africa's fourth longest river) below us. The pilot banked the plane in a wide semicircle before taking us down. The gravel airstrip started near the edge of the river, just past a herd of hippopotamuses. We landed without incident and slowed to a stop.

Waiting for us by the airstrip, in an open-top Land Rover, was Brian Worsley, our African guide. Although Skip was also a guide, his primary duties for this trip were organizational in nature. Skip had worked with Brian in the past and made special arrangements for him to lead our expedition.

I had a mental picture of Brian before we met but had leaped to a conclusion about his race. Now that we were face-to-face, I was surprised to be shaking the hand of a white man who instantly reminded me of Teddy Roosevelt. This time I kept my observation to myself.

The eight of us waved good-bye to the pilot before departing in the Land Rover.

"Keep an eye out for elephants," said Brian. "There were several on the airstrip a few minutes ago."

"What would have happened if they hadn't moved by the time we were ready to land?" I asked.

"Elephants are quite common on the airstrip. The pilot can usually scare them away by making a close pass before landing."

I looked around. The bowling-ball-sized droppings scattered about left no doubt as to what kind of animal had been in the area.

My first impression of Mana Pools National Park was that its landscape resembled a forest and a desert combined. A thin layer of reddish sand covered the ground, and the trees were thick with green foliage. The timing of our trip coincided with the start of the dry season. In another month or so, the leaves would be dropping from the trees, and the park would have an entirely different look.

As I would observe in the coming days, Mana Pools supports a wide variety of habitats. Collectively known as "bushveld," or simply "the bush," the land had clusters of tall acacia trees, which would give way to bushes and scrub, which would give way to a water-hyacinth-covered waterhole, which would give way to a dried-up riverbed, which would give way to open grassland, which would give way to the hippo-dotted Zambezi River. Overall, the terrain was flat, but often in sight were the purple mountains on the Zambia side of the river valley.

From the airstrip, we had a short ride to the Chikwenya Safari Camp on the western edge of Mana Pools. We'd spend the night there and start our hike across the park in the morning.

Even though Deb and I were new to Africa, we had international travel experience our companions lacked. This became evident as we bounced down a rutty dirt road with Jill and Susan giddily reacting to every new sight and sound. Their enthusiasm was delightful and infectious.

Since we weren't in a hurry, we made several stops along the way. First, we checked out a baobab tree, which was so big it would have taken five or six of us to reach around it. Then we paused to watch a herd of nearly twenty impalas. Seeing impalas for the first time was a thrill. Little did we know, we'd see literally hundreds of them during our expedition.

When a troop of baboons crossed the road, Brian turned off the Land Rover so we could take some photos. I stepped out of the vehicle for a better angle, but the baboons disappeared before I could push the shutter button. As I climbed back into my seat, the Land Rover's leaf springs creaked.

"What's that!" screamed Jill. "It sounded big!"

"Leaf springs," I said.

"No, it sounded like an animal." The springs creaked again. "Oh, yeah. You're right."

I chuckled to myself, remembering a similar experience I had had in Peru—I was sure that stick in the river was an anaconda. False alarms were to be expected until everyone grew accustomed to the sights and sounds of the bush.

The road ended at the Chikwenya Safari Camp. Our accommodations were the opposite of what I would have expected to find in a remote region of a depressed country. The well-maintained camp overlooked the Zambezi River and reminded me of the Borneo Rainforest Lodge. It had a sheltered open-air area for drinking, lounging, and dining, and to either side were raised walkways leading to screen-walled cabins. In all, it would be a comfortable place to recover from our jet lag and prepare for the long days of hiking ahead.

We ate lunch before settling in. Then Brian gave us the option of retiring to our cabins or spending the afternoon at a viewing platform in the bush. All of us were too keyed up to relax—Africa was waiting for us.

Jill, Sam, Deb, and I were crusty from our long overseas flights and in desperate need of a shower. Joe, Susan, and Skip, on the other hand, had arrived in Zimbabwe a few days ahead of us and were dressed in clean clothes and ready to go. Rather than make the fresh members of our group wait, Brian offered to drive them to the platform while we crusties cleaned up.

I walked out to the Land Rover with Joe and Susan as they told me about their stay in Harare. I was curious about life in the city, but they weren't able to give me much information. When they checked into their hotel, the management told them not to leave the premises, because the city was too dangerous for foreigners.

Susan always had a smile on her face—and rightfully so. This trip was her fiftieth birthday present—or at least that was the justification she used to convince Joe to take time off from work. Like me, Joe was in the telecommunications business. His official title was "economist," but his unusual job revolved around being an expert witness in telecommunications court cases. Seeing him with his wavy brown hair, dressed in a casual shirt and zip-off-leg pants, I had a hard time imagining him testifying in a three-piece suit. I could tell, however, that he must have been good on the witness stand, as he had an extraordinarily quick wit.

Once Joe, Susan, Skip, and Brian departed for the viewing platform, I hurried down the walkway to join Deb. The porch attached to our cabin had a three-walled outdoor shower with the open side facing the floodplain of the Zambezi River. This would be the first of many showers I'd take in front of an audience. In this case, Birft, the resident Cape buffalo, watched me from forty feet away as he leisurely chewed his cud. The camp staff had named Birft for the grunting noise he made, but he wasn't a pet—our cabin just happened to be within his territory.

If I had had a pen on my body, I could have checked off the first animal on my Africa's "big five" list. What began years ago as a list of the most dangerous animals to hunt has now been adapted as a spotting goal for nonhunting safaris such as ours. The big five are Cape buffalo, elephant, leopard, lion, and rhinoceros.

After our showers, Deb and I waited in the lounge area for Sam and Jill. Sam was an executive for a large corporation and Jill was in sales. Both were in their early thirties and physically fit. When they finally joined us, I had to raise an eyebrow. Decked out in designer safari clothes, they were the best-dressed couple I'd seen in seven continents of travels.

We joined Brian in the Land Rover and weaved down the rutted road toward the viewing platform. Trees and bushes paralleled us for the first mile of our drive.

"Keep your eyes open," said Brian. "We're coming upon some grassland where we usually see a few animals."

Moments later, my eyes widened to take in a sight I had seen in photographs but never expected to see in person: elephants, waterbucks, impalas, vervet monkeys, and chacma baboons all shared the landscape. I had observed moose and deer together outside my house but couldn't think of any time I had watched more than two large mammal species in the wild without having to turn my head.

"A *few* animals, huh, Brian?" said Deb.

Brian smiled. "It's pretty good today, yeah?"

As the expedition progressed, we'd see similar scenes with different combinations of animals. The most consistent grouping would be impalas with baboons. Both animals were common in the bush, but that's not why we'd see them together so often. When I think of animals with symbiotic relationships, what comes to mind are birds that pick ticks off hoofed animals and cleaner wrasses that remove parasites from the gills of other fish. With impalas and baboons, no physical contact takes place—it's lookout duties that are shared symbiotically.

I wouldn't notice the connection between the two species right away, but when I did, I mentioned it to Brian. Not only did he agree that predator detection was the reason for the relationship, but he also added some interesting insights: "Baboons have incredibly sharp eyes, plus they are often up in the trees, which gives them a better vantage than the impala. Impalas also glean seedpods and fruit, which baboons drop while feeding in the trees. Baboons don't seem to gain much from the relationship, but they do occasionally prey on young impalas."

The five of us watched and photographed the animals on the grassy plain for a while before proceeding to the viewing platform. I expected to see Skip, Joe, and Susan when we arrived, but Brian had decided to take us to a different location. We climbed the steps to the ten-foot-high wooden platform, cracked open some soft drinks, and waited for the animals to appear. After seeing all the wildlife on the plain, I expected the platform to be equally productive. Instead, our only visitor was a Cape buffalo, peering at us from the edge of a reedy swamp.

Eventually Brian announced, "We better go find the others. They were expecting us a half hour ago, and they're probably wondering what happened to us."

We returned to the Land Rover and rumbled toward the other viewing platform. Soon we came upon two greater kudus. When we stopped, roughly forty feet away, I expected them to run. Instead, they stood perfectly still. Kudus are members of the antelope family. They have oversized ears, delicate faces, and a tuft of mane between their shoulders that gives them a hunched-back appearance. The most unforgettable feature of these graceful animals is their horns. While females are hornless, males grow spiraled horns that can exceed five feet in length— the longest of any antelope. The kudus we were watching, though not fully mature, were an impressive sight.

This was not a day for lingering too long on any one species of animal. As soon as I squeezed off a few kudu photos, Brian glanced behind us and spotted a small herd of zebras grazing at the far edge of some grassland. Zebras are one of the most recognizable animals in the world. Although I had seen them in zoos, in photographs, and on television, watching them in the wild was a completely different experience. I hadn't appreciated just how bright their coats were until I saw them against the dusty browns, grays, and greens of the African bush.

No one knows for sure why zebras have stripes. One theory is that when zebras stand together, predators have a difficult time determining where one animal ends and the next one begins. The prevailing theory is that since each zebra has a unique stripe pattern, the stripes help herd members identify one another. Of the two theories, I personally think the first one is most logical. I could see with my own eyes how difficult it was to make out individuals when members of the herd stood together. And if zebras truly need stripes to tell one another apart, why aren't horses perpetually confused?

I tried to creep up on the zebras for a frame-filling photograph, but the skittish ungulates spotted me and drifted into the bush. I hopped into the Land Rover only to jump back out again when we encountered more elephants and baboons.

"This is unbelievable!" said Deb.

"Everywhere I look, there's another animal," added Sam.

"When you took Joe, Susan, and Skip to the other platform, did you come across as many animals as we have?" I asked.

"No, we didn't see a thing," said Brian.

"Maybe we shouldn't tell them what we saw," I suggested.

"You're right," agreed Jill. "They'll be disappointed if they know."

Now, way behind schedule, we beelined for the platform—well, we did have to pause to watch a waterbuck (a heavy-bodied antelope with tall ringed horns) trot across our path.

When we arrived, Skip, Joe, and Susan waved to us from atop the platform. As I stepped out of the Land Rover, I scanned the landscape for wildlife—not even an impala in sight.

"We were beginning to wonder if you'd ever show up," said Skip.

"Sorry, we got distracted," said Brian.

"How was your wildlife viewing?" I asked.

"We saw quite a few birds, but no mammals," said Skip. "How'd you guys do?"

"Well . . . um . . ."

We returned to camp and drank a few beers while discussing our eventful afternoon. Joe and Susan were gracious about missing out on the wildlife the rest of us had enjoyed—we *had* to tell.

After a bit, Brian announced, "We can relax here until dinner or eat a little late and squeeze in a night drive. It's your choice."

Pacing ourselves was the last thing on our minds. And the sooner Joe and Susan saw more animals the better we'd all feel. We piled into the Land Rover and headed off in a new direction.

We still had more than an hour of light left, and in that time Joe and Susan rapidly caught up on their wildlife viewing. In fact, the only animals they didn't see that we saw earlier were Cape buffalo and zebra. We also enjoyed several animal spottings that were new for all of us.

"Warthog!" said Brian in a hushed shout.

"Oh, isn't he cute!" proclaimed Susan before the animal dashed out of sight.

When people discuss warthogs, *ugly,* not *cute,* is the word most commonly used to describe them. I prefer Susan's word choice and frown whenever anyone describes an animal as "ugly." There are no ugly animals—just ask their mates.

Warthogs belong to the pig family. These handsome animals can weigh up to 220 pounds, and their upward-facing tusks can reach eight inches in length. We won't talk about the "warts" below their eyes.

In my opinion, warthogs and hippos are the most comical animals in the wild kingdom. I'll tell you why hippos make me laugh later. As for warthogs, it's the cartoonish way they run that cracks me up. Reaching a top speed of thirty-four miles per hour, they run with their tails standing at attention and their short stiff legs in a blur beneath their stocky bodies.

Brian shared a story with us from the Tonga tribe, which explains why warthogs run with their tails in the air: "The river god Nyaminyami decided to use gray hide when making the hippo, rhino, elephant, and warthog. He made the first three animals so big that by the time he got to the warthog, only a small scrap of hide remained. To make the scrap cover the warthog's body he had to stretch it mightily. Warthogs are low to the ground, so they squint to protect their eyes from thorns and sticks when they run through the bush. Since their skin is so tight, squinting pulls their tails straight up."

Beyond the warthog, we encountered more elephants, baboons, and impalas. Upon reaching a spot without animals, Brian stopped the Land Rover so we could release our beers back into the wild. While the men stood behind a large tree and the women squatted behind a tepee-sized termite mound, a call came over the radio.

Brian answered the call and repeated the news to us: "One of the other guides spotted a leopard between here and the river ten minutes ago. If we're lucky we can find it before dark."

Everyone's face lit up with excitement. The elusive leopard is the ultimate safari animal. Even guides who have worked in the bush for years get excited when they spot one.

Brian turned the Land Rover around, and we headed off road into a ravine lined with grass and scrub. We stopped where the leopard was last seen, then continued up the ravine's far slope. When the terrain leveled off, we veered left and slowly proceeded down a wide field of short grass bounded by the Zambezi River on one side and a six-foot-tall wall of adrenalin grass (an informal name for *Vetiveria zizanioides*) on the other side.

"The leopard is probably long gone," said Brian, "but scan along the edge of the tall gra—there he is!"

"Where?" I asked. "I don't see a thing."

"He's lying just inside the edge of the adrenalin grass."

"I still don't see him."

"I'm pointing directly at him. He's about fifty meters away."

"Oh, there he is!" (Similar exchanges would take place several times a day between members of our expedition. Birds and small mammals in trees were particularly difficult to spot.)

Brian eased us in closer before turning off the engine. When the leopard sat up, we didn't dare make a sound. Though the big cat appeared to be unconcerned about our presence, he eventually rose to his feet and crossed a section of short grass. For just a moment, we had a full view of his body; then he cut back into the tall grass.

Everyone exhaled and broke into smiles.

"What a beautiful animal!" exclaimed Deb.

Leopards are such magnificent creatures that spotting one takes your breath away. They're so powerful they can kill an impala and drag it up a tree for an uninterrupted meal. They've also killed humans, but such attacks are extremely rare. As for our leopard, he had been eyeing a lone impala, which was stubbornly standing out in the open. We moved to the riverbank so the cat could resume his hunt.

Our timing was perfect: each of us grabbed a beer and raised a toast to our first African sunset. Once darkness set in, Brian switched on his spotlight, and we began searching for animals working the night shift.

The last time Deb and I went on a night drive was in Borneo. Here, our spotting results were about the same—the few animals we saw were barely recognizable in the spotlight's halo. At least this time we weren't choking on diesel fumes.

Even though the nighttime portion of our drive wasn't as productive as we had hoped it would be, we returned to camp excited by a day that had far exceeded our expectations. Within eight hours of arriving at Mana Pools, we had seen the following animals: African elephant, African hoopoe, African wood owl, brown snake-eagle, Burchell's zebra, Cape buffalo, cattle egret, chacma baboon, fiery-necked nightjar, gray tree frog, greater kudu, hamerkop, hippopotamus, impala, large-spotted genet, leopard, rainbow skink, red-billed hornbill, red-billed wood-hoopoe, side-striped jackal, Southern African tree squirrel, vervet monkey, warthog, waterbuck, and white-necked raven.

Dinner was served soon after we arrived. As would be typical of all our evening meals, we dined outdoors at an elegant candlelit table with formal place settings and crisp linens. Our food on this night included tigerfish fresh out of the Zambezi River, vegetables, soup, and rice. I flashed back to a meal during my childhood. I had grown full before finishing, and my father was scolding me: "Think of all the starving people in Africa who would just love to have the food on your plate!" Though my father's words were meaningless to me back then, now that I was actually in Africa, I tried to take only as much as I could eat.

Twenty minutes later, I pushed my plate aside and scolded myself—my eyes were still bigger than my stomach.

Deb and I awoke at sunrise, eager to begin our trek across Mana Pools National Park. The 542,000-acre park was only thirty miles wide, from west to east, but we wouldn't be walking in a straight line and expected to double the mileage. Although the hike would be the longest either of us had ever attempted, it would also be the cushiest. Each day, while we were hiking, the camp staff would be moving the entire camp—including our gear—to our evening destination. Other than water and a camera or binoculars, we wouldn't need to carry a thing.

Our expedition departed shortly after breakfast. Brian took the lead position, followed by me, Deb, Jill, Sam, Susan, Joe, and Skip. While our trek would ultimately head west across the park, for part of the first day we'd walk in the opposite direction. The purpose of our hike was to see wildlife—not just traverse from one point to another—and Brian felt the bush east of Chikwenya Safari Camp would be particularly productive.

Brian carried a high-powered rifle as a defense against animal attacks. He paused to warn us about animals that could force him to use it: "Contrary to what you might think, lions aren't the biggest danger in the bush. When lions charge, they're usually bluffing. Cape buffalo, on the other hand, will run right over you. Buffalo, and to a lesser extent elephants, are the most dangerous animals we'll encounter."

I had to ask the obvious question: "Have you ever used your gun to protect your clients?"

"Several times," he replied.

"Do you fire a warning shot first?"

"If an animal charges, there's no time. I always shoot to kill."

I looked at Brian's gun. "Your rifle looks powerful enough to handle a buffalo, but could you drop an elephant with it?"

"Yes, in fact I had to use it once to kill an elephant."

We walked in silence for a bit, while I considered our conversation. I understood why the gun was necessary, but if I had my way, I would have preferred taking my chances without it.

I posed another question: "When you hike on your own—without clients—do you ever go without a gun?"

"Sometimes, if I'm feeling particularly bullish."

I loved listening to Brian talk. I couldn't remember the last time I heard someone use the word *bullish* without referring to the stock market. Since Zimbabwe is a former British colony, he and most of the other local people I met sounded as if they were from England. I especially enjoyed Brian's colorful British slang, such as when he complained about a bottle of wine tasting "dodgy."

Deb and I would spend this entire trip with a single group of people. Group trips can be fun because of the social aspect, but they can also be complicated because of differing priorities. While we all wanted to see the big mammals, our other animal interests, at least initially, seemed incompatible. This was particularly the case with me, who wanted to find a snake, and Jill, Sam, and Skip, who wanted to find birds.

We all laughed upon realizing how different our objectives were: the birders had set a goal for the trip of spotting 150 bird species, and the herper—that would be me—had set a goal for the trip of spotting just one of the "glamour snakes."

I made up the term *glamour snake* while trying to explain that I wouldn't be satisfied with finding the snake equivalent of a robin. On this expedition, only a big or dangerous snake, such as a python, boomslang, cobra, or mamba would do.

During the course of our expedition, I'd occasionally grow impatient with my companions and their birding, especially when they'd spend an excessive amount of time staring through binoculars at small, plain-looking birds in faraway trees. Conversely, I'm sure my companions grew equally impatient with me and my herping, as I'd frequently scamper off whatever animal trail we were following (we seldom followed human trails) to check out fallen trees, termite mounds, and other likely snake hiding spots.

In reality, our wildlife-spotting activities were more compatible than they seemed. My best chance to find a snake was to pay attention to the birds, as some species would noisily announce the presence of predators. If the right bird squawked at the right snake, we'd all win.

Twice, early in our hike, birds proclaimed that a predator was in the area. The first time their warning produced a large-spotted genet (a small catlike member of the Viverridae family), and the second time we couldn't locate what they were screeching at.

Of the many birds we'd spot on this day, our best find was a southern ground-hornbill. The bird was all black, except for a deep-red face and throat, and it exceeded three feet in length from the tip of its tail to the tip of its beak. Hornbills are one of my favorite bird families, because each member species has an interesting natural history. In the case of the southern ground-hornbill, they're perfectly capable of flight, but they prefer to walk and put on many miles each day. In the bush, however, it's not the hornbill's walking that gets your attention—it's a call they make that sounds like a lion's roar.

After seeing so many mammals from the Land Rover on the previous day, I was surprised how few we were seeing on foot. The only large mammals we saw before noon were a herd of twenty or so Cape buffalo. We did our best to stalk the herd, but as soon as we got close, they bolted in the opposite direction.

Cape buffalo, incidentally, are quite different from what we call buffalo in the United States (which are actually American bison). Although the two species are similar in size, a Cape buffalo has a shorter coat, larger horns, and a cowlike body. On a male Cape buffalo, the horns start in a rock-hard boss (helmet) at the top the forehead before curving down and up like giant hooks. On a female, the boss is incomplete and the horns are smaller.

Shortly after noon, we stopped for a break by a shallow waterhole to watch a troop of about thirty chacma baboons. By far Mana Pools' most common monkey, chacmas have boxy doglike muzzles, long tails, and two-tone brown fur with a hint of black. When full-grown, males weigh seventy or more pounds, and females weigh half that. Experts are divided as to whether chacmas are a subspecies of the savannah baboon or a species unto themselves. Either way, they're the world's largest baboons.

We sat quietly on the far side of the water as the chacmas treated us to a scene featuring a near-complete life cycle of activity. A tiny baby clung to his mother's chest, while another rode on her mother's back; subadults methodically fed on aquatic plants; and in the middle of everything, a large uninhibited male had sexual intercourse with a female in estrus.

Eventually we rose to our feet and hiked for another hour. Then, as we would do each afternoon, we took a two-hour break in the shade of some trees for lunch and siesta. The range of temperatures on this gorgeous sunny day was typical of what we'd experience during the rest of our visit: low seventies in the morning, mid-eighties by midafternoon, and a return to the low seventies by bedtime.

In addition to the ideal weather, the lack of annoying insects contributed to a near-perfect environment. During certain months, Zimbabwe's bugs get nasty, but this wasn't one of those months. On average, I would get one or two tsetse fly bites a day.

Now that I've visited all seven continents, I can officially confirm that the area surrounding the Essen family cabin in northern Minnesota has the worst biting insects on Earth. My doctor once showed me an X-ray of a compressed disc in my neck and asked if I'd ever fallen on my head. "As a matter of fact," I said, "when I was a young boy, playing on our cabin dock, a cloud of horseflies and mosquitoes picked me up and started carrying me away. My big sister saved my life by spraying me with Raid, but by the time the bugs dropped me I was already several feet in the air!"

Okay, in the interest of accuracy, I must confess: I exaggerated the above for dramatic effect. To even suggest that anything less than napalm would have resulted in me being dropped is an insult to the bugs of northern Minnesota.

Here in bug-free Zimbabwe, we concluded our first hike at five o'clock. Susan had brought a pedometer along, so we'd know how far we walked each day. Today's distance was seven and a half miles.

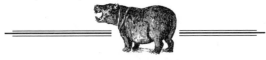

Our camp sat near the edge of a riverbank that dropped abruptly into the Zambezi, ten feet below. Paralleling the river, from east to west, were five dome-shaped tents, a bucket shower, a dinner table, and a campfire. A portable outhouse stood twenty paces south of the tents, and the kitchen and the camp-staff tents were situated forty paces west of the outhouse.

Every night our mobile camp had a similar setup. Each couple shared a tent, and Skip and Brian had their own tents. As for the shower and the outhouse, both had three canvas walls for privacy. The difference was that the open side of the outhouse faced the bush, and the open side of the shower faced the Zambezi. If anyone wanted to take a shower, he or she would inform the camp staff, and someone would promptly fill the suspended bucket with warm water.

On this night, showering commenced shortly after we reached camp. The men, feeling chivalrous, suggested the women go first. When Deb's turn arrived, she stripped off her clothes and stepped under the bucket.

"Huh, huh, huh, huuuuuuuuuuh!" Grunting, reminiscent of a college-aged man cheering on a strip show, emanated from the river.

Deb reached up and turned the spigot. As water dribbled over her body, others joined in a chorus of grunts: "Huh, huh, huh, huuuuuu-uuuuh! Huh, huh, huh, huuuuuuuuuuuh!"

When Deb started laughing, the rest of us, who were enjoying drinks by the campfire, looked toward the shower.

"You have a fan club!" I shouted.

"I don't know whether to feel flattered or embarrassed!" Deb shouted back.

"Enjoy it while you're still young!" yelled Susan.

The source of the grunting was a small group of hippos gazing up from the river. They continued their serenade through the rest of our showers, but Deb was definitely their favorite.

Hippos are creatures of contrast. Even though they're herbivores closely related to whales, their nasty temperament makes them one of Africa's most dangerous mammals. Weighing in at over five thousand pounds and equipped with lower canine teeth that can exceed a foot in length, they have the tools to get what they want. Despite all this, I found hippos to be endearing creatures, and they instantly became one of my favorite animals. Not only are they just plain goofy looking, but their repertoire of humorous grunts and snorts can make even the grumpiest person smile.

As we prepared for our first night in tents, some members of our group were apprehensive. Brian tried to put everyone's mind at ease by explaining that each tent was equipped with an air horn. In an emergency, we could sound the horn and he'd come running with his gun. "Just don't mistake the air horn for underarm deodorant like one of my previous clients did!" he said.

The mental picture of someone confusing an air horn for spray-on deodorant would have us chuckling for days.

Brian went on to say that if we had to go to the bathroom we could either step outside the tent or stay inside and use the chamber pot. While Deb and I would always brave the outdoors, some of the others would take advantage of their chamber pot. Frankly, I couldn't have used the pot if I wanted to—the tinkle of urine hitting the bottom of the little metal container would have promptly frozen me up. And believe me, when someone used the chamber pot, *every* awake person could hear it. Tents placed eight feet apart meant no privacy from sounds louder than a whisper.

Canvas tent walls also meant everyone could clearly hear the sounds of the bush. Although hippos seem to be awake twenty-four hours a day, technically they're nocturnal, and after dark they come ashore to feed on grasses. On this night, we could hear them walk past our camp, snort, roar, fight, and call out to Deb for another nudie show. Perhaps the best indicator of their proximity to our tents was the near-constant sound of their chewing.

Hippos weren't the only animals making noise. Occasionally we'd hear lions roaring, hyenas whooping, and who-knows-what snapping and crackling through the bush. In all, our first night in tents reinforced just how low we were on the natural food chain.

Deb and I awoke at sunrise to the gentle gurgle of water poured by one of the camp staff into the washbasin outside our door. After he finished, he scratched lightly on our tent and said in a soft voice, "I've brought warm water for your face." Subsequent mornings would start the same soothing way. Even Deb liked waking up.

One by one people gathered by the campfire for their morning coffee. Each time someone new arrived, he or she would mention the various animals heard during the night. Lions, hippos, hyenas, and frogs made everyone's list.

Once we were all together I asked, "Did anyone hear the elephant trumpeting last night? I swear one walked right through our camp."

When everyone answered a collective "no," I felt embarrassed and decided I must have fallen victim to an overactive imagination.

Forty minutes later, we hiked out of camp and nearly tripped over a freshly deposited one-foot-high mountain of elephant dung. To my relief (I think), my hearing had been proven accurate.

Brian had warned us that on this day we'd be passing through an area where we wouldn't see many mammals. Although his prediction held true early, our luck improved after siesta. Mammals observed for the first time included mongooses, dwarf mongooses, and elands. Repeat sightings included impalas, zebras, and waterbucks.

All day long, the birders had a grand time adding to their species list. Today's top find was a marabou stork. With a wing span that can reach ten feet, marabous are the world's largest storks. Other than size, what makes these birds unusual is that they seem to think they're vultures. Rather than feeding on small wetland creatures, like respectable storks, they prefer to get down and dirty with the hyenas and scavenge carcasses.

We often recognized birds by their calls. For instance, trumpeter hornbills sounded like human babies crying, and gray louries sounded like children telling us to "go away." Of all the birds, Cape turtledoves had the most prevalent call. They kept insisting that we "work harder, work harder, work harder. . . ."

Joe finally had enough and announced that the turtledoves' calls were inappropriate for our expedition. What they were really saying was "drink lager, drink lager, drink lager. . . ."

Skip agreed that the turtledoves weren't demanding we work harder. However, he maintained that they weren't asking us to drink lager either—even if it was a fine idea. Instead, the true interpretation of their calls was "Skip Horner, Skip Horner, Skip Horner. . . ."

By the end of the day, we had walked ten miles. More important than the distance was that the birders had opened up a substantial lead over the herper. Their bird count already exceeded one hundred species, and my snake count was holding steady at . . . well, zero.

"I don't understand your fascination with snakes," said Joe, "but I admire your persistence. If I were you, I'd be very frustrated by now."

"If this were my first or second trip with snake finding as one of my goals, I would be frustrated," I said. "But I've learned that the snake gods like to make me suffer for a while. Today was only our second day of hiking. The gods won't let me see a snake until at least day five."

Brian always paced our hikes so we'd arrive at camp near five o'clock. That gave us an hour before darkness to shower and change clothes. Then we'd eat dinner and spend the rest of the evening relaxing around the campfire, enjoying drinks, and telling stories.

On this night, Brian told us more about life in Zimbabwe under Mugabe. Fuel shortages and school closings were two of many problems he grappled with on a daily basis. Because service station tanks were often empty, he'd order private fuel shipments and store the gas himself. The shipments always arrived weeks late and at a much higher price than agreed upon. But as he said, "I have no choice other than to pay whatever they ask." The school situation was particularly sad. Mugabe wouldn't allow education funding to rise with inflation. As a result, schools were closing all over the country, and the one attended by Brian's children was struggling to remain open.

Brian always acted cheerful until the discussion turned to events in his country; then he'd grow quiet and depressed. I wanted to learn as much as I could about Zimbabwe but had to balance my curiosity against his feelings. I found the best approach was to ask a few questions and then change the subject. If nothing else, the nearby hippos had a knack for keeping the mood light: "Huh, huh, huh, huuuuuuuuuuh!"

Monday morning was the beginning of our fourth day in Zimbabwe. I enjoy the company of people, as long as I don't have to go too long without some private time. As the saying goes, "Fish and guests smell after three days." When Deb and I traveled with others on the Amazon and Antarctica expeditions, we both had opportunities to spend time alone. Here, so far, we had always been with the group (our tent could scarcely be considered a place for privacy).

Having reached my togetherness tolerance maximum, I was feeling a bit antisocial and allowing even little things to get on my nerves. I tried to improve my frame of mind by telling myself how lucky I was to be with such an outstanding group of people, but sometimes a mood just has to run its course.

No one knew how I was feeling until an hour into our hike. We were in the midst of crossing a large area comprised of adrenaline grass, streams, and mud. This was my kind of territory. I loved the adventure of walking through adrenaline grass and the sensation of sloshing through muddy streambeds. The problem was that some in our group were doing everything possible to stay clean. I have nothing against cleanliness, but when I'm exploring, getting dirty makes me feel like I'm part of nature rather than just an outside observer.

When we made a course adjustment to avoid an area where people might get dirty, I silently fumed. Shortly thereafter I watched Sam and Jill, in their spotless safari clothes, warily tiptoe around a section of mud. In contempt, I walked straight through where they had side-stepped and allowed the mud to cover my boots and splatter my calves.

Unaware that I was trying to send a not-so-subtle message, Susan approached me from behind and said, "Here, Marty, would you like a wet wipe?"

"We're in Africa on safari," I barked. "We're *supposed* to get dirty!"

I immediately felt terrible for what I said. Susan was just trying to be nice. I vowed to concentrate on not snapping again. No one was responsible for my mood but me.

Brian's job was to protect us, and in doing so, he kept us on a tight leash. Since he had the only gun, we needed to stay close enough for him to react in time if an animal attacked. Despite the danger, I never felt uneasy in the bush and found myself pushing his boundaries. To Brian's credit, he gave me a little more slack each day.

I decided to start using siestas to create my own private time. While others napped, I headed out looking for snakes. The chances of finding anything during the midafternoon heat were almost nil, but this was one time where success was unimportant. I enjoyed being able to thoroughly search an area without the guilt of holding others up and loved the feeling that came over me when I worked my way out far enough that I couldn't see anyone—I was alone!

Later that afternoon, we had to deal with the thickest stand of adrenaline grass so far. Brian did his best to lead us into open areas, but sometimes we had no choice but to push through grass that towered above us. I was surprised how bravely everyone handled the situation. We all knew the danger, yet it seemed to exhilarate us. If anyone was nervous, it was Brian. He had previously experienced the terror of an animal charging him through a wall of grass and was mindful of what would happen if he had to use his gun and one of us ended up in his line of fire. While we normally walked in silence to avoid spooking animals, here Brian encouraged us to engage in lively conversation.

Eventually we cleared the grass and found ourselves on the broad floodplain of the Zambezi. From there, we headed toward camp, stopping only long enough to observe a herd of about thirty Cape buffalo.

Overall, we had a slow day of animal watching. Other than the Cape buffalo, our mammal sightings included our daily dose of impalas, waterbucks, and hippos. Our hike covered a respectable eight miles, and because several people wanted to wash clothes, we pushed hard near the end and pulled into camp a half hour early.

For me, being alone with my wife was just as important as being by myself. Since Deb and I hadn't had a private conversation in four days, we took advantage of our early arrival and walked a short distance downriver to become reacquainted.

At the beginning of the expedition, I asked Brian if we could go on a night walk. I wasn't surprised when he told me the activity would be too risky, but I was surprised when he said he had never gone on one himself.

The location of our current campsite presented a unique nighttime opportunity. Our tents sat on a high riverbank that dropped down to marshy floodplain bounded by a narrow river channel. I could hear a breathy voice calling out to me from the baseball-diamond-sized marsh: "If you explore it, they will come."

I approached Brian shortly before sunset. "I know you said night walks are too dangerous, but the marshy area below looks like great snake territory, and there aren't any trees or adrenaline grass where large animals can hide. With your permission, I'd like to go down with my flashlight after dark. The danger would be minimal."

Brian surveyed the marsh and the ten-foot-long crocodile on the far side of the channel before answering, "Let me know when you're ready. I'll go with you."

"I'll go too," said Skip.

I waited until thirty minutes after sunset, to give the nocturnal creatures a chance to wake up, then asked Joe and Sam if they'd like to join our exploration party.

"We'll wait here by the fire with our drinks," said Sam. "If you find anything good bring it up to us."

"And besides, someone has to stay to guard the women," added Joe.

I flashed a grin and shuffled down the steep bank, followed by Skip and Brian. As soon as we reached flat land, I realized finding a solid surface to walk on would be more difficult than expected. I took several steps in ankle-deep mud before suddenly sinking to my knees in water. My trusty Danner hiking boots had protected my feet on every continent. I loved my boots, but I was asking a lot of them to keep me dry while being totally submerged. I hopped onto a clump of grass and wiggled my toes—still dry!

Brian, Skip, and I serpentined across the marsh—stepping mostly on patches of soggy grass—until we reached firmer ground near the edge of the channel. Along the way, we saw many frogs but no snakes.

"Crocodile!" yelled Brian.

"Where!" I shouted.

"On the point just ahead of us!"

Brian and I took off running—*toward* the crocodile—with a surprised Skip close behind. Although Brian and I moved fast for men in our early forties, we didn't have a chance—the three-and-a-half-foot-long croc slipped into the water before we could get close.

"We missed him, but there might be more around here," said Brian.

"Catching a croc would be *soooo* great!" I said.

Two nights earlier, I had told Brian and Skip about a three-foot-long American alligator I caught in the Florida Everglades and mentioned that I hoped to catch a similar-sized Nile crocodile in Zimbabwe.

Upon hearing my desire, Skip had asked me, "Don't you think a three-foot-long croc would be too big to handle?"

"No," I answered. "As long as I can reach around the back of its neck with one hand and grab the base of its tail with the other I should be okay. I could handle a four-footer, but that would be as big as I'd attempt out here."

Although I sounded confident at the time, I really wasn't sure how big of a croc I could handle. How could I know unless I tried?

The three of us continued searching the marsh until we had another croc in sight. This one, unfortunately, was already in the water, and it submerged as soon as we moved toward it.

While the crocs were easily avoiding us and the snakes were successfully hiding from us, the meaning of the message from the breathy voice was now quite clear. Mosquitoes, which were absent atop the riverbank, had come in droves and were rapidly scoring some bites. We were in a malaria area, and though I took my pills religiously, no antimalarial is 100 percent effective. This was no place to take an *unnecessary* risk. We gave up our search and sloshed back to camp.

"Tomorrow we hike past the first Mana pool," said Brian. (In the Shona language, "mana" means four, as in four pools.) "You might have another chance to catch a croc when we get there."

We departed camp at seven-thirty on Tuesday. A series of animal trails led us across grassland dotted with clusters of tall broadleaf trees. Other than a few birding stops, we hiked steadily and just enjoyed the beautiful sunny morning.

Around noon, we reached the first Mana pool. If I was a good swimmer, I could have easily swum across the narrow body of water—albeit the crocodiles and hippos might have severed a limb or two along the way. As for the pool's length, it stretched on for a half mile before curving out of sight.

Brian spotted a large elephant a short distance from the water, still wet from crossing the pool. On our first day in Zimbabwe, we had been able to get relatively close to elephants, because the Land Rover provided some safety. Now, on foot, we had to be more cautious. Brian's rule for elephant encounters was the opposite of what I had expected: we would give cows a wide berth, as they were too dangerous, but we would move in on bulls, as they were more tolerant.

Since the elephant before us was a bull, we snuck up, using a termite mound as a screen, then moved a few feet to either side for an unobstructed view. The big bull had three-foot-long tusks, and though he was aware of us and could have been on us in seconds, he didn't seem to mind our presence. His attention was devoted to devouring as many apple ring acacia tree leaves as possible. With his trunk he'd reach high above his head, pull down clumps of leaves, and stuff them into his mouth. For us to be able to watch such a majestic animal from only sixty feet away was truly a privilege.

Once the elephant moved on, we hiked a little farther before taking our customary two-hour break for lunch and siesta. We plopped down in the shade of some tall trees bordering a slightly rolling meadow. A more peaceful place would have been hard to find. I had a quick bite to eat, tried to relax for a moment, then reviewed my boundaries with Brian and set off on my own. Because the trees in this area were moderately spaced and the undergrowth was minimal, I had more room to roam than usual.

I crossed the meadow to some fallen trees and worked a wide circle. No snakes, of course, but I received a tremendous consolation prize when I looked up and realized a bull elephant was directly ahead of me. At first, I thought he was the same bull we had seen by the pool, but this one had a broken tusk.

Like the other bull, he was too busy eating to be concerned about humans and just meandered along, grabbing trunkfuls of leaves. I hadn't truly appreciated how big elephants were until that moment. Without a Land Rover or a termite mound to provide a measure of safety, I felt extremely insignificant.

I continued on my circle and soon spotted Joe and Susan. They had also seen the elephant and were now watching a small herd of zebras in the opposite direction. I crept alongside the couple and observed the herd for a while. Since I still didn't have a good zebra photo, and these weren't quite in range, I decided to move closer. Though I was already at the edge of Brian's boundary, I trusted the zebras would warn me of any predators.

I approached, using scattered trees as cover, and waved for Joe and Susan to follow me. They declined. Here I was, forty-two years old, and I felt like I was back in grade school, sneaking one block farther from home than my parents told me I could go.

I photographed the zebras, while leaning around the last tree before a wide gap of open land. After several clicks of the shutter button, I heard a loud crack to my left and jerked toward the sound.

At first I didn't see anything. Then I saw them, slowly emerging from behind the trees. One, two, ten, fifteen—a troop of chacma baboons and their good friends the impalas were cutting across the meadow to join the zebras. I aimed my camera and captured a few more images before turning around to look at Joe and Susan—they were grinning like politicians at a fund-raiser.

I rejoined the beaming couple.

"This is unbelievable!" said Joe. "I haven't moved for fifteen minutes and the animals have come to me."

"I know," I said. "The wildlife here is incredible!"

I left Joe and Susan, and returned to the siesta site, where the others were waking from their naps.

"Any luck?" asked Brian.

"Oh, just the usual boring stuff—baboon, impala, zebra, and elephant," I said in a monotone before cracking a smile.

Near the end of the day, our hike paralleled one of the Zambezi's many side channels. We decided to take a break and draped our legs over the edge of the high, sheer riverbank. Directly across from us, on the opposite bank, was a troop of baboons. One of the baboons noticed us and became curious about our curiosity. She moved as close to the edge of the riverbank as she could and sat facing us with her legs pulled up to her chest and her arms wrapped around her legs. The watchers were now the watched.

Moments later, Susan had the best herpetofauna sighting of the trip so far: a five-foot-long Nile monitor lizard. As the expedition's official herp photographer, I snuck up behind a tree, peeked around the trunk, and clicked two quick shots before the lizard plunged off the cliff into the river.

We pulled into camp tired but happy after our ten-and-a-half-mile hike. As with the previous nights, we savored a multicourse dinner, quaffed drinks by the campfire, and collapsed in our tents for the night.

Two hours after I fell asleep, I was startled awake by the loudest, most intense roar I'd ever heard—a lion was next to our tent!

The incessant roaring pierced the thin canvas—no, the roar was too deep and too powerful to come from a lion.

I sat bolt upright. Now, fully alert, I reasoned that only a hippo would be capable of such noise. It was more than a roar—it was a cry of pain.

Unless I left the tent to investigate—and no way was I doing that—I could only speculate on the cause of the noise. My mind raced through possible incidents that could make a hippo bellow in agony. I could tell it was struggling, as its roar rose and fell in intensity and pitch. Was a young rival in the grasp of a dominant male's twelve-inch-long canine teeth?

Since the confrontation was taking place on land, my main worry was this: what if the hippo makes a run for it and our tent is in its way? A typical hippo weighs more than a Chevy Blazer!

I aimed my flashlight on Deb; she was sound asleep. How could anyone sleep through noise louder than a freight train! Then, as if the train had entered a tunnel, silence cloaked the camp.

I waited a moment, pulled down the tent door zipper, inhaled deeply, and stepped outside. I shined my flashlight in all directions, but whatever was making the noise had vanished into the night. I took the opportunity to water a nearby bush before crawling back into the tent and falling asleep.

In the morning, I found Brian by the campfire sipping his coffee. "Did you hear that loud, pained roaring last night?" I asked.

"I didn't hear anything," he said. "I nodded off right away and slept straight through the night."

When Skip joined us, I asked him the same question.

"No, I didn't hear a thing," he said.

As others emerged from their tents, I asked them as well. Everyone had quickly fallen sound asleep from either exhaustion or sleeping pills.

On our first night in tents, when I was the only one who heard the elephant, a pile of dung had proven the accuracy of my hearing. While this time I knew it was a hippo that had awakened me, I couldn't find any physical evidence to confirm the event. Part of me envied those who were taking sleeping pills each night before bed. If a hippo or an elephant were to trample Deb's and my tent, I'd prefer to be snoring when it happened.

As we prepared for our hike, Joe pointed to a small shed snakeskin behind his tent and said to me, "We haven't seen a snake yet, but this proves they're here."

"Remember earlier, when I said the snake gods wouldn't let me see a snake until at least five days into our trek?"

"Of course."

"Today is the day. We may not see a glamour snake, but we *will* see a snake."

During our previous hikes, we had found many beautiful feathers on the ground. The best feathers, such as those from lilac-breasted rollers, were picked up and stuck into hats. Almost everyone had feathers in their caps, except me.

Though I had confidence in my day-five prediction, a tribute to the snake gods seemed like a fitting precaution—and besides, why should the birders have all the fun? I picked up the snakeskin, rolled the tail end between my fingers, and pulled it partway through an air hole in my baseball cap. When I returned the cap to my head, I had a snakeskin ponytail.

Each morning we departed from camp a little later, as some got ready a tad slower and lingered over breakfast a bit longer. My consistent desire was to hit the trail early, because the snakes would slither for cover as the day heated up. On this morning my impatience showed— I was vibrating with anticipation. If today was going to be *the* day, I didn't want to miss a minute of it.

I settled down once we got going. After a half-mile hike to an acre-sized, oval-shaped waterhole, I was only thinking of the sights and sounds around me. The waterhole looked like an ideal place for herpetofauna. Brian, Deb, and I explored the far shore—the side with the best snake hiding spots—and everyone else explored the near shore. Brian's excellent tracking skills soon had us following the fresh indentation of a medium-sized snake. We followed the track until it reached hard-packed ground and vanished. "Damn!" I thought. "If we had just left camp a little earlier. . . ."

Past the waterhole, we hiked into a large section of open grassland. Brian looked at me over his shoulder while he pointed in the opposite direction. "See that fallen tree at the edge of the grass? Let's check it out. The birds over there are squawking, and it looks like a great place for a snake."

At that moment, I realized just how frustrated I had become. Three days earlier I would have sprinted the 250 feet across the grass, but now, despite my prediction of success, I walked. When Brian and I reached the tree, he took the far side and I took the near side. The large tree had recently fallen and still had its full complement of leaves. I lifted and looked under each branch, but my side was definitely snake free.

"Marty, come here," said Brian. The hushed tone of his voice indicated he had probably found a small lizard or rodent for me to see. I checked a final branch and walked around to where he was standing.

"See that cluster of leaves? Duck down and look at what's lying on top of the large limb just below it."

"Oh, my god! It's an African rock python!"

The stunning creature before me had gold-colored skin accented by brown saddle markings. She glowed iridescently in the stray shafts of sunlight that pierced the foliage. My initial instinct was to grab the glamour snake and pull her into the open. Then I thought of Joe, Susan, Jill, and Sam—none of them shared my fascination with reptiles. If they could see what I saw, perhaps they'd develop a glimmer of appreciation for snakes. I couldn't risk botching the capture and losing the educational opportunity.

I stepped back and called my companions forward. After everyone had a look—and uttered the appropriate "oohs" and "aahs"—I surveyed the branches to figure out the best way to catch the python. Even though I could only see the front part of her body, I could tell she would be by far the biggest snake I'd ever caught.

Brian suggested I come down from the top, but I decided to do the opposite, and come up from below. I'd have to grab her high on her neck, but doing so would take all my nerve. On my approach, I'd have to move slowly, so she wouldn't spook. Once in position, I'd have to move quickly, before she could strike. If my technique wasn't perfect, instead of my fingers grasping the snake, a mouthful of teeth would grasp my fingers.

I lunged!

"Yesssssssssss! I've got her!"

Grabbing the python's head was just the first step. I knew from experience that pulling a snake out of a tree against its will could be a battle. Not because the snake would overpower me, but because tugging too hard could injure it. I pulled, expecting the python to wrap her tail around a branch to halt her slide, but instead she came straight out.

"Wooohooooo!" I howled. "Look at her! She's *huge!*"

Rock pythons are Africa's largest snakes. They can exceed twenty feet in length and are nonvenomous. Though their preferred food is small to medium-sized mammals, full-grown specimens will eat animals as large as an impala. The rock python in my hands was seven and one half feet long, about the same length as the amethystine python found on the Australia trip. This find, however, was more special. Unlike in Australia, where my guide, Chris Leach, grabbed the snake and handed it to me, here in Africa I caught the snake myself. For me, this was the single most satisfying moment of all our trips. Personally catching a big boa or python had been one of my lifetime dreams.

The python became aggressive as soon as I moved her away from the tree. First she tried to bite me; then she discharged her spooge (a mixture of excrement and musk from her cloaca). While I was able to avoid her teeth, her spooge soaked my T-shirt.

After a few minutes, she settled down, allowing me to release my grip around her neck. I held her with her chin resting on my forearm and her body wrapped around my upper arm and shoulder. As we posed for pictures, some in our group approached to touch a snake for the first time (people are always surprised that snakes are smooth and dry, not slimy). Once everyone was finished, I gently grasped the python by her neck again and planted a big kiss on her forehead!

The python had given me a greater gift than her little brain could comprehend. The best way to thank her was to let her go. I held my arms out in front of me and allowed her to crawl through my hands and descend to the ground. As soon as she was free, she curled into a defensive position and struck at me to announce our love affair was over. I snapped a few photos and backed away so she could return to her tree.

"That was a *hundred* times better than sex!" I exclaimed.

"Thanks a lot!" said Deb.

"I didn't mean it that way."

"Marty gets the first shower tonight!" proclaimed Jill.

"Are you kidding, Jill? I'm not showering or changing my shirt for the rest of the trip!"

My feet wouldn't touch ground for the remainder of the day, except when I'd spontaneously break into a little dance. To accompany my dancing, the B-52's song "Rock Lobster" played in my head—with "Python" substituted for "Lobster," of course.

We took a break by an oblong, three-acre-sized waterhole. Across the water from us were more than ninety chacma baboons—some were on little islands, feeding. This was the largest gathering of baboons we had seen yet. I screwed my monopod/walking stick onto my camera and started shooting photos.

"Marty, there's a crocodile in the water!" yelled Brian as he pointed. "He's about four feet long. I'm not sure if you can get to him."

I looked through my camera's zoom lens and spotted the crocodile. He was floating next to an island midway from shore. "That croc is mine! I think I can find enough firm ground to zigzag my way out there."

"If you catch a croc and a python on the same day, I'll just die," said Deb.

While everyone watched from shore, I started toward the crocodile. As with many of the waterholes we came across, vegetation covered much of its surface, creating the illusion of a field dotted with large puddles. I progressed by stepping wherever the footing looked the firmest. Often I'd find myself on a tiny island of plant-covered mud and have to hop over a vein of deep water to reach the next island. The problem with leaping from one spot to the next was that I was never sure of what I would land on—or where the young croc's fifteen-foot-long parents were lurking.

The crocodile was just off the far side of a ten-foot-wide island. The sections of terra firma near the middle of the waterhole were farther apart, but if I made a long jump onto a three-foot-wide island, I could still reach the croc's island with a final leap. I only had enough room for two short steps but was able to take to the air with just enough speed to land on the edge of the small island. For a second I thought I'd stay dry, then the soggy edge crumbled beneath me and I sank to my thighs in muddy water.

After I scrambled onto the island, Brian shouted, "The crocodile went underwater!"

"There's a surprise," I shouted back. "My approach was so 'stealthy'!"

As I slogged my way to shore, adult baboons, who had been watching my awkward leaps, were pointing at me and laughing, telling their offspring: "I know it's hard to believe, but we evolved from *that* creature six million years ago!"

My disappointment in not catching the crocodile was soon overshadowed by a delightful afternoon of animal sightings. We hiked a short distance to another waterhole, spotted four warthogs and 130 baboons, and didn't even attempt to count all the impalas. Then, an hour later, we snuck up on a herd of nine zebras and enjoyed a close-up photo session.

Fifteen minutes from camp, our thoughts turned to removing our daypacks, showering, and relaxing by the campfire with some drinks. As we cut across a large oval of open grassland surrounded by deciduous forest, we were already discussing the highlights of our incredible day.

Woof!

"Everyone, sit!" whispered Brian. "A pack of Cape hunting dogs is directly in front of us!"

The dogs were an animal I had hoped, but never expected, to see. Cape hunting dogs are also called African wild dogs, African painted wolves, or just about any combination of the three names. I prefer calling them "painted dogs."

Yet another animal some people consider homely, painted dogs are gorgeous to my eyes. They're big eared, long legged, and gangly. Each dog has a unique coat pattern. It's almost as if someone took a canvas of short brown fur and created a work of abstract art by splashing it with blotches of black, gray, yellow, and white.

The IUCN classifies painted dogs as an "endangered species." An estimated seven hundred remain in Zimbabwe and only four thousand exist in all of Africa. Habitat loss, hunting, trapping, and other human-related activities have collectively diminished the population of this intelligent animal.

Even though painted dogs are part of the canine family, their genetic line is unique. They're also very social animals who work cooperatively for the good of the pack. After returning from hunts, the dogs will regurgitate part of their prey for those who were left behind because of age or injury.

The pack standing in front of us consisted of eighteen individuals, and when we sat to watch them, they sat to watch us. While people kill painted dogs out of fear, we had nothing to worry about—painted dogs don't kill people. Like the wolf in North America, they're victims of human ignorance.

Our group was well aware of the rare treat before our eyes. The pack, on the other hand, wasn't nearly as impressed with us as we were with them. After several minutes of mutual staring, they lost interest and paraded to the far side of the grassland to lie down. We followed, but not so closely that we'd disturb them.

Soon after we returned to the ground and resumed our staring, a suicidal impala trotted to the edge of the trees, screamed an alarm call, and retreated. When the dogs didn't respond, the impala returned to repeat his call. All animals have their jobs, and in Africa an impala's job is to be the prey. Still, taunting painted dogs takes work ethic just a little too far.

Eventually the pack had enough of us and leisurely walked off in the direction of the impala. This time we didn't follow.

What a great day! Though we had covered eight miles, I was so energized by all the animal encounters that I felt as fresh as when I left camp in the morning. Others, however, disputed my freshness. In deference to them, I took the first shower—the hippos grunted their approval.

On Thursday morning, we had a nine-mile hike to the Ruckomechi Camp on the western edge of Mana Pools National Park. To stay on schedule, we had to hike fast and had little time for animal watching. We did have one memorable experience though, as Brian had to ready his gun for the first time.

After following a path down between some thick bushes, we popped out on a dry riverbed next to a wallow and its resident hippo.

"Get up on the bank!" yelled Brian, taking aim as the hippo reared out of the wallow. Lucky for all, the hippo wanted no part of us and charged off in the opposite direction.

We reached camp by lunchtime—weary but proud of our accomplishment. We had hiked a total of fifty-three miles and successfully traversed Mana Pools National Park on foot!

At that point, everyone was thinking about how good it would feel if we could relax for the remainder of the day. Ruckomechi was similar to the Chikwenya Safari Camp, and it currently housed only two overnight guests. The staff opened the vacant cabins, so we could take showers and naps, but after a two-hour break, we'd have to hike to the canoe landing and begin our journey down the Zambezi River.

I was looking forward to a nap until Ashley, the camp manager, mentioned over lunch that she had recently seen both a Mozambique spitting cobra and a spotted bush snake on the camp's grounds. No way could I sleep now. I quickly finished my meal and began my search. Poor Brian; he could have used a nap like everyone else. But with a cobra in the area, he felt obligated to accompany me.

Finding the spotted bush snake was easy. First, we checked the last place Ashley saw it. When it wasn't there, we walked toward the open-air lounge just in time to see it glide across our path and crawl into a mass of shrubbery.

I feared the snake had disappeared for good and was surprised when he stuck his head out the top of a shrub to check me out. He looked as if he were saying, "Hi, I'm a spotted bush snake, what are you?"

After shooting the snake's portrait, I debated whether to catch him. I turned to Brian and asked, "Is he venomous?"

"I don't think so, but he may be rear fanged with mild venom."

The thin three-foot-long snake was bright green with specks of black. He was one of the prettiest snakes I'd ever seen. He also closely resembled one of the glamour snakes on my list: the deadly boomslang.

I flashed back to my experience on the island of Borneo when I picked up the incorrectly identified, highly venomous banded coral snake. Consequently, I decided a cautious capture attempt would be my best approach. If the snake gave me a clear path to his head, I'd grab him. Otherwise, I'd let him be.

Halfhearted efforts are seldom successful. When I reached for the snake, I hesitated for the tiniest moment. That was all he needed to avoid my grasp and retreat into the shrubbery.

Since the snake was out of reach, I stepped over to the lounge library and grabbed the *Field Guide to Snakes and other Reptiles of Southern Africa.* I confirmed the snake's identity by comparing the photo in the book with the image on my digital camera screen. Next, I turned to the photo of the boomslang. The spotted bush snake was a close mimic indeed. Head shape (a boomslang's head is rounder) and a subtle variation in markings were the only differences I could see between the snakes.

Spotted bush snakes don't have venom glands, but according to *A Field Guide to the Reptiles of East Africa,* their saliva appears to be toxic to frogs. This got me to thinking: perhaps in its quest to mimic the boomslang, the spotted bush snake may continue its evolution and someday develop venom glands of its own.

Our search for the spitting cobra was unsuccessful. I did, however, encounter another mimic. I was crossing the grass between the lounge and the cabins when a water pipe, protruding from the ground, froze me in my tracks. The spigot atop the vertical pipe was at the perfect angle to create the illusion of a hooded-up cobra, ready to spit.

After our break, we all met in the lounge for instructions on our three-day canoe trip. Humphrey Gumpo, a specialized canoe guide, would be joining us for the journey. The twenty-five-year-old native Zimbabwean had stopped by our camp a few days earlier, so we were already familiar with his instantly likeable, happy-go-lucky personality. He could be serious when necessary but often told elaborate stories that sounded convincing—until he flashed a wide grin.

As Humphrey warned us about hazards on the river, his seriousness was unquestionable: "There are four dangers you need to be prepared for, but they're not in the order you'd expect. The greatest danger is the sun, because you can quickly become sunburned or dehydrated. Be sure to put on lots of cream and drink plenty of liquids.

"Snags, such as submerged trees, are the second greatest danger. Brian and I will point out snags as we see them. Give them a wide berth. But if you can't steer out of the way, hit them straight on. The water current is moderately fast, and if you drift into a snag off center, your canoe could capsize. If you do get caught, lean into the current until we arrive to assist you.

"The other two dangers are crocodiles and hippos. The main thing with crocodiles is to avoid dangling your feet or hands in the water—like bait. We will have close encounters with hippos. The important thing to know is that hippos always move to deep water. Most of the time, we'll be canoeing in shallow water. If hippos block our way, we'll stop to give them time to move. The one place we don't want to be is between a hippo and deep water. We also need to be careful near high riverbanks, as we can't always see what's on top. If we startle a grazing hippo, it will plunge into the river unaware that we're below it in our canoes."

Jill and Susan gasped.

"Finally," continued Humphrey, "a hippo could surface under your canoe. This is very rare, but if it happens you'll feel a little bump, and the hippo will go back down until you pass over it."

When Jill and Susan gasped again, Brian did his best to calm their fears: "I've been doing this for eighteen years, and I've never had a client in the water. Once we start paddling, your nerves will settle down and you'll be surprised how safe and easy the canoeing is. Just relax and enjoy the scenery."

While on the Zambezi, we would paddle approximately forty miles, pass fifteen hundred hippos, and float over hundreds—possibly thousands—of crocodiles. I wasn't as nervous about the dangers ahead as Jill and Susan were, but I was definitely on edge. Though I was technically just another member of the expedition, with no leadership duties, if it wasn't for me, none of us would be here. Therefore, I felt obligated to put on a stoic front.

Since Jill seemed to be the most nervous of all, as we walked the half-mile trail to the canoe launching area, I said to her, "Deb and I have canoeing experience. We can canoe ahead of you, or if you prefer, between you and hippos. Just let me know how we can help."

"Thank you," she said. "I'll let you know."

One by one we pushed off from shore onto a narrow channel of flat water. Humphrey and Brian led our convoy of five canoes, followed by Deb and me, Susan and Joe, Jill and Sam, and Skip.

I hadn't canoed since Belize and was looking forward to using the initial unchallenging section of river to hone my strokes. On the Zambezi, however, even the most placid water can become challenging in a hurry. We were only ten minutes into our journey when we encountered our first hippo. My paddling refresher course would have to wait.

A young bull was in shallow water, caught between us and a herd of hippos with a dominant male. When he stood his ground and roared at us, we paddled to the riverbank and held on to the long grass. He continued roaring as he considered his options. He obviously preferred to deal with us rather than the dominant male downriver but eventually chose a third option and climbed onto the opposite bank. As we floated by, he opened his mouth in a classic "yawn" of aggression—yes, his big tusks were quite intimidating.

Slipping past the young bull was one thing. Now we had to face down the dominant male and six other hippos who were blocking our entrance to the main river channel. As we floated toward thirty-five thousand pounds of snorting attitude, I wondered how we'd reach camp before nightfall. Surely, these hippos weren't going anywhere.

Then, in what seemed like a miracle, the hippos did what they were supposed to do—they submerged. Canoeing past an underwater herd of hippos for the first time was the ultimate exercise in trust. Although Brian and Humphrey had floated the river numerous times, could anyone really predict how a hippo would react? I gripped my paddle as if it were a rope in a game of tug of war.

The tension I felt paled in comparison to how Joe and Susan felt. The typically jovial couple had virtually no canoeing experience, and Susan disliked water even more than I did. I could hear them bickering behind me. No matter what Joe did, Susan retorted it was wrong, and vice versa. They reminded me of the first time Deb and I canoed together, except their pitch was much more fevered.

The current in the main channel was faster than I expected. We moved along at a good clip with a minimum of paddling.

"There's a snag to the right!" shouted Humphrey.

"I see it!" yelled Deb.

As we drifted past the snag, I turned from my position in the stern, pointed at the low-floating tree trunk, and shouted to Joe and Susan, "Watch out for the snag! It's right there!"

All they needed to do was steer two feet to the left, but instead they veered just enough to hit the trunk off center. I cringed as I watched their canoe turn sideways.

"Aaahhhhhhhhhhhhhhhhh!" screamed Susan.

"Brian! Humphrey! Joe and Susan are caught on the snag!" yelled Deb.

Joe shouted to Susan, "Lean into the current!" but she was too terrified to react. Their canoe listed precariously downstream.

We had all seen huge crocodiles along the riverbanks, and now in Susan's mind even bigger crocs were waiting to rip her to shreds the moment she splashed into the water. "Oh my god! Oh my god! We're gonna tip over! Oh my god! Oh my god! We're gonna tip over! Oh my god! . . ." she chanted.

"You're gonna be okay!" yelled Humphrey. "Just lean into the current!"

"Oh my god! Oh my god! We're gonna tip over! . . ."

Brian and Humphrey paddled upstream of the frightened couple's canoe and attempted to dislodge it—the heavy current held it in place.

"Aaahhhhhhhhhhhhhhhhh!" screamed Susan as the canoe rocked.

Humphrey jumped into the dark four-foot-deep water and pushed on the bow—it wouldn't budge. He repositioned himself and wiggled the stern—the canoe slipped free!

Two tense situations in a short amount of time had raised everyone's anxiety level. Moments after we continued on our way, Susan, still panic-stricken, pointed at a ripple in the water and screamed, "There's a hippo right there! He's swimming straight toward us! Aaahhhhhhhhhhhhhhhhh!"

"It's just the current, Susan!" yelled Joe. "*Calm down!*"

A bit farther downstream, the river widened to a quarter mile across and the current slowed. Per Humphrey's instructions, we changed the order of our single-file paddling. Joe and Susan moved up to second in line, Jill and Sam maintained their third spot, Deb and I lingered in the fourth position, and Skip brought up the rear.

As the sun dropped in the sky, an idyllic calm came over the river, and a gentle breeze kept us comfortable. Best of all, the hippos were spread out and moving to deep water without much fuss. I could feel the tension melt off my shoulders. Others in our group seemed to relax as well. The adventure part of our canoe trip was surely behind us, and from now on sunburn would be our greatest worry. A smile creased my face as I thought about what the next few days would be like: my feet would be enjoying a well-deserved break, the wildlife sightings would be spectacular, and the hippos would be serenading us along the way. Ah, life on the river would be sweet!

The depth of the Zambezi wasn't always proportional to the distance from its banks. Sometimes we canoed inches from land and were unable to touch bottom with our paddles; other times we'd nearly run aground at midstream. Actually seeing bottom was rare, however, as the water's visibility was little more than a foot.

Deb and I were canoeing next to a low, flat riverbank when we felt a sharp bump. Perhaps we'd hit a rock. We were too close to land for it to be a—

Grrrrraaaarrrrrrrrrrrrrrrrrrr! Something huge chomped through the middle of our canoe and thrust us into the air!

At first, I thought it was a crocodile. Then I saw a hippo's giant mouth!

As we continued skyward, my eyes shifted to Deb, who was rising higher than I was. At peak height, the canoe rolled shoreward, dumping us like a front-end loader would. I hit the ground first, followed by Deb—who landed on her side with an eerie thud!

The hippo dropped the canoe and vanished into the river.

Fearing the worst, I scrambled to my feet, calling to my wife, "Deb, are you okay? Deb, are you—"

She jumped up and we both wheeled toward the river, ready to spring out of the way if the hippo came at us again.

"Yes, I think so," she said while scanning the water. "I'm gonna have some bruises, but nothing feels broken. How 'bout you?"

"I twisted my back, but I'll be fine."

The hippo had dumped us on a shallow bed of mud. Though we looked like pigs after a good wallow, we couldn't have landed in a better spot. Adding to our good fortune was that despite the ferociousness of the attack, it was over before we fully realized what had happened.

Once we were sure the hippo wouldn't return, we hugged, whispered "I love you" to each other, and burst into laughter.

"We were attacked by a *fucking* hippo!" I chortled.

"I know," said Deb between giggles, "and we're just filthy!"

"I can't believe you got up after that fall."

"Mud is wonderful stuff!"

"A *fucking* hippo attacked us!"

As we stood by the river, giggling, Skip came running. "Are you guys okay? Is anyone hurt?"

"We're gonna be a little sore," said Deb, "but other than that we're *great!*"

When Skip realized we were laughing, not crying, he grinned and said, "I saw the entire attack! The hippo lifted your canoe six feet into the air—it was *soooo* cool!"

When the hippo struck, the rest of our group was ten canoe lengths downriver. After pulling ashore, they ran back to us.

"Deb, Marty, are either of you injured?" asked Brian.

"No, we're fine," I said. "Look at what the hippo did to our canoe!"

We had been paddling a heavy-duty, wooden-keeled, fiberglass Canadian canoe. The hippo's upper teeth had snapped the gunwale, and its lower teeth had smashed through the bottom of the canoe, ripped out a sixteen-inch-long section of keel, and pierced my dry bag and day-pack. The canoe was beyond repair, but we could mend the dry bag and daypack once we reached camp.

"Eighteen bloody years, and this has *never* happened before!" said Brian.

"Sorry to break your winning streak," said Deb.

The attack troubled Brian so much that he immediately conferred with Humphrey to figure out what they, as guides, had done wrong. Jill, Sam, Joe, and Susan were also troubled and obviously debating internally whether to continue on the canoe trip. As for Deb and me, we were still giggling away.

"I can't believe you two are laughing about this," said Jill. "If the hippo had attacked Sam and me, we'd be totally freaked out."

"The only way I can explain it, Jill, is that Deb and I have just lived through something very few people have ever experienced. I feel like we've been given a gift."

"All I can say is that it happened to the right couple," said Joe. "If it had happened to Susan and me, we'd be done. As it is, we may still be done."

"Yes, we're very fortunate the hippo chose your canoe," added Skip. "You two have handled the situation perfectly."

"What are we gonna do with our canoe?" I asked.

"Leave it here for now," said Brian. "Tomorrow we'll send someone down from Ruckomechi with a boat to pick it up."

We continued downriver arranged quite differently from how we had started. Humphrey paddled alone, Jill and Sam maintained their original partnership, Joe and Susan shared a canoe with Brian, and Deb and I shared a canoe with Skip.

When I noticed Deb and Susan were sitting in the middle seat of their respective canoes, I joked—a little too loudly—that they were both occupying the "death seats." Deb laughed, but when Skip shushed me,

I realized I had to be careful about what I said from now on. The hippo attack had confirmed Susan's worst fears.

The Zambezi serves as the border between Zambia and Zimbabwe. Motorboats were a rare sight on the river and were restricted to the Zambian side. Therefore, I was startled when a speedboat with several men in it raced up alongside Humphrey's canoe. Were they river bandits? Were they the unpredictable military personnel the U.S. Department of State had warned me about? I looked on with trepidation as a suspicious-looking man held up something white and cylindrical.

My paranoia, of course, was unnecessary. The men in the boat had witnessed the hippo attack from the Zambian shore and motored over to offer their assistance. Though we had already departed by the time they arrived, they stopped anyway to take a closer look at the bite holes in the canoe. The white cylinder was my teleconverter lens, which they had found embedded in the mud. I was grateful to the Zambians for their act of kindness and waved to them as they sped back to their side of the river.

That night at camp, Deb and I were bush celebrities as we told the camp staff about our adventure and in general were the subject of every conversation. Sam even gave the hippo attack a name. From that point on it was known simply as "the incident."

When Susan didn't join us for cocktails around the campfire, I asked Joe if she was okay.

"She's pretty shook up," he said.

"Is she gonna continue on the canoe trip?" (Anyone unwilling to return to the river had the option of traveling on land with the camp staff.)

"She's not going to decide until morning, but I'd be surprised if she ever gets back in a canoe."

I had mixed feelings about what Joe said. Though I'd feel bad if Susan didn't continue, I worried she'd panic at the next snag or hippo and end up dumping herself and others into the river.

I doubt many people slept well that night, including those with sleeping pills. Deb and I had spent most of the evening laughing about the incident, but once we were alone in our tent, reality set in: we had to face the hippos again in the morning.

My fitful night of sleep was interrupted before sunrise by the loud splashes of hippos returning to the river after a night of grazing. I couldn't tell how many there were, but there must have been dozens, as the splashing continued for several minutes. When I tried to picture the scene, the only image I could conjure up was comical. I could see them parading to the edge of the riverbank, flashing wide toothy grins, and doing flips and cannonballs into the river—"Huh, huh, huh, huuuuuuuuuuuh!"

Our morning start was delayed by a half hour while a fresh canoe was brought down from the Ruckomechi Camp for Deb and me to use.

As we waited, Deb pulled me aside and bared her hip so I could see the largest of her angry purple bruises. "Look at my hippo souvenir!" she said.

"Ouch! Are you gonna be able to sit in a canoe all day?"

"I think so. It's pretty much on my side. How 'bout you? How's your back?"

"I'm a little stiff, but I'll loosen up once we start paddling."

When the time came to launch the canoes, I looked on with admiration as Susan grabbed a paddle and took her seat. Conquering fears has been a recurring theme in this book. On several occasions, I've had to deal with my own fears, but never was I as terrified as Susan was at that moment—she was shaking uncontrollably. Though I'm sure I wasn't the only person who thought she'd be better off onshore, her determination to continue was an inspirational display of courage and tenacity.

For the remainder of the trip, Joe and Susan would paddle in separate canoes, partnering with Humphrey and Brian respectively. On this day, Brian deserved triple his normal guiding fee. Not only did he put himself at risk by being in a canoe with a client who would likely react unpredictably at the next dangerous situation, but he also filled the roles of cheerleader and psychologist.

While Deb and I were both apprehensive about returning to the river, we didn't admit it to anyone—including each other. We knew we had to set an example and that concealing our fear would have a calming influence on our fellow travelers.

Despite our brave faces, a hint of our true feelings was exposed when we encountered the first hippos of the morning—we paddled so close to the riverbank that we were almost on land. Raising our stress level was a persistent headwind that threatened to swing us the wrong way at the worst possible moment.

Repressing my feelings shortened my temper. Deb and I were second in line, behind Joe and Humphrey and in front of Jill and Sam. Since we were paddling single file, our canoes occasionally bumped into each other. To avoid colliding with Joe and Humphrey, Deb and I stayed several lengths back. Jill and Sam, on the other hand, didn't give Deb and me nearly as much space and unintentionally rammed us several times. After one too many jolts, I barked at them to give us some room and eventually maneuvered our canoe to switch places in line with them. Shortly thereafter, Deb and I miscalculated *our* momentum and rammed Jill and Sam. I felt like such an ass.

The only thing worse than being in front of a tailgating canoe was being in front of Brian and Susan's canoe. Susan had channeled her fear into a nervous chuckle. Since she was in the bow of her canoe and I was in the stern of mine, her nonstop tittering was always directly behind me. After a half hour, all I wanted to do was turn around and yell, "Shuuuut uuuuuup!" This time, however, I kept my mouth closed. Susan was doing what she needed to do to cope with a stressful situation, and I couldn't fault her for that. Still, if we could just switch places with Skip. . . .

We stopped for a snack on a high, flat riverbank. The morning had been a miserable ordeal of repressing nerves, fighting wind, and avoiding hippos. I ate in silence while staring at the river and trying to get myself out of the foul mood I'd slipped into.

As my thoughts wandered, I said to myself, "I need something to make this trip fun again—something spectacular."

"Asssssk and ye sssssshall receive," replied a booming voice.

"Who are you? You're not one of the *normal* voices in my head."

"You've been a dedicated herper, and we appreciate the sacrificesssss you've made for usssss during the passssst three yearsssss. And that nifty sssssnakeskin you're wearing in your cap, it'ssssss sssssure to become a new fasssshion trend. Therefore, we, the sssssnake godsssss, have decided to sssssend you a messssssenger—a BIG messssssenger!"

Suddenly the heavens opened up and a swarm of locusts—no, make that birds—descended onto a lone tree near the riverbank.

"Marty, there's a huge python!" shouted Brian, jolting me back to reality.

"Where?"

"See that tall tree, one hundred meters downriver? He's next to it, out in the open."

"How'd you spot him?"

"The birds gave him away. Come on, let's go!"

I grabbed my camera and followed Brian, running at full speed. The African rock python was stretched out on the hard-packed dirt, sunning himself, when we arrived.

"He must be at least ten feet long!" I exclaimed.

Not only was he longer than the python I had caught two days earlier, but he was also thicker—about as big around as a roll of toilet paper. After catching the first python, I joked that I wanted to capture a bigger snake—one that would push me to the limit. I never seriously expected to have the opportunity.

While I stood admiring the python, he slowly turned and crawled toward the tree. I should have immediately grabbed him behind the head, but as with the previous python, I wanted to give my companions an opportunity to "ooh" and "aah" before making a capture attempt. The problem with my plan was that everyone was approaching at a leisurely pace.

If I didn't do something, the python would escape. I grabbed his tail and started pulling him away from the tree—he turned and raced back along his body!

I let go just before he tagged me.

As my heart pounded, the python crawled against the tree and curled into a defensive position—I'd blown my chance for an easy capture.

I circled the python, planning my next move.

"Haven't you caught the snake yet?" asked Deb as she arrived with the others.

"No. When Brian and I got here, the python was sunning himself. I figured he'd stay put. Obviously, I was wrong. I'm gonna try to catch him now, but he's quite agitated."

I decided to try the direct approach. Since the python's strike range was approximately one third his length, I couldn't reach him without risking a bite. I inched to within three feet from his coils and bent forward, hoping to snatch his neck with a sweep of my hand.

The python lashed out!

I jumped back with my arms flying open!

If you've ever watched Steve Irwin attempting to catch a snake on *The Crocodile Hunter,* that's exactly how I looked. I leaned in again and flew back to avoid another strike. My moves would have made great television, and I was having loads of fun, but my goal was to catch the snake, not tease it. I had to find a better, more humane approach.

"Deb, will you please hand me my walking stick."

My walking stick, which often doubled as a monopod for my camera, would now have a third use as a snake stick. I grasped the pointed end and used the side of the handle end to pin the python's head to the ground. The maneuver worked, for a split second; then he freed himself with a flick of his head. I tried again. Same result.

"Why don't you slide the wrist strap over his head?" suggested Jill.

"Good idea," I said.

Well, maybe not. Pythons don't particularly like to be lassoed. As soon as I lowered the wrist strap in front of his face, he struck at it and caught a tooth.

I lunged for the capture!

He freed himself and lunged at me!

I sprang back just in time!

I turned to Brian and said, "The only way I can catch him is if you distract him from the front and I reach around from behind the tree and grab him."

"Okay," he said. "Let's try it."

Brian squatted into position, but the python was too smart to fall for our trick. Every time I made a move, he snapped his head toward me. No way could I grab him without him grabbing me first.

I knew if I didn't catch the snake, I'd kick myself all the way back to Montana. On the other hand, receiving a bite from a python so large could be serious. If he got me, he wouldn't let go, and his razor-sharp teeth would shred my skin.

"I don't know," I said, "he may be uncatchable." I rounded the tree looking for an opening. "Damn!"

I was upset with myself. I had wished for a snake that would push me to the limit, and now that I had one, I was faced with being the loser. I *had* to go for it.

I grabbed the python by his tail and pulled him away from the tree. *Whap!*

I let go just in time to avoid his strike.

While I counted my fingers, the snake slithered back to the tree and started to climb—this was my last chance! With all the nerve I could muster, I seized his neck.

"I've got him!" I yelled.

The python turned his head to bite me, but I had him just right. Disengaging him from the tree, however, would be a three-person operation. I lifted his front, Brian supported his midsection, and Deb threaded his tail through some branches. Once he was free, we carried him into the open so I could hold him.

As I took his entire body in hand, he released his spooge—a big snake holds a lot of spooge! I deftly avoided his initial discharge, but when I wrapped his body around my back, he released his reserve supply—dark-brown spooge dripped down my biceps.

"That was a quality at bat!" said Skip as he snapped photos of me with the snake.

"I hadn't thought about it that way, but you're right. For a while I was worried I'd strike out."

I wanted the python to stay wrapped around me (I wasn't worried he'd squeeze too tight), but he wouldn't cooperate. The only way I could hold him with the proper amount of support was by sitting on the ground and letting his tail go free. Like the first python, this one quickly settled down, allowing me to loosen my grip on his neck.

Snakes are wonderful animals, when you understand them. While capturing the python had turned out to be an adventure, keep in mind that when I first approached him he moved away to avoid a confrontation. Only when he felt his life was in danger did he become aggressive. Now, resting in my arms, he sensed I wasn't going to hurt him, and his aggression dissipated.

I held the python until I noticed my companions were growing impatient. Although I wanted the moment to last longer, I thanked the snake gods for their generosity and kissed their messenger good-bye.

"Wait! I forgot to get a measurement."

I carefully stretched out the python, and Brian paced alongside him. "He's ten and one half feet long," he announced.

"Cool! And I bet he weighs close to fifty pounds."

When Brian and I stepped back, I expected the python to make a rapid departure. Instead he lay motionless, exhausted from the fight of his life. Several minutes would pass before he'd slither away.

The delayed morning start, steady headwind, and feisty python had combined to put us behind schedule. For most of the day, the hippos had been well behaved—relatively speaking, of course—but the lower the sun dipped in the sky, the higher their aggression level climbed.

Several times we paddled through channels where we encountered barricades of territorial hippos with their giant heads just above water. Sometimes they'd submerge, only to surface moments later much closer than we expected. I felt as if we were in a live video game, where monsters popped out around each corner. To win the game we'd have to reach camp before nightfall, but each monster we sneaked by slowed our progress.

Remember when I told you that hippos were one of my favorite animals? The past two days hadn't changed my opinion. But when we were paddling on the dark side of twilight, and all that stood between us and camp was one last pissed-off hippo, I wished just once they'd return the love.

We awoke early on Saturday to get on the river in time to watch the sunrise. The Zambezi at dawn was a breathtaking experience. No one said a word, as we slowly paddled on a watery mirror toward a fiery ball of red.

Occasionally during our floats, we'd "raft up" by arranging our canoes side-by-side and flipping our legs over the neighboring gunwale. Sometimes the purpose for pulling together was to drift with the current, and other times it was to hear instructions more easily.

We were passing through a channel shortly after sunrise when Humphrey ordered a raft-up for morning announcements. Our canoe sandwich had Skip on the outside, then Humphrey and Joe, Deb and me, Jill and Sam, and Susan and Brian.

"We will continue quietly through this channel," said Humphrey. "After that the river will get much wide—"

Grrrrrraaaarrrrrrrrrrrrrrrrrr! A hippo surfaced with a mighty roar!

"My, he's a little grumpy this morning. As I was saying, once we get past this section, the river will get wider and—"

Grrrrrraaaarrrrrrrrrrrrrrrrrr!

After a night of grazing, hippos are supposed to be sluggish and mellow. One lesson we had learned, however, was that hippos make their own rules. The channel we were in was narrow, perhaps four times wider than our raft, and the hippo was downstream from us, near the opposite bank. As the gentle current pushed us closer, he let loose a fierce medley of snorts and roars.

"We'll hold here for a bit," said Humphrey as he motioned for Brian and Susan to grab onto the riverbank. "He's not too happy about sharing the river with us. He must have had a rough night."

Our impasse lasted for several tense minutes. Then our morning bad boy ducked underwater.

—Cue theme music from the movie *Jaws.*

Duuuuu-uunt, duuuuu-uunt.

A wave headed toward Skip's canoe!

Duuuuu-uunt, duuuuu-uunt, duuuuu-uunt, duuuuu-uunt.

Forty feet!

Dunt-dunt, dunt-dunt, dunt-dunt . . .

Thirty feet!

Dunt-dunt, dunt-dunt, dunt-dunt . . .

A look of fear washed over Skip's face!

Dunt-dunt, dunt-dunt, dunt-dunt . . .

Ten feet!

Dunt-dunt—

Smack! Skip and Humphrey whacked the water with the broadside of their paddles.

Everyone held their breath. . . .

The wave turned and headed for the opposite bank.

"That was a wee bit close," I said.

"No kidding!" said Skip.

Now, fully awake, we continued through the channel—but not for long.

"Lions!" announced Humphrey in a hushed shout.

Everyone wanted to see lions. If we could have bellowed out a loud cheer without alarming them, we would have. Instead, we pulled ashore with quiet whispers of excitement.

The channel arced like the letter C, with the lions on a small hill at the top of the letter and us on the far bank at the bottom of the letter. In the middle of the C was a sixty-foot-wide field of scrubby vegetation. Brian had warned us that lions usually take off as soon as they see people, so we were surprised when they ignored us.

The reason for our good fortune was that they were stalking a Cape buffalo. We counted seven lions in the hunting party (all females), and as the drama unfolded, the buffalo quickly gained the advantage. First, the buffalo crossed a side channel. When the lionesses followed, they had to make a hasty retreat to avoid a crocodile. Moments later, a second buffalo stepped into view to join the first one. Eventually some of the lions crossed the channel, but for the time being they were unwilling to move in for the kill.

After watching the standoff for a while, we returned to our canoes. The course of the river took us directly past the animals. Six of the lions disappeared from sight before we drifted by. The youngest, however, didn't have the hiding skills of the others and "hid" by crouching behind a tiny clump of grass. I'm not sure if she truly believed we couldn't see her, but her pose was perfect for some humorous pictures.

The next several hours were uneventful, so let's talk about bodily functions—okay, just one. Before the trip, I wondered how members of our mixed-sex expedition would relieve themselves in a flat, sparsely forested area. The answer to my question evolved as we grew more comfortable with each other. During the first few days, if someone had to answer nature's call, he or she would walk at least thirty feet away and hide behind a tree or termite mound. Now that we had been together for nine days, ten feet away, with nothing to hide behind, was sufficient. The one constant was that the men always had to turn away from the women—no matter which sex was urinating.

As we neared the end of the canoeing portion of our journey, the river widened to a mile across, and we spent much of our time rafted up. Everyone seemed to be feeling more comfortable on the water, including Susan, who had stopped her nervous chuckling.

I was in a great mood, enjoying the tranquil river, when we approached three lines of hippos, all facing in our direction. The first line had five hippos, with three together in the middle and one spaced out on each end; the next line had three hippos evenly spaced out; and the back line had two hippos spread far apart. They were missing a player, but the football formation was unmistakable.

"Hey, Joe!" I shouted. "Look, they're in a prevent defense!"

"Yes, and the safety is cheating in!" he added.

Even though I loved to joke about hippos, somehow I knew they wouldn't let us complete our trip without a final drama. If there's anything predicable about hippos, it's that they grow more cantankerous as sunset approaches. We were paddling through a bend in a narrow channel, less than a mile from camp, when we came upon two hippos fighting. Rather than squeezing by and risking their wrath, we opted to pull ashore to try and wait them out.

As we watched the giant beasts go at each other, an adorable calf popped up and down in the water next to them.

"I can't understand why the baby is staying so close to the fight," said Sam.

"It must be a custody battle," I suggested.

Though the fracas was entertaining to watch, we grew concerned when we realized it could go on for hours. If we didn't get past the combatants soon, we'd end up paddling in the dark.

As our leader, Brian had the difficult decision to make. Finally, he announced, "We'll walk on land past the hippos, and Humphrey will paddle our canoes down to us."

Though Brian had come up with a good solution, I couldn't help feeling disappointed. I had paddled this far on my own and wanted to finish what I started. After all, what were the chances of a hippo attacking Deb and me twice on the same trip?

"Can Deb and I paddle our own canoe?" I asked. "I think we'll be okay."

Brian hesitated before answering, "Yes, if you want."

Since the start of our travels, Deb had never backed down on anything because of fear. This time, however, passing within twenty feet of two brawling hippos exceeded her bravery threshold.

"I'm staying on land," she said. "Let Humphrey paddle our canoe. I don't need to be macho."

"Come on. We can do it," I said. "We'll be fine."

"I don't *need* to do it," she said as she shot me one of her unmistakable *knock it off* looks.

I considered proceeding by myself, but I hadn't solo paddled a canoe in years and wasn't confident I could steer past the hippos with the necessary precision. I reluctantly followed Deb downriver and waited for Humphrey to bring us our canoe.

We arrived at camp with no further incidents. After a final shower and nudie show for the hippos, we gathered around the campfire to celebrate crossing Mana Pools National Park twice without touching a motorized vehicle and—most importantly—retaining all our body parts in the process.

With drinks in hand, we raised a toast to Mana Pools and said farewell to Humphrey. We had all bonded with our canoe guide and were sad he wouldn't be joining us on the morning bush flight southwest to Matusadona National Park.

A broad smile lit up Humphrey's face when he thought of a way to make sure he'd be with us in spirit. Matusadona had one animal that Mana Pools lacked: the critically endangered black rhinoceros. So far, we had seen four of the "big five," and a rhino would complete our list. Knowing we had a difficult task ahead, Humphrey put Brian's reputation on the line by nonchalantly declaring, "Any proper guide can find a black rhino."

Everyone laughed at Humphrey's proclamation, except Brian. As I was just beginning to learn, Brian had a relationship with the various local guides that included competition, practical jokes, and general tomfoolery. If he couldn't track down a rhino, Humphrey and the others would find out, and he'd be subjected to a good-natured ribbing.

We arose at sunrise and commenced a four-mile hike east to the airstrip. Brian led us through an area where he had seen black mambas in the past. This of course had me bubbling with anticipation, but today was Sunday, and the snake gods were resting.

Our best find of the morning was a Land Rover parked beside a rutty road. One of the other guides had driven his clients into the bush, left the vehicle, and continued on foot.

"I have to leave my calling card," said Brian as he scanned the ground. "Oh, good! There's some—and it's still fresh!"

He reached down with his bare hands, picked up a mountain of elephant dung, and placed it on the driver's seat. While I'm certain Brian would face retaliation for his "card"—especially if the guide sat on the seat before looking—revenge would have to wait, as we'd soon be flying high above the park.

When we reached the airstrip, I expected to see the same plane that had dropped us off. Instead, our transportation had been upgraded to a newer, dual-engine model. Although the plane looked better, the pilot's takeoff method didn't change. He gunned the engines before releasing the brake, and we took to the air just in time to buzz a small herd of hippos.

Seventy minutes later, we landed near Lake Kariba, a 175-mile-long reservoir formed by the damming of the Zambezi River. A Land Rover was waiting by the airstrip to take us to the lake, where a boat was waiting to take us across a bay, where another Land Rover was waiting, which Brian would drive to our bush camp. The precision of our transfers was amazing.

The twenty-mile-long gravel road to our camp ran east, parallel to Lake Kariba, through a section of heavily forested land. Because the roads within Matusadona National Park were only minimally maintained, we had to contend with massive ruts and washouts, which made our short drive take more than an hour.

Unlike Mana Pools, where we slept at a different location each night, here we'd have a stationary camp for our entire stay. The tents in the seldom-used bush camp had been set up just prior to our arrival and weren't nearly as nice as the ones we had been staying in. Deb's and my tent was worn, and it had holes in the floor that tiny red ants quickly discovered.

We did, however, have a new luxury. Behind our tent was a private canvas-walled, dirt-floored bathroom complete with a bucket shower and a flush toilet (a fifty-gallon drum on stilts provided water for the toilet). Unfortunately, some flattened, slightly decomposed elephant dung made the first step out of our shower a tricky maneuver.

The primary disadvantage of the bush camp was that we didn't have the Zambezi nearby for water. Our tents sat on the edge of a dried-up river, and the staff had to get us our water the same way the elephants got theirs—by digging a hole in the riverbed. We did have bottled water for drinking, but our washbowl and shower bucket were always filled with the silty water from the hole. As Susan found out, if you did laundry in the washbowl, your whites became browns.

Although rain hadn't fallen since we arrived in Zimbabwe, Matusadona looked substantially drier than Mana Pools. Other than Lake Kariba, which was two miles north of camp, I didn't see any bodies of water, and all the riverbeds were dry except for an occasional puddle. The vegetation, which consisted mostly of closely packed trees and dense thickets of thorny shrubs, also differed from Mana Pools.

Our next two and a half days would follow a similar routine. We'd depart from camp with a mission to find a black rhino and return with little more than scrapes on our legs. Since only about seventy black rhinos live within Matusadona National Park's 348,000 acres, the odds of success weren't in our favor. Adding to our frustration was that other animal sightings were also in short supply. As Brian said after our first day of tracking, "You pay a price to find a black rhino. They live in the thickest part of the bush, where few other animals go."

Elephants were one animal we did see while rhino tracking, as they were often in the riverbeds digging for water. In places where the riverbanks were as tall as the elephants, we would perch on top and watch their activities from close range. While sometimes the elephants would charge us, they couldn't climb the steep banks to get to us. The effect was like having behind-the-plate seats at a baseball game—you know foul tips against the backstop can't hit you, but that doesn't stop you from flinching.

In the ongoing competition of the birders versus the herper, I was now behind by 138 bird species to two snake species. The birders were determined to add twelve more to their list, and I hoped to add one more to my list. The birders would eventually achieve their goal, but not until adding birds they found in the city of Victoria Falls.

I reached my goal, on our second day in Matusadona, by adding another glamour snake to my list. We were crossing a wide, sandy riverbed, when Brian spotted a black mamba sunning herself.

According to the *National Audubon Society Field Guide to African Wildlife*, the black mamba "is the largest and most dangerous poisonous snake in Africa, and is considered to be the world's fastest." Although reference sources seldom agree when discussing snake superlatives, who am I to dispute the National Audubon Society?

The mamba was in the middle of the riverbed, seventy feet away. I crept closer, hoping to get a good picture. When she spotted me, she raised her head several inches, then bolted for the bushes bordering the riverbank.

The race was on! I sprinted toward her—shooting photos along the way—but I was no match for her speed. She was thirty feet ahead of me when she disappeared into the bushes. I considered following but knew Brian would probably shoot my legs out from under me if I did.

Since the mamba had left a trail in the sand, I was able to review the photos on my digital camera screen and estimate the original location of her head and tail. Brian paced between the spots and announced a length of fourteen feet. If the measurement was accurate, the mamba was at the generally accepted maximum length for the species. I rechecked my camera screen and decided I couldn't be sure of the exact spot where her tail had been. To be conservative, I deducted two feet from the measurement.

Regardless of the snake's length, chasing after a black mamba won't go down as one of the brightest moments in my life. It did, however, prove that even the largest mambas will go out of their way to avoid a confrontation. Had I cornered her, she would have defended herself, but since she had an escape route, she took it. So much for the mamba's reputation as a snake looking for a fight.

After the mamba sighting, we returned to the bush camp for siesta. Joe, Susan, Deb, and I relaxed in lawn chairs on the camp's riverbed "beach" while the others retired to their tents. We were enjoying some cool drinks when a Land Rover pulled up and parked on the far riverbank. A stocky middle-aged man stepped out of the vehicle and walked over to us.

"Hello, my name is Obert," he said with a wide grin. "I'm the guide for the camp down the road, next to where the boat dropped you off yesterday. Is Brian around?"

"I think he's in his tent, sleeping," I said.

"Are you people enjoying your day?"

"Yes, very much," said Deb. "It feels good to just sit here and do nothing."

"Has Brian found you a rhino yet?"

"No, not yet," said Susan, "but he's working on it."

"I've seen a rhino every day during the past week—not far from here. I'm sure he'll be able to track one down for you."

"That would be wonderful!" said Joe.

"If you need to speak with Brian, his tent is the last one on the end," said Deb, pointing over her shoulder.

"Thank you. I hope to see you all again soon." He flashed another smile and walked toward Brian's tent.

Little did we know, we had played right into Obert's game. Like Humphrey, Obert wanted us to believe that "any proper guide could find a black rhino." Consequently, when Brian joined us an hour later, we enthusiastically brought up the news of Obert's sightings.

Rather than being encouraged, Brian furrowed his forehead and said, "Obert *always* tells everyone he's seen rhinos. He loves to give me grief!"

Shortly thereafter, we headed back into the bush to resume our rhino search. This time Brian found tracks, but none were fresh. We returned to camp at last light, frustrated but hopeful that tomorrow would be our lucky day.

Because of a scheduling mix-up, Sam and Jill's return flight to the United States left a day earlier than originally planned. Since the couple wanted enough time to enjoy Victoria Falls, they decided to cut a half day from the Matusadona portion of their trip.

For that reason, we got up extra early on Tuesday morning to make another attempt at tracking down a black rhino. Brian did his best, but after several hours of hard hiking, we ran out of time.

We dropped Sam and Jill off at Lake Kariba, where a boat was waiting to take them back across the bay. They were great sports about not seeing a rhino and wished the rest of us luck for the remainder of our stay. Everyone exchanged good-byes as the boat pushed off from the landing, but we wouldn't be apart for long. We'd see each other again the following day in Victoria Falls.

Deb and I had worked with several wonderful guides during our seven-continent journey. One trait all our best guides had in common was their determination to succeed. In Brian's case, not finding a black rhino bothered him to the point that his good-humored nature had become starkly serious.

When I noticed his personality change, I said to him, "Don't worry about finding a black rhino. Our wildlife spottings have far exceeded our expectations, and we have to leave *something* unseen for a return trip.

I'm content spending the rest of our time watching baboons, elephants, or zebras."

Although Brian continued to keep an eye out for rhino tracks, we ended up doing what I suggested. We enjoyed an extended visit with a herd of nine elephants on a riverbed and then took the Land Rover north to Lake Kariba, where we watched a herd of eight zebras elegantly silhouetted by a stunning sunset.

When we returned to camp for our final outdoor supper, I asked Susan for the latest reading on her pedometer. I added the figure to the log I had been keeping and announced that since the start of our expedition we had walked a total of seventy-seven and a half miles. Everyone was mildly disappointed about not reaching eighty, but when we included our forty miles in canoes, we were suitably impressed.

On Wednesday morning, we packed our gear and loaded the Land Rover for our return to civilization. The coolest temperatures of the trip, combined with the open-top vehicle, meant we were in for a miserable ride to the Lake Kariba boat landing.

Deb and I snuggled in next to each other and gritted our teeth as the wind whistled through our lightweight fleece shirts. If only we had something to distract us—something to get the blood rushing through our bodies.

"Hyena!" shouted Brian.

Though we had often heard hyenas at night, this was our first opportunity to see one. A wave of warmth washed over me for a split second; then the hyena disappeared into the bush.

"All I saw was a flash of fur," I said to Brian. "I'll take your word for it that it was a hyena, but I can't count it as a personal sighting since I didn't see enough of the animal to recognize it."

Then, as if on cue, the hyena cut in front of the Land Rover and ran down the middle of the road.

"Now I can count it!"

The hyena sighting made us all feel warmer, though the wind was still a bit chilly. Twenty minutes from the boat landing, Brian stopped the Land Rover to radio ahead our arrival time. I couldn't hear his conversation over the engine noise, but when he finished, he turned his head and looked back at us in shock. "There's a black rhino, not far from here! We still have time to see it if we hurry."

The rivalry between guides never reached the point where it disadvantaged the client, but in this case, Brian obviously had mixed feelings—the man on the other end of the radio conversation was Obert.

"You have no idea how hard it is for me to bring you to see another guide's rhino!" he said.

Ten minutes later, we spotted Obert on the side of the road. He was wearing a "gotcha grin" almost as broad as his plump face. Brian wouldn't live this one down for a long time.

We climbed out of the Land Rover and followed Obert a short distance into the bush. He pointed straight ahead and whispered, "She's lying in that thicket of small trees."

"I don't see anything," I whispered.

"Below that large branch, ten meters away."

This was camouflage at its best. A 2,500-pound animal was directly in front of me and I couldn't see it—at least for a few seconds. Once my eyes adjusted, I could make out most of the rhino's huge gray body. Much of her head, however, was hidden behind a cluster of vegetation.

"Can I move closer?" I asked.

"No. She'll charge if she sees you. Come over here, for a better angle."

Black rhinos have keen senses of smell and hearing, but poor eyesight. As I moved, the rhino jerked her head toward me but didn't get up. From my new location, I could see her big ears tracking me like radar dishes and her massive horns ready to lead a charge. Though my view was still partially obstructed, I could now count the rhino sighting with a clear conscience.

Like Africa's painted dogs, black rhinos are on the brink of extinction. From 1970 to the present, their numbers have dropped from 65,000 to 3,100. Many areas that once supported large populations are now completely barren. A case in point is Mana Pools National Park, where poachers were so successful that the government had to relocate most of the black rhinos to "Intensive Protection Zones."

As for those that weren't relocated, Brian told me, "The last time I saw a rhino in Mana Pools was about 1992. There was one individual hanging around, but she was poached soon after."

Gram for gram, rhino horns are worth more than gold. In some Middle Eastern countries people carve them into dagger handles, and in China people grind them up for their alleged medicinal properties.

I believe in sensitivity to other cultures up to the point where they adversely affect other living beings. In this instance, we are well beyond that point. So to the cultures that still see rhino horn as a commodity, I'll put it bluntly: Come on, people! Use your big brains! A rhino-horn dagger is not worth the extinction of a species, and a ground up horn is not going to cure *anything!*

When discussing the value of rhino horn as medicine, Brian put its effectiveness in perspective when he said, "Ground up fingernails are basically the same substance."

The time had come to depart Matusadona National Park. As I indulged in one last look at Obert's rhino, I felt privileged to be viewing such a magnificent animal in the wild and prayed the poachers would never find her.

We returned to the Land Rover and whisked toward Lake Kariba. The wind felt so warm.

Our flight southwest to Victoria Falls would take ninety minutes, and this time I got to sit in the co-pilot's seat. Since the Zambezi River was still high from the past rainy season, the views out my window were spectacular. A half hour before landing, I could already see the spray rising from Victoria Falls. It looked like someone had aimed thousands of fire hoses toward the sky and cranked on the water.

When our pilot circled the falls, I could see the reason for the erupting water. The Zambezi meanders over miles of flat land before dropping abruptly into a deep, T-shaped, steep-walled canyon. After the river plunges over the top of the T, the narrow canyon walls stop all forward motion and funnel the water out through a single small exit. The sudden restriction and abrupt change in direction combine to send sheets of water shooting skyward.

We touched down at the Victoria Falls airport early in the afternoon and took a shuttle van to our hotel. Because the city of Victoria Falls is Zimbabwe's most economically important tourist destination, it has been spared some of the hardships that are prevalent in other parts of the country. Even so, many of its 35,700 residents have had to resort to street peddling.

Deb and I checked into the hotel and headed directly to our room. Our accommodations were well-appointed but not luxurious. After spending twelve nights with companions in the bush, just having the privacy provided by solid walls and a door was all the luxury I needed.

Deb took the first shower. When she emerged ten minutes later, she announced, "Now that I've grown accustomed to showering under a bucket, having an unlimited supply of hot water felt so wasteful."

"Yeah, it's amazing the things we take for granted," I said.

Following my shower, we decided to walk the streets and check out the village market. As we stepped into the hallway to leave, we ran into Sam.

"Hi! Welcome to Victoria Falls," he said. "When did you get here?"

"A little over an hour ago," said Deb.

"Did you guys ever find a black rhino?"

"Well . . . um . . . ." I hated to blurt out our good fortune. "Yes, we did, but it was in a thicket, and it was *really* hard to see."

"Good for you," he said graciously. "Jill and I hoped you'd find one. Well, I just ran in to grab my camera. Jill is waiting for me. I'll catch you later."

Deb and I proceeded to the lobby and stopped at the front desk to ask for directions to the market. When an American tourist overheard our inquiry, he approached us and said, "Be careful. The people in the market are *animals!*"

We were already aware of the market's reputation and were unconcerned about it. Our previous experiences in similar markets in other countries had taught us that the two best ways to handle persistent peddlers were either to ignore them or to have fun and talk with them. We preferred using the second method whenever possible.

The market had the city's highest concentration of people hawking arts and crafts, but in reality, there was scarcely anyplace other than hotel property where tourists could escape high-pressure sales pitches. All the hotels had private security guards to protect their customers from being harassed, and all the peddlers knew exactly how close they could approach before the guards shooed them away.

We encountered street peddlers (who were all men in their late teens or early twenties) as soon as we crossed our hotel's "invisible line of tranquility." I could understand why some tourists would feel intimidated, but the men were poor, not criminals. I admired their crude but effective salesmanship. Purchasing one item was never enough. Their standard pitch was, "Buy more, and I give you one price."

The concept of invisible lines also applied at the market. Each peddler had a shop where he displayed his wares. Although the shops were simply newspapers spread over the ground, they represented exclusive territories. Each peddler pitched us only while we were in front of his particular shop. If we moved even an inch into an adjacent territory, he'd immediately stop speaking and the neighboring peddler would take over. The cooperation between the men was absolute.

We wandered through the market, talking with people, and buying way more than we needed. The hand-carved stone and wooden animal sculptures we purchased were all ridiculously inexpensive—especially considering how much work went into creating them. More important than the deals, however, was that the money we spent would help the men feed their families.

Major foreign currencies were the preferred method of payment in Zimbabwe. Peddlers loved taking American money, and by law we couldn't pay for our hotel room with Zimbabwean dollars. Even the Zimbabwean government refused to take its own currency. For instance, all foreigners entering Victoria Falls National Park were required to pay the entrance fee with money from their home country. The government had a logical reason for snubbing its own currency: it needed an influx of foreign money for trade.

I picked up a Zimbabwean five thousand dollar bill as a souvenir. While at the time it was worth less than one American dollar, it would soon be worthless, as it had an expiration date printed on its face of December 31, 2004.

Our walking tour of Victoria Falls graphically illustrated the country's deteriorating financial situation. The city had an elegant appearance and at one time was a haven for the wealthy. In fact, many of the traditional stores outside the market area still tried to sell upscale goods. What the city was missing were people with money to spend. This was especially true for the hotels. Deb and I meandered through two huge luxury hotels that were impeccably maintained yet eerily vacant.

With our arms full of treasures, we strolled back to our modest hotel. There we ran into Jill and Sam, who had just returned from viewing Victoria Falls (which was a ten-minute walk from our hotel). Both wore harried expressions as they told us about street peddlers who had hassled them so badly near the entrance to the falls that they had to ask for a security guard escort.

While Deb and I would never experience a similar situation, we did grow weary of all the in-your-face-peddlers. The next time we walked the streets, we dealt with the problem by making friends with a young peddler named Freedom. In exchange for some purchases and a tip, he became our private bodyguard. With Freedom by our side we had the liberty to go wherever we wanted without anyone hassling us.

Although the aggressive sales pitches had shaken Jill and Sam, they quickly recovered. When they departed for the airport on Thursday morning, their smiles looked as if they'd last for the entire flight home and then some. Zimbabwe had provided them with the trip of a lifetime.

As for me, I contemplated where Zimbabwe would rank on my seven continents travel list. Had we saved the best for last? Since the list was mine, so were the rules—and this time they wouldn't be strict. Today Zimbabwe would hold the top spot, but I reserved the right to change my mind depending on the trip I was reminiscing about at the time. In fact, all the trips for this book had produced such special memories that almost any one of them could end up as my definitive favorite. For now, I'd just enjoy basking in the afterglow of what had been an incredible adventure.

Before saying good-bye to Zimbabwe, Joe, Susan, Deb, and I walked over to Victoria Falls National Park. After seeing the falls from the air, we were all eager to experience them up close.

Victoria Falls produces the largest curtain of water on earth and is one of the Seven Natural Wonders of the World. For comparison, they're a little more than twice as wide and twice as high as Niagara Falls. In addition to size, what made the falls so breathtaking was that we could stand on the long wall directly opposite them and watch the water rush toward us before it plunged into the narrow canyon.

The spray from the falls, which varied from a light mist to a drenching downpour, had created a miniature rainforest within the park. Perhaps nowhere else in the world is there a more abrupt change in ecosystems. It was almost as if someone had taken a small slice of the Amazon rainforest and dropped it onto the Great Plains.

Like most visitors, my companions wore raincoats to stay dry. I, on the other hand, decided that since the temperature was a perfect eighty degrees, my T-shirt and shorts would be sufficient.

We started our tour on the far western end, where several brilliant rainbows framed our view down the length of the falls. From there, we hiked east along the ridge in front of the falls. The mist intensified as we progressed. Had the falls been located in the United States, massive guardrails would have kept us safely away from the edge. Here in Zimbabwe, however, a few flimsy sticks merely suggested that we not get too close—because they sure as hell weren't going to stop us if we slipped. *Whoooooooosh!*

A wave of spray washed over us and soaked me to the skin. Perhaps I should have worn a raincoat. Nah! Getting wet, albeit a bit chilly, was way too much fun. Soon another wave approached—we screamed with laughter and braced for impact!

Whooooooosh!

The falls were the perfect place to conclude our seven continent journey—soaking wet, laughing, and enjoying the company of new friends. The only question was: where do we go next?

Afterword

The most important thing to remember is,
no matter what anybody tells you, it is never, ever unpatriotic
or un-American to question anything in a democracy.

—STEVE EARLE

As I was working on this book, I realized I didn't have the picture I wanted for the front cover. I planned to use a shot with a tailless whip-scorpion on my face, but the only one I had was taken from a bad angle. To get a proper photo, my best options were either cheating, by purchasing a whip-scorpion from a breeder, or returning to the Amazon rainforest.

Our 2001 Amazon expedition had produced only two tailless whip-scorpions. As much as I hate cheating, I pondered the advisability of a trip with the primary goal of finding an elusive arachnid. After all, nothing in nature comes with a guarantee.

"If we can't find a whip-scorpion I'll eat my shorts," said Dr. Devon Graham.

Okay, almost nothing.

In April 2005, Deb and I returned to the Amazon. Not only did we have the pleasure of seeing Devon again, but Laurel from the Antarctica trip joined us as well. The combination of Devon's sense of humor and Laurel's laugh—and just a little whiskey—made for some memorable evenings.

Since most of the Peruvian staff from our previous expedition were also along, the trip felt like a family reunion. Segundo had been promoted to boat captain, and Cesar still has the best eyes in the rainforest. In the all-important category of snake finds, however, I'm pleased to report that on this trip I was Cesar's equal. I found and caught two Amazon tree boas, while he found one unidentified snake that got away and a small anaconda, which I subsequently caught.

Yes, we did find a whip-scorpion. In fact, we found four. All of them—sometimes two at once—took turns crawling on my face as Deb shot roughly two hundred photos. They loved settling directly over my eyes, giving me a much-too-close view of their large fangs. Whip-scorpions aren't supposed to bite, but keeping my eyes open was definitely an exercise in trust.

Our trip took place during the rainy season. Consequently, the biting insects (mosquitoes and no-see-ums) were much worse than in 2001—though still not bad enough to wrest the "Worst bugs on Earth" title away from northern Minnesota. Because much of the rainforest was flooded, we were able to kayak among the trees. This was a strange experience. In many places, the water was so deep that I couldn't touch the forest floor with my seven-foot-long paddle!

The Madre Selva Biological Station had grown during the four years we were away. The sleeping platform is now a screened-in dining hall, and a dormitory and classroom were added to accommodate groups of students. In addition, descendants of the outhouse spider had to find alternative living quarters, as their home had been torn down and replaced by a new building with four flush toilets and four cold-water showers.

As Deb said to Devon, "This is very nice, but it's kind of like returning to your childhood home and finding it completely remodeled."

While writing *Cool Creatures, Hot Planet,* I verified my facts with multiple sources whenever possible. I was especially careful to be accurate with animal natural history, as the animals were the stars of my travels.

If you recall in the Amazon chapter, when the bullet ant stung me, I speculated—in jest—that someone must have done a pain comparison test before naming the ant. Though my research uncovered many instances of people *claiming* the ant's sting felt like a hit from bullet, I couldn't find any examples of an actual side-by-side comparison—until now.

When Devon, Laurel, Deb, and I were in Iquitos, we had dinner with a Peruvian herpetology student. With Devon serving as interpreter, I learned that the young man had recently been shot in the leg after accidentally stepping into a shotgun-armed armadillo trap.

Naturally, I had to ask him, "Have you ever been stung by a bullet ant?"

"As a matter of fact," he said, "a bullet ant stung me in the shoulder moments before I walked into the trap!"

After we all cringed and agreed that we'd never again complain about having a bad day, I continued. "Which pain felt worse, the shotgun wound or the bullet ant sting?"

"Without a doubt, the bullet ant," he said. "Even after the doctor gave me morphine for my leg, my shoulder still throbbed."

So there you have it: a bullet ant's sting is more painful than a close-range shotgun wound. Remember, you read it here first.

I began this book with an old quote from Mark Twain, and I'm ending it with a new quote from Steve Earle. The world changed dramatically between the time of the Belize trip and when I am writing this now, in February 2006. The Iraq war was started with a lie, and thousands of people have died as a result. In addition, the Bush administration has been mortgaging the world's environmental future to satisfy the greed of a select few.

My most vivid memory from our seven continents of travels isn't of an animal encounter. It's of a photo I saw in a Malaysian newspaper of an Iraqi man carrying a young girl whose legs had been reduced to bloody stumps in a U.S. led air strike. To the best of my knowledge that graphic photo (and others like it) was never shown by the mainstream media in the United States. Instead, Americans were spoon-fed "Shock and Awe" and stories of war heroes that turned out to be fabrications. As much as I blame the Bush administration for what they've done, I also blame the mainstream media for not having the balls to report the realities of war. Imagine how long *any* war would last if color photos of all the children caught in the cross fire were printed daily on the front page of every newspaper.

We live in a democracy, and it's our right to question *our* government. In addition to demanding a full and truthful answer from the Bush administration about its motivation for war, we are also entitled to ask, repeatedly: Why are environmentally harmful programs, such as the Clear Skies and Healthy Forest Initiatives, so often hidden behind misleading names? Why hasn't the United States joined other nations in signing the Kyōto Protocol? Why must we allow oil drilling in ANWR?

I became a grandfather shortly after returning from our Borneo expedition. Though I feel way too young to be called "grandpa," I must now think further ahead than just the world my son's generation will inherit. What will the Amazon rainforest, Arctic tundra, and Antarctic glaciers look like thirty years from now if global warming continues unabated? How can the world's natural resources handle a human populace that is increasing at a dangerous rate? How many of the animal species I enjoyed during my travels will be extinct by the time my granddaughter reaches my age? These questions involve more than just the

United States, but as the richest and most powerful nation on earth we must lead by example. A "do as I say, not as I do" method of leadership is insulting to people in other countries.

I close by asking for your help. Some people believe that working to better our world is a wasted effort, as "one person can't make a difference." I know from experience, such beliefs are unfounded. Please, recycle, teach a child the importance of respecting and protecting our wildlife, give generously to humanitarian and environmental organizations, write pro-conservation letters to newspapers and elected representatives, volunteer to work on campaigns for conservation-oriented political candidates, run for office, and of course, vote.

Acknowledgments

Writing *Cool Creatures, Hot Planet* would have been much more difficult without the contributions of others. I sincerely thank the following individuals:

For believing in this book from early in its development, and for her outstanding editing: Marjorie Weber.

For suggesting I write the Amazon story that started it all: Rod Daniel of the Ravalli Republic newspaper.

For manuscript reading and constructive comments: Cyndy Boehm, Rod Daniel, Deb Essen, Sean Essen, Dr. Devon Graham, Dale Morrow, Laurel Pfund, and Dr. Bryan Spellman.

For fact-checking help: Gary Bondeson, Dr. Devon Graham, Carsten Jensen, Lawrence Mason, and Brian Worsley.

For her exceptional writing coaching: Laurie Rosin.

For his encouragement at just the right time: Senator George McGovern.

For their ongoing encouragement: Mom, Dad, and Milt and Meredith Froehlich.

For running my office, so I could write: Nicole Nelson and Dr. Bryan Spellman.

For being a part of this adventure: all the people I met during my travels.

Back-of-the-book thank-yous are traditionally reserved for humans, but I'm going to make an exception. Only one individual was by my side for all of the many thousands of hours I put into writing this book. Only one individual listened to me read the same paragraphs aloud over and over without feeling as if she had to leave the room screaming. That individual was Annie.

I was two weeks away from finishing this book when I learned that Annie had cancer throughout her body. She bravely held on until I completed my manuscript. Then, three hours later, she took the portal to Idaho for the final time. I will always have dogs in my life, but none will ever be as special as she was.

Thank you, Annie, for your loyal friendship—I'll miss you.

Selected Bibliography

African Horizons. "Zimbabwe's Parks and Reserves." http://www.africanhorizons.com.

African Safari Consultants. "National Parks and Game Reserves in Zimbabwe." http://www.classicsafaris.com.

Alaska Department of Environmental Conservation. "Statewide Summary of Oil and Hazardous Spill Data: Fiscal Years 1996–2002." http://www.state.ak.us/dec/index.html.

Alden, Peter C., Richard D. Estes, Duane Schlitter, and Bunny McBride. *National Audubon Society Field Guide to African Wildlife.* Fourth Printing. New York: Alfred A. Knopf, Inc., 2001.

Antarctic Explorer. Chichester, UK: Ocean Explorer Maps, 2002.

Areste, Manuel, and Rafael Cebrián. *Snakes of the World.* New York: Sterling Publishing Co., Inc., 2003.

Associated Press. "Two Sue Feds Over Anti-Bush T-Shirt Arrest." *FoxNews.com,* September 15, 2004. http://www.foxnews.com/story/0,2933,132425,00.html.

Australian Government, Department of Environmental Heritage. "Wet Tropics of Queensland." http://www.deh.gov.au/heritage/worldheritage/sites/wettropics/index.html.

Australian Tropical Research Foundation. http://www.austrop.org.au.

Being Caribou. http://www.beingcaribou.com.

Black Hills Reptile Gardens, Inc. "The Deadliest Snakes in the World." http://www.reptile-gardens.com/reptile/topten.html.

Botting, Douglas, ed. *Wild France: A Traveller's Guide*. New York: Interlink Publishing Group, Inc., 2000.

Branch, Bill. *Field Guide to Snakes and other Reptiles of Southern Africa*. Third Revised Edition. Sanibel Island, FL: Ralph Curtis Books Publishing, 1998.

British Antarctic Survey. *Whalers Bay*. Undated informational sign.

Burnie, David, and Don E. Wilson, eds. *Smithsonian Institution Animal: The Definitive Visual Guide to the World's Wildlife*. London and New York: DK Publishing, Inc., 2001.

Campbell, Elaine J. F. *A Walk through the Lowland Rain Forest of Sabah*. Kota Kinabalu, Sabah: Natural History Publications (Borneo) Sdn. Bhd., 1994.

Carlsson, Olle, and Stefan Lundgren. *Antarctica: Souvenirs from the Seventh Continent*. Second Edition. Sweden: Ice Is Nice Publishing House, 2001.

Castillo de la Triste Condesa. http://web.jet.es/mdelgado/vchachi/arqui/chcasti.html.

Castillos de Espana. http://jirm_38.eresmas.com.

CBC News. "Locked Horns: The Fate of Old Crow," *CBC News*, June 4, 2003. http://www.cbc.ca/witness/oldcrow.

CBS News. "Hybrid Gas Mileage Falls Short," *CBS News*, May 28, 2004. http://www.cbsnews.com/stories/2004/05/28/eveningnews/consumer/main620265.shtml.

———. "Wild Wolves," *CBS News*, April 14, 2000. http://www.cbsnews.com/stories/2000/03/20/60II/main174111.shtml.

Central Intelligence Agency. "The World Fact Book." http://www.cia.gov/cia/publications/factbook/index.html.

City Council of Arenas de San Pedro. "Arenas de San Pedro." http://www.ayto-arenas.com.

Clutton-Brock, Juliet, and Don E. Wilson. *Smithsonian Handbooks: Mammals.* London and New York: DK Publishing, Inc., 2002.

Cohen, Leon J., and A.C. Rogers. *Say it in Spanish.* New York: Dover Publications, Inc., 1960.

Columbus Zoo & Aquarium. "African Forest: Rainforest Facts." http://www.colszoo.org/animalareas/aforest/effect.html.

Community for Coastal and Cassowary Conservation Inc. http://cassowaryconservation.asn.au.

Cooke, Fred, Hugh Dingle, Stephen Hutchinson, and others. *The Encyclopedia of Animals: A Complete Visual Guide.* Berkeley and Los Angeles: University of California Press, 2004.

Corwin, Jeff. *Living on the Edge.* Emmaus, PA: Rodale Press, Inc., 2003.

Couvrette, Phil. "U.N Report Says Biodiversity on Decline." *Associated Press,* May 20, 2005. http://abcnews.go.com/Technology/wireStory?id=774760&CMP=OTC-RSSFeeds0312.

Cox, Merel J., Peter Paul van Dijk, Jarujin Nabhitabhata, and Kumthorn Thirakhupt. *A Photographic Guide to Snakes and Other Reptiles of Peninsular Malaysia, Singapore and Thailand.* Sanibel Island, FL: Ralph Curtis Publishing, Inc., 1998.

Cross, Robert. "Amazon Q&A." *Chicago Tribune,* November 5, 2000.

Daintree Cape Tribulation Tourism. "The Cassowary." http://www.daintreecoast.com/cassowary.htm.

Daly, Margo, Anne Dehne, David Leffman, and Chris Scott. *The Rough Guide to Australia.* Fifth Edition. London and New York: Rough Guides, LTD., 2001.

Defenders of Wildlife. "Arctic National Wildlife Refuge." http://www.defenders.org.

Dey, Phoebe. "Bighorn Sheep Suffering Decline of the Fittest." *University of Alberta ExpressNews,* December 10, 2003.

DK Travel Writers Staff. *DK Eyewitness Travel Guide: Australia.* London and New York: Dorling Kindersley Publishing, 2000.

Easton, Adam. "Rainforest May Hold Key to New Drugs." *BBC News World Edition,* October 8, 2002. http://news.bbc.co.uk/2/hi/health/2308743.stm.

Elliot, John L. "In Search of the Deadly Jelly." *National Geographic,* July 2005.

Encyclopedia Britannica, Inc. *Encyclopedia Britannica 2003 Ultimate Reference Suite.*

Estes, Richard D. *The Safari Companion: A Guide to Watching African Mammals.* Revised Edition. White River Junction, VT: Chelsea Green Publishing Company, 1999.

Eungella National Park. http://www.brokenrivermr.com.au.

Evans, Clay. "The President Cries Wolf!" *Boulder Daily Camera,* October 24, 2004.

Extreme Science. "Amazon River. How Great is Great?" http://www.extremescience.com/AmazonRiver.htm.

———. "Rhinoceros Beetle." http://www.extremescience.com/ StrongestCreature.htm.

Eyes on Africa. "Zimbabwe's National Parks: Safari Information." http://www.eyesonafrica.net/african-safari-zimbabwe/ zimbabwe-safari.htm.

Federation of French Regional Parks. "Parc Naturel Regional de Camargue." http://www.parcs-naturels-regionaux.tm.fr/fr/accueil.

Fernando, Prithiviraj, T.N.C. Vidya, John Payne, Michael Stuewe, Geoffrey Davison, and others. "DNA Analysis Indicates that Asian Elephants are Native to Borneo and are therefore a High Priority for Conservation." *PLOS Biology,* October 2003.

Finlay, Hugh, Andrew Humphreys, and Mark Armstrong. *Lonely Planet Queensland.* Second Edition. Footscray, Victoria: Lonely Planet Publications, 1999.

Francis, Charles M. *A Photographic Guide to Mammals of South-East Asia.* Sanibel Island, FL: Ralph Curtis Publishing, Inc., 2001.

Game-Reserve.com. "Zimbabwe." http://www.game-reserve.com/ zimbabwe.html.

Gibson, John. *Anatomy of the Castle.* New York: MetroBooks, 2001.

Goodwin, Peter. "Zimbabwe's Bitter Harvest." *National Geographic,* August 2003.

Gottlieb, Sheldon H. "Vipers, Venom and Life-Saving Snakes." *Diabetes Forecast,* November 2001.

Gould, Edwin, and George McKay. *Encyclopedia of Mammals: A Comprehensive Illustrated Guide by International Experts.* Second Edition. San Diego and San Francisco: Academic Press, 1998.

Government of Yukon, Department of Environment. "Mammals." http://www.environmentyukon.gov.yk.ca/mammals.html.

———. "Thinhorn Sheep." http://www.environmentyukon.gov.yk.ca/sheep.html.

Government of Yukon. *Places to Go on Yukon Time.* Undated booklet.

Grafe, Kris Valencia, ed. *The Milepost: Trip Planner for Alaska, Yukon Territory, British Columbia, Alberta & Northwest Territories.* Augusta, GA: Morris Communications, LLC., 2002.

Gray, Gary. *Running With the Bulls: Fiestas, Corridas, Toreros, and an American's Adventure in Pamplona.* Guilford, CT: The Lyons Press, 2001.

Greenpeace. "Don't Move that Blubber!" *Greenpeace,* October 30, 2002. http://whales.greenpeace.org/news/30oct2002.htm.

Grunfeld, Frederic V. *Wild Spain: A Traveller's Guide.* New York: Interlink Publishing Group, Inc., 2000.

Gwich'in Renewable Resource Board. "Fall Movements of the Porcupine Caribou Herd Near the Dempster Highway August 2000." http://www.grrb.nt.ca.

Halliday, Tim, and Kraig Alder, eds. *Firefly Encyclopedia of Reptiles and Amphibians.* Buffalo and Toronto: Firefly Books, LTD., 2002.

Harris Interactive. "The Harris Poll #57." http://www.harrisinteractive.com/harris_poll/index.asp?PID=487.

Holladay, April. "Chapter 8: Life is Hard for Arctic Plants and Animals." Complete Idiot's Guide Clips, 2003. http://www.wonderquest.com/april-writer/ch8-plants-animals.htm.

Hoffman, Eric. *Adventuring in Belize: The Sierra Club Travel Guide to the Islands, Waters, and Inland Parks of Central America's Tropical Paradise.* San Francisco: Sierra Club Books, 1994.

Human, Katy. "Alpinists' Ice-dreamy Mountains Melting Away." *The Denver Post,* January 12, 2005.

International Mountain Caribou Technical Committee. http://imctc.com.

International Union for Conservation of Nature and Natural Resources. "2004 IUCN Red List of Threatened Species." Downloaded on June 18, 2005. http://www.redlist.org.

International Whaling Commission. http://www.iwcoffice.org.

International Wolf Center. "Are Wolves Dangerous to Humans?" http://www.wolf.org/wolves/learn/intermed/inter_human/dangerous.asp.

Issacson, Rupert. *Cadogan: Southern Africa on the Wild Side.* London: Cadogan Guides, 1998.

Ivereigh, Djuna. "It Takes a Forest." *Nature Conservancy Magazine,* Volume 53, Number 2, Summer 2003.

Japan Whaling Association. "Questions & Answers." http://www.whaling.jp/english/qa.html.

Kane, Joe. *Running the Amazon.* New York: Vintage Books, 1989.

———. *Savages.* New York: Vintage Books, 1996.

Kauffman, Murray S. *Reefs and Rain Forests.* Beverly Hills: Reefs and Rain Forests Publications, 2002.

Kiley, David. "Hybrid Car Owners Wonder: Where's the Mileage?" *USA Today,* February 3, 2004.

King, Anna. "Oregon Prepares for Wolves' Return." *Tri-City Herald,* January 3, 2005.

Kirby, Alex. "Whaling Ban Should Stay." *BBC News,* June 12, 2000. http://news.bbc.co.uk/1/hi/sci/tech/787748.stm.

Kricher, John. *A Neotropical Companion: An Introduction to the Animals, Plants, and Ecosystems of the New World Tropics.* Second Edition. Princeton, NJ: Princeton University Press, 1999.

La Alvarada. "Don Álvaro de Luna." http://www.alvarada.com/alvaro.htm.

Lambertini, Marco. *A Naturalist's Guide to the Tropics*. Chicago and London: University of Chicago Press, 2000.

Lansing, Alfred. *Endurance: Shackleton's Incredible Voyage*. Twenty-second printing. New York: Carroll & Graf, 1959.

Lewis & Clark Law School. "International Environmental Law Project: Whaling and the International Whaling Commission." http://www.lclark.edu/org/ielp/whales.html.

Mahler, Richard. *Belize: Adventures in Nature*. Second Edition. Santa Fe, NM: John Muir Publications, 1999.

Mallan, Chicki, and Patti Lange. *Belize Handbook*. Fourth Edition. Emeryville, CA: Moon Travel Handbooks, 1998.

Margarita Tours, Inc. http://www.amazon-ecotours.com.

Marshal Vauban Website. "Villefranche-de-Conflent: Rousillon." http://www.geocities.com/Pentagon/6750/fvillefr.htm.

Martin, R.D. "Are Fruit Bats Primates?" *Science Frontiers Online*, Jul-Aug 1986. http://www.science-frontiers.com/sf046/sf046p09.htm.

Mason's Tours. http://www.masonstours.com.au.

Medieval Spain. http://es.geocities.com/endovelico2001/med/index.html.

Menkhorst, Peter, and Frank Knight. *A Field Guide to the Mammals of Australia*. Oxford, NY: Oxford University Press, 2001.

Merriam-Webster Inc. *Webster's Third New International Directory*. Unabridged on CD-ROM. Springfield, MA: Merriam-Webster Inc., 2000.

Microsoft Corporation. *Microsoft Encarta Reference Library 2003*.

———. *Microsoft Encarta Reference Library 2004*.

Milbank, Dana, and Mike Allen. "Bush Urges Commitment to Transform Mideast." *Washington Post*, November 7, 2003.

Minnesota Wolf Alliance. "Myth vs. Fact." http://www.mnwolfalliance.com.

Montgomery, Sy. *Journey of the Pink Dolphins: An Amazon Quest*. New York and London: Touchstone, 2001.

Morgan, Randy C. "Giant Tropical Bullet Ant, Paraponera Clavata, Natural History and Captive Management," 1997. http://www.sasionline.org/antsfiles/pages/bullet/bulletbio.html.

Murdock, Elizabeth, and Rebecca Harrison. *Keep the Wild Alive.* Reston, VA: National Wildlife Federation, 2001.

New Straits Times Press, April 11, 2003.

Nielsen, Lloyd. *Daintree: Jewel of Tropical North Queensland.* Mount Molloy, Queensland: Published by Author, 1997.

Nolting, Mark W. *Africa's Top Wildlife Countries.* Fifth Edition. Fort Lauderdale, FL: Global Travel Publishers, Inc., 1997.

Northwest Creation Network. "Biblical Chronology." http://www.nwcreation.net/biblechrono.html.

O'Byrne, Denis, Joe Bindloss, and others. *Lonely Planet Australia.* Tenth Edition. Footscray, Victoria: Lonely Planet Publications, 2000.

Office de Tourisme. *Villefranche de Conflent.* Undated brochure.

O'Hanlon, Redmond. *Into the Heart of Borneo.* New York: Vintage Books, 1984.

Orangutan Foundation UK. "Adventure with a Capital A." http://www.orangutan.org.uk.

O'Toole, Christopher, ed. *Firefly Encyclopedia of Insects and Spiders.* Buffalo and Toronto: Firefly Books, LTD., 2002.

Painted Dog Research Project. Brochure and http://painteddogconservation.iinet.net.au.

Patterson, José Ramón L., and Luis Mario Arce, *Asturias.* Spain: Ediciones Júcar, 1992.

Payne, Junaidi. *Wild Malaysia: The Wildlife and Scenery of Peninsular Malaysia, Sarawak and Sabah.* Cambridge, MA: The MIT Press, 1990.

Pearson, David L., and Les Beletsky. *Perú: The Ecotravellers' Wildlife Guide.* San Diego and San Francisco: Academic Press, 2001.

Perrins, Christopher, ed. *Firefly Encyclopedia of Birds*. Buffalo and Toronto: Firefly Books, LTD., 2003.

Pettigrew, John D. "Are Flying Foxes Really Primates?" *Bat Conservation International*, June 1986. http://www.batcon.org.

Pickerell, John. "Borneo Elephants: From Pest to Priority?" *National Geographic News*, September 4, 2003. http://news .nationalgeographic.com/news/2003/09/0904_030904_ borneoelephant.html.

Plater, Greg de. "The Venom of the Platypus." http://www .kingsnake.com/toxinology/old/mammals/platypus.html.

PR Services LTD. *Watson Lake Map-Attraction and Service Guide 2002*.

Project Amazonas, Inc. http://www.projectamazonas.com.

Public Library of Science Biology. "Priority for Conservation," *Public Library of Science Biology*, August 18, 2003. http://biology .plosjournals.org/perlserv/?request=get-document&doi=10.1371/ journal.pbio.0000007.

Rand McNally Road Atlas. Skokie, IL: Rand McNally, 2000.

Rehabilitation of Orangutans at Sepilok, The. http://www.sabah .org.my/bi/know_sabah/wildlife/orangutan_conservation.asp.

Reptile House, The. "World's 10 Most Deadliest Snakes." (Compiled from Steve Irwin's *10 Deadliest Snakes* Video, 1996.) http://www .reptileallsorts.com/deadliest-snakes.htm.

Reuters News Service. "Trophy Hunting Depletes Genes for Big Horn Sheep." *Planet Ark,* December 12, 2003. http://www .planetark.com/dailynewsstory.cfm/newsid/23098/story.htm.

Ricketts, Bruce. "Klondike Kate." Mysteries of Canada. http://www .mysteriesofcanada.com/Yukon/klondike_kate.htm.

Ritz, Stacy. *Hidden Belize*. Berkeley, CA: Ulysses Press, 1999.

Robinson, Alex, and Gardenia Robinson. *The Amazon*. Guilford, CT: The Globe Pequot Press, 2000.

Ryan, Michelle, and Chris Burwell, eds. *Wildlife of Tropical North Queensland*. South Brisbane, Queensland: Queensland Museum, 2000.

SabahTravelGuide.com. "Sepilok Orang Utan Rehabilitation Centre." http://www.sabahtravelguide.com/mapguide/ default.asp?page=Sepilok.

——. "The Danum Valley Conservation Area." http://www .sabahtravelguide.com/mapguide/default.asp?page=danum.

Save Alaska. "Arctic National Wildlife Refuge." http://www.savealaska .com/sa_anwr.html.

Schmidt, Karen J. "Glacier National Park: Biodiversity." http://www.nps.gov/glac/resources/bio7.htm.

Scientific Committee on Antarctic Research. "Signatories to the Antarctic Treaty." http://www.scar.org/treaty/signatories.html.

Shine, Richard. *Australian Snakes: A Natural History.* Ithaca, NY: Cornell University Press, 1995.

Shorter, Damon. "Great Australian Bites. Three of the Worst." *Australian Broadcasting Corporation,* 1998. http://www.abc .net.au/science/slab/shorter/story.htm.

Sierra Club. "Debunking the 'Healthy Forests Initiative.'" http://www .sierraclub.org/forests/fires/healthyforests_initiative.asp.

——. "Facts About the Bush Administration's Plan to Weaken the Clean Air Act." http://www.sierraclub.org/cleanair/clear_skies.asp.

Sierra Club of Canada. "Caribou Commons Project." http://www.cariboucommons.com.

SIL International. "SIL International Presents: Ethnologue." http://www.ethnologue.com.

Sitwell, Nigel, and Tom Ritchie. *Antarctic Primer.* Darien, CT: Quark Expeditions Inc., 1997.

Slater, Candace. *Entangled Edens: Visions of the Amazon.* Berkeley and Los Angeles: University of California Press, 2002.

Sleeper, Barbara. *Primates: The Amazing World of Lemurs, Monkeys, and Apes.* San Francisco: Chronicle Books, LLC., 1997.

Smith, Amber. "Things That Go Bump: Facts About Phobias." *Discovery Health Channel, Discovery.com, Inc.,* 1999-2001. http://health.discovery.com.

Smith, Donald. "Canada's Hardy Inuit Hope for Better Times." *National Geographic News,* May 8, 2000. http://news .nationalgeographic.com/news/2000/05/0508_inuit.html.

Spawls, Stephen, Kim Howell, Robert Drewes, and James Ashe. *A Field Guide to the Reptiles of East Africa.* San Diego and San Francisco: Academic Press, 2002.

Steves, Rick. *Rick Steves' Spain & Portugal 2002.* Emeryville, CA: Avalon Travel Publishing, 2002.

Stewart/Hyder International Chamber of Commerce. http://www.stewart-hyder.com.

Strahan, Ronald. *A Photographic Guide to Mammals of Australia.* Sanibel Island, FL: Ralph Curtis Books, 1995.

Stuebing, Robert B., and Robert F. Inger. *A Field Guide to the Snakes of Borneo.* Kota Kinabalu, Sabah: Natural History Publications (Borneo) Sdn. Bhd., 1999.

Swan, Gerry. *A Photographic Guide to Snakes & Other Reptiles of Australia.* Sanibel Island, FL: Ralph Curtis Books, 1995.

Thailand Hornbill Project. http://www.thai.to/hornbill/eend.htm.

Town of Inuvik. http://www.inuvik.ca/index.html.

Trewby, Mary, ed. *Antarctica: An Encyclopedia from Abbott Ice Shelf to Zooplankton.* Buffalo and Toronto: Firefly Books LTD., 2002.

Tucker, Brian. "Australian Railways." http://www.btucker.albatross .co.uk/Queensland.htm.

Twain, Mark. *The Innocents Abroad or The New Pilgrim's Progress.* Special Edition. New York: Airmont Publishing Company, Inc., 1967.

Tychostup, Lorna. "The Costs of War." *Chronogram Magazine,* April 2003. http://www.chronogram.com.

Udvardy, Miklos D. F. *National Audubon Society Field Guide to North American Birds: Western Region.* Eighteenth Printing. New York: Alfred A. Knopf, Inc., 1992.

Unwin, Mike. *Southern African Wildlife: A Visitor's Guide.* Guilford, CT: The Globe Pequot Press, Inc., 2003.

U.S. Department of State, Bureau of Consular Affairs. "Consular Information Sheet on Malaysia," April 7, 2003. http://travel.state.gov/malaysia.html.

———. "Zimbabwe." http://travel.state.gov/zimbabwe.html and http://travel.state.gov/Zimbabwe_warning.html.

U.S. Fish & Wildlife Service. "Potential Impacts of Proposed Oil and Gas Development on the Arctic Refuge's Coastal Plain: Historical Overview and Issues of Concern." January 17, 2001. http://arctic.fws.gov/issues1.htm.

U.S. Fish & Wildlife Service-Alaska. "Arctic National Wildlife Refuge: Frequently Asked Questions About Caribou." http://arctic.fws.gov/carcon.htm.

U.S. Fish & Wildlife Service-Pacific Region. "Selkirk Mountains Woodland Caribou." http://idahoes.fws.gov/Fact/Caribou.html.

USA Today. "Campaign 2004. U.S. Senate. Conrad Burns (R) Incumbent." *USA Today.* http://asp.usatoday.com/news/politicselections/CandidateProfile.aspx?ci=1732&oi=S.

Valhouli, Christina. "World's Most Dangerous Travel Destinations 2004." *Forbes.com,* 2004. http://www.forbes.com/2004/03/25/cx_cv_0325feat.html.

Village des Tortues. http://www.villagetortues.com.

Wagner, Doug. *Boas, Everything about Selection, Care, Nutrition, Diseases, Breeding, and Behavior.* Hauppauge, NY: Barron's Educational Series, Inc., 1996.

Wallechinsky, David. "The World's 10 Worst Dictators." *Parade,* February 22, 2004.

Walt Disney Pictures. *Never Cry Wolf,* 1983.

Wet Tropics Management Authority. http://www.wettropics.gov.au.

Wetzler, Brad. "The Wild File." *Outside Magazine,* February 2004.

Wever, Ernest Glen. "Hearing in the Crocodilia." *Proceedings of the National Academy of Sciences of the United States of America,* July 1, 1971. http://www.pnas.org/cgi/content/abstract/68/7/1498.

Whitaker, John O. *National Audubon Society Field Guide to North American Mammals.* Third Printing. New York: Alfred A. Knopf, Inc., 1997.

Whitfield, John. "Ram Cull Dents Gene Pool." *News@Nature.com,* December 11, 2003. http://www.nature.com/news/2003/031208/full/031208-10.html.

Wignall, Jeff. "The Last Wilderness." *Outdoor Photographer,* February 2005.

Wild Africa CC. http://www.wildlifeafrica.co.za.

Wolf Trust. http://www.wolftrust.org.uk.

WolfRivals.org. http://www.wolfrivals.org.

World Gazetteer, The. http://www.world-gazetteer.com.

Young, Allen M. *Tropical Rainforests.* New York: St. Martin's Press, 2001.

Yulsman, Tom. "Meltdown." *Audubon,* December 2003.

Zimmer, Carl. "Beetle of Burden." *Discover Magazine,* April 1996.

About the Author

M arty Essen lives in Montana with his wife, Deb, two dogs, two cats, and two rainbow boas. When not traveling, he runs Essen Communications Corporation, a local telephone company.

Readers wishing to communicate with the author may do so via e-mail: Marty@CoolCreaturesHotPlanet.com.

Please visit www.CoolCreaturesHotPlanet.com for information on author slide shows and appearances, travel and conservation links, additional photos, signed copies of this book, etc.